P9-AGO-342

*f*P

THE HUMAN CHRIST

THE SEARCH FOR THE HISTORICAL JESUS

CHARLOTTE ALLEN

THE FREE PRESS
NEW YORK LONDON TORONTO
SINGAPORE SYDNEY

THE FREE PRESS
A Division of Simon & Schuster Inc.
1230 Avenue of the Americas
New York, NY 10020

Designed by Carla Bolte

Manufactured in the United States of America

10 9 8 7 6 5 4 3 2 1

Library of Congress Cataloging-in-Publication Data

Allen, Charlotte, 1943–
The human Christ: the search for the historical Jesus/
Charlotte Allen.
p. cm.
Includes bibliographical references and index.
1. Jesus Christ—Biography—History and criticism. 2. Jesus
Christ—Historicity. I. Title.
BT301.9.A45 1998 97-46463
232.9′08–dc21 CIP

ISBN 0–684–82725–5

TO MY PARENTS,

ELMER CARLTON LOW

AND

MARIA VIRGINIA DEL RIO LOW

"Mrs. Rose, we are going to have a picnic on Monday in the Valley of Jehoshaphat; will you and your young ladies join us? We shall send the hampers to the tomb of Zachariah."

"Thank you, Miss Todd; we should have been so happy; but we have only three days to do Bethlehem, the Dead Sea, and Jericho. We must be off tomorrow."

"Mamma, I lost my parasol somewhere coming down the Mount of Offence. Those nasty Arab children must have stolen it."

"They say the people in Siloam are the greatest thieves in Syria; and nobody dares to meddle with them."

"But I saw it in your hand, my dear, at the Well of Enrogel."

"What, no potatoes! There were potatoes yesterday. Waiter, waiter; who ever heard of setting people down to dinner without potatoes?"

"Well, I didn't know what to say to it. If that is the tomb of Nicodemus, that seems to settle the question. May I trouble you for the salt?"

"Mr. Pott, I won't have anything more to say to you; you have no faith. I believe it all."

"What, all? From Calvary upstairs in the gallery down to the dark corner where the cock crew?"

"Yes, all, Mr. Pott. Why should not a cock crow there as well as anywhere else? It is so beautiful to believe."

—Anthony Trollope, *The Bertrams*

They'll no get him a' in a book I think
Though they write it cunningly;
No mouse of the scrolls was the Goodly Fere
But aye loved the open sea.

—Ezra Pound, "The Ballad of the Goodly Fere"

CONTENTS

ACKNOWLEDGMENTS

Every book is to some extent a collaborative effort, and this one could not have been written without my deep immersion in the writings of New Testament scholars and historians of Christianity far more learned and perspicacious than I. Martin Hengel's *Crucifixion* provided an encyclopedia of historical detail about this grisly practice, and his immensely erudite *Son of God* provided baseline insights into the specifically Jewish theological context in which the earliest Christians (who were Jews) worshipped the crucified Jesus as a figure who sat at God's right hand. The work of James H. Charlesworth (particularly his *Jesus Within Judaism*) and Alan Segal (particularly his *Paul the Convert* and *The Other Judaisms of Late Antiquity*) introduced me to the richness and range of the noncanonical Jewish literature that circulated widely during Second Temple times and contained tantalizing parallels to the Christological imagery in Paul's letters and the Gospels. (Few Christians or Jews know much about the Old Testament Apocrypha and Pseudepigrapha, and they should.) I have also drawn on N. T. Wright's observations about the prophetic context in which Jesus might have operated among his fellow-Jews, along with his conclusion (shared by Segal and W. D. Davies) that Paul's Christian theology was thoroughly grounded in the Judaism of his time. As for first-century Judaism itself, the work of Seán Freyne, Lester L. Grabbe, Michael Grant, Harold W. Hoehner, Richard A. Horsley, Joachim Jeremias, Jacob Neusner, John Riches, Samuel Sandmel, E. P. Sanders, and E. Mary Smallwood all taken together painted a vivid picture of the tumultuous, socially and spiritually variegated, and ultimately tragic history of Jesus' homeland before, during, and after his ministry. Martin Hengel (in his voluminous studies of Judaism and Hellenism) and J. N. Sevenster (in his well-documented demonstration that most Jews of Jesus' time spoke some Greek) effectively shattered the long-standing assumption that Palestinian Judaism during Second Temple times was largely unaffected by the Hellenistic culture that surrounded it. Geza Vermes's many books on the Dead Sea Scrolls were indispensable, as was Hershel Shanks's reader *Understanding the Dead Sea Scrolls.* W. F. Albright, Jack Finegan, and Yigael Yadin introduced me to the archaeological record of first-century Palestine. *Jesus and His World* by John J. Rousseau and Rami Arav provided a wealth of detail on such various matters as Roman construction techniques, the ancient olive oil industry, and the kinds of fish caught in the Sea of Galilee.

For the social and doctrinal history of early Christianity I drew largely on the work of Henry Chadwick, Robin Lane Fox, W. H. C. Frend, Robert M. Grant, Arland Hultgren, Abraham Malherbe, Wayne A. Meeks, Rodney Stark, Timothy Ware, and Robert L. Wilken. All those writers brought home to me the high level of intellectual, economic, and scientific sophistication that prevailed in the ancient Roman world. J. Stevenson's *Creeds, Councils and Controversies,* a compilation of the key documents of early Christian history, was always close at hand as a source book, as were M. R. James's *The Apocryphal New Testament,* Maxwell Staniforth's *Early Christian Writings,* James M. Robinson's *The Nag Hammadi Library,* Helmut Koester's *Ancient Christian Gospels,* and John S. Kloppenborg's *Q Parallels*. Bruce Metzger's work on the formation of the New Testament canon was invaluable. Beryl Smalley's *The Study of the Bible in the Middle Ages* amply documented the erudition of medieval exegetes, while V. A. Kolve's *The Play Called Corpus Christi* and Rosemary Woolf's *Art and Doctrine* demonstrated the way in which medieval theological preoccupations dealing with Jesus' humanity found their way into the popular arts.

As for the story of the search for the historical Jesus, Albert Schweitzer's *The Quest of the Historical Jesus* (1906) is still a researcher's main resource after nearly a century. However, there now exist several important supplements to Schweitzer's magisterial book, which covered only the hundred-odd years between Hermann Samuel Reimarus and Wilhelm Wrede. William Baird's *History of New Testament Research,* volume one (the second volume is still unpublished), introduces the reader to the English deist Jesus-searchers who preceded and influenced Reimarus, most of whose books have not been republished since the 18th century (however, fortunately, the Library of Congress has an ample collection of them in first edition). The *Life of Jesus* series edited by Leander E. Keck comprises contemporary editions of seven literary classics of the search for the historical Jesus, including Reimarus's *Fragments* and David Friedrich Strauss's *Life of Jesus* as translated by George Eliot.

Werner Georg Kümmel's *The New Testament: The History of Its Investigations* summarizes and reprints excerpts from quest-for-Jesus literature through the 1960s (as well as short biographies of the key questers), while Warren S. Kissinger's *The Lives of Jesus* is an excellent bibliography and summary of quest-for-Jesus literature through the 1970s. Otto Betz's *What Do We Know About Jesus?,* Marcus J. Borg's *Jesus in Contemporary Scholarship,* Hendrikus Boers's *Who Was Jesus?,* Howard Clark Kee's *Jesus in History* and his *What Can We Know About Jesus?,* and Ben Witherington III's *The Jesus Quest* all effectively (if sometimes tendentiously) summarize quest literature up to the very recent past. Bruce Chilton and Craig A. Evans's *Studying the Historical Jesus* is a useful scholar's guide. Luke Timothy Johnson's *The Real Jesus* and N. T. Wright's *Who Was Jesus?* offer acidulous critiques of the Jesus Seminar and other adventurous manifestations of the quest during the 1980s and 1990s. Donald A. Hagner's *The Jewish Reclamation of Jesus* helpfully summarizes the various Jewish contributions to the quest. The text, footnotes, and appendixes of Raymond E. Brown's *Death of the Messiah* and recent *Introduction to the New Testament,* along with John P. Meier's *A Marginal Jew: Rethinking the Historical Jesus,* are treasure-troves of minute data about questers and quest theories, as well as information about Jesus' own time.

Besides being in debt to the above scholars who have researched the search for the historical Jesus so meticulously, I also could not help but be influenced by several intellectual historians who have offered percipient critiques of the course of biblical criticism since the Enlightenment. Among them especially: Henry E. Allison, Owen Chadwick, Hans Frei, Vincent McCarthy, Alister McGrath, Stephen Neill, John Redwood, and Henning Graf Reventlow. The insights in J. C. O'Neill's *The Bible's Authority,* a collection of essays on New Testament commentators ranging from Gotthold Lessing to Rudolf Bultmann, were especially useful in helping me formulate my ideas about these personages, as there exist to date no authoritative biographies in English of many of them, including Bultmann. Edwina Lawler's and Marilyn Chapin Massey's commentaries on David Friedrich Strauss are nearly the only first-rate English-language critical work on Strauss to date, and I am grateful to both. *Nineteenth Century Religious Thought in the West,* edited by L. Ninian Smart and others, is a compendium of provocative studies on which I relied shamelessly. Edward Said's *Orientalism* helped focus my thoughts about Western seekers in the Near East, and Estelle Jussim's *Slave to Beauty* introduced me to the life and photography of the unjustly all-but-forgotten F. Holland Day.

Many people helped me with this book in countless ways. My interest in the search for the historical Jesus began with an article for *Washington City Paper* in 1992. I am grateful to *City Paper*'s then-editor, Jack Shafer, for assigning me the piece and editing it with enthusiasm. More recently and with equal enthusiasm, Cullen Murphy and Susan Parilla of *The Atlantic Monthly* and Alexander Star of *Lingua Franca* edited portions of the book that appeared in somewhat altered form in those two magazines. During the three years I spent researching, writing, and revising the manuscript, many other editors—notably Steve Coll, T. A. Frail, Jeffrey Frank, Susannah Gardiner, Liza Mundy, and Judith Shulevitz—provided me with assignments that were welcome distractions to my obsessive focus on this one large project. Among the many fellow-writers to offer constant professional encouragement were Thomas Alderson, Katharine Boo, Michael Dolan, Tom Dunkel, Eric Felten, Alan Green, Charlotte Hays, Philip Terzian, and Alona Wartofsky.

To Jude R. Dougherty, dean of the school of philosophy at the Catholic University of America, I am grateful for extending me the privileges of a scholar in residence from 1994 to 1997, and to Ralph McInerny of Notre Dame University's medieval studies program for recommending me to Dean Dougherty. The library staff at Catholic University was especially helpful in finding books for me, and I also obtained good service from librarians at the Library of Congress, Georgetown University, and Wesley Theological Seminary. Leander Keck (of the Yale Divinity School), Luke Johnson (of Emory University's Candler School of Theology), and Richard Horsley (of the classics and religion departments at the University of Massachusetts in Boston) have all agreed to read and comment on the galleys of this book—although I take full responsibility for all errors that remain after their perusal. Andrew Ferguson agreed to read the manuscript from a literary perspective. Mark Jay Mirsky, director of Jewish studies at the City College of New York and an old, dear friend, read the first draft of my section on the Jewish reclamation of Jesus, and his blunt, astute comments were invaluable for my revisions. A beloved former teacher, Charles R. Beye of the City University of New York classics program, advised me on Greek translations and transliterations. Stephen Morrow, Loretta Denner, and Judyth Schaubhut Smith of The Free Press edited my manuscript with extraordinary care. Ms. Smith in particular drew on her thorough knowledge of German and French to ensure the correctness of my grammar, spelling, and accenting in those languages. Michael Morris of the Graduate Theological Union at Berkeley introduced me to some of the artists who were obsessed with the historical Jesus. Paula Trotto hunted down the illustrations for this book with surehandedness and dispatch. My agents, Lynn Chu and Glen Hartley, provided substantive as well as sales help, alerting me, for example, to Oscar Wilde's interest in the historical Jesus. I also wish to extend heartfelt appreciation to my teachers: to Charles Beye and the late Edwin J. Doyle and Hazel Hansen for reawakening my lifelong love of the Greek and Latin classics, and to William Alfred, V. A. Kolve, and the late William Ackerman and Morton Bloomfield for grounding me in medieval literature. Without their mentoring so long ago I could not have written this book's early chapters.

Finally, the writing of this book would have been impossible without the steadfast love of my large family and many dear friends, especially Diane Bettencourt, Cathy Colloff, Mary Jane Lafferty, Linda Simmons, and Jeffrey and Hilary Tucker. To my husband, Don, whose heart is ever with mine in the Highlands whence our ancestors came and in California where we were born, and who endured my daily agonies as a writer with limitless patience and a constant stream of wise counsel, I owe the greatest debt of love and gratitude of all. *Dónal, 'se Dónal, 'se Dónal a rinne an bhainis.*

INTRODUCTION

Crucifixion is one of the cruelest forms of execution ever devised. Impaling someone, arms outstretched, on a tree or intersecting stakes, was meant to bring about a prolonged, painful, and highly public death, the cause of which was probably an agonizing process of asphyxiation as the victim struggled to push upward with his legs in order to counteract the crushing weight of the upper torso on the lungs. It took several days for the stronger victims to die. Those who were more fortunate had been flogged so badly beforehand that they expired within hours; or their bodies were pushed upward after being partially nailed, and twisted, causing excruciatingly painful muscle spasms that interfered with their efforts to breathe and thus hastened death; or their legs were broken on the cross, and they died immediately because breathing became impossible.

Crucifixion was practiced throughout the ancient world—in India, Scythia, Mesopotamia, northern Africa, Greece, and Rome, and among the Celts of northern Europe—from the seventh century B.C.E. to the fourth century C.E. Reserved for egregious felons, rebellious slaves, non-Roman citizens convicted of crimes against the empire, and enemies captured in war, it was often the subject of gallows humor in Roman comedies and graffiti. Among the Jews, although it was not one of the penalties listed in the Mishnah, the rabbinic legal code of 200 C.E., it was practiced nonetheless. At least one of the Dead Sea Scrolls alludes to crucifixion as a punishment for high treason against Israel, and the Jewish king Alexander Jannaeus (reigned 103–76 B.C.E.) is reported to have crucified as many as 800 Pharisees. The Book of Deuteronomy reminds Jews of the disgrace of being crucified, declaring that "anyone hung on a tree is under God's curse."[1]

Among the countless victims of crucifixion in ancient times, the most famous was the Galilean Jew Jesus of Nazareth, who was nailed to a cross outside Jerusalem on a Friday during Passover toward the end of the reign of the Roman emperor Tiberius (42 B.C.E.–37 C.E.). His cross bore the superscription King of the Jews, which seemed to indicate that he had been taken for the Messiah, the Anointed One, the Royal Savior of Israel prophesied in the Hebrew Scriptures, and had been seen as an enemy of Rome. He had obviously been a figure of controversy, and his crucifixion was clearly designed to put an end to whatever aspirations he had held. After Jesus' death his followers, who had at first gone into hiding, began acting in a surprising way. They evidenced no shame at having been associated with a convicted felon, or fear at having consorted with a known traitor. They were all Jews, but they did not believe Jesus' death was a locus of God's curse. On the contrary, they considered it a cause for *celebration.* They were boldly certain that Jesus, who they knew had died like any other man, was alive, and therefore akin to God. He was in their very midst, a powerful reality that gave them enormous confidence, even though their numbers were pitifully small and their cause—trumpeting a dead criminal as the risen Messiah—seemed patently absurd. They sang hymns of joy in his honor rather than dirges of mourning.

The oldest extant Christian artifact is one of these hymns, composed no more than 20 years after Jesus' death. It survives because Paul of Tarsus, a Pharisee who had joined Jesus' followers after a conversion experience, quoted it in a letter written around 55 C.E. to a Christian community he had founded at Philippi, a Macedonian port city and Roman colony. Arranged in two thematically symmetrical stanzas of almost equal length, it had this to say about Jesus:

who, though he was in the form of God,
did not regard equality with God
as something to be exploited,
but emptied himself,
taking the form of a slave,
and being born in human likeness.
And being found in human form,
he humbled himself
and became obedient to the point of death—
even death on a cross.

Therefore God also highly exalted him
and gave him the name
that is above every name,
so that at the name of Jesus
every knee should bend,
in heaven and on earth and under the earth,
and every tongue should confess
that Jesus Christ is Lord
to the glory of God the Father.[2]

In all probability, the Christians of Philippi were mostly Jews, representatives of a widespread Diaspora that had ringed the Mediterranean with synagogues. The composer of the hymn, a poet of considerable talent, was almost certainly a Jew.

The hymn is saturated with allusions to characters from Jewish Scripture, including Adam, who had desired to be the equal of God and had sinned (in contrast to Jesus, who *was* the equal of God and had humbled himself), and the Suffering Servant of the Book of Isaiah, who "poured himself out to death" and "was wounded for our transgressions / crushed for our iniquities . . . he bore the sin of many."[3] In Isaiah's prophecy, God had promised to turn the Servant's pain into joy ("therefore I will allot him a portion with the great"; "to me every knee shall bow / every tongue shall swear"),[4] and he had fulfilled his vow by exalting Jesus after his death. The poet calls Jesus "Christ," Greek for the Anointed One, or the Messiah. Even "the name / that is above every name" is an oblique reference to the sacred Tetragrammaton, the ineffable and unutterable name of the God of Israel. The images with which the author of the hymn clothes Jesus come directly from the Hebrew Bible, as well as the Greek-language Septuagint Bible read in many Diaspora synagogues.

Linking God's name to that of Jesus, and calling Jesus "Lord," which was God's own title *(Adonai)* in the Hebrew Scriptures, was tantamount to saying that Jesus *was* God, or at the very least, someone "in the form of God" who had descended from heaven. At first glance, this might seem incompatible with Jewish monotheism. In point of fact, the Jewish religion of Jesus' time was filled with imagery that made it easy for certain Jews to adopt a theology that regarded him as divinely sent without compromising their belief in one God. They read in their Scriptures about living figures that personified divine attributes. The Book of Proverbs portrayed divine wisdom (*ḥokhmah* in Hebrew; *sophia* in Greek) as a powerful female personage who was with God at the very creation. The Book of Genesis depicted the "wind from God" (the Spirit, *ruaḥ,* another female) as sweeping over the waters when God made the world.[5] The Book of Daniel contained a vision of "one like a son of man," perhaps an angel or the Messiah, who would come down from heaven and rule the earth forever.[6] The authors of these passages may well have been influenced by polytheistic modes of thinking, because Jews living both within and without the Holy Land had been exposed to Hellenistic culture for three centuries by the time Jesus was born, and had deftly incorporated polytheistic imagery into their strictly monotheistic theology.

During Jesus' time, a large number of other religious Jewish texts, known as the Old Testament Apocrypha and Pseudepigrapha, were circulating in the Holy Land and elsewhere. The canon of the Hebrew Bible was not "closed" in Jesus' day, and Jews were still writing works that many of their readers considered to be Holy Scripture in the years before, during, and after Jesus' ministry. Some of them embroidered on the visionary and apocalyptic themes of the Book of Daniel, including that of the Son of Man. A favorite character was the patriarch Enoch, who had ascended to heaven in the Book of Genesis, and was described in the Pseudepigrapha as having been made into an angel who sat on God's own throne. The religious imagery employed was often so similar to that of the early Christians that scholars still argue over whether particular texts are Jewish or Christian, as James H. Charlesworth of Princeton Theological Seminary has noted.[7] One of these texts, a hymnbook known as the Odes of Solomon, which dates from around Jesus' time, refers to the "Bridegroom." Is this an allusion to the bridal imagery of the Song of Solomon, or to Jesus, whom Paul's letters and the Gospels draped with bridal metaphors? Another contemporary Jewish text, the Prayer of Manasseh, speaks of human sinfulness, charity to others, and the forgiving and fatherly love of God in language that resembles that of the Lord's Prayer. Nearly all Jews in Jesus' day believed in the resurrection of the dead, especially in the case of martyrs. It is therefore not surprising that certain of them imagined that Jesus had returned to life in glorious form.

Christianity's oldest and most puzzling paradox is that of the crucified man who was celebrated in song as being "in the form of God." The Gospel of Matthew would later declare that Jesus had been born of a virgin, without a human father, and the Gospel of John would describe him as the son of God from the beginning of time. In the fourth century, the Nicene Creed would clothe this proposition in technical terminology: Jesus was "very God and very man," fully divine and fully human. Throughout nearly 2,000 years of Christian history, his dual identity has been a source of mystery, meditation, theological investigation, and troubling inquiry. In our own theoretically post-Christian age (at least in the industrialized West), Jesus is still the *ur*-icon of civilization, the enigmatic figure who continues to fascinate our imagination. Because we live in an age when science and scholarly research are supposed to supply answers to all our questions, for the most part we are unwilling to accept such a paradox. The search for the "historical" Jesus—the human being who walked the roads of Galilee 2,000 years ago—has thus become a hallmark of modernity, an obsession that has gripped the minds of intellectuals for nearly three centuries.

I am not a biblical scholar, and this book is not an attempt to offer a theory of who the historical Jesus was, or whether he actually said or did those things attributed to him in the Gospels. Rather, it examines the way in which the image of Jesus has functioned as a vehicle for some of the best and worst ideas of Western civilization over the past 2,000 years. To a greater or lesser degree, the quest for the historical Jesus has intrigued some of the most provocative figures of modern times, including Baruch Spinoza, Isaac Newton, Voltaire, Edward Gibbon, Tom Paine, Thomas Jefferson, Immanuel Kant, G. W. F. Hegel, Karl Marx, Friedrich Engels, George Eliot, Gustave Flaubert, Oscar Wilde, William Butler Yeats, Cecil B. DeMille, and Norman Mailer. Jesus scholarship has been shaped by nearly every intellectual fashion of the past three centuries: English deism, Enlightenment rationalism, philosophical Idealism, Romanticism, Darwinism, existentialism, Marxism, and feminism. The liberal Protestant outlook of the 19th century, the "social gospel" of the early 20th century, the "God Is Dead" movement of the 1960s, and the liberation theology of the 1970s and 1980s have all cast long shadows on the search for Jesus. In 1909, the Modernist Catholic theologian George Tyrrell complained that the liberal German biblical scholars of his day had reconstructed a historical Jesus who was no more than "the reflection of a liberal Protestant face, seen at the bottom of a deep well."[8] In other words, the liberal searchers had found a liberal Jesus. The same can be said of the Jesus-searchers of every era: the deists found a deist, the Romantics a Romantic, the existentialists an existentialist, and the liberationists a Jesus of class struggle. Supposedly equipped with the latest critical and historical tools, the "scientific" quest for the historical Jesus has nearly always devolved into theology, ideology, and even autobiography.

Besides falling prey to faddishness, the results of each epoch of Jesus research have become dated at an alarming pace. The biblical scholars of the 19th-century German universities were the most learned, meticulous, hardworking, and critical-minded in the world. They produced multi-volume, exhaustively annotated "lives of Jesus" that ran to thousands of pages each. The fruits of all that toil are now gathering dust—unread, for the most part untranslated, and largely irrelevant to 20th-century historians. As for the English deists who launched the quest for the historical Jesus in the early 18th century, there is not even a modern edition of most of their tracts. No one has ever bothered to edit, much less translate, the bulk of the *Apology* of Hermann Samuel Reimarus, the iconoclastic pioneer of German Jesus scholarship, and it is likely that no one ever will. No one besides cultural historians reads David Friedrich Strauss nowadays. The works of Ernest Renan are still worth reading—as literature, not scholarship—as is Wilhelm Bousset's balmy *Kyrios Christos,* a kind of nonfiction *Marius the Epicurean* for buffs of *belle-époque* aestheticism. Rudolf Bultmann is an important name in 20th-century theology, but his own students have rejected nearly all his theories, including his Christian existentialism, which was the talk of the universities only a few decades ago. The output of the New Hermeneutics movement of the 1960s is hardly illuminating today. The latest array of "New Quest" Jesuses—the Cynic sage, the shaman, the "spirit person," the wisdom teacher—will undoubtedly look touchingly quaint within a generation or two. The Jesus of liberation theology is fading fast, as Pentecostalism, not Marxism, rides the religious wave in Latin America. Regarding deconstructionism, the latest fashion in biblical criticism, Society of Biblical Literature members, take note: It is already past noon for deconstructionism elsewhere in academia.

The quest for the historical Jesus has produced surprisingly little genuine and uncontroverted new knowledge over the past three centuries about the man and his time. We still do not know where the four canonical Gospels were written, or when, although it is fairly certain that all of them existed in something like their present form by the end of the first century. We can only make educated guesses as to how they were composed and what source materials their authors used. Although the majority of biblical scholars believe that Mark's Gospel was the first to be written down, a respectable minority holds otherwise. To this day, nearly our only sources of information about Jesus remain the Gospels and the other Christian writings of the first century, which have been available for more than 1,900 years.

Despite these considerations, I do not believe that the search for the historical Jesus has been in vain. Indeed, it has recently come full circle in recognizing and exploring Jesus' Jewishness. For most of its history, Christianity's sin was that of having forgotten its Jewish roots. In some ways, this was understandable: The Christian Church soon became overwhelmingly Gentile; Jerusalem, where it had been born, was physically obliterated by the Romans at the beginning of the second century, and its Jews were driven from memory. Christians retained the Psalms in their liturgy and the Old Testament in their Bibles, but they chose to ignore the fact that Jesus and his earliest followers had been steeped in an intense and intellectually creative Jewish religiosity that had translated itself into the earliest Christian theology of the crucified Messiah. By and large, the secular quest for the historical Jesus has carried on the old, erroneous Christian tradition of regarding Jesus as an opponent of Judaism. Even today there is a tendency among avant-garde Jesus-searchers to view him as an anti-establishment figure with respect to the institutions of his own religion. The most fruitful branch of Jesus research in recent years has centered on his status as a figure (albeit problematic) *within* Judaism.

One final word: As a Catholic, I am certain that my own theological presuppositions have colored my presentation of the people I have surveyed, just as their theological and ideological presuppositions have colored their presentations of Jesus. However, as I read their books and biographies in the course of my research, I found myself entering the sometimes tragic, sometimes comic, but always interesting mental worlds of Edward Gibbon, Voltaire (that lovable rascal!), David Strauss, George Eliot, Ernest Renan, Gustave Flaubert, Oscar Wilde, Albert Schweitzer, Rudolf Bultmann, Paul Winter, James M. Robinson, Norman Mailer, and many others. I have tried to write about the subjects of this text at least partly from their own point of view, with sympathy as well as critical detachment.

1

JESUS' JEWISH WORLD

Jesus was born in Roman-ruled Palestine, a small, predominantly Jewish backwater in a vast empire that completely encircled the Mediterranean, encompassing Egypt, Greece, the Balkans, and the entire Near East, and extending far into northern Europe and even Britain. We of the modern world know a great deal about the Holy Land during the first century, including its politics and religions, its incessant civil unrest, its constantly changing procession of rulers both local and Roman, and its humiliating fate after the Jewish population's revolt against Rome led to the destruction of Jerusalem in 70 C.E. This knowledge does not come solely from the New Testament. The Jewish historian Flavius Josephus (37–100 C.E.), commander of the Galilean forces during the early years of the revolt, and later a protégé of the emperor Vespasian (9–79 C.E.), wrote four long historical and autobiographical works in which he recounted the story of the Jews, especially during his own fateful century, when the Second Temple, the proud handiwork of a people returning to their land after the Babylonian captivity, was burnt to the ground, never to be rebuilt.

Josephus had little interest in Jesus, whom he referred to briefly as a wonder-working wise man, said by some to be the Messiah, who had been betrayed by Jewish leaders and was survived by a corps of devoted followers in Jerusalem and elsewhere. What gripped Josephus was the total destruction of the Jewish world into which Jesus and Josephus himself had been born. His was the tragic tale of Jerusalem's fall at Roman hands following a grisly starvation siege and the wholesale slaughter of its inhabitants, which nearly destroyed Judaism in the process, and the parade of imperious, eccentric, brave, ruthless, and fanatically patriotic personalities who had played out their parts in the city's demise. Some of the Zealot Jewish nationalists who had governed Jerusalem during the siege fled to the deserts and caves around the Dead Sea, where Roman troops hunted them down like animals. Their last stand was in 73 C.E. at Masada, a mountaintop fortress near the Dead Sea, where 1,000 men, women, and children committed mass suicide rather than surrender to the Roman Tenth Legion.

Many modern historians accuse Josephus of having exaggerated his country's importance to Rome and its rulers, probably out of a sense of religious loyalty. By contrast, the Roman secular historians who covered the century—Livy, Tacitus, Suetonius, and Dio Cassius—dealt with Palestine only in passing. By their accounts, Pontius Pilate, the Roman governor of Judea and Samaria who sentenced Jesus to death, was essentially a nobody who had a few good friends in Rome. Pilate's title of "prefect," which was later upgraded to "procurator," denoted a second-rate civil-service post awarded to members of the equestrian, or knightly, class of Roman nobility, whose bloodlines were considered inferior to those of the ruling senatorial class. Even more humbling, the governor of Judea answered to the governor of Syria, a blueblood of the senatorial class, as Syria was a larger and more important Roman province whose chief cities, Antioch and Damascus, were major trade *entrepôts* with the East.

The Caesars consistently made poor or mediocre choices for the governors they assigned to the Jewish homeland during Jesus' time. Stationed not in Jerusalem but in Caesarea, a port city on the Samaritan coast, most of the Judean prefects and procurators served suspiciously short terms of two or three years, either because the post was hardship duty or because they were unfit administrators. Pilate, appointed by the emperor Tiberius, was probably in the middling ranks of competence. He lasted a full 10 years, an extraordinarily long term for a Judean prefect. There was no love lost between Pilate and his Jewish subjects. Josephus and another first-century Jewish intellectual, Philo of Alexandria, report several bloody crackdowns on religious Jews, and the Gospel accounts of Jesus' passion depict a Pilate who taunted Jewish officialdom by dangling in front of it the prospect of freeing Jesus. For the most part, however, Pilate did what was necessary in order to keep the peace. Tacitus, who devotes part of his *Histories* to Jewish affairs, notes that

Pilate's term, as well as that of his predecessor, Gratus, another Tiberian appointee, was by and large uneventful. "Sub Tiberio quies," comments Tacitus in the terse Latin style for which he is famous: "Under Tiberius, all was quiet."[1]

The last of the Roman procurators, Gessius Florus, who served from 64 C.E. until war broke out in 66 C.E., was a dismal failure. Incapable of maintaining law and order (raging nationalist sentiment had spawned terrorist attacks on officials and civilians), he was also unspeakably brutal. According to Josephus, Florus levied punishment for a riot in Jerusalem by randomly arresting, flogging, and crucifying 3,600 residents, including women, children, and even Roman citizens of Florus's own equestrian class, who were supposedly exempt from crucifixion. "The Jews' patience lasted until Gessius Florus became procurator," notes Tacitus in another of his dry comments.[2] The only Roman governor of Judea who made an effort to understand Jewish religious beliefs and customs was Tiberius Julius Alexander (46–48 C.E.), during whose reign escalating Jewish-Roman hostilities enjoyed a brief respite. The succession of inept Roman rulers indicated that the Caesars troubled themselves little to find appropriate governance for Palestine.

Although small and relatively remote, the Jewish homeland was nonetheless vital to Roman interests as a strategic frontier territory. In the desert just beyond its boundaries (and those of Syria to the north) lay Parthia, Rome's most powerful enemy, and the only significant contender for hegemony over the Eastern Mediterranean. Parthia's empire extended from the head of the Euphrates River (nearly abutting Syria) to the Indian Ocean, encompassing nearly all of present-day Iraq, Iran, and Afghanistan, as well as parts of northern India and Pakistan. With occasional allies in the independent kingdom of Armenia to its north and several small buffer-kingdoms along its borders, Parthia completely controlled the overland trade routes that brought raw silk from China and spices from India to the Roman Empire via Syria. In the vast Arabian desert and along the approximate boundary of today's Turkey (then called Asia Minor), Rome's writ stopped running and Parthia's began.

A semi-nomadic people famous for their horsemanship and skill with the bow and arrow, the Parthians had originally come from a region south of the Caspian Sea that had belonged successively to the Assyrian and Persian empires, and to the "Macedonian" empire that Alexander the Great had patched together from his conquered territories in the early fourth century before Jesus. Around 250 B.C.E., the Parthians wrested their independence from the Greek-speaking Seleucid monarchy that Alexander had established in Syria to govern the Near East. They then embarked on their own course of empire-building.

The Parthians practiced a monotheistic but highly dualistic religion (featuring a powerful devil-figure named Ahriman) founded by the teacher Zoroaster, who had lived in Persia during the sixth century B.C.E. Mithra (who had originated as the Hindu god Mitra), one of the subdivinities of the Parthian heaven, was worshipped as an independent deity from Assyria to India, in Armenia and Asia Minor, and among the numerous Asians serving in the Roman army.

During Jesus' time, the Jewish Diaspora was extremely widespread. Some six million of the eight million Jews of his day resided outside the Holy Land, the majority of them living under Parthian, not Roman, rule. More than three million Jews inhabited the Mesopotamian cities at the western end of the Parthians' domain, including an enormous Jewish population in Babylon. These were descendants of the Jews whom the Babylonian king Nebuchadnezzar had deported from Judea after his sack of Jerusalem during the early sixth century B.C.E.

About 50 years before Jesus was born, the Romans, who had been pushing their way east ever since the Parthians had bolted from the Seleucids, set their sights on the Parthian Empire. Under the leadership of the warlord Pompey (108–48 B.C.E.), they had already annexed Syria in 64 B.C.E. and Palestine in 63 B.C.E., taking boatloads of captured Jews back to Rome as trophies. Pompey's wealthy and glory-hungry rival Marcus Licinius Crassus, best known for his friendship with Julius Caesar and his crushing of Spartacus's slave rebellion in southern Italy, had led a massive Roman army into Parthian-ruled Mesopotamia in 54 B.C.E. After several easy victories, Crassus's troops had been routed and nearly destroyed by Parthian archers, resulting in his disgrace and eventual murder. The Romans and Parthians continued to battle sporadically over Mesopotamia and Syria for the next 250 years. By the time of Jesus' birth, although the Parthians were on a course of slow decline, they were still a formidable enemy.

Palestine was thus an important border state that kept the Parthians and their Armenian allies out of the Mediterranean and secured Rome's domination of Syria's important trade centers. There was no natural geographic border between Palestine and Syria, whose boundaries encompassed all of present-day Syria and Lebanon (known as Phoenicia), as well as parts of today's Iraq. The Roman treasury was fat with revenues from Syria's trade connections with the East and the Phoenician ports of Tyre and Sidon.

In Jesus' day, the Jewish homeland covered considerably more territory than the current state of Israel. It was even larger than the ancient kingdom of David and Solomon, which had extended down both sides of the Jordan River to the Dead Sea and well up into what are now Lebanon and Syria all the way to Damascus. Only certain portions of the coastal plains along the Mediterranean had belonged to non-Israelite peoples in the days of King David. These were the Philistines to the south around Gaza and the Sidonians around Tyre to the far north. After Solomon's death, the Hebrew kingdom had split into two separate monarchies: Israel, encompassing the land north of the Dead Sea, including Samaria and Galilee, and Judah, embracing Jerusalem and the hilly region between the Dead Sea and the Philistine coastal cities.

In 722 B.C.E., the Assyrians had conquered the kingdom of Israel and deported some, but probably not all, of its Hebrew population. More than 100 years later, in 597 B.C.E., after having annexed most of the Assyrian Empire, the Babylonian king Nebuchadnezzar absorbed the kingdom of Judah, destroyed the Temple built by Solomon, and deported many of Jerusalem's inhabitants. In 539 B.C.E., 24 years after Nebuchadnezzar's death, Cyrus the Great of Persia overthrew the Babylonians and allowed Babylonian Jews to return to Judah. Under the Persians, Judah—or Judea, as the Greeks and Romans came to call it (the word "Jew" comes from the Greek *ioudaios,* meaning inhabitant of Judea)—was reduced to no more than a strip of towns and villages clustered around Jerusalem. Judea remained under Persian rule after the fall of Babylon, but the Persian kings allowed the Jews to restore the Jerusalem Temple and manage their internal affairs through the high priest. In 333 B.C.E., Alexander the Great wrested Judea from the Persians on an upward swing from Egypt to Tyre. The tiny territory of the Second Temple Jews fell first under the control of the Ptolemaic monarchs whom Alexander had set up to rule Egypt, and then under that of the Seleucids.

Except for the Jews of Jerusalem and its environs, the Ptolemaic and Seleucid rulers of Palestine nearly obliterated the land's ancient Hebrew identity. (Greek and Roman writers of the time combined Syria and Solomon's old kingdom geographically under the name Coele-Syria.) In Jerusalem, many members of the Jewish upper class adopted Greek names and customs, and some highborn young Jews even tried to reverse their circumcisions with an operation so as to compete naked in athletic contests without being ridiculed by the Gentiles. In 169 B.C.E., the Seleucid king Antiochus IV attempted to push assimilation a step further by abolishing Jewish holidays, banning Jewish observances, and setting up an altar to Zeus in the Temple. This perceived blasphemy sparked a guerrilla revolt led by Judas Maccabeus ("Judah the Hammer"), the son of a rural priest. Judas took Jerusalem from Antiochus, rededicated the Temple, and established a tiny, Seleucid-beleaguered theocracy centered in Jerusalem. After the scepter had passed from Judas to his four brothers and their heirs, known as the Hasmoneans (after their ancestor, Ḥashmon), the new Jewish rulers of Judea gained independence from the Seleucids, and began calling themselves both kings and high priests.

They also set out to reconquer Solomon's old kingdom, pushing north to annex Samaria and Galilee, south to annex Idumea (biblical Edom and part of the old kingdom of Judah), west to the Mediterranean coast, and east across the Jordan. By this time, the religion and culture of these sections of the former Judah, Israel, and Philistia were largely Syrian-Hellenistic. Ten cities along the Jordan—independent city-states known collectively as the Decapolis—were famous centers of Greek literature and philosophy. Gadara, across the Jordan River from Galilee, spawned several important Hellenistic poets and philosophers. The major coastal cities of Palestine—Gaza, Jamnia (or *Yavneh*), and Joppa (modern Haifa, now part of Tel Aviv)—had never been part of Solomon's kingdom. In Samaria, where many descendants of the old Israelites still worshipped the God of Israel in their own temple on Mount Gezirim, hatred of the Jews and their Temple in Jerusalem was rampant. Even in Judea, the Hasmoneans, who had also begun to adopt Greek names and ways (such as the keeping of royal concubines), were regarded by many of their pious Jewish subjects as decadent and irreligious.

The Hasmonean monarchs were not descendants of David, nor were their high priests of the hereditary line of Zadok, who had been high priest under David and Solomon, causing certain Jews to refuse to accept their legitimacy. However irreligious, when it came to fighting for Judaism and their ancient land, the Hasmoneans were persistent to the point of ruthlessness. They tried to stamp out the Samaritans' religion by demolishing the alternative temple at Mount Gezirim, and forced the Idumeans and Galileans to covert to Judaism (by having them circumcised) on pain of deportation. They also dissolved the independent governments of the Decapolis cities, dispersed their inhabitants, and installed Jewish settlers throughout the recaptured lands. As noted by historian E. Mary Smallwood, when the aggressive Hasmonean king Alexander Jannaeus (*Yannai* in Hebrew) died in 76 B.C.E., the Jewish kingdom was almost as extensive as it had been under David and Solomon.[3]

During the reign of Herod the Great, an Idumean chieftain who had used Roman support to seize the monarchy from the Hasmoneans in 37 B.C.E., and presided over Jerusalem as a Roman client-king when Jesus was born, the Jewish territory became more vast. Because Herod had proved himself adept at suppressing brigandry, his patron, the emperor Augustus (63 B.C.E.–14 C.E.), transferred a long swath of bandit-plagued land to him in southern Syria that ran eastward from the Golan Heights (then called Gaulanitis) into the Arabian desert. This entire region remained more or less in the hands of Herod's numerous descendants for several generations after his death in 4 B.C.E. Judea, Idumea, and Samaria, which Herod had willed to his son Archelaus, were the only Jewish domains of Jesus' time to fall under direct Roman rule as an imperial province. Archelaus had proved to be so brutal, slaughtering thousands of Jews and Samaritans alike, that Augustus removed him in 6 C.E., replacing him with a line of prefects that included Pilate.

Just to the south of Herod the Great's kingdom, spanning the Sinai desert and northern Arabia, lay the fabulously wealthy kingdom of Nabatea, which controlled the north-south spice-trade routes between the Red Sea and Syria. Nabatea was theoretically another Roman client-monarchy like that of Herod, but the Nabatean kings, ruling from their splendid Greek-style city of Petra, exercised a good deal of independence from Rome. They occasionally made war on their own initiative (strictly *verboten* under the Roman magisterium), and forged various alliances with the Parthians. Malchus, one rather truculent Nabatean ruler, especially enjoyed persecuting Herod. Because Nabatea was not entirely under Rome's thumb in Jesus' day, Roman control over Palestine was all the more critical.

During Judas Maccabeus's time, the Jews of Palestine had considered Rome a benevolent ally against the Seleucids. Rome, in turn, needed Maccabeus and his family; the militarily powerful kingdom of Judea was a Roman thorn in Syria's side. Syria grew progressively weaker, however, wracked by dynastic quarrels that led to its invasion and occupation by Tigranes, the king of Armenia, in 83 B.C.E. Tigranes and his self-aggrandizing father-in-law, King Mithridates VI, who reigned over the tiny monarchy of Pontus on the Black Sea, soon loomed as a greater threat to Rome than Seleucid Syria. After gradually annexing most of Asia Minor to his Black Sea mini-kingdom, Mithridates began skirmishing with the Roman army in Greece, only to be squelched (along with Tigranes) by Rome in the end. It was in an effort to batten down security that Pompey took Syria from Tigranes as part of his spoils in 64 B.C.E. and turned it into a Roman province.

It was only a matter of time—one year, in fact—before Pompey initiated similar action in Palestine. Alexander Jannaeus's two sons, Hyrcanus (the elder and heir to Jannaeus's titles) and Aristobolus (the younger and more aggressive), were threatening the *Pax Romana* as they warred bitterly over which of them would assume his late father's throne and high priesthood. Ignoring a century of Jewish-Roman friendship, Pompey marched into Jerusalem and stormed the Temple itself. He then divided the Jewish kingdom into four administrative districts, "liberated" the Syrian-Hellenistic coastal cities from Jewish control (although all had sizeable Jewish populations), restored self-governance to the Decapolis, and forced Palestinian Jews to start paying Roman taxes for the first time in history. Aristobolus, who had forced Hyrcanus to abdicate from his dual office four years earlier as part of their fraternal feud, was sent with his family in chains to Rome as part of Pompey's triumphal parade. Thousands of his supporters were also transported to the imperial city and sold into slavery. Pompey gave the high priesthood back to Hyrcanus, a more pliant character than his younger brother, but refused to let him reassume the monarchy.

The economic damage suffered by the Jews from the loss of their maritime ports was heavy, and the humiliation of having their homeland politically dismantled was crushing. Even under Herod the Great a generation later, when the Romans restored much of the Jewish kingdom to Jewish hegemony, they never returned the Decapolis, which remained under the Syrian governor's administration throughout Jesus' youth and ministry.

The Jewish kingship went to Herod thanks to the manipulations of his father, Antipater. Antipater's own father had maneuvered his way into Alexander Jannaeus's favor, and Jannaeus had rewarded him by naming him governor of Idumea. Antipater had continued the family tradition of cozying up to the powers-that-be by ingratiating himself first with Hyrcanus and later with Pompey, who gave him the title "governor of the Jews" after taking over Palestine in 63 B.C.E. When Pompey died and his rival, Julius Caesar, gained control of Italy, Antipater (and Hyrcanus) rapidly switched their allegiance to Caesar by sending him Jewish reinforcement troops for an Egyptian campaign. Out of considerations of political expediency as much as gratitude, Caesar traveled to Palestine, where he granted Roman citizenship to Antipater, conferred on Hyrcanus the title of "ethnarch" (a close approximation to kingship), restored the port of Joppa to the Jews, and allowed the rebuilding of the Jerusalem walls, which Pompey had destroyed in his ravages.

By judiciously performing favors for whichever Roman happened to be holding the reins, over a period of about 75 years Antipater and Herod the Great threw their weight behind a total of five different Roman strongmen: Pompey, Caesar, Caesar's assassin Cassius (who gave Herod permission to launch a personal vendetta after Antipater was murdered in a palace intrigue in 43 B.C.E.), Caesar's avenger Mark Antony (who made Herod and his elder brother, Phasael, administrators over Palestine), and Mark Antony's nemesis, Octavian, a nephew of Caesar who later became the emperor Augustus and Herod's most generous benefactor.

Not long after Antipater's death, Hyrcanus, by then quite elderly, gave the hand of his granddaughter Mariamme to Herod, at the same time naming him legal guardian of Mariamme's 10-year-old brother Aristobulus, the heir-apparent to the Hasmonean kingship. As well as being a titled Hasmonean, Mariamme was considered a great beauty. Herod already had a wife, Doris, but no matter: he divorced Doris overnight. He now had a ticket to the Judean throne. However, there were others ambitious for the kingship besides the boy Aristobulus. One of the pretenders was Antigonus, son of the other Aristobulus, Hyrcanus's exiled and now dead younger brother Antigonus raised an army from a Palestinian Jewry overwhelmingly supportive of his royal claims. In 40 B.C.E., three years after Antipater's death, the Parthians overran Syria and invaded Galilee, where they joined forces with Antigonus's rebel troops. Together they stormed the countryside of Herod's native Idumea and marched on Jerusalem, where they promptly installed Antigonus as king. They also cut off the ears of Hyrcanus, thus rendering him unfit to serve as high priest, and captured Herod's brother Phasael, who took his own life.

Herod managed to escape from Jerusalem and rushed to Rome, where Antony and Octavian named him "king of the Jews" and led him to the Capitoline Hill to offer a sacrifice to Jupiter. It was rather an odd ceremony for a Jewish monarch, but Herod wore his Judaism lightly (his mother, an Arabian, was not even Jewish). The Roman army then drove the Parthians out of Syria and installed Herod on the Jerusalem throne after bombarding the city and slaughtering countless numbers of its inhabitants. Antigonus, who had personally surrendered to the Roman commander Sosius, was taken to Rome, where he was executed by Mark Antony.

Herod still had powerful enemies, both real and perceived, many of whom were his own Hasmonean relatives (via marriage to Mariamme) and their sympathizers. One of his first acts of state was to execute 45 well-placed supporters of Antigonus, in the process ravaging the Sanhedrin, an administrative body drawn from the Jerusalem religious aristocracy that held court, levied taxes, and performed whatever other governmental functions the Romans permitted. This bloody purge, accompanied by Herod's stripping the Sanhedrin of certain powers, fatally weakened the local Jewish leadership class, which never fully recovered. Such acts paved the way for the takeover of Jerusalem by the intransigent Zealots and other rebels many decades later, which led to the city's eventual destruction.

Herod's next target was his brother-in-law and ward, Aristobolus, then 16 and an obvious candidate for the high priesthood and even the kingship itself. Herod arranged a fatal swimming accident for the teenager and appointed an apolitical candidate who was not of the Hasmonean family as high priest. With Aristobolus gone, the aged and earless Hyrcanus, whom Herod had rescued from the Parthians and brought back to Jerusalem, proved to be immensely popular with the Jews of Palestine, who persisted in viewing their new Idumean king as a foreign interloper. Herod had Hyrcanus executed on a trumped-up charge of collaborating with his archenemy, Malchus of Nabatea. Next to go was Mariamme. Hyrcanus's granddaughter had never cared much for her Idumean husband, and after her brother's murder, she despised him. Herod's initial infatuation with her had evolved into a complex passion in which love alternated with sexual jealousy and suspicion of her Hasmonean family loyalties. In 29 B.C.E. he had Mariamme executed on a specious adultery charge. Remorse over her death tormented Herod for the rest of his life, but he consoled himself somewhat with at least nine other wives and concubines, including Doris, whom he had reinstalled in the palace, and a second Mariamme, who was the daughter of one of his handpicked high priests.

Herod's Jewish subjects never stopped loathing him. Nonetheless, he was a generally fair ruler, even if brutally intolerant of anyone who challenged his legitimacy or disturbed the public order. At his own expense, he rebuilt the Second Temple on a lavish scale, and commissioned other public works that provided employment to many Jerusalemites. According to certain scholars, he even reduced his subjects' tax burden to Rome.

Toward the end of his life, Herod deteriorated both mentally and physically. He fell out of favor with Augustus after having launched an unauthorized military foray against his nemeses in the Sinai, the Nabateans. He felt constantly threatened by the growing numbers of Hasmonean pretenders, including his own five children by Mariamme I. While still in Augustus's good graces, he had tried to persuade the emperor to have his two eldest sons by Mariamme executed for treason. When Augustus refused to comply, Herod called for a trial of the two princes before the Roman governor of Syria, who duly condemned them to death. He also had Antipater, his son by Doris, executed on charges of plotting his murder. In a moment of rage, he ordered a group of young Pharisees to be burnt alive because they had destroyed a golden eagle (a Torah-forbidden graven image with symbolic overtones of Roman imperialism) that he had affixed over the Temple doorway. Finally, he stipulated that a number of prominent Jews whom he had imprisoned in Jericho were to be killed immediately following his death so as to ensure that people would mourn. The story in Matthew's Gospel of his massacre of baby boys in Bethlehem after having learned of a likely rival's birth is in line with the bloodthirstiness and paranoia that marked his last days on the throne. Upon his demise, there were nationwide riots that required three Roman legions under the Syrian governor to dispel.

The stories of Herod the Great and his father Antipater are graphic examples of the way in which the fortunes of Jewish monarchs, and even ordinary Jews, were intertwined with those of influential Romans of their day. Indeed, during Jesus' time the Holy Land was hardly the remote outpost that tradition would have us believe. The sea voyage from Rome via Alexandria to the ports of Joppa and Caesarea (the latter of which Herod had built and named after his patron, Augustus) took only two weeks or so at the height of the summer season. Thanks to Roman muscle, anyone with means could—and did—book passage on a boat or join a trade caravan and traverse the Mediterranean periplus with very little fear of molestation. As Yale University professor of religion Wayne Meeks has pointed out, it was not until the invention of the steamboat in the 19th century that Mediterranean travel would become more brisk than it had been during the first few centuries after Jesus' birth.[4] Every good-sized city in the Roman Empire bustled with official emissaries, itinerant craftsmen, traders in goods and slaves, wandering poets and philosophers, and religious pilgrims. Mail delivery was also remarkably efficient for an era in which there was no government postal service. Records of contemporary Egyptian papyruses, for example, indicate an active correspondence with Rome, the Arabian peninsula, and Cilicia in Asia Minor.

The friendship between Augustus and Herod was genuine enough while it lasted, although always colored by expediency and decidedly tilted in Augustus's favor. Herod, who considered himself a proper, cosmopolitan Hellenistic monarch, avidly promoted Greek culture and architecture, even building a theater and stadium in Jerusalem. He financed public works all over Greece, even in Athens and Sparta, and once sponsored the Olympic Games. On the island of Rhodes, where he subsidized the restoration of a temple to Apollo that had been destroyed by fire and helped underwrite the maintenance of the world-famous Rhodian fleet, his name may well have been as familiar as that of Augustus. In Sebaste, a Greek-style city he founded in Samaria and named after Augustus (*Sebastos* is Greek for "Augustus"), as well as in Caesarea, he installed theaters, stadiums, gymnasiums, and other Hellenistic accouterments. Thanks to his industry, the kingdom of Judea enjoyed a short-lived international panache.

Herod traveled frequently to Rome and other sites where Augustus happened to be encamped. He sent at least six of his many sons to the imperial court for a combination of education and political palm-greasing. One of his grandsons (by the first Mariamme), a charming profligate named Agrippa after Augustus's favorite general, spent his entire early manhood in Rome, where he ran up debts and became an intimate of Tiberius's son Drusus and the future emperor Claudius. When Drusus died, Agrippa turned his attentions to Tiberius's grandnephew Gaius, nicknamed Caligula, who succeeded Tiberius as emperor and rewarded Agrippa handsomely for his solicitousness. Agrippa's mother and grandmother had both been confidantes of Claudius's mother Antonia and grandmother Livia. Except for Cleopatra of Egypt, an archrival of Herod who had persuaded a besotted Mark Antony to give her a huge tract of revenue-generating balsam groves in Herod's territory, no ancient royalty other than the Herods hobnobbed so extensively with the rulers of Rome. The ministry of Jesus thus took place not on the sidelines of history, but on a great world stage where Pompey and Caesar, Antony and Cleopatra, and Augustus, Tiberius, and Caligula trod the boards at various times.

When Herod died in 4 B.C.E., Augustus, who had never reconciled with him after his unauthorized Nabatean incursion, refused to ratify his will, which had left his entire kingdom to his son Archelaus by a Samaritan wife, Malthace. Augustus limited Archelaus's realm to Judea, Idumea, and Samaria, and divided the northern half of Herod's territory into two independent "tetrarchies," one of which went to Archelaus's elder brother Antipas, and the other to his half-brother Philip. As I noted previously, Archelaus proved to be both unnecessarily harsh (at one point he sent a detachment of troops into the Temple, provoking a riot during which his soldiers killed 1,000 Jews) and impolitic with his peers. He even quarreled with Sabinius, the Roman military head of Syria, who thought he also had a mandate to assume trusteeship over the whole of Herod's former domain.

By 6 C.E., the situation in Jerusalem had become so poisonous that Varus, the Roman governor of Syria, installed a garrison of Roman troops to maintain law and order, touching off a Palestine-wide guerrilla war that was especially fierce in Galilee, where the bandit chieftain Judas the Galilean led an insurgent army from his headquarters in Sepphoris, four miles from Jesus' hometown of Nazareth. When Varus finally squelched the rebellion, he ordered Sepphoris burnt to the ground, and 2,000 of Judas's troops were crucified. The boy Jesus might have seen the crosses. Archelaus was so universally hated that the Jews and Samaritans temporarily buried their religious antagonisms and sent a joint delegation to Rome to lodge a protest with Augustus and petition for direct Roman rule. The emperor complied, cashiering Archelaus to Gaul, and creating a new Judean-Samaritan province called "Judea."

Augustus allowed Antipas and Philip, who had demonstrated capable leadership, to retain their tetrarchies. Antipas's territory encompassed Galilee, a rural area of approximately 750 square miles with a population of around 200,000, and Perea, an 850-square-mile tract running along the east side of the Jordan River down to the Dead Sea. Philip had inherited a sprawling swath of southern Syria, including Gaulinitis. Antipas's two realms, Galilee and Perea, were not contiguous. Between them, spanning the Jordan where it flowed out of the Sea of Galilee, lay the Syrian-ruled city-states of the Decapolis.

Like his father before him, Antipas astutely flattered whoever ruled in Rome: first Augustus, and then his successor, Tiberius. He gave the name Tiberias to a new capital city he built on the Sea of Galilee's western shore. Earlier he had founded a city in Perea called Livias Julias after Augustus's empress Livia. While Philip's tetrarchy was mostly Gentile (with a sizeable Jewish minority), and thus disinclined to resent the Herodian dynasty and the Hellenophile culture it championed, this was not the case in either Galilee or Perea, where Antipas tried to respect his subjects' religious sensibilities. Unlike his half-brother, Antipas did not have graven images stamped on his coins. Although not a particularly observant Jew, especially in private life, he was careful not to flaunt his impieties.

Once again like his father, Antipas would brook nothing that smacked of political dissent. The famous bandits of Galilee, half insurgents and half highwaymen in the tradition of Judas, kept a low profile during his 44-year rule. Both the Gospels and Josephus recount that Antipas imprisoned and decapitated John the Baptist, who had centered his ministry along the Jordan in Perea, because he considered the popular prophet a threat to his sovereignty. Also according to the Gospels, Antipas kept a wary eye on Jesus, who in turn gave him a wide berth. (As related by Luke, Jesus once paid Antipas a back-handed compliment, calling him "that fox" in reference to his cunning wit and his relatively minor status in the Roman order.)[5] Antipas's attitude toward Jesus was undoubtedly a mixture of fear that he might be another putative threat to his throne and curiosity about his supposed miracles and exorcisms.

Philip managed to die on his throne in 34 C.E. Antipas would probably have done so as well had he not decided after Tiberius's death that he wanted to be a real king, not just a tetrarch. Early in his career, he had tried unsuccessfully to persuade Augustus to appoint him sole ruler of Herod's kingdom. Egging on Antipas was his social-climbing niece and second wife, Herodias, another of Mariamme I's grandchildren. Herodias had been married to her uncle Herod Philip, one of Mariamme II's sons by Herod the Great, but had divorced this obscure prince (not the same man as Philip the tetrarch) in order to marry Antipas, by far the most fortunate of her uncles. Marriages between close relatives of different generations were a common occurrence among the Herodians. Herodias's daughter by Herod Philip, Salome—the girl in the Gospel stories who danced in front of Antipas and was rewarded with the head of John the Baptist on a platter—married first her uncle Philip the tetrarch, and then a cousin of the Hasmonean line who was in all probability young enough to be her son.

Gaius Caligula, who became emperor after Tiberius, was not sympathetic to Antipas's royal aspirations. After Philip's death, Gaius named his former mentor Agrippa, who was Herodias's brother, as heir to Philip's tetrarchy, giving him the title of king that Antipas himself had so desperately craved. As Tiberius had recalled Pontius Pilate to Rome just before he died, it appeared likely that Gaius's next move would be to restore the Jewish throne in Jerusalem and seat Agrippa upon it. Herodias decided that the moment had arrived for her husband to make his own bid for the monarchy. When Agrippa learned of Antipas's maneuvers, he retaliated by bringing charges of treason against him, including complicity with the Parthians. Gaius promptly deposed Antipas (in 39 C.E.), exiled him to Gaul (where Augustine had sent Archelaus), and handed Galilee and Perea over to Agrippa. Antipas died in obscurity in a village on the Spanish frontier. Despite his humiliating end, however, he had managed to reign for an unusual length of time amid the political turmoil of his age. He had also afforded Galilee the same measure of relative peace in Jesus' day that Gratus and Pilate had provided for Judea. Thanks to the pro forma independence he had secured for his tiny domain, no Roman troops were garrisoned in Galilee, even though its inhabitants undoubtedly saw Roman soldiers marching along the Jerusalem-Damascus highway that wound through its center.

Other than the politics of Antipas's reign, surprisingly little is known about first-century Galilee, a hilly agricultural region of the old kingdom of Israel that had been surrounded on three sides by Gentiles since the first Hebrew occupation. (In Hebrew, Galilee's name meant "circle" or "district.") Geographically, Galilee was part of southern Syria, and in ancient times the Syrian port of Ptolemais lay due west of Galilee's orchards and fields. Due to the Assyrian deportations in the eighth century B.C.E., the centuries of Gentile occupation, and the Hasmoneans' forced conversion of many Galileans when they had reconquered Galilee 100 years before Jesus' birth, certain scholars have speculated that the Galileans were not related to the Jews of Judea, and that their Judaism was superficial and separatist.[6] Fueling these suppositions is an ongoing debate among archaeologists as to whether or not there were any synagogues in Galilee in Jesus' day. The custom of using the synagogue as a place of worship outside the Temple, which was a consequence of the Diaspora, came late to Judea. To date, archaeologists have unearthed only three pre-70 Palestinian synagogues. One of these, however, is at the site of the ancient town of Gamla in Gaulanitis, the birthplace of Judas the Galilean, which suggests that adjacent Galilee in all likelihood had synagogues of its own and that its residents were conventionally observant Jews.

Furthermore, unlike the Samaritans, who genuinely hated the Jews, the Galileans did fight the Romans alongside the Judeans throughout the First Jewish War. The efforts of Antipas, at least in public life, to accommodate his subjects' prohibition against graven images also indicates that they took their religion seriously. Following Antipas's exile, a Galilean mob led by a radical named Jesus of Tiberias burnt down his palace in order to destroy certain animal murals, graven images that had been painted on the inside walls. Most Galileans seem to have faithfully paid the tithes that supported the Temple. Those who could afford it regularly walked 75 to 100 miles south to Jerusalem for the Jewish festivals. Finally, they often named their children after nationalist Jewish heroes. One of the most popular of these names was

"Judas," in memory of the Maccabean leader as well as one of Israel's twelve patriarchs. Jesus had two or perhaps three apostles called Judas (the Syrian Christian tradition lists Judas as the real name of the apostle Thomas, whose byname was the Aramaic word for "twin"). Jesus' own name, a variant of Joshua, after the great Jewish general, was also highly popular in Galilee and Judea. The early Christian belief that Jesus was of the tribe of Judah and the house of David, mentioned both in Paul's letters and in the Gospels, may well have stemmed from his being the offspring of Jewish settlers in Galilee during Hasmonean times.

In matters other than religion, Galilee was surprisingly cosmopolitan for such a rural hinterland (it had no coastline, and Sepphoris and Tiberias were its only real cities). Major trade routes linking Egypt, Syria, Jerusalem, and the Palestinian ports crisscrossed Galilee, doubtless providing a constant stream of fresh news and entertainment. The Jerusalem-Damascus highway ran through Nazareth's urban neighbor Sepphoris (rebuilt under Antipas) before swinging eastward to Tiberias and then due north. Even the most isolated farmers probably caught glimpses of exotic caravan goods and shambling gangs of chained slaves being driven to the markets of Alexandria or Antioch. Directly abutting Lower Galilee was the Decapolis, with its pronouncedly Greek culture. Galileans had far more direct exposure to the languages and customs of the Gentiles than did the Judeans to the south.

It is safe to speculate that even the lowliest Galilean peasants knew at least a few words and phrases of Koinē Greek, the *lingua franca* of the ancient Mediterranean world. Anyone having regular dealings with Gentiles probably spoke Greek fairly fluently; those who were literate most likely wrote serviceable Greek as well. It is not inconceivable that Jesus and his disciples, although mere fishermen and farmers, were fluent both in their local tongue, Aramaic, and in Greek. Given the fact that Gentiles and Jews lived side by side in first-century Palestine and its environs, even the most devout Jews imbibed Hellenistic culture and ways of thinking. Moderns are accustomed to viewing ancient Western societies through the eyes of the second-century Christian theologian Tertullian, who characterized "Athens and Jerusalem" as symbolic polar opposites, the one Hellenic, intellectual, and agnostic, and the other anti-Hellenic, anti-intellectual, and pietistic. In many ways, Jerusalem *was* Athens in Jesus' day. Thanks to Herod, all its public buildings except for the Temple were constructed in the international Hellenistic style. Its wealthier residents also saw to it that their children were given classical educations, as did upper-class Jews elsewhere in the Roman Empire.

Greek was indubitably the first language of Diaspora Jewry in the Roman world. Especially during Passover, as many as half a million pilgrims inundated Jerusalem, large numbers of whom spoke Greek. In his 1968 book titled *Do You Know Greek? How Much Greek Could the First Jewish Christians Have Known?*, J. N. Sevenster presents evidence of widespread fluency and even literacy among first-century and early-second-century Jews from a wealth of funerary inscriptions, government edicts, business records, legal documents, and personal letters found within and without Palestine.[7] With the exception of the cities of Jerusalem, the cities of ancient Palestine founded by the Ptolemies, the Seleucids, and the Herods were predominantly non-Jewish, while the countryside was overwhelmingly Jewish. However, even Caesarea, where the Roman prefect had his headquarters and Roman troops were garrisoned, maintained a large Jewish community; Tiberias and Sepphoris, despite their Hellenistic architectural trappings, were heavily Jewish in population. Andrew and Philip, two of Jesus' Galilean disciples mentioned in the Gospels, had Greek names. Only in the smallest, most remote villages did Jews and Gentiles live separate lives. The few Jews who were not directly exposed to Greek culture almost certainly had contact with others who were.

According to Duke University scholar E. P. Sanders, the Jews of Palestine probably dressed like Greeks as well.[8] Textile remnants found in the Dead Sea caves of Judea, and wall paintings depicting members of the Jewish community of the ancient Mesopotamian city of Dura-Europos, suggest that first-century Palestinian Jews wore the same Graeco-Roman clothing that had been common to the Mediterranean world and its environs for hundreds of years. Men's wear consisted of a belted tunic (*chitōn* in Greek), a garment made from two pieces of fabric sewn together (more expensive tunics were made from a single, seamless piece of cloth). Depending on the length of the tunic and the way in which it was folded, it fell either above or below the knee. Over this garment they wore a long cloak (*himation* in Greek) that was wrapped around the body and thrown over the head in cold or inclement weather, or even used as a blanket. Winter apparel was usually made from woolen fabrics that were sometimes dyed in a rainbow of yellows, browns, reds, blues, maroons, and purples. In summer, they dressed in linen that had been bleached as white as they could afford (flax was a major Palestinian crop), or perhaps imported cotton (which the climate of Palestine was too dry to cultivate domestically). Underneath these garments they wore loincloths. Their feet were shod in sandals, or if the paintings from Dura-Europos are any guide, short leather boots. Again, judging from these wall paintings, which date from the third century but depict attire that had been used for centuries, men wore their hair fairly short, and had either shaven faces or short beards.

First-century Jewish women garbed themselves in longer, more colorful, and more generously cut tunics. When elaborately folded over and under several belts, these became graceful, ankle-length gowns. Wool and linen were also their most popular fabrics (only royalty and the very rich could afford silk, which was fabulously expensive, imported raw from China, and then rewoven into cloth of gossamer fineness). Footwear was generally embroidered, trimmed with beads, or dyed in bright colors, with cork or wooden "platform" soles, and accessories were as sumptuous as money could buy. Rabbinic literature (admittedly from centuries later) speaks of the "golden city," or "golden Jerusalem," an elaborate hair ornament worn by the women of Jerusalem that was probably a type of crown or high comb. Most women covered their heads with a veil, or a hairnet resembling a Victorian snood that held up their long tresses at neck or shoulder level, or both.

According to later rabbinic literature (which may be anachronistic), upper-class Jewish women were not permitted to leave their homes unless they were swathed in veils to the point of unrecognizability. Among the wealthiest women of Jerusalem, some may even have been sequestered entirely in luxurious domestic quarters. However, Josephus, the Gospels, and the letters of Paul, as well as letters and legal documents found in the Judean deserts, all suggest that first-century Jewish women of the lower classes, perhaps out of economic necessity, enjoyed remarkable independence, sartorially and otherwise. Many of them worked alongside their husbands as farmers, artisans, street hawkers, traders, and shopkeepers, while others operated their own businesses. They also filed lawsuits, funded charitable works, and traveled freely with or without their mates, both in the cities or on pilgrimages and visits to distant kin.

Galilee was a cultural crossroads due in part to an astonishing abundance of crops that fed the entire Middle East and beyond. Thanks to excellent soil (which is still the case today, despite centuries of deforestation and erosion), a mild climate, and a long growing season, the valleys north of the Sea of Galilee produced so much wheat that the Roman and Herodian royal families maintained granaries of their own. The land was such a valuable agricultural resource that it was rarely used for pasturage, and herds of sheep and goats were far more common in Syria and Judea. Galilee also had the finest wines in Palestine, and its vast date-palm, fig, and walnut orchards were famous throughout the ancient world. Most lucrative of all for the export trade, however, were the Galilean olive groves. As historian Fernand Braudel has noted, their fruit was an integral part of a distinctly "Mediterranean" way of life in Europe, Asia, and Africa, in the lands that lay between the northernmost habitat of the olive tree and that of the date-palm.[9] People not only cooked with olive oil and ate the fruit pickled in brine, but they also lit their homes and public places with olive-oil lamps, rubbed olive oil on their wounds, and bathed in olive oil when they were ill. The town of Gischala in Upper Galilee produced such huge quantities of oil that it was sold in bulk as far away as Laodicea in the western part of Asia Minor. In Jotapata, which was not far from Gischala, there were so many vats of oil on hand during the First Jewish War that the town's defenders heated large pots of it to the boiling point and poured them over the walls onto the Roman attackers.

The fishing industry, which figures so prominently in the Gospels (there are 45 references to fishing boats and fishermen in connection with Jesus, most of them uncannily accurate in detail), was Galilee's other mainstay. Under the early Israelites, most of whom were farmers and herdsmen, the Sea of Galilee (now Lake Kinnaret) had been little more than a geographical marker. During the third century B.C.E., the region's Ptolemaic governors recognized the lake's commercial potential, and began stocking it with fish (some which come from Egypt) and curing the catch for export. Their staple was a species of fresh-water sardine *(Anocanthobrana Terrae Sanctae)* that was sold in every marketplace in Palestine, and possibly exported to markets as far away as Antioch, Alexandria, and Rome, in salted, pickled (in jars), or smoked form. Other popular fish included several species of carp and *Tilapia Galilaea,* or Saint Peter's fish. Wherever one looked along the shores of the Sea of Galilee, there were probably hundreds of single-masted fishing boats, 20 to 30 feet in length, docked at the villages strung around the lake. These were first-century Cannery Rows whose inhabitants were mostly engaged in some aspect of fishing and fish-processing industries.

One of the towns on the Galilean side of the lake, where the emperor Vespasian would convene a hasty treason trial for Galilean rebels during the war, was Magdal Nunia (or "tower of fish," from the Hebrew *magdal* and the Aramaic *nunia*). Its Greco-Roman name was Taricheae, from the Greek word *tarichos,* "smoked fish." Given her surname, Jesus' follower Mary Magdalene may well have been a fish-monger's runaway daughter. At the top of the lake lay the larger town of Capernaum, where according to Luke's Gospel, the fisherman Zebedee, father of Jesus' disciples James and John, owned a boat in partnership with two of Jesus' other disciples, Simon Peter and his brother

Andrew. Other than their proprietorship of the boat, which implies some modest means, it is difficult to understand the social status of these first-century fishermen. Unlike the herding and butchering of animals, fishing and fish-processing were not among the large number of "despicable trades" that relegated Jews to an inferior social class (as affirmed by the later-written Mishnah).

Nonetheless, working with one's hands and the sweat of one's brow has never been a mark of exalted social standing. Fishing was also an occupation with somewhat disreputable connotations: off-again-on-again work schedules, especially for the pickup crews of day laborers who manned the boats, and leisure hours whiled away in dubious company at the dockside taverns that abounded in the ancient world as they do now. In any case, there was probably good money to be made in Jesus' time from fishing. The catch of 153 "large" fish (most likely carp and tilapia) made in less than 10 minutes, which John's Gospel describes as Jesus' last miracle, would have retailed for at least $5,000 at today's prices.

One result of the thriving agricultural industry was "agribusiness," which came early to Galilee (and even more markedly to Judea), where it persisted as a social blot on a landscape that must once have seemed like a rustic paradise. (The term "agribusiness" was used by the biblical scholar Seán Freyne to denote a concentration in land ownership and rise in state-run monopolies in Palestine that had been widely promoted by the Ptolemies and Seleucids three centuries before Jesus was born.) The kingdoms of Israel and Judah had been commonwealths of family farms, and this ancient pattern of smallholding was undoubtedly still prevalent in Jesus' day. Josephus regularly referred to the "Galileans" as independent-minded rural yeomen who lived comfortably, if primitively, on their own land (the father of the prodigal son in Luke's parable was probably an example of such an individual). However, Alexander the Great had already begun the tradition carried on by the Ptolemies and Seleucids of confiscating land in conquered territories, claiming it for the crown, and distributing it in large tracts as a reward for military service. As time went on, more and more of Palestine was transformed from small farms into vast estates worked by tenant farmers, hired hands, and even slaves, a system that continued through Hasmonean and Herodian times. Some of the huge landholdings, especially in Judea, were the property of the crown (at one point, Herod the Great personally owned two-thirds of Judea).

Furthermore, grain, oil, and other commodity markets were strictly regulated by the governments in power, which granted trade monopolies to local brokers in return for pledges of loyalty and services rendered. Under the Ptolemies, this policy was to become blatantly mercantilistic: Egypt literally milked Palestine for foodstuffs. Although the governors from Alexandria and Antioch introduced Greek-style innovations in livestock breeding, cultivation, irrigation, and marketing, it is unlikely that anyone but the brokers, large landholders, and government officials benefitted much from enhanced productivity and expanded international markets. In contrast to the Ptolemies and Seleucids, the Romans tended to respect traditional land-holding arrangements, and neither Herod the Great nor Antipas was inclined to upset the peace by dispossessing peasants. In Galilee, numerous independent, family-tilled plots coexisted with a handful of large estates. In Judea, there were far fewer autonomous farmers. In his studies of first-century Galilee, Freyne paints a dismal picture of the Galilean fishing industry, with large-scale enterprises siphoning off profits from those who actually caught the fish.[10]

In all likelihood, conditions were somewhat less grim and more entrepreneurial than Freyne makes them out to be. As already noted, the Gospels depict Zebedee and Simon Peter as business partners who co-owned a fishing boat. According to Luke's Gospel, Simon was also a homeowner. If the Gospels are to be believed, he and the other disciples fished when they felt like it rather than every day, indicating that their condition was not destitute. Recent excavations of a first-century fisherman's house in Bethsaida, a town on the Sea of Galilee just across the Galilean border in Philip's realm (which, according to John's Gospel, was the birthplace of Peter, Andrew, and the two Zebedee brothers), reveal that its owners lived a comfortable life in relatively spacious quarters. Its larders and others like it in Bethsaida also contained large numbers of animal bones and wine jars, suggesting plentiful amounts of food and drink.

It is equally clear from reading Josephus, however, that many lower-class Galileans were only one bad harvest away from destitution, despite the richness of their soil and the profusion of its crops. Taxes were high. The precariousness of economic life undoubtedly accounted for the persistence and popularity of the bandits who infested the hills of Galilee and Philip's tetrarchy across the lake. These were probably local Zapatas—highwaymen who doubled as guerrilla warriors.

What was the lifestyle of the average Galilean—or Judean—in Jesus' day? By modern standards, it would be considered rather squalid. There was virtually no middle class, although in the cities skilled craftsmen and shopkeepers made decent livings, and some merchants became quite wealthy by acquiring monopoly rights in commodities or making shrewd investments in luxury goods and spices. Outside the cities, the overwhelming majority of Palestinian Jews were small farmers or sharecroppers. Like peasants elsewhere in the Mediterranean basin, they undoubtedly inhabited a one-room, mud-brick structure above a ground-level barn that housed their domestic animals. They had almost no furniture, and slept on mats or mattresses laid on the floor. Those who were farther up on the social ladder owned larger homes with rooms arranged around a central courtyard. The truly wealthy possessed imposing dwellings fitted with swimming pools.

Except for the poorest of the poor, few people went hungry in Galilee, even though most ate red meat only on feast days, and chicken and fish only on the Sabbath. Bread, beans, eggs, olives, and sheep or goat cheese were the dietary staples, supplemented by vegetables and fresh or dried fruit. Wine, which was the chief beverage, was in plentiful supply. Presumably few people went cold either, as Palestine abounded in sheep, especially in the hill country of Judea. The Mishnah, while admittedly not a document contemporary with Jesus, prescribes working with wool—spinning, weaving, sewing, embroidering, and mending—as a pursuit with which all Jewish housewives, rich and poor alike, should fill their spare time, since "idleness leads to unchastity."[11] There is no reason to believe that the production of wool clothing by local womenfolk was not as ubiquitous in Jesus' day as it was when the Mishnah was codified in approximately 200 C.E.

Daily life, even for the most humble, was certainly not all drudgery. Once a week, Jews relaxed on the Sabbath, a practice otherwise unknown in the ancient world. In addition, there was a liturgical calendar of holy days that were occasions for celebration. Weddings were another frequent and pleasant excuse to take a day off. As the Gospels point out, nuptials were village-wide social events involving every shirttail relative and friend of a friend who could claim some relation to the bride or groom. Another diversion was making pilgrimages to Jerusalem for the three great Jewish festivals of Passover, Pentecost, and Sukkot. Indeed, the Book of Deuteronomy *commanded* Jews to partake in the Passover feast in Jerusalem if they could afford to do so, and allowed them to count the money they had spent entertaining themselves in the holy city as a tithe. Entire families or groups of families made the Passover journey on foot along the dirt roads leading to Jerusalem from Galilee or Idumea, camping out at night. The poorer classes doubtless had neither time nor money for more than one pilgrimage a year (a travel rate of 15 miles per day and a week spent in Jerusalem took three weeks out of their lives). Religious junkets therefore doubled as annual vacations for those of modest means. These were times for praying in the Temple, but also for gabbing with relatives and gawking at the luxury wares of the merchants and skilled craftsmen whose shops lined the narrow streets of a city swollen with wealth from a Temple tax that Jews around the world were obliged to pay. To some extent, such sojourns probably resembled the pilgrimage in Chaucer's *Canterbury Tales:* a combination of praying, hymn-singing, joshing, tall-tale-telling, eating, drinking, and camaraderie. E. P. Sanders writes: "Jewish festivals were like Christmas: a blend of piety, good cheer, hearty eating, making music, chatting with friends, drinking and dancing."[12]

Thus, while it can be said that the ordinary Jews of Jesus' time lived under physical conditions resembling those of southern sharecroppers during the Great Depression—primitive housing, few changes of clothing, simple food, and truncated educations, if any—their existence, centered on kinship, worship, the land, and the festive cycles of the agricultural and liturgical year, was far from miserable. The vast majority of people in the ancient world were no better off than they, and even the wealthiest took for granted living conditions that moderns would find intolerable. The upper classes' swarms of servants, lavish meals, and bejeweled apparel hardly compensated for the dusty roads, insects, uncomfortable beds, lax sanitation, dearth of central heating, and untreatable diseases.

It is safe to say that there were no atheists, or even agnostics, among the Jews. Atheism was the ultimate evil for an ancient, giving license to amoral acts. However, it is difficult to generalize about the kind of Judaism that Jesus' contemporaries practiced. Until recently, most biblical scholars tended to read the directives of the Mishnah and the two Talmuds, all three codified several centuries after Jesus, as though they described the religious norms of his own time. Scholars also once assumed that the Judaism practiced by the Pharisees (the forebears of the rabbis of today's Judaism) was the "orthodox" Judaism of Jesus' day. They surmised that the many prescriptions and proscriptions of rabbinic tradition were in full force when Jesus preached several decades before there were rabbis. They contrasted the teachings of Jesus, which emphasized love and forgiveness, with the rigid Judaism that hypothetically prevailed at the time, which they called "late" Judaism because to them it represented a lapse into decadent legalism. They were aided in this misperception by the Gospels, which give the Pharisees a central role as "hypocrites" who are Jesus' chief debating opponents. Early biblical studies, some of which had an overt anti-Semitic bent, and later works by Jewish scholars aiming to restore the Pharisees' good name as proto-rabbis, both reached the conclusion that the Pharisees actually controlled Palestinian Judaism in Jesus' day. They indiscriminately identified all pious Jews mentioned by Josephus as "Pharisees," and used the words "Pharisee" and "rabbi" interchangeably.

However, the Judaic scholar Jacob Neusner has ably demonstrated that the anti-Judaic 19th-century experts who cast Jesus as a free-thinking opponent of lifeless legalism, as well as the pro-Judaic authorities who came to the Pharisees' defense, were probably wrong. Neusner concluded—and most scholars nowadays agree—that there was no concept of "normative" or "orthodox," much less "late" Judaism, during Jesus' time.[13] Instead, there were many forms of "Judaism" within and without Palestine, encompassing a wide variety of sects, philosophies, and interpretations of the Jewish Scriptures. In Neusner's view, the Pharisees, who probably never exceeded 10,000 in number, exemplified only one of these "Judaisms."

The Pharisees were the spiritual descendants of the pious, learned *Ḥasidim,* whose outrage at the Seleucid pollution of the Temple had eventually led to the Maccabean revolt. Lay people devoted to the Law (or Torah), they were not of the highest social standing. The Judean aristocracy, including the Temple priests, belonged to the Sadducees (so called after Zadok, David's high priest), a religio/socioeconomic faction whose Judaism was focused solely on Temple ritual and cared little about morality or the hereafter. The Sadducees also believed in accommodation at all costs with occupying foreign powers, as any other stance was a threat to the continued existence of the Temple. Although highly erudite, the Pharisees probably struck the sophisticated Sadducees and the rest of the Hasmonean court as rather brash and self-righteous.

The Pharisees were the first to develop the idea of an "oral Torah," a tradition of interpreting and supplementing the written Torah, which they said dated back to Moses himself. They believed as well that the complex rules and regulations laid down by the Book of Leviticus for the Temple priests applied to all Jews, and that strict observance would set them off from their neighbors as God's chosen people to preserve them from corruption by an alien Hellenistic civilization. Most important, they thought that obedience to Torah laws was the result of proper teaching (ironically, the notion of inculcating virtue through education, or *paideia,* was actually Greek).

The Pharisees had begun as a political faction in the Hasmonean court, hoping to influence the monarchy to make their doctrine of the oral Torah the law of the land. As politicians, they were unsuccessful. After falling out with Alexandra Jannaeus during the early first century B.C.E., some 800 were crucified en masse. While Alexander's queen and successor, the pious Alexandra Salome, had restored them temporarily to privilege and power, by the time of Jesus they were out of favor with both Herod and the Roman governors. Most likely under the leadership of Hillel, the greatest of the Pharisaic teachers (who died during Jesus' boyhood), the Pharisees gave up politics altogether and became what Neusner has called a "table-fellowship sect."

Strict observance of dietary laws, regulations concerning marriage, worship, ritual, and tithing, and restricting one's mealtime companions to those who were similarly meticulous were the hallmarks of the Pharisees of Jesus' time. Their obsession with detail undoubtedly pleased some of their Jewish countrymen and annoyed others. There were, however, genuinely revered teachers within their midst who gathered bands of disciples: Hillel, who taught a version of the Golden Rule similar to that of Jesus; Shammai, Hillel's rival; and Gamaliel I, whom Paul of Tarsus, a former Pharisee, claimed as his mentor.

As the Pharisees' base of operations was Jerusalem, some scholars have questioned whether they were active as far north as Galilee in Jesus' day (which would make the Gospel accounts of Jesus' debates with them fictional). We do know that at least two Pharisees lived in Galilee during the mid–first century: Yoḥanan ben Zakkai, founder of rabbinic Judaism after the destruction of the Temple in 70 C.E., and his wonder-working disciple Ḥanina ben Dosa.

Most Jews, however, were neither Sadducees nor Pharisees. Nor were they radical separatists like the Essenes (whose secret communities near the Dead Sea and elsewhere totaled only 4,000 during Herod the Great's time, according to Josephus). Some espoused what Josephus disdainfully termed "an intrusive fourth philosophy," whose invention he credited to the bandit-chief Judas the Galilean and a renegade Pharisee named Saddok.[14] Driven by fierce religiosity and radical patriotism, its adherents believed that God alone should rule the Jewish homeland, and that the Roman imperium was illicit and should therefore be overthrown. Such revolutionary sentiments, fueled by eschatological hopes, eventually coalesced into the radical political faction known as the Zealots, who were a major faction in the insurrection against Rome in 66 C.E. and the rebel takeover of Jerusalem.

The rest of the ordinary, largely illiterate population that the rabbis later called the *ammei ḥa-aretz* (the people of the land)—followed a wide array of itinerant teachers, prophets, exorcists, baptizers (like John of the desert in the Gospels), and reputed miracle-workers who appeared regularly on the local landscape, and just as regularly disappeared. Their dispersion was often at the hands of the Herodian rulers and Roman governors, who regarded any prophet with too large a following as a possible source of sedition. Astrology was also popular, although theoretically not in accord with Judaism. On the sidelines were magicians, dealers in talismans, and charismatic preachers.

The most arresting feature of first-century religious life in Palestine was its widespread intellectual and spiritual ferment. The Jews had a homeland, and a rich, imposing Second Temple, but they were also under the heel of unsympathetic foreign rulers and puppet kings and tetrarchs who were only nominally Jewish. Most must have longed for the deliverance that they believed God had promised to his people. Everywhere in Palestine and beyond, groups of Jews were claiming that their own particular form of Judaism would bring about deliverance: the Sadducees advocated Temple rites, the Pharisees fidelity to Torah, the Essenes alternative communities of the purified, and the followers of the "fourth philosophy" the overthrow of the Romans and establishment of the kingdom of God.

The "apocalyptic" literature of the day, which typically described an individual's mystical journey from a world ruled by evildoers and pagans to a paradisical world ruled by a God who would set all things right, was extremely popular. The New Testament Book of Revelation is the best-known example of this prolific genre. James H. Charlesworth of Princeton Theological Seminary has estimated that there were at least 60 apocalyptic and related works written between 250 B.C.E. and 100 C.E.[15] The canon of the Hebrew Bible was not fixed until nearly 100 C.E., and many Jews undoubtedly revered these accounts as Holy Scripture. We know about some of them because certain Christian churches incorporated them into their Bibles, while others have turned up among the Dead Sea Scrolls.

As I mentioned in my Introduction, first-century Jews loved to hear and tell stories about Enoch, the father of Methuselah, who ascended alive into heaven. According to Jewish tradition, Enoch ultimately became the Metatron, or greatest of all the angels, and sat on God's throne as a near-divinity. One of the Books of Enoch that circulated during Jesus' day contained a series of parables (much like those of Jesus in the Gospels) that spoke of the "Son of Man," the deliverer of Israel mentioned in the Book of Daniel. The Parables of Enoch identified the Son of Man with the Messiah, who would also deliver his people from oppression.

Despite their many differences, first-century Jews held certain common articles of faith. They believed in an omnipotent God who had elected the descendants of Abraham as his chosen people and had promised them a land of their own. In return, they were to abide by his law. As a sign of this sacred covenant, they circumcised their sons, kept the Sabbath as a day of rest, and celebrated Jewish holy days. Although most did not abide by the strict dietary regimen of the Pharisees, no practicing Jew would eat pork. The majority probably abstained from eating other foods forbidden by the Scriptures, such as catfish, which was in abundant supply in the Sea of Galilee but lacked the scales dictated by the Book of Deuteronomy. Recent excavations of numerous immersion pools from the Golan Heights in the north to Qumran and Masada in the south suggest that ordinary Jews in Palestine engaged in the ritual purifications mandated by the Book of Leviticus. Diaspora Jews may have been less compunctual about purity, although there is some mention of immersion in ancient writings, and certain synagogues were located near rivers or the sea.

The most sacred rite of the Jews was the daily sacrifice of animals at the Jerusalem Temple. For many moderns, it is difficult to understand how butchering and burning bulls, sheep, goats, and turtledoves to express thanksgiving or offer retribution for one's sins was anything other than barbaric at worst, and vacuously ritualistic at best. For Jews, Temple sacrifice involved participation in a tradition established in the earliest days of the Israelite monarchy, when the king had stood beside the high priest before the altar of God. The closest contemporary religious analogue would be the Roman Catholic Mass coupled with confession. As Lester L. Grabbe of the University of Hull explains: "It was not the activity itself that was holy but the meaning invested in it. The temple site was holy because it had been declared holy, not because of some innate quality. . . . Slaughter of bulls, sheep, and goats was sacred in the temple because this was what God had commanded. The sacrifice was *ex opere operato*—the action itself had been vested with sacral meaning by age-old tradition, and performing the sacrifice was a holy and efficacious act in and of itself. The offering of a sin offering resulted in the forgiveness of sin. . . . Guilt was removed, the proper relationship with God reestablished, and the cosmic balance correctly realigned."[16]

The hordes of first-century Jews, Palestinian and Diaspora alike, who made pilgrimages to the Temple for sacrifice and paid their tithe in its support are indicative of widespread fervor. Their religion, in its myriad manifestations, was alive and vigorous. Although the "infancy" stories in the Book of Luke—the tale of Elizabeth, the priest's wife who gave birth to John the Baptist in her old age, and that of Mary, the teenage prophetess who sang hymns of joy when she became pregnant with Jesus—have been called fictional by many scholars, their portrayal of first-century Jewish family piety, centered in Temple, prayer, and eschatological longing, does not ring false. As I mentioned previously, another expression of religious devotion was the naming of children in memory of kings, patriarchs, soldiers, and prophets from the Hebrew Scriptures and the tales of the Maccabees. Mary was named after Moses' sister, Miriam, and Elizabeth in remembrance of Elisheva, the wife of Moses' brother, Aaron.

Within two generations after Jesus' death, the Jewish state was in a shambles. Agrippa, the grandson of Herod the Great whom the emperor Gaius had named king of Galilee and its environs in 37 C.E., was immensely popular with his Jewish subjects although an extravagant spender (as a young man, he had been hounded from country to country by his creditors, and as king, he could scarcely pay his bills out of his royal revenues). The fact that he was a descendant of Mariamme I, and thus of Hasmonean as well as Herodian blood, undoubtedly helped. Like the rest of the Herods, Agrippa paid no more than lip service to Judaism and even encouraged his Gentile subjects to worship him as a god. However, one year after ascending the throne, he intervened personally with Gaius to prevent him from installing a statue of himself in the Jerusalem Temple, a desecration that would probably have triggered a nationwide revolt. This genuine act of courage (Gaius was a megalomaniac who brooked no opposition) was followed by other efforts by Agrippa to protect Jews throughout the Roman Empire from Gentile molestation. Gaius was assassinated in 41 C.E., and his successor, Claudius, enlarged Agrippa's kingdom to include Judea and Samaria, thus restoring the monarchy to Jerusalem after nearly 40 years of direct Roman governance.

Agrippa did not reign for long. In 44 C.E., he died in Caesarea from a mysterious stomach ailment. His only surviving son, Agrippa II, was a boy of 16 completing his education at the Roman imperial court. Claudius at first refused to let the youth inherit his father's kingdom and it reverted to the status of a Roman province. Claudius and his successor, Nero, later granted Agrippa II domain over the cities of Tiberias and Taricheae (Magdala) and the surrounding countryside, parts of Perea, and portions of Philip's old tetrarchy. Some of these land transfers were Nero's reward to Agrippa II for having supplied troops to help fight the Parthians, who were once again making trouble on the eastern frontier. As for Judea, Agrippa became a kind of honorary king, frequently visiting Jerusalem, and even lodging there for long periods of time. Unmarried, he was often seen in the company of his sister Berenice, the young widow of their paternal uncle Herod, who had been ruler of Chalcis, a tiny kingdom abutting Lebanon. In ancient times, it was highly unusual for a monarch not to have a wife, and rumor had it that the beautiful, headstrong Berenice, who acted as queen and hostess for her brother, was also his mistress. Their sister Drusilla was married to the Roman procurator Porcius Festus.

During this second round of direct Roman rule, the Jewish homeland deteriorated into political chaos, social unrest, and outright violence. Bands of urban terrorists known as *sicarii* (after the *sica,* or curved-blade dagger they carried concealed under their cloaks) mingled with the crowds of pilgrims in Jerusalem and stabbed to death suspected Jewish traitors, including a former high priest. In the countryside, there were constant skirmishes between Jews and Samaritans led by agitators promising an end to Roman dominion. There were also bandit raids on wealthy landholders believed to be Roman collaborators, and street fights in Jerusalem among rival nationalist groups.

The completion of Herod the Great's Temple-rebuilding project in 64 C.E. created enormous unemployment that further exacerbated public discontent. After long-simmering feelings of hostility between Greeks and Jews in Caesarea erupted into a full-fledged riot in the summer of 66, the procurator Gessius Florus had several prominent Jews arrested. When he then removed a large sum of money from the Temple treasury to cover his administrative expenses, Jerusalem residents protested in the streets by "panhandling" for alms for the impecunious procurator. Florus retaliated with mass floggings and crucifixions. Berenice herself risked execution by interceding for the condemned prisoners, but to no avail. Another riot ensued, including an assault on the Roman garrison Antonia, which forced Florus to retreat with some of his troops to Caesarea.

When Agrippa tried to impress upon the Jewish nationalists that they were headed for direct confrontation with an enemy that would not accept defeat, his warnings went unheeded. Shortly afterward, a band of *sicarii* seized the Roman fortress at Masada and massacred its command, while in Jerusalem the Temple priests suddenly discontinued their practice of offering a daily sacrifice for the health of the Roman emperor. A coalition of nationalist insurgents thereupon seized the city, burnt down the public archive that stored debt bonds (which made the rebels popular), murdered the Temple high priest for having acted as a peacemaker with the Romans, and captured the Antonia, where they slaughtered two entire Roman units.

Not all Jews supported the Roman-Jewish War that followed. Most Sadducees and Pharisees persisted in their loyalty to Rome, as did a handful of Jewish cities, including Sepphoris in Galilee. The majority of Diaspora Jews remained neutral, and the Samaritans refused to lend their support. Elsewhere in Palestine, however, there were seizures of Roman garrisons, gruesome ethnic/religious fracases in the coastal cities where Greeks and Jews had lived side by side for centuries, and the bloody rout of the Syrian governor Cestus Gallus, who had sent 30,000 men down from Antioch hoping to put a quick end to the Jerusalem rebellion.

After Gallus's defeat, the emperor Nero himself intervened. He appointed one of his top commanders, Titus Flavius Vespasian, to replace him. In the spring of 67, Vespasian assembled nearly 60,000 men (three Roman legions and numerous auxiliary troops) and proceeded to reconquer Palestine, beginning with Galilee and ruthlessly working his way south. (The fortress he reclaimed at Jotapata was commanded by Josephus, whom he took prisoner and later freed.) The cruel and vainglorious Nero, hated and feared by an increasingly mutinous Roman populace, killed himself in 68 C.E. Galba, his immediate successor, was assassinated, and a few months later Galba's successor, Otho, committed suicide. Thereupon the Roman legions of the Eastern Mediterranean proclaimed Vespasian emperor.

By the time Vespasian returned to Rome and placed his son Titus in command of Judean repacification, Jerusalem had been torn apart by internecine warfare. Three different rebel armies had taken command of the city, bloodying each other and terrorizing civilians in the process. One of these factions was a gang of bandits headed by the Galilean olive-oil tycoon John of Gischala. The second faction, the Zealots, delighted in torturing and slaying moderates who sought peace with the Romans. The third was a ragtag force led by a nasty character named Simon, Son of Gioras. In the course of their frequent skirmishes, they set fire to large numbers of buildings and grain warehouses, causing panic among the citizenry.

With four Roman legions at his disposal, Titus encircled the city in the spring of 70 to prevent the importing of provisions. His troops began hacking away at the walls with battering rams, as stones, javelins, and lighted torches rained down on the residents within. During the long, demoralizing siege, Titus first tried negotiations, and then mass crucifixions in view of the walls to compel the insurgents to surrender.

Having finally breached the walls in August, Titus worked his way to the Temple, which he ordered incinerated. Within a month of the Temple's destruction, Roman troops had reduced the entire city to flames. Among the survivors were John of Gischala and Simon, who had joined forces the preceding Passover to lure many of the Zealots into the sanctuary of the Temple and slaughter them unarmed. Titus clapped John and Simon into irons and shipped them to Rome to head his triumphal parade. He also garrisoned a Roman legion in Jerusalem for the first time in the city's history. Except for the "Wailing Wall," where Jews still go to lament the city's fall, he knocked down Jerusalem's massive ramparts.

At the end of the war, bands of *sicarii* who had fled Jerusalem holed themselves up in the badlands near the Dead Sea, maintaining strongholds in several fortresses that Herod the Great had built to defend his kingdom against Nabatean incursions. It took more than three years for the Romans to starve or burn the rebels out. Eleazar, Son of Jairus, or Jair, and grandson of Judas the Galilean, was the commander of Masada, the last of the these outposts to be defeated. After an unsuccessful five-month siege, the Romans mounted a full-scale assault. When it became apparent that escape was impossible, the defenders first burnt all their possessions and then killed themselves and their wives and children rather than submit to Roman capture and a life of slavery. The mass suicide at Masada at Eleazar's urging marked the end of first-century Jewish resistance.

With the obliteration of the Temple, the cultic center of worldwide Judaism, the Romans had perhaps hoped to accomplish the dissolution of Judaism itself. Despite the religious crisis occasioned by the cessation of daily Temple sacrifice, the Jewish faith was far from destroyed. The Pharisee named Yoḥanan ben Zakkai, who had managed to slip out of Jerusalem just before the end of the war and surrender to the Romans, was given permission to establish a school of disciples in the coastal city of Yavneh. Yoḥanan believed that Temple sacrifice was not the only means of reconciling God and Israel. In keeping with the ancient Pharisaic notion that all Jews were a priestly people and every Jewish home was a temple, he taught his followers that private acts of piety and sacrifice for others were as efficacious as any Temple sacrifice in Jerusalem. "If one wants to do something for God in a time when the Temple is no more, the offering must be the gift of selfless compassion," the Judaic scholar Jacob Neusner wrote. "The holy altar must be built in the streets and marketplaces of the world, as the purity of the Temple formerly had to be observed in the streets and marketplaces of Jerusalem."[17] Under the leadership of Yoḥanan and the rabbis who succeeded him, the myriad "Judaisms" of the first century gradually became the rabbinic Judaism of today.

In return for Yoḥanan's avowed apoliticism, the Romans permitted the Jews of Palestine a measure of self-government under their rabbis, and made no effort to ban Jewish observances or the teaching of the Torah. Although Vespasian had expropriated large tracts of Judean land immediately after the war, the rabbinic literature suggests that within a decade or two, much of this acreage was again under Jewish ownership, and the country was recovering fairly well. While Vespasian had made it clear that he would never allow the Temple to be rebuilt or Judea to enjoy self-rule, he did reward Agrippa II for his loyalty during the war by augmenting his kingdom, although not in the vicinity of Jerusalem.

When Agrippa died childless shortly before 100 C.E., his realm was divided between the Roman provinces of Judea and Syria. Having wearied of client-kings, Rome annexed Nabatea outright in 106, renaming it the province of Arabia, and garrisoning another legion there. Agrippa's sister, Berenice, had fallen in love with Titus. She followed him to Rome, where she installed herself as his mistress in the imperial palace and tried to persuade him to marry her. The Romans did not approve of his liaison with a foreign woman. When Titus succeeded his father as emperor in 79, he was forced to send Berenice back home.

Before his death, Vespasian had converted the Temple tithe into a compulsory Roman head tax known as the *fiscus judaicus,* payable by every Jew of every age in the empire. Titus's younger brother Domitian, who had succeeded him as emperor in 81 C.E., then launched a systematic campaign of persecution against both Jews and Christians, charging anyone who would not worship him as a god with atheism and treason (both of which were crimes punishable by death). Assassinated in 96, Domitian was succeeded by a Roman nobleman named Nerva, who put a stop to the Jewish persecutions. By the time Nerva's adopted son Trajan succeeded him in 98, the Jews of the Diaspora, who had remained quiescent during the Palestinian rising two generations earlier, were engaged in a series of revolts throughout the empire, including Alexandria, Cyrene, Cyprus, and Mesopotamia, the last of which Trajan had temporarily wrested from the Parthians. The reasons for those insurgencies are not entirely clear. They seem to have been the result of ethnic tensions with Gentiles in the Hellenistic cities, and a messianic hope of recapturing Palestine.

The last Palestinian revolt occurred in the spring of 132 C.E., during the reign of Trajan's successor Hadrian, when a young man named Shimeon Bar Kokhba raised a rebel Jewish army and recaptured Jerusalem from the Romans. Shimeon began ruling the city like a king, even to the point of minting his own coins, and he may well have thought of himself as the Messiah (his patronymic "Bar Kokhba" meant "Son of the Star," signifying the tribe of Judah from which David had come). It took three years for the Roman legions to drive his forces back to the caves and ravines of the Dead Sea, where the last of the Zealots had perished some 60 years earlier. As the Romans gradually searched them out, Shimeon himself was killed in August 135 during the merciless siege of Bethar, the final Dead Sea stronghold.

In retaliation, Hadrian ordered nearly all surviving residents of Jerusalem to be sold into slavery. After razing the city to the ground, he built a new Roman-style city, Aelia Capitolina, with a central forum. There were baths, along with an amphitheater and cultic sites for various Roman gods. On the site of the old Jewish Temple, he constructed temples dedicated to Jupiter and himself. All Jews were then banished, as well as Christians of Jewish blood. For the first time since Jesus' death, the Christian bishop of Jerusalem was not of Jewish lineage. Even the Samaritans, who had not participated in Shimeon's revolt, were punished during the sweeping reprisals, suffering the ultimate humiliation of seeing a second temple to Jupiter built atop their sacred Mount Gezirim. As a final castigation of the Jews, Hadrian renamed Judea as Syria Palestina.

One hundred years after Jesus' death, his people had lost their land, and their culture had been irrevocably changed, but their Judaism, as transformed by the rabbis, had survived and was actually thriving. In the words of Jacob Neusner, rabbinic Judaism "for 20 centuries illuminated the humble and, from a worldly viewpoint, unimportant affairs of a homeless, often persecuted, despised, and alien nation, dwelling alone among other nations."[18]

2

THE QUARRELS OF THE ANCIENTS

Within 35 years of Jesus' death, a religious movement bearing his name extended from Jerusalem to Italy. By 70 C.E., there were at least three dozen Christian communities in Judea, Galilee, Samaria, and certain coastal cities of Palestine, in the provincial capitals and ports of Syria, Asia Minor, and Greece, in the port city of Puteoli (modern Pozzuoli) near Naples, and in Rome itself, a sprawling megalopolis with a population of more than one million. By the end of the first century, there were similar groups in Egypt, Mesopotamia, and along the southern shore of the Black Sea. For decades, the members of these societies still called themselves Jews, because the majority of the first Christians were indeed Jewish.

Wherever there were first-century urban Jews—in Jerusalem, Antioch, Corinth, or Alexandria—there were certain to be Christians among them. Rome's Christian community was in the Trastevere, which was home to the descendants of the Jewish slaves Pompey had brought back in 63 B.C.E. Nearly all the earliest Christians had practiced Judaism before their conversion, and most continued to observe the feast days, attend synagogue, and obey the dietary laws for the rest of their lives.

Even Gentiles who converted to Christianity shared many of the Jewish traditions, as witnessed by Christian doctrinal debates of the time. Although exempt from circumcision and dietary restrictions, they were required to immerse themselves in the Jewish Scriptures. It must have seemed strange for a Gentile Christian from Ephesus, for example, whose mother tongue was Greek, and whose psychic landscape was dominated by the temple and giant statue of the great mother-goddess that drew pilgrims from all over the Hellenistic world, to be studying the history of an alien people whose own divinity was never depicted. Among the earliest Christians, Jew and Gentile alike believed in the God of Israel who had made a covenant with his chosen people, and regarded the pagan gods with horror. What distinguished Christians from Jews was their conviction that Jesus, whom they called the Christ (*ho christos,* or the Anointed One, which was Greek for Messiah), represented the fulfillment of God's promise. They interpreted the Jewish prophecies as referring specifically to Jesus' coming and thought of the Jewish patriarchs, prophets, and kings of the Scriptures as allegorical and typological prefigurations of Jesus himself.

These were shocking assertions for most Jews, who accused the Christians of willfully misinterpreting the Scriptures. In their minds, considering Jesus the means of ultimate salvation rather than the Temple and Torah was nothing short of blasphemy. As relations between the two religious groups quickly devolved into open antagonism, in Jerusalem there were incidents of violence against Christians, including Paul of Tarsus, the Jewish Pharisee who had converted to Christianity and who occasionally excoriated his fellow Jews for refusing to accept Jesus.

Certain of the inevitability of Jerusalem's destruction, which had been prophesied by Jesus himself as punishment for its inhabitants' wickedness, many Christians left the city when the first war against the Romans broke out in 66 C.E., refusing to fight alongside the Jews. The Diaspora Jews and most of the Pharisees in Palestine had also declined to support the rebellion, but the Christian exodus from Jerusalem was a dramatic symbol of Jewish-Christian estrangement. It is possible that the authors of the canonical Gospels, which probably date from the period of the war or the first few decades thereafter, were Jewish, but they, like Paul, insisted that Jews who rejected Jesus were misguided and even sinful. During Christianity's early centuries, anti-Jewish polemic was a staple of literature and sermonizing. One of the most vituperative pieces of anti-Judaic Christian oratory, a fourth-century sermon by the bishop of Constantinople—called John Chrysostom ("golden-mouthed") for his rhetorical gifts—exhorted Christians to stop celebrating Jewish holidays because the Jews had killed Christ.

The Jews, in turn, created a body of anti-Christian folklore. As early as the second century, one of the favorite Jewish tales about Jesus was that he had not been born of a virgin, but was instead the bastard son of an adulterous Jewish woman and a Roman soldier. They also dwelled on the fact that he had done nothing to indicate he was ever the great priest or royal son of David that the Scriptures described. He was not even a glorious failure like Shimeon Bar Kokhba, but rather an ignominious failure who had perished on a cross.

Most Jews thought of the Christians as a band of Gentiles who were using the Jew Jesus to destroy his people's ancient faith. Jewish parents no longer called their sons *Yeshu,* the shortened form of *Yeshua* (or Joshua), which translated into *Iēsous,* or Jesus, in Greek. The rabbis of Yavneh suppressed the Greek version of the Bible known as the Septuagint (after the 70 holy men who had written it), which many Diaspora synagogues had used for centuries, and commissioned a new translation. The Christians then made the Septuagint Bible their own, adding a number of other Jewish texts that they interpreted as containing direct references to Jesus. The rabbis excluded these books from the Hebrew canon.

As both faiths competed aggressively for converts among the Gentiles, they were both generally regarded with equal contempt. The pagans despised the Jews for their clannishness and refusal to worship any other god besides their own. Even the most sophisticated intellectuals among the pagans who viewed the pantheon of gods as images of the one great unknowable God were repulsed by the Jews' rejection of the supernatural beings who from time immemorial had safeguarded the homes, cities, and civic institutions of the Hellenistic world. In their eyes, the Christians were even worse. Not only was their religion exclusivist like that of the Jews, but their religious practices were reputed to be immoral. The secret Christian rites (no outsiders were permitted to attend the eucharist) prompted speculation that the liturgy, which was said to include the consumption of Jesus' body and blood, actually involved orgies or even human sacrifices.

The second-century Roman orator Cornelius Fronto, who served as the emperor Marcus Aurelius's tutor, described the eucharist as the ritual murder of an infant whose blood the Christians then drank. "This is the victim by which they seal the covenant," Fronto was quoted as saying in a book written by Minucius Felix, a contemporary Christian lawyer.[1] According to Minucius, Fronto went on to describe a lurid Christian festival featuring the head of an ass (which Jews were rumored to worship as well) and the genitals of a priest.

After a drunken banquet, claimed Fronto, the Christians snuffed out the lights and engaged in a sexual free-for-all that included even the orgiasts' mothers and small children. "In the shameless dark and with unspeakable lust they copulate in random unions, all being equally guilty of incest, some by deed but everyone by complicity," wrote the horrified Fronto.[2] The Romans, who revered the family, and who (despite the debaucheries of certain of their emperors) were almost prudish in their standards of decency, found such reports utterly shocking. For Fronto and other highborn Romans (including Tacitus), however, the most disgusting aspect of Christianity was the very object of Christian veneration: Jesus, the crucified criminal.

The early Christian communities included representatives of all social classes. Among the members of his congregation, Paul of Tarsus counted wealthy merchants and dowagers, learned synagogue leaders, and at least one public official. Certain relatives of the emperor Domitian himself may have been Christians as well. Nonetheless, their ranks were disproportionately filled with the so-called dregs of society. The second-century philosopher Celsus wrote a diatribe against Christianity titled *On the True Doctrine* that included a contemptuous survey of Christian demographics. Celsus viewed the Christians as a subversive network of shoemakers, wool-workers, laundresses, yokels, and slaves that ran through the back alleys, shops, and servant quarters of the great private houses of the Roman Empire.

Christians were also regarded, sometimes with good reason, as lunatics. Many were convinced that the world was coming to an end, and that Jesus would return in their own lifetimes. Paul of Tarsus devoted one of his letters to an unhinged Christian community in the Greek port of Thessalonica, urging them not to leave their jobs because the apocalypse might not be so close at hand as they imagined. Late in the second century, in the final years of Marcus Aurelius's reign, a Christian preacher named Montanus, who claimed to be in direct contact with the Holy Spirit, announced that the Second Coming was about to take place in Phrygia in central Asia Minor. Accompanied by two flashily dressed prophetesses, Prisca and Maximilla, who had left their husbands to join his entourage, and drawing huge crowds (and collections) wherever he went, Montanus was the ancient world's equivalent of a televangelist. Thousands of mesmerized followers deserted their families and homes to listen to the call of these three charismatics for fasting, sexual abstinence, and even voluntary martyrdom in preparation for the Armageddon and millennium that Montanus assured them lay just around the corner. The Montanists established their own churches in Phrygia, centered on prophecy and possession by the Holy Spirit. Although Montanus and Maximilla are said to have hanged themselves while in an ecstatic trance, at the height of their celebrity their numbers included the brilliant North African lawyer Tertullian, who had earlier been merely a mainstream Christian apologist of a puritanical bent.

Not surprisingly, Christians quickly gained a general reputation as mindless fanatics. "A class of men given to a new and murderous superstition," wrote the historian Suetonius in his early-second-century biography of the emperor Nero, who had tried to stamp out Christianity in Rome.[3] After blaming the Christians for a fire that destroyed nearly half the city in the summer of 64 C.E., Nero rounded them up by the hundreds and executed them theatrically: crucifying some, dressing others in animal skins for dogs to attack in the arena, and coating still others with pitch for use as human torches in his garden. The Christians were already so unpopular among the Romans that few complained about this blatant scapegoating, even though it was widely rumored that Nero, who was universally despised as a tyrant and a lecher, had started the fire himself in order to indulge his ambitions as an urban planner. In his own chronicle of Nero's reign, Tacitus noted disdainfully that Nero had "punished with the most excruciating tortures those whom the rabble called 'Christians,' hated because of their shameful crimes. . . . The originator of their name was Christ, who had been punished himself when Pontius Pilate was procurator during the reign of Tiberius."[4]

In a similar vein, the mid-second-century satirist Lucian of Samosata penned a mock biography of a Cynic philosopher, *The Passing of Peregrinus,* that japed Christians for their gullibility in worshipping a man whom he regarded as a species of fraudulent philosopher:

> The poor wretches have convinced themselves, first and foremost, that they are going to be immortal and live for all time, in consequence of which they despise death and even willingly give themselves into custody, most of them.
>
> Furthermore, their first lawgiver persuaded them that they are all brothers of one another after they have transgressed once by denying the Greek gods and by worshipping the crucified sophist himself and living under his laws.[5]

Aristocrats like Lucian, Tacitus, and Fronto were not alone in finding the Christian deification of a condemned man highly offensive. A surviving third-century graffito scrawled on an imperial building on Rome's Palatine Hill lampoons Jesus' crucifixion by depicting a man with an ass's head nailed to the cross, with the following phrase in Greek: "Alexamenos worships God."

Both Alexamenos and the graffiti artist were probably soldiers in the Roman army.

Brutal suppression of alien religions that threatened the social and political order had always been the Roman way. In 186 B.C.E., the Senate had bloodily squelched a mystery cult of the Greek wine god Bacchus in southern Italy, believed to be part of a populist conspiracy to burn down the city of Rome. Nero's reprisal against the Christians after the 64 C.E. fire may well have been inspired by the Bacchanalian massacre two centuries earlier, which had been chronicled in detail by Augustus's court historian, Livy. His mass crucifixions set a precedent for a lengthy, if sporadically enforced, imperial vendetta against Christians who refused to recant their faith and worship the Roman gods, especially the deified emperor himself. The punishment for declining to curse Christ and offer the required pinch of incense was almost invariably death.

The earliest large-scale Christian persecution, carried out by the emperor Domitian at the end of the first century, included the Diaspora Jews whose growing numbers and obvious prosperity after the devastation in Jerusalem had become cause for considerable alarm to their Gentile neighbors. Domitian's successors Trajan and Hadrian were the first to draw a clear distinction between Jews and Christians, in terms of government policy. While they harassed the former, they unofficially tolerated the latter, with the exception of individuals whose names were reported directly to the authorities. Imperial liberalism with respect to Christianity ended when Marcus Aurelius took office in 161.

Marcus, a practitioner of the Stoic philosophy, developed a reputation for erudition and high-mindedness during his 19-year reign. Where Christians were concerned, however, his policies were anything but tolerant. In 177, a pogrom against Christians in the Rhône Valley in Gaul, most likely prompted by the fact that many were wealthy immigrants from Asia Minor, caused the provincial governor in Lyons to write for instructions from Marcus, who was campaigning against the Germans along the Danube. The emperor responded by ordering that the entire Christian community be accused of high treason, which meant that their slaves were tortured into giving evidence against them and they themselves were hunted down and tortured until they recanted or died. These grisly interrogations of suspected Christians and their servants, accompanied by whips, the rack, and red-hot irons, were carried out in front of howling xenophobic crowds throughout the summer of 177 both in Lyons and across the Rhône in Vienne. The hundreds of victims—Christians who either had refused to renounce their faith or had renounced it and then changed their minds—included teen-agers and housewives, Pothinus, the 90-year-old bishop of Lyons, who was beaten to death by a street mob, and the community's unofficial leader, a small, plain-looking young slave woman named Blandina, who proved to be the hardest of all to kill. Over a period of several weeks, she was tortured, hung from a post in the Lyons arena as bait for the lions, and finally, when her body was thoroughly mangled and covered with burn marks, placed in a basket and thrown to the bulls to be gored to death. The charges against Blandina and the other Lyons martyrs were the usual ones of incest and cannibalism of children. When the carnage was over, the authorities refused to let the victims' bodies be buried. They threw the corpses of those who had died in jail to the dogs, and left the severed heads and dismembered trunks of those who had been killed in the arena on the ground for nearly a week before burning the body parts and tossing the ashes into the Rhône.

When Marcus died in 180, his elder son, Commodus, who succeeded him as emperor, adopted a more moderate stance. Commodus had a reputation for depravity (he considered himself to be an incarnation of Hercules, and he liked to dress up as a gladiator), but his mistress, Marcia, was sympathetic to the Christian cause. After Commodus's death by assassination in 193, his successors resumed Marcus's efforts to stamp out Christianity. The most severe periods of persecution were the reigns of Septimius Severus (193–211), Maximinus (235–238), Decius (249–251) (who set up commissions throughout the empire to oversee sacrifice tests designed to ferret out Christians), Valerian (253–260), and finally Diocletian (286–305), a devotee of the Parthian god Mithra. After initiating a purge of the army and civil service in 296, he extended his campaign of persecution to the entire Roman empire, especially in the Eastern Mediterranean. From 303 until his abdication in 305 because of poor health (he probably had malaria), Diocletian and Galerius, his second-in-command in the East, oversaw the systematic destruction of churches, confiscation and burning of Gospel books, and arrest, torture, and execution of thousands of Christians who had refused to renounce their faith.

By this time Christianity was thoroughly entrenched in the countryside as well as the cities and it managed to survive Diocletian's bloodbath. After Diocletian stepped down from the throne, Galerius took over the eastern half of the empire and enlisted the aid of his kinsman, Maximinus Daia, in pursuing the cause of repression. In 311, however, an aspiring despot named

Constantine, whose father, Constantius Chlorus, had ruled the West as Diocletian's second-in-command, launched a military-political campaign that would eventually result in his becoming sole emperor of East and West. When he defeated one of his rivals in a key battle at Rome's Mulvian Bridge, he credited his victory to a dream of Christ on the cross. Not long afterward, at his insistence, the Roman Empire embraced a policy of religious tolerance. While Constantine himself did not convert to Christianity until he was on his deathbed, he made the once-hounded faith the state religion when he ascended the throne.

During the periods of relative calm in the more than two centuries of sporadic persecution, Christians practiced their religion openly, erecting shrines and churches. Christian bishops moved about freely, Christian sects quarreled over doctrine and jostled for power, Christian intellectuals wrote apologias defending their faith, and the Christian population swelled to such a point that it is not surprising that such emperors as Decius and Diocletian came to regard Christianity as an institutional threat rather than an agglomeration of contumacious citizens. As time passed, Christian churches became repositories of wealth and works of art. Prosperous Christian merchants and artisans began to flaunt their worldly goods in ways that their critics found most un-Christian.

The third century Christian theologian Origen of Alexandria wrote, "Come, wild beasts! Come crosses! Come fire! Come torture! I know that as soon as it is over, I depart from my body. I am in peace with Christ."[6] Origen did not actually die a martyr, but repeated torture sessions under Decius's interrogators broke his health and led to his death at age 69. Most Christians were not so eager to have their faith tested. When Decius instituted his empire-wide sacrifice test in 250, and even more dramatically, when Diocletian launched his anti-Christian pogrom at century's end, the vast majority chose to apostasize, if only temporarily, rather than face torture.

Christians celebrated the feast days (execution dates) of their favorite martyrs with picnics at their graves, and compared their bravery to that of the Jewish martyrs under Antiochus IV. However, when their own necks were on the block, many chose to risk the punishment of eternal damnation, the scorn of those who had suffered, and the jibes of friends and enemies alike if they could escape with their lives. During Diocletian's persecution, Christians lined up by the hundreds to sign certificates attesting that they had duly sacrificed to pagan gods, or paid ringers to forge their names to these testimonials. The total number of Christians executed during nearly 300 years of imperial persecutions was probably no more than 3,500 (although thousands of others were condemned to hard labor in the imperial mines).

The question of what to do about defectors once Constantine had declared a general amnesty provoked a series of schisms within the Christian Church, especially in North Africa, where a populist cult of the martyrs was particularly widespread. Certain clergymen were agreeable to the idea of granting absolution to contrite apostates willing to do penance, while others insisted that the only way to keep faith with the martyrs was to limit the Church to those prepared to die a martyr's death.

During the first centuries of Christianity, the disputes among pagans, Jews, and Christians over the identity of Jesus had a curiously modern flavor. Many of the objections that Jews and pagans raised about the believability of the Gospels were exactly the same as those voiced by many "searchers for the historical Jesus" today. By and large, the non-Christian ancient world was convinced that Jesus' father had been a mere mortal, that he was born in Nazareth (or some other village) and not in Bethehem, that he had worked no miracles, and that his resurrection from the dead had been a matter of wishful thinking on the part of his disciples. It is customary nowadays to imagine the ancients as having been far more gullible than the moderns. On the contrary, their own writings indicate that they knew perfectly well how babies were made, and they knew that the dead stayed dead. They lived too closely with their animals, and with the messy, smelly detritus of childbearing and dying, to imagine much if any direct supernatural interference with ordinary life.

Indeed, few modern skeptics about Jesus have improved on the theories of the early pagan critics. These included the argument that the tales of Jesus' miraculous healings had been borrowed from the legends of the wonder-working Asclepius, the half-divine physician of the *Iliad* whose temples in Epidaurus and elsewhere had attracted thousands of worshippers who hoped to have their ailments cured by prayer. Further, the Christian ritual of baptism (the pouring on of water to cleanse away sins) had surely been inspired by lustration, the Roman ritual of purification. The eucharist bore more than superficial resemblance to a secret rite of the cult of Mithra, who was said to have slain a bull that disgorged wheat and wine from his wounds. The doctrine of Jesus' virginal conception seemed to have been borrowed from the Greek myth of the virgin Danäe, who conceived the hero Perseus by Zeus after he had gained entry to her bedchamber in the form of a shower of gold.

During the second century C.E. a self-styled "apologist" for the Christian faith named Justin attempted to refute these arguments. A native Palestinian,

Justin was born at Nablus in Samaria just after 100 C.E. to pagan Greek parents who in all probability were among those subsidized by the emperor Titus to colonize the new Samaritan city (literally "Flavia Neapolis") that he had established after the First Jewish War on the site of the biblical Shechem. Justin's parents afforded their son a first-rate classical education in Asia Minor, after which the young man became a wandering philosopher, drifting from town to town and from one philosophical school to another. In this golden age of Hellenistic learning and literature, his contemporaries included the Stoic philosopher Epictetus, the historian Plutarch, and the anatomist Galen, a provincial doctor who had specialized in treating gladiators and had gone on to become court physician to Marcus Aurelius. Around the year 130, Justin met an old man in Ephesus who told him about Jesus and Christianity. Justin converted to the new faith, calling himself a Christian philosopher and devoting his life to trying to make Christianity intellectually palatable to his educated contemporaries. Clad in his distinctive philosopher's cloak and amiably willing to take on all debaters, he continued his wanderings until settling in Rome, where he founded a school of philosophy. When Marcus Aurelius's campaign against Christians finally caught up with Justin in 165, he was beheaded along with five companions (four men, one woman), who most likely were his students. After his death, his admirers gave him the title of "Martyr."

Justin Martyr wrote two Apologies, or defenses of Christianity, intended for pagan readers in general, and the emperor, Antoninus Pius (Marcus Aurelius's adoptive father) in particular. Laced with direct and indirect quotations from Greek literature and philosophy, the Septuagint Bible, its haggadah, and at least three of the canonical Gospels (which he generally referred to as the "memoirs" of the apostles and their successors), these works were more high-spirited than intellectually persuasive. His response to the charges that the Gospels had borrowed from pagan cults and myths was to assert that certain demons had introduced these parallels into the legends in an effort to discredit Christianity. He further contended that the Gospel stories of the incarnation, crucifixion, and resurrection were indeed historical because they had fulfilled divinely inspired biblical prophecies.

What is most interesting about Justin's writings are his allusions to the parallels between the Gospels and Greek mythology. In his first Apology, he wrote:

> And if we declare that the Word of God was begotten of God, not in the ordinary but in the extraordinary manner, as we stated above, this may be com-

> pared to your claim that Mercury is the announcing word of God. And should anyone object that He [Christ] was crucified, this indignity may be compared to that of Jupiter's sons [Bacchus, Asclepius, and Heracles], as you call them. . . . If we state that He was born of a Virgin, this may be compared to what you admit of Perseus. When we say that he cured the lame, the paralytics, and those blind from birth, and raised the dead to life, we seem to attribute to him actions similar to those said to have been performed by Asclepius.[7]

Justin did not rely solely on prophecy in arguing for the historicity of the Gospel stories. In support of the assertion that Jesus was born in Bethlehem (and not Nazareth), as prophesied by Micah, he went so far as to suggest that Antoninus might wish to refer to the census data of Quirinius, the legate of Syria, contained in the imperial archives. He was convinced that his biographical account of Jesus' life could be confirmed by independent historical sources—a very "modern" response to the very "modern" form of skepticism that his opponents demonstrated.

In another apologetic work, the *Dialogue with Trypho,* Justin described a debate he claimed to have had in the year 135 C.E. with one of several learned Jews who had fled Palestine for Ephesus after Bar Kokhba's fall. After befriending Trypho (who may actually have been a famous Palestinian rabbi named Tarphon), Justin tried to persuade him to accept Jesus as Messiah by adopting his usual argument that Jesus had fulfilled the Hebrew prophecies. Although his proselytizing proved unsuccessful, he and Trypho remained on cordial terms.

The most intriguing aspect of the *Dialogue* is Trypho's catalogue of objections to the Gospel's historicity, which is extremely modern in tone. His contention that the evangelist Matthew had relied on a Septuagint mistranslation into Greek of the relevant Hebrew passage in the Book of Isaiah when he wrote that Mary's virginal conception of Jesus fulfilled Isaiah's seventh-century B.C.E. prophecy is one that biblical skeptics still make to this day. In regard to the verses "Look, the virgin shall conceive and bear a son, / and they shall name him Emmanuel,"[8] Trypho noted that the word "virgin" (*parthenos* in the Greek of Matthew and the Septuagint) was incorrect, since Isaiah had used the Hebrew word *almah,* which means "young woman" or "maiden," and not "virgin." He insisted that the passage in Isaiah referred not to the birth of Jesus, but rather to that of Hezekiah, a king of Judah during Isaiah's lifetime who had campaigned successfully against the invading Assyrians.

What was really at issue in the debate between Trypho and Justin was the profound difference between Jewish and Christian interpretations of the *sub-*

stance of Isaiah's prophecy. Trypho accused the Christians not only of misinterpreting an obvious reference to Hezekiah, but also of borrowing the virgin-birth motif from the Greek myth of Zeus and Danäe—the very same charge that had been made by Justin's *pagan* opponents. In Trypho's own words:

> You Christians should be ashamed of yourselves, therefore, to report the same kind of stories as these men, and you should, on the contrary, acknowledge this Jesus to be a man of mere human origin. If you can prove from the Scriptures that he is the Christ, confess that he was worthy to be chosen because of his perfect observance of the Law, but do not also speak of miracles, less you be accused of talking nonsense, like the Greeks.[9]

The rabbi Trypho was obviously scandalized by what he viewed as the Christians' deification of a mere mortal by embellishing his life story with mythological lore borrowed wholesale from the Hellenistic polytheism that the Jews so despised. In his view, Jesus was nothing more than a Jewish male, and as such should be judged strictly in terms of his faithfulness to the Torah. His was an argument that any modern-day Jew might make.

Perhaps a dozen years after Justin's execution, Celsus wrote his famous diatribe against Christianity, *On the True Doctrine.* Like Trypho and the anonymous pagans of Justin's first Apology before him, he accused the Christians of adorning Jesus with attributes from Greek mythology. While making it quite clear that he detested the Jews, he insisted that the Christians were even more despicable inasmuch as they also believed in the mythological lore that no educated pagan would ever take seriously. Celsus equated the Christians with the worshippers of Mithra and other new deities from the Middle East, whose cults were corrupting traditional religion.

Little is known about Celsus, since the only portion of his treatise to survive is contained in a point-by-point refutation entitled *Against Celsus,* which was written by Origen in the middle of the third century. Celsus may well have been a friend of the mid-second-century satirist Lucian of Samosata, who made mention in his *Alexander, the False Prophet* of "a certain Celsus" who had written an exposé of magicians—a possible reference to *On the True Doctrine.*[10] Perhaps Celsus might best be described as an archconservative who considered Christianity a threat to traditional ties between the age-old polytheistic religions and the social order. Most likely he did not believe in the physical reality of the ancient gods, whose names he viewed as interchangeable appellations for a greater divine presence. He was, after all, a Platonist who understood the radical disjuncture between the ideal world created by the abstract God of the philosophers and the imperfect world of the statues and temples in his midst. The particulars of his screed against Christianity, however, are "curiously modern," according to his translator R. Joseph Hoffman.[11] In depicting the Gospels as missionary propaganda rather than sacred biography, Celsus was "the first of the New Testament demythologizers, a title he shares in the history of the church with Porphyry, Voltaire, Tom Paine, D. F. Strauss, Arthur Drews, and Rudolph Bultmann," notes Hoffman in the introduction to his recent translation of *On the True Doctrine.* Celsus even called Christianity "the cult of Christ," a term adopted by a number of 20th-century scholars.[12]

Like many moderns, Celsus was convinced that only the ignorant and uneducated could possibly view the Gospels as literal truth. He himself wrote, "One can even say [Christianity] spreads because of the vulgarity and illiteracy of its adherents."[13] Furthermore, his own interpretations of the circumstances surrounding the biblical accounts of Jesus' life anticipate precisely the assertions about the "historical" Jesus that would dominate Enlightenment and post-Enlightenment thinking about the New Testament:

— *Jesus was illegitimate.* After having become pregnant by the Roman soldier Pantera (a borrowing from Jewish anti-Christian folklore), his mother fabricated the story of the virgin birth—and a fanciful genealogy for her bastard son—when her carpenter husband drove her out of the house as a common adulteress.

— *Jesus was not divine.* His followers created the myth of his divinity from legends of Hercules, Asclepius, and other Greek heroes who were worshipped as gods after their deaths.

— *Jesus was not born in Bethlehem.* His actual birthplace was an obscure village somewhere in the countryside.

— *The story of the Magi and Herod's massacre of the innocents was a Christian fabrication.*

— *Jesus worked no miracles* (although he may have had some knowledge of magic or sorcery).

— *Jesus did not foresee or foretell his own passion and death.*

— *The Christian teaching that God allowed Jesus to die in order to atone for mankind's sins is perverse.* "Is there any human father so ruthless as your god?" Celsus asked the Christians,[14] anticipating by 18 centuries the theory of "divine child abuse" adopted by a number of feminist theologians who reject the atonement doctrine on the ground that it encourages violence against women and children.

— *Jesus' resurrection was a mere fantasy on the part of his grief-stricken disciples.* They were "so wrenched with grief at his failure that they hallucinated him risen from the dead by a sort of wishful thinking."[15]

Celsus had no degree in biology or grief psychology, nor had he taken courses in New Testament criticism. He lived long before Newton, Darwin, Durkheim, and Freud. Nonetheless, he was the first scholar in Western history to conduct a thoroughgoing "search" for the "historical Jesus," the human being behind the "Christ of faith" depicted in the Gospels. In their different ways, Celsus and Trypho, like many other ancients, were baffled by the paradox of Jesus' humanity as an object of Christian devotion. The most profound dilemma for Celsus, and for Tacitus and Cornelius Fronto before him, was the apparent *unworthiness* of a crucified felon. As Celsus himself observed:

> A true son of God, like the sun that illuminated the world by first illuminating itself, ought first to have been revealed as a true god. The Christians put forth this Jesus, not only as the son of God but as the very Logos—not the pure and holy Logos known to the philosophers, mind you, but a new kind of Logos: a man who managed to get himself arrested and executed in the most humiliating of circumstances.[16]

The conundrum described by Celsus was troubling to Christians as well. It was difficult for even the most pious and philosophically sophisticated among them to imagine a being who was "equal to God," the "Son of God," or, as the Gospel of John avowed in Platonic-sounding language, the "Logos" (the Word), who was "with God" and who "was God"—but who also "became flesh and lived among us."[17]

In attempting to solve this enigma, the philosopher Justin Martyr had concluded that Plato and the evangelist John had actually been saying the same thing, and that the Greek philosophers had been Christians before their time. In so doing, he completely ignored the fact that no Platonic or Stoic philosopher had ever conceived of the Logos as a material entity, much less a human being. When Trypho learned that Justin had equated Platonism with Christianity, in all likelihood he was amused, for he and other Jews believed the Messiah would be a man, not a disembodied "Logos" or "Word." According to historian of Christianity W. H. C. Frend, Justin "laid himself open to his Jewish opponent Trypho's well-directed thrust that the Christians 'by receiving a worthless rumour, shape a kind of Messiah for themselves and perish for him blindly' (*Trypho* 8.4) and that they were trying to prove 'impossibilities that God had endured to be born and became a man' (*Trypho* 68.1)."[18]

The early history of Christianity might well be described as a centuries-long debate over Jesus' theological identity that began during its very first decades. In a letter written in 55 C.E. (or perhaps earlier) to a Christian community in Galatia (an ethnically Celtic region of central Asia Minor encompassing modern Ankara and its environs), Paul of Tarsus warned that "there are some who are confusing you and want to pervert the gospel of Christ."[19] In the second of his two letters to the Christians of Corinth, which dates from around the same time, Paul referred to "false apostles, deceitful workers, disguising themselves as apostles of Christ."[20]

What these "false apostles" taught is not clear from the context. However, other early Christian documents confirm that by the end of the first century, many of the ancients who called themselves Christians could not bring themselves to believe that the Jesus who had died on the cross was the same person as the mystical Christ who was the "Son of God." If Jesus were divine, they concluded, he must only have *seemed* to suffer and die. This form of reasoning, which is called "docetism" (after the Greek word *dokein,* meaning "to seem"), plagues Christianity to this day.

Another New Testament document, the Second Letter of John, appears to have been addressed to docetic Christians. "Many deceivers have gone out into the world, those who do not confess that Jesus Christ has come in the flesh," the author cautions.[21] In a companion New Testament document, the First Letter of John, the writer repeatedly exhorts his readers to remember that "the blood of Jesus [God's] son cleanses us from all sin."[22] These were undoubtedly attempts to assure the faithful that the human Jesus who had shed his blood and the divine Christ whom they considered their savior were one and the same.

By the second century, the notion of a radical disjunction between Jesus the man and Christ the savior had become the basis for a dissident Christian sect that stretched from Rome and North Africa to Edessa in Mesopotamia just east of the Euphrates River. Its leader was a bishop's son and wealthy shipowner named Marcion, who was born around 85 C.E. As a theological dualist, he believed there were two gods: the evil, ignorant God of Israel, who had created an imperfect material world, and a benign, omnipotent "unknown God" who had sent Jesus as savior. Marcion excised the entire Old Testament from the Christian Bible, and most of the New Testament as well. His biblical canon contained only the Gospel of Luke (who seemed to be addressing a Gentile readership) and certain of Paul's letters that emphasized salvation through faith in Jesus rather than obedience to Jewish law.

Although rigorously ascetic (only the unmarried were eligible for baptism), Marcion's brand of Christianity attracted numerous followers because it provided an answer to the question that has continued to plague monotheists: If God is good, why is there such a thing as evil? However, as Tertullian pointed out, in assigning the blame to the God of Israel, Marcion severed Jesus from his Jewish past and transformed him from a human being into a "mere phantasm" who had taken his flesh "on loan from the elements."[23] In short, Marcion's Jesus was not human at all.

Others among the early Christians imagined a Jesus who was quite the opposite: profoundly human and profoundly Jewish. One of these sects, known as the Ebionites (from the Aramaic word for "poor"), seems to have originated on the eastern shore of the Jordan River (there may have been Ebionite communities west of the Jordan during the first century, but there is no evidence for their existence). Never more than a splinter faction, Ebionite Christianity first surfaced in the writings of second-century church fathers, and was defunct by the fourth century. Unlike the Marcionites, who totally rejected any relationship with Judaism, the Ebionites attempted to be both Jews and Christians by keeping the Sabbath and also holding Sunday services that resembled eucharistic celebrations. As for Jesus, they believed that he was an ordinary man whom God had chosen as his own son on the occasion of his baptism in the Jordan. Repudiating all four canonical Gospels, they produced their own Gospel of the Ebionites, a small portion of which has survived in the form of quotations preserved in other writings long after the Ebionites themselves had died out.

A third group, the Gnostics, were an intellectual elite who resolved the paradox of Jesus' identity (and the problem of evil) by severing the human Jesus, whom they viewed as the offspring of mortals, from the immortal Christ, a divine being who "emanated" directly from God. At the height of its popularity in the mid–second century, Gnosticism had its headquarters in Alexandria, a center of culture for the ancient world with its famous library and flourishing school of philosophy. The Gnostics produced dozens of esoteric, often highly poetic texts, many of which were recovered from the Egyptian desert only in this century.

Gnosticism was extremely eclectic, drawing on Jewish, Christian, and Platonic theology and imagery. While certain members did not even consider themselves Christians, others practiced secret Gnostic rituals alongside (or on top of) those of conventional Christianity; still others who called themselves Christians declined to have anything to do with ordinary Christian life or liturgy. All Gnostics believed, however, that salvation ultimately depended not on Jesus' atonement for their sins, but rather on the "knowledge" (*gnōsis*) that Jesus as "Savior" would make available to enlightened initiates. Like the Marcionites, many also accepted the idea of two supreme beings: the inferior "demiurge" described in the Jewish Scriptures, and a superior, unaccessible "God."

In *The Apocalypse of Peter,* a fourth-century Gnostic text discovered at Nag Hammadi, near the Nile River, in the mid-1940s, the apostle Peter has a vision of two Jesuses on the cross, a "living" spiritual Jesus who feels no pain and makes merry at his own crucifixion, and a fleshy "substitute" who suffers and dies. In his confusion, Peter asks:

> "What do I see, O Lord, that it is you yourself whom they take, and that you are grasping me? Or who is this one, glad and laughing on the tree? And is it another one whose feet and hands they are striking?
>
> The Savior said to me, "He whom you saw on the tree, glad and laughing, this is the living Jesus. But this one into whose hands and feet they drive the nails is his fleshly part, which is the substitute being put to shame, the one who came into being in his likeness."[24]

Since the material world was hopelessly corrupt, the only way to imagine Jesus as both human and divine was to separate his mortal self from his immortal self, as Peter had done in his schizophrenic vision.

The Gnostic theory of the two Jesuses had the paradoxical effect of making the Christian story more palatable to skeptics. Unlike other Christians, Gnostics were not obliged to take Jesus' incarnation and resurrection literally. They could instead assign his divinity to an entirely spiritual realm. Furthermore, they did not have to face the taunts of their pagan neighbors over their worship of a crucified man, since that had been the shameful fate of his "substitute."

All three separatist groups—the Marcionites, Ebionites, and Gnostics—had more or less vanished by the time Constantine seized control of the Roman Empire at the beginning of the fourth century, although Marcionism persisted in Syria for some time and there were still a number of isolated Gnostic enclaves. Marcionism and Gnosticism evolved into an even more radical form of quasi-Christian dualism known as Manicheism, which spread as far east as China and reappeared under various guises in Europe throughout the Middle Ages (such as the Albigensians of southern France and the Bogomils of Serbia).

The vast majority of early Christians belonged to none of these three sects. Instead, they professed a congeries of beliefs about Jesus that the Lutheran scholar Arland Hultgren has defined as "normative." They viewed the God of Israel as the benevolent father of a human Jesus, who had redeemed the human race through his genuine suffering on the cross. They also believed that Jesus was in some sense divine.

By the mid–second century, those Christians who accepted the "normative" beliefs expressed in a variety of creeds beginning with the letters of Paul were known as "orthodox," while others were identified as "heretics." However, even the so-called "orthodox" could not agree on exactly what these assertions meant. The problem of Jesus' identity continued to plague the Christian churches in the first centuries after Christ, generating bitter theological disputes, accusations of heresy, mutual anathemas, and painful schisms, all of which were seemingly based on technical terms that eluded definition. If Jesus was God, as John's Gospel appeared to say, did that mean there was more than one God? Were there actually three Gods if one took into account the Holy Spirit? Or were these names—"father," "son," and "holy spirit"—simply a reflection of the different attributes of a single divine entity? If they were more than names, and Jesus really was the "Son of God," was he not a lesser being than God, and therefore not God at all? If Jesus was not God, what was the significance of John's Gospel? These conundrums began to resemble a never-ending game of scissors-paper-stone.

During the second and third centuries, dozens of obscure Christian factions, all of which hewed to the "normative" tradition, began battling with each other over the precise calibration of humanity and divinity in Jesus. Among them were the Monarchians (who believed that God the father, Jesus, and the Holy Spirit were one and the same person); the Trinitarians (who believed in one God in three separate persons); the Modalists (sometimes called Sabellians after one of their bishops, who tried to reconcile Monarchianism and Trinitarianism by asserting that the Trinity represented three aspects of the same God and not three separate persons); the Subordinationists (who believed that Jesus as "son" was inferior to God the father); and the Adoptionists (who believed, like the Ebionites, that Jesus was a mere human being whom God had later infused with the divine Logos).

Paul of Samosata, a leading third-century Adoptionist or near-Adoptionist who was to become bishop of Antioch, was among the many theologians of

Antioch who, like the Ebionites, focused on the majesty and transcendence of God. The Antiochenes asked: How could the human Jesus have the qualities of God the father? Could a human Jesus have existed before all time, as had God the father? In typically Antiochene fashion, Paul of Samosata reasoned that the divine Logos of John's Gospel might well have preexisted Jesus' birth, but the human Jesus had not. Paul referred to Jesus simply as "the Nazarene," a human being like everyone else who had had to grow into his divine role, noting that even the Gospel of Luke declared that the boy Jesus had "increased in wisdom and in years, and in divine and human favor."[25] Paul was brash, tyrannical, and eccentric, and generally disliked. His enemies accused him of using his office to enrich himself, of refusing to allow hymns to Christ to be sung in his church, and of living at his sumptuously appointed bishop's house with two pretty young women whom he called "spiritual brides." Paul's relationship with the "brides" was innocent, but it created scandal. A synod of bishops eventually deposed him.

Paul was not the only early "orthodox" Christian theologian to have fallen into one heretical trap by trying to avoid another. Justin Martyr had sometimes sounded as though he did not believe that Jesus was fully human. Tertullian, who had promoted Trinitarianism (which became a core orthodox doctrine), eventually fell into Montanism. In writing to combat the Gnostic teaching that Christ had been merely an "emanation" from God, Origen had seemed to say that Christ and God were two separate deities.

A third-century bishop of Alexandria named Dionysius, who was later to be martyred under the emperor Valerian, was one of Paul of Samosata's chief opponents. Dionysius also warred against the Monarchians and their belief that God the father and Jesus were the same person. However, he went so far in his condemnation of the Monarchians as to call Jesus a "creature" in attempting to differentiate him from God the father. The word "creature" provoked the ire of Dionysius, the bishop of Rome, and the two theologians began hurling accusations at one another. Dionysius of Rome accused Dionysius of Alexandria of having misinterpreted the Trinity, while Dionysius of Alexandria charged Dionysius of Rome with promoting Monarchianism, or at the very least Modalism.

In the early fourth century, an Alexandrian priest named Arius, who was reputed to be a brilliant logician, endeavored to strike a balance between Adoptionism with its all-too-human Jesus and Modalism with its all-too-divine Christ. He maintained that Jesus had indeed been the Son of God from the moment of conception. However, although Jesus was the Logos made flesh, the Logos itself was not exactly divine. Great as it was, it *had* to have been a creation of God. Arius's Jesus was neither the human being of the Adoptionists nor the divine Christ of the Modalists. He was instead a sort of angel, or superman.

After publishing his theory, Arius was condemned and sent into exile by a council of bishops in the year 319. In turn, he accused the bishops of practicing Modalism. The animus behind this war of words was only partly theological. At one time a member of an ultra-conservative Christian community in Egypt known as the Meletians, who were opposed to forgiveness for Christians who had apostasized during Diocletian's persecution, Arius had later switched sides. In retaliation, the rigorist Meletians threatened to denounce Bishop Alexander of Alexandria as a heretic if he did not take immediate action against the priest.

In 325 the emperor Constantine, who was by then solidly ensconced as ruler of the entire Roman world, convened an ecumenical council of 230 bishops in the port city of Nicea in Bithynia. Like many of his successors among the Byzantine emperors, Constantine had no qualms about meddling in church affairs. (Although unbaptized, he had styled himself as the "bishop of bishops.") His aim at Nicea was not only to rid the Church of Arius and his novel theology, but also to encourage a compromise between the Modalists, who held sway in much of northern Africa, and the Adoptionists, who were still a powerful presence in Antioch and its environs. Constantine urged the bishops to accept a doctrine of Jesus based upon his being "of the same essence" as God the father. As such, he was both fully divine and uncreated (in order to trounce Arius and appease the Modalists) and a separate human being who had suffered and died (in order to satisfy the Adoptionists and the Antiochene theologians, who veered toward Adoptionism). The emperor managed to secure a near-unanimous vote in support of Jesus' divine essence, which the bishops defined as his "consubstantiality" with God the father. This profession of faith became the foundation for the Nicene Creed, which is still recited in Roman Catholic, Eastern Orthodox, Anglican, and many Protestant churches.

Practically speaking, however, routing Arianism proved to be far more difficult than Constantine had anticipated. Arius's Jesus might not have appealed to other theologians, but he had an immense popular following. For many Christians, it was easier to comprehend a numinous superhero who was rather like Hercules than the puzzling Jesus of Christian orthodoxy, whose precise measure of humanity and divinity was so troublesome. The novelist E. M. Forster wittily summed up Arianism's lure to the ancients: "By making Christ younger and lower than God it brought him nearer to us—indeed it tended to level him into a mere good man and to forestall Unitarianism. It appealed to the untheologically minded, to emperors and even more to empresses."[26]

In time, even Constantine himself warmed up to Arius (the fact that one of his sisters was a leading Arian advocate certainly helped). A decade after the Council of Nicea, the emperor ordered Bishop Alexander of Alexandria's successor, Athanasius, to restore Arius to St. Mark's, his old parish church. When Athanasius, who had the toughness of a street thug, refused to obey, Constantine promptly banished him from his see. Upon Constantine's death in 337, his three sons wrested control of his empire from several other contenders and divided it among themselves. Amid the political chaos, Athanasius quietly returned to Alexandria.

The new emperor of the East, Constantius II, ruling from the imperial capital of Constantinople on the Black Sea, fancied himself a mediator in matters theological in the grand tradition of his father. In an effort to reconcile Arianism and orthodoxy, he proposed a Jesus who was not of the "same" but of a "similar" essence as God the father. After Athanasius protested violently, Constantius banished him twice, and even tried to have him arrested (Athanasius fled to the desert and hid among friendly monks along the Upper Nile). The stubborn Athansius was to endure two more banishments during his 46 years in office, bringing the total to five. The fourth banishment came under the emperor Julian, a nephew of Constantine who tried to restore the old paganism during his brief reign from 361 to 363. Athanasius was banished for the fifth and final time under Valens, Eastern emperor from 364 to 378, who also favored (as did many bishops) the doctrine of "similar" over "same."

Although Arius himself had long since died, his teachings were acquiring a substantial following in the West. Justina, the second wife of Valentinian I, Valens's older brother and the emperor of the West, had definite Arian leanings. When Valentinian died in 375, Justina became regent over the Balkans, where her five-year-old son, Valentinian II, was technically emperor. Under Justina's auspices, Arianism and quasi-Arianism filtered through the Balkans, where they became the local variants of Christianity, to the Germanic tribes who were streaming unchecked over the old Roman frontier along the Rhine and Danube rivers by the end of the fourth century. Over the next century, as the Germans swept across Gaul and Spain and down into Italy and North Africa, much of western Europe and northern Africa, including Rome, became Arian territory. In 476, Romulus Augustulus, the last Roman emperor of the West, was deposed by his German (and Arian) overlord Odoacer.

The various Germanic tribes—the Ostrogoths in Italy, Visigoths in Gaul and Spain, and Vandals in northern Africa, among others—were duly impressed by the image of Jesus as superhero that the Arian bishops preached. Their native polytheism, like that of the Greeks, had embraced a class of heroic figures, such as Siegfried, conceived through miraculous unions and occupying places midway between gods and men. Arianism flourished in the West until the mid–sixth century, when the German chieftains were eventually conquered or assimilated by the Catholic Christians whom they ruled.

Even in non-Arian lands, the Nicene Creed that Constantine had sponsored in 325 continued to be a bone of contention. Once the bishops had sailed back to their own sees from Nicea, the old Modalist-Adoptionist controversy reappeared, although in more refined theological language. Many theologians objected strongly to the phrase "of the same essence," arguing that since it was not in the New Testament, it could hardly be the basis for an article of Christian faith. To their minds, such an epithet reduced Jesus to a mere manifestation of God, similar to the burning bush in the Book of Exodus. Even Athanasius, the Nicene Creed's most vigorous defender, confessed in a letter written in 371 that it was difficult to reconcile "of the same essence"—a declaration of Jesus' divinity—with the equal reality of his humanity.

As a growing schism threatened to divide eastern Christianity between Alexandrian theologians such as Athanasius, who emphasized Jesus' divinity, and those from Antioch, who emphasized Jesus' humanity, Apollinaris of Laodicea, a Syrian bishop, devised a reformulation that he hoped might satisfy both sides: Jesus had possessed a human body and a divine soul. A bishops' synod promptly condemned the hapless Apollinaris, accusing him of stripping Jesus of his human soul and turning him into a semi-divine monster. Somewhat later, two Cilician bishops of the Antiochene school in southeastern Asia Minor, Diodre of Tarsus and Theodore of Mopsuestia, postulated that Jesus was a single person with two separate natures, one fully human and the other fully divine.

A protégé of Theodore named Nestorius, who served as bishop of Constantinople in the early fifth century, attempted to elaborate on Theodore's dual-nature theory. In so doing, however, he often sounded as though he were talking about Jesus as two separate persons who were imperfectly united. When he contended, for example, that Jesus' mother, Mary, a mere mortal herself, could not have been the "bearer of God," but only the "bearer of man," or at best, the "bearer of Christ," he succeeded in provoking the wrath of Cyril, the new bishop of Alexandria, home to a flourishing Marian cult based on the title "Theotokos," or "bearer of God." Both high-handed and irascible (although indubitably pious), Cyril railed intemperately against pagans, Jews, and heretics alike. When a Christian mob lynched the

Neoplatonist philosopher Hypatia on an Alexandrian street in 415, Cyril was widely (although probably falsely) suspected of having contrived her murder. In 431, Cyril fastened his sights on Nestorius, first issuing an anathema-laden broadside against him, and then convening a bishops' council at Ephesus, almost a straight sail across the Mediterranean from Alexandria. Although Nestorius had theological allies among the bishops of Antioch and points east, before his supporters (and a papal delegation from Rome) could reach Ephesus via laborious land and sea routes, Cyril was already rounding up votes to depose him. Several days later, Nestorius's eastern allies arrived and promptly voted to depose Cyril himself. Some two weeks thereafter, the papal contingent landed at Ephesus, whereupon it confirmed the council's condemnation of Nestorius, and formally declared that Mary was indeed the "bearer of God," as the Alexandrians had maintained. At that point, the fed-up Eastern emperor Theodosius II had both Cyril and Nestorius arrested and thrown into prison until matters could calm down.

As had been the case at Nicea, a compromise document eventually emerged from Ephesus that supposedly reconciled the Alexandrians and Antiochenes: Jesus was "one person," representing a "union" (to appease the Alexandrians) of "two natures" (to satisfy the Antiochenes). Many of the Antiochenes did not care for this language, which did nothing to lift the previous condemnation of Nestorius. A bloc of churches in Cilicia, eastern Syria, southern Armenia, and Persia hived off to pursue a separatist "Nestorian" Christianity that has lasted to this day. Despite their so-called compromise position, the Alexandrians and Antiochenes redoubled their mutual accusations of heresy and blasphemy.

A second and even less successful council was held at Ephesus in 449, during which Dioscurus, Cyril's successor as Alexandrian bishop, maintained his predecessor's militant anti-Antiochene posture. Jesus had but a single nature, Dioscurus argued, which was a fusion of the human and the divine. In collaboration with an abbot named Eutyches who enjoyed Theodosius's favor, Dioscurus also secured the instant dethronement of several Nestorius-sympathizing prelates, one of whom was Flavian, Nestorius's successor as bishop of Constantinople. Theodosius's soldiers promptly clapped Flavian in chains and dragged him out of the council chamber so roughly that he died of his injuries not long afterward.

Shortly before the council, Pope Leo I had written a treatise titled the *Tome,* whose eloquent defense of the dual-nature theory was praised even by the elderly Nestorius, exiled to Egypt after losing his see. Few bishops in the

East, however, paid any attention to the Latin-speaking pope, particularly in light of a long-simmering dispute between Rome and Constantinople over the status of the see of Constantinople that had already soured relations between East and West.

A year after the second Ephesian council, Theodosius abruptly died when he was thrown from his horse in a hunting accident. His capable older sister, Pulcheria, who had served as regent during his boyhood while she herself was still in her teens, decided to succeed him along with her husband, a general and respected war veteran named Marcian. After their coronation, Pulcheria and Marcian purged the court of certain of Theodosius's more obnoxious favorites, including Eutyches, and tried to encourage a rapprochement between Pope Leo and Anatolius, the new bishop of Constantinople, who was also intent upon settling the Antiochene/Alexandrian theological conflict once and for all. Furthermore, both East and West were bracing themselves for an invasion by the Huns, ruthless hordes from the Russian steppes who were sweeping across eastern and central Europe under the warlord Attila, dispossessing the Germans and pushing them farther south into Roman territory.

In 451, Marcian convened a council at Chalcedon, across the Bosporus from Constantinople. Some 520 Eastern bishops attended, along with a handful of Westerners and a papal delegation from Rome. When the truculent Dioscurus arrived from Alexandria, he immediately went on the offensive, excommunicating Leo for heresy. This time, however, the bishops' sentiments were against him. His victim Flavian, whose body Pulcheria had ordered brought back to Constantinople and triumphantly interred, had nearly achieved the status of martyr. Although Dioscurus valiantly invoked the names of Athanasius, Cyril, and other church fathers to support his anti-dual-nature position, the council was determined to hammer out a reconciliation between Alexandrians and Antiochenes that would finally stick. To Dioscurus's dismay, the bishops voted overwhelmingly in support of a formal statement to the effect that there was no inconsistency between Cyril's theology and that of Leo.

The resulting document came to be known as the "Chalcedonic Definition." Using dual-nature language borrowed from Leo's *Tome,* while at the same time ratifying Mary's title as "bearer of God" as a bone to the Alexandrians, the bishops declared that Jesus was:

> truly God and truly man, the same consisting of a reasonable soul and body, of one substance with the Father as touching the Godhead, the same of one sub-

> stance with us as touching the manhood, like us in all things apart from sin . . . one and the same Christ, Son, Lord, Only-begotten, to be acknowledged in two natures, without confusion, without change, without division, without separation, the distinction of natures being in no way abolished because of the union but rather the characteristic property of each nature being preserved and concurring into one Person and one subsistence, not as if Christ were parted or divided into two persons, but one and the same Son and Only-begotten God, Word, Lord Jesus Christ.[27]

As can be seen, the Chalcedonic Definition offered verbal concessions to Jesus-as-God and Jesus-as-man partisans alike.

The theological conflicts that the Chalcedonic document had papered over reemerged as soon as the bishops returned home. Safe inside their own territory outside the empire's eastern frontier, the Nestorians ignored Chalcedon and all that it stood for. The Egyptians, and large numbers of Ethiopians, Syrians, Armenians, and other Easterners who favored a single-nature Jesus, regarded the Definition as heretical. Within a century after Chalcedon, Eastern discomfiture over the dual-nature formulation had crystalized into a separatist "Monophysite" (from the Greek for "one nature") movement. Most of the Eastern flank of the church gradually defected and set up its own hierarchy, forming a Monophysite "empire," in W. H. C. Frend's words, stretching from Ethiopia to the eastern end of the Black Sea, and outsizing the Latin and Eastern Orthodox territories combined. Even Theodora, the courtesan who married the sixth-century Byzantine emperor Justinian, considered herself a Monophysite Christian.

Elsewhere in the remains of the old Roman Empire, the Chalcedonic Definition held fast. Despite differences in ecclesiastical language (Greek in the East, and Latin in the West—and few people knew both), liturgical style, and theology, Eastern and Western Christians agreed that Jesus, son of God yet born of a woman, mysteriously incorporated a divine and a human nature.

It is customary for moderns to regard the ancient conflict over Jesus' identity as a no more than thinly veiled political struggle with humorous overtones. Indeed, vicious quarreling and overt political maneuvering were very much a part of the councils that proclaimed the Nicene and Chalcedonic doctrines. In view of the fact that the Eastern emperor regarded himself as an arm of the church, the Monophysite movement in Egypt represented a revolt against Greek hegemony. Furthermore, certain of the Greek technical terms used in the debate, such as *homoousios* (of the same essence) and *homoiousios* (of similar essence), sound archaic and even silly to today's ears. Finally, for many in the 20th century, the very idea of a "creed"—a set of required beliefs—smacks of authoritarianism.

Moderns tend to view the Christological controversies of the first five centuries through the lens of Edward Gibbon, who sneered at all things Christian, especially bishops. Gibbon believed that the Greek-speaking hair-splitters at Nicea and Chalcedon were trying to graft an arcane and irrelevant Platonism onto a simple Jewish preacher named Jesus. "The profane of every age have derided the furious contests which the difference of a single dipthong excited between the Homoousians and the Homoiousians," Gibbon chuckled.[28] In the same vein, the late-19th-century liberal German church historian Adolf von Harnack observed: "The Christian religion was mixed up with the refined asceticism of a perishing civilization, and a foreign substructure given to its system of morality, so earnest in its simplicity."[29] In his 1992 study of Jesus, the British novelist A. N. Wilson commented: "If it were even half possible that an historical personage existed who said the words attributed to him in the Gospels, there could be no greater insult to his memory than to recite the creeds, invented in a Hellenized world which was, imaginatively speaking, light years away both from Jesus and from ourselves."[30]

It is important to remember, however, that during these early centuries (and for many centuries thereafter), the linguistic debates over Jesus' identity that consumed the bishops also obsessed humble, illiterate lay Christians. It was not unusual for ancient mobs to hurl imprecations and heavy objects at theologians whom they considered heretical. Gregory of Nyssa, a fourth-century bishop from Cappadocia in eastern Asia Minor, noted that Christological arguments rang through the streets of Constantinople when he visited the city for an ecumenical council in 381. Among the food vendors, old-clothes-dealers, and money-changers of the city's marketplaces and alleyways, theological debates never stopped: "If you ask someone to give you change, he philosophizes about the Begotten and the Unbegotten; if you inquire about the price of a loaf, you are told by way of reply that the Father is greater and the Son inferior; if you ask, 'Is my bath ready?' the attendant answers that the Son was made out of nothing."[31]

For Gregory and others of his era, defining Jesus' identity was of the utmost importance inasmuch as they believed that their own salvation depended on imitating his blameless life. If he, a human being, had risen from the dead, so would they at the end of time. Rowan A. Greer, a professor of early Christian literature at Yale University, described this way of thinking in an essay on Gregory of Nyssa:

> First, since Christ is the Savior and since only God can save, Christ must somehow be God. Second, since the only way God can save us is by touching us and our human condition directly and fully, Christ must somehow be identified with our humanity. Third, these two aspects of Christ's identity must be kept distinct but must not compromise his unity. . . . The church's theological task, then, was to sort out and make sense of these apparently contradictory assessments of Christ. Moreover, the task was more than a theoretical one, since it was designed to define Christ as the object of Christian piety, worshipped in the liturgy and imitated in the Christian's life. Were he not God and distinct from the Father, he would not be a worthy and clear object of worship. Were he not a human, he would not bring salvation to his worshippers and would not supply them with a paradigm of true humanity to assist them in their lives.[32]

The Chalcedonic Definition remained the basis for profound religious meditation on Jesus' humanity up to the very brink of the modern era. Nonetheless, while orthodox Christians of East and West regularly recited the Nicene Creed (and still do), the old distinction between Jesus-as-God Alexandrian Christianity and Jesus-as-man Antiochene Christianity—or "Christology from above" and "Christology from below," as they are sometimes called—lingered on in a number of subtle ways.

The focus of Eastern Christianity was on Jesus' incarnation, the process by which the divine being descended from heaven to become a man. The growing devotion to icons—likenesses of Christ and the saints—stemmed directly from this incarnational emphasis. Although the Book of Deuteronomy had forbidden Jews to make artistic representations of God (and many Christians believed that this prohibition applied to them as well), the Eastern theologians taught their followers that the fact that God had become human in Jesus meant that he could be portrayed through depictions of Jesus.

The eighth-century theologian John of Damascus wrote: "But now when God is seen in the flesh and conversing with men, I make an image of the God whom I can see."[33] John's declaration was a stirring affirmation of the holiness of all creation, including the human body. It was also an attack (as noted by Oxford University scholar Timothy Ware) on a puritanical dualism that has periodically resurfaced in Christianity: the belief that the material world is evil, and that it is sinful to enjoy it.[34] However, it is interesting that John used the phrase "image of . . . *God,*" and not simply "image of Jesus."

The figures in Eastern iconography have always possessed an exalted, hieratic quality. While mere human beings, they are also endowed with a sacred aura. The quintessential Orthodox icon is the omnipresent Christ the Pantocrator, the ruler of all creation. With his piercing eyes, his halo and beard, and his holy Gospel book in hand, he is at once stunningly virile and authoritatively divine. He exemplifies "Christology from above," an image of God incarnate, whose human and divine natures are fused into one person.

By contrast, Western Christianity has nurtured the Antiochene image of a Christ with two natures so distinct from one another as to be nearly disjoined. Pope Leo's *Tome* was a dramatic example of the paradoxical approach to Christianity that still marks the West. Leo wrote:

> To hunger, to thirst, to be weary and to sleep, is obviously human; but with five loaves to satisfy five thousand people and to bestow on the woman of Samaria that living water, a draught of which will cause the drinker to thirst no more; to walk upon the surface of the sea with feet that do not sink, and to calm the rising waves by rebuking the tempest, is without question divine . . . [I]t does not belong to the same nature to weep for a dead friend with emotions of pity, and to recall the same friend from the dead with a word of prayer when the stone was taken away which had covered the grave for four days. . . .[35]

Leo used specific events from Jesus' life as recorded in the Gospels—his falling asleep on a boat, his miraculous feeding of the multitudes, his dialogue with the oft-married Samaritan woman at Jacob's well, his raising of Lazarus from the dead, and his thirsting on the cross—to illustrate that Jesus had separate human and divine natures.

In his portrayal of Jesus, Leo drew not on theological speculation, but rather on what he considered to be the sacred biographies of a Jesus who had actually lived in history, and as such had been fully engaged in the ordinary activities of human beings: eating, thirsting, weeping, and dying. At the same time, he delineated a divine figure who had walked on water and raised the dead. He made no effort to reconcile the two aspects of Jesus as presented in the Gospels, except to assert that they pertained to the same person. His was a typical example of Western "Christology from below," focusing on specific aspects of Jesus' humanity.

Whereas the quintessential religious image of Eastern Christianity was the icon of Christ the glorious God-man, that of the West was the crucifix, the symbol of Jesus, the Son of God, who had suffered and died like any other man. During the Middle Ages, the passion of Christ, as depicted in paintings, sculptures, music and works of poetry, books of meditation, and religious dramas, became a virtual obsession. In contemplating the figure on the cross, medieval Westerners—even the semi-literature tradesmen who produced the English mystery plays of the 13th and 14th centuries—could identify their own day-to-day tribulations with those of the Christ who had suffered out of love for them. They also found cause for joy in the knowledge that they had been redeemed by his sacrifice. To some extent, this explains why medieval literature shifted so readily in tone from the exalted to the jocular, or even the bawdy (Chaucer's *Canterbury Tales* is a prime example). In his 1966 study of English mystery plays, the medievalist V. A. Kolve examined the way in which authors wove broad farce into their dramas, such as the jests of Roman soldiers who were tormenting Jesus, without sacrificing reverence. "So thoroughly is the theological background assimilated that we seem to be in the presence of nothing more than ordinary life, closely observed and represented," Kolve wrote.[36]

Through the image of Jesus on the cross, medieval theologians of the West tried to reconcile the age-old paradox of his dual identity. Meditating on Jesus' human suffering gave them a way of seeing—or at least saying—how God himself, unchanging and immortal, could suffer and die. In the words of the 13th-century scholastic theologian Thomas Aquinas, "The Passion is to be attributed to the suppositum of the Divine Nature, not because of the Divine Nature, which is impassible, but by reason of the human nature."[37]

This sort of theological speculation translated into an emotion-drenched body of sacred texts that explored the shocking contrast of Jesus' divinity with the brutality of his human passion on the cross. "They seized almighty God . . . they laid him down limb-weary and stood around his head / and beheld the lord of heaven," wrote an eighth-century Anglo-Saxon poet.[38] According to the late Rosemary Woolf of Oxford University, "The theological point that the Christ who endured the Crucifixion is fully God and fully Man is thus perfectly made and with it the imaginative effect . . . is attained, the astonishment at the great paradox of Christianity that God should endure such things."[39]

Beginning with Pope Leo, Western Christians had made no real attempts to resolve this "theological point" intellectually. Like the anonymous Anglo-Saxon poet of the cross, they were content to meditate upon the dramatic and emotional images of the crucified Jesus as God experiencing human pain and evil. Even among Protestants, who have never venerated the crucifix, Leo's paradox has been portrayed through the medium of music. The Passions and cantatas of the devout Lutheran, Johann Sebastian Bach, would be grossly sentimental were they not so sublime. In America, Pentecostal and African-American hymns dealing with the human sufferings of Jesus have provided a wellspring of religious experience for the Christian believer.

Nonetheless, the Christian creedal paradox that Jesus is both fully divine and fully human has continued to defy human understanding. Over the millennia Christian believers have regularly yielded to the temptation to view him as more divine than human. Docetism—the belief that Jesus only *seemed* human—has been on the sidelines of Christian theology since New Testament times. At the beginning of the second century, the church father Ignatius of Antioch warned a Christian community in Ephesus that it was pointless to speculate on how Jesus as God could have died a human death, or how his virgin mother had come to bear him. These were "mysteries" or "secrets" beyond human understanding and known only to God.[40] By the end of the century, a large body of pious but not officially sanctioned literature called the "apocryphal Gospels" had begun circulating throughout the Christian world, claiming that Jesus had not been physically born to Mary; that as a child he had made clay birds fly and had struck playmates dead on a whim; or that he had later functioned as a mystical surrogate for the apostle Thomas (his "twin"). In the mid–20th century, the religious theorist Mircea Eliade described the folklore of the Orthodox peasants of his native Romania as having transformed the historical Jesus who had lived and died into a cosmic lord of nature who eternally renewed the earth.[41]

The fault line between the divine and the human Jesus has always been implicit in Christian doctrine. However, it was not until the 18th century, when educated Western Christians began leaving the Church en masse, that this fault line became a gaping abyss. As the divine Jesus simply fell away and disappeared, the human Jesus continued to fascinate. This phenomenon, coupled with a new-found faith in science, would become the basis for the search for the "historical" Jesus. No longer would Western intellectuals seek to understand Jesus' humanity experientially or theologically. Rather, they would seek to know him "historically." They had come to believe that history itself was a branch of science, and as such, it could even explain religious experience.

3
THE PARADIGM SHIFT

Most people believe that the search for the historical Jesus began in Germany toward the end of the 18th century. Their belief stems from the assertions of Albert Schweitzer, the celebrated medical missionary and theologian. Schweitzer (1875–1965) was born in Alsace, which had been annexed by the German victors of the Franco-Prussian War in 1871, and he imbibed German triumphalism with his mother's milk. In 1906, he published his famous *Quest of the Historical Jesus,* in which he affirmed on the very first page that "the greatest achievement of German theology is the critical investigation of the life of Jesus."[1]

Schweitzer's text explored the lives and works of more than 200 academic Jesus-searchers, almost all of whom were Germans, up to his own time. He also identified Hermann Samuel Reimarus (1694–1768), a professor of Oriental languages at the Gymnasium Johanneum, a secondary school in Hamburg, as the first person to have formed "a historical conception of the life of Jesus."[2] Indeed, the original German title of the *Quest* was *Von Reimarus zu Wrede,* or *From Reimarus to Wrede* ("Wrede" being the German scholar Wilhelm Wrede, whose book titled *The Messianic Secret and the Gospels* appeared in 1901).

Reimarus had pride of place in *The Quest of the Historical Jesus.* From the years 1774 through 1778, the German dramatist and philosopher Gotthold Lessing (1729–1781) had published seven anonymous excerpts from the deceased Reimarus's private writings under the title *Fragments of an Unknown.* These were also called the *Wolfenbüttel Fragments,* after the market town in the duchy of Braunschweig where Lessing was serving as ducal librarian at the time of their publication.

Reimarus's *Fragments* contained material that was shocking to pious Christians and Jews. In one instance, he poked fun at the narrative of the parting of the Red Sea in the Book of Exodus, speculating that such a horde of humans and animals, especially in the lazy Orient, could never have crossed the sea in a reasonable length of time. In July 1778, the publication of the seventh *Fragment,* which concerned Jesus and his mission, prompted a scandalized Duke of Braunschweig to order Lessing to surrender the texts.

In this last *Fragment,* which was titled "Concerning the Intention of Jesus and His Teaching," Reimarus accused Jesus of having deliberately deceived his followers in portraying himself as a miracle-worker. In an earlier *Fragment* published in 1777 called "On the Resurrection Narratives," Reimarus had pointed out 10 contradictions in the Gospel accounts of Jesus' rising from the dead. Treating the canonical evangelists like alibi witnesses in a criminal case, Reimarus had sarcastically concluded that all four stories were total fabrications. In the seventh *Fragment,* he also theorized that after Jesus' death, his disciples had made him into a divine figure and invented a religion they called Christianity in order to sponge off the collection plate. "They had grown out of the habit of working," Reimarus noted wryly.[3]

Such heavy-handed irony was typical of Reimarus's style. Outwardly a rationalist but churchgoing Lutheran, he secretly detested Christianity and poured out his loathing in his private papers. Schweitzer termed Reimarus's seventh *Fragment* a "masterpiece" of anti-Christian polemic, adding, "Seldom has there been a hate so eloquent, so lofty a scorn."[4] His characterization of Reimarus's sarcasm-dripping seventh *Fragment* as the first "critical investigation" into the life of Jesus was taken up by both laymen and biblical scholars.

Because of Schweitzer's influential book, many people now believe that the "historical Jesus" had to have been a radically different figure from the Jesus of the Gospels. According to Reimarus, the historical Jesus was a failed political revolutionary with some sound ethical teachings whose disciples had turned him into a god. Robert Funk, founder of the iconoclastic Jesus Seminar, and his colleague Roy W. Hoover wrote in their introduction to the Seminar's *Five Gospels:* "A close study of the New Testament gospels convinced Reimarus that what the authors of the gospels said about Jesus could be distinguished from what Jesus himself said. It was with this basic distinction between the man Jesus and the Christ of the creeds that the quest for the historical Jesus began."[5]

Furthermore, Funk and Hoover, like many who have read Schweitzer's book, consider the quest for a non-Christian "historical" Jesus initiated by Reimarus and other disbelievers to be the underpinning of modern "critical" New Testament scholarship, which examines texts in ways not necessarily in accord with traditional religious interpretation. Once again in their introduction, they wrote: "In the course of the modern critical study of the Bible, which was inspired by the Reformation (begun formally, 1517 C.E.) but originated with the Enlightenment (about 1690 C.E.), biblical scholars and theologians alike have learned to distinguish the Jesus of history from the Christ of faith."[6] In other words, "critical" biblical scholarship was largely a product of the Enlightenment and its exaltation of rationalism and empiricism, and all truly "critical" biblical scholars were (and still are) radical skeptics like Reimarus.

Although admittedly widespread, these presuppositions are erroneous. The first "critical" biblical scholars were not Enlightenment skeptics but rather a Parisian Roman Catholic priest who lived during the reign of Louis XIV, and several German Pietists, practitioners of a flourishing late-17th and early-18th-century Lutheranism that emphasized the believer's personal relationship with Jesus and the Holy Spirit. Although they all lived during the post-1690 era that Funk and Hoover designate as the Enlightenment, they did not share the movement's hostility toward Christianity.

The Catholic cleric Richard Simon (1638–1712), who has been called the "father of Biblical criticism" for his series of detailed and erudite *Histoires critiques* of Old and New Testament texts, pioneered the modern "historical-critical" analysis of the Scriptures in 1678 by his reading of the Bible through the lenses of history and literary criticism. Brilliant but somewhat tactless, Simon soon ran afoul of France's most powerful bishop, Jacques Bénigne Bossuet (1627–1704), an advocate of absolutist government and absolutist Christianity. Bossuet, who had no mean mind himself (and was an eloquent writer), first banned and then censured Simon's works, which had to be published in Protestant Holland and smuggled back into France.

While Simon believed that the Scriptures were divinely inspired, he was also convinced that a good scholar needed to examine the history of their texts, which had undergone numerous linguistic changes throughout the centuries in the process of being recopied. He also maintained (and this infuriated the traditionalist Bossuet) that the exegetical interpretations the early church fathers had given to Scriptural passages were not necessarily as insightful as those of modern scholars armed with better texts and more exhaustive learning. Simon's falling-out with Bossuet was ironic, because one of his aims as a Catholic was to refute the Protestant doctrine of *sola scriptura* (the Scriptures as the sole religious authority) by demonstrating that the muddled textual history of the Bible had produced a number of unreliable readings.

Among the several leading Pietist biblical scholars, Johann Albrecht Bengel (1687–1752) undoubtedly left the greatest mark. Head of a rigorous preparatory school at Denkendorf and fluent in Latin, Greek, and Hebrew, Bengel virtually invented the modern science of identifying authoritative biblical texts. He also instituted a system of classifying the more than 5,000 extant manuscript versions of the New Testament (no two of which contained precisely the same wording) by establishing textual "families" based upon geographical provenance. Bengel's principles are still in use today, as are certain of his criteria for determining whether a variant reading represents a scribe's corruption or a truly authentic rendition. One of his precepts that continues to be utilized is based on his theory that many of the scribes tended to alter the texts in order to make them more readable. Bengel credited the more difficult readings with greater reliability. To some extent, both Simon and the Pietists drew on a tradition of careful textual interpretation of the New Testament that harked back through the Renaissance and the Middle Ages to the era of the church fathers.

Contrary to what Schweitzer believed (or chose to believe), Hermann Reimarus was not a particularly original thinker. The quest for the historical Jesus had actually been set in motion in England during Reimarus's boyhood by a coterie of coffee-house freethinkers known as deists, who held that Christianity (together with all other organized faiths) was no more than a web of superstition woven by power-hungry ecclesiastics. Institutionalized religion represented a corruption of what the deists called "natural religion," the informal worship of a benevolent but distant Supreme Being who could be known only through human reason and an innate moral sensibility that lay inside every human heart. Several of them reconstructed their own historical Jesus—a preceptor of morals, as might be expected—who antedated Reimarus's Jesus by several decades. The English deists specialized in the same type of ridicule and anti-Christian rhetoric that Schweitzer later found in the *Fragments*.

On the Continent, the deists influenced several important intellectuals of the Enlightenment, most notably Voltaire (1694–1778), who had lived in

England from 1726 to 1728 while on the lam from the law after having fought a duel with a French aristocrat. Voltaire returned to France possessed by an "infatuation" with England and its rationalist philosophies, in the words of historian Peter Gay.[7] Reimarus himself, who had visited England and Holland in 1720 and 1721 and had become enthralled with deism and its faith in progress and human reason, wrote a treatise on natural religion.

By and large, the English deists were not intellectuals, much less biblical scholars. Most were simply autodidacts with a flair for pamphleteering. As Peter Gay has noted, "Among the deists, only Anthony Collins (1676–1729) could claim much philosophical competence; only Conyers Middleton (1683–1750) was a really serious scholar." It was the opponents of the deists—David Hume, who was a more thoroughgoing skeptic, and the poet (and sometime deist sympathizer) Alexander Pope, who was a wittier writer—who possessed superior learning and argumentation skills. In their battles against Christianity, Gay writes, the deists could "muster only common sense, a healthy skepticism, some knowledge of religious history, some telling abuse, and a certain brutish, patient obsession with their polemics against 'superstition.'"[8]

One of the most famous deists—and probably the originator of the quest for the historical Jesus—was Thomas Chubb (1679–1747), a glovemaker from Salisbury who knew neither Latin nor Greek but who read voraciously in rationalist philosophy and became a pet of the London salons, where the idea of the noble savage was much in vogue. During the 1730s, Chubb was to London intellectual society what Benjamin Franklin was to the French court during the American Revolution: an amusing "natural." In several of his writings, including a posthumously published essay titled "Of the Personal Character of Jesus Christ" (which will be discussed in greater detail in the next chapter), Chubb limned a historical Jesus who bore a remarkable resemblance to Reimarus's Jesus of two or three decades later: a teacher of simple moral truths who "walked by the sea of Galilee"[9] dispensing maxims to his disciples and comfort to the poor. Like his successor Reimarus, Chubb did not believe in miracles (he had published a notorious tract ridiculing them in 1741), nor did he have any use for the supernatural. He mocked the Gospel accounts of the virgin birth, and declared that Jesus' resurrection from the dead was impossible. As the New Testament historian William Baird has noted, Chubb turned Jesus into "a sort of first-century Palestinian deist, garbed in the seamless robe of reason and natural religion."[10] Once again like Reimarus, he concluded that Jesus had never intended to found a religion, and that his disciples should be held responsible for the spread of Christianity after his death. For Chubb, the real villain was Paul of Tarsus, whom he accused of having invented the Christian doctrine of Jesus' death as an atonement for human sin (Chubb was too optimistic to take sin seriously, and he considered Jesus' death to have resulted from his being a political scapegoat of the Pharisees).

Besides being the first modern to search for a non-Christian historical Jesus, Chubb was the first to articulate the proposition, still widely disseminated, that Paul of Tarsus was to blame for distorting Christianity into something radically different from the religion that Jesus himself had believed in and taught. As can be seen from Chubb's example, one did not need to be an intellectual or professional biblical scholar to embark on a quest for Jesus the mere man.

In contrast to Chubb and most of the other English deists, Hermann Reimarus was a genuine (and prolific) scholar whose specialties were philosophy and ancient history. During a long and fruitful career at several academic posts in Germany, he wrote treatises on logic and the theories of Machiavelli, and edited the works of the third-century Roman historian Dio Cassius. However, in his writings on the historical Jesus, Reimarus was playing an amateur's game. He did not need his vast learning in order to have written his incendiary seventh *Fragment*. He needed only Thomas Chubb's equipment: a copy of the New Testament and a thoroughgoing deist outlook.

As can be seen from the examples of Reimarus and Chubb, the preoccupation with disentangling the "historical" Jesus from Christian faith was not the result of more sophisticated research during the late 17th and early 18th centuries, but rather the reflection of a dramatic and all-encompassing change of mindset that accompanied, or perhaps fueled, the rise of what we call modernity.

The 17th and 18th centuries are remembered as an age of great scientific advancement. In 1774, the same year in which Lessing began publishing Reimarus's *Fragments,* the English amateur scientist Joseph Priestley conducted a series of chemical experiments that isolated the element oxygen. At one time a Presbyterian minister, Priestley had lost his Christian faith, become a Unitarian, and launched his own search for the historical Jesus. It was not scientific progress alone that had turned Priestley into a nonbeliever.

There was something larger at work in his culture: a shift in or a substitution of mythologies, the phenomenon that Thomas Kuhn called a paradigm shift.

In 1941, nearly 200 years after Chubb's death, the famous German theologian Rudolf Bultmann (1884–1976) delivered a much-debated paper concerning Christianity and the modern age titled "New Testament and Mythology." Chubb, Reimarus, and even Priestley, would have agreed with his thesis, despite their unfamiliarity with 20th-century scientific inventions. Bultmann declared: "We cannot use electric lights and radios and, in the event of illness, avail ourselves of modern medicine and clinical means and at the same time believe in the spirit and wonder world of the New Testament."[11] Like his predecessors of the 18th century, Bultmann had come to *believe* that modern science was incompatible with belief in supernatural phenomena. In defining as "mythology" the traditional Christian stories about Jesus that entailed the intervention of supernatural powers, especially those of the virgin birth and the resurrection, he assumed that no rational 20th-century person could credit such tales. He considered it the task of Christian theologians to "demythologize" the Gospels, by first explaining the reasons why they portrayed miracles, and then purging them of these miracles in order to make Christianity more palatable to the modern mind. Bultmann, who was an existentialist, believed that the "demythologized" Jesus was also an existentialist, whose message was absolute trust in an unknowable God.

In formulating his theories about mythology and demythologizing, Bultmann himself (along with Chubb and Priestley) subscribed to a myth: scientific progress had so transformed modern men and women that mythical thought patterns had simply disappeared from their consciousness. Bultmann could not have been more wrong. As the French social theorist Jacques Ellul has pointed out, the modern age, far from desacralizing people's thinking, has merely substituted a new set of sacred myths for the old ones. The current sacral worldview, as defined by Ellul, includes a fervent belief in progress and the continual betterment of the human condition; a worship of science as "a sort of awe-inspiring and benevolent divinity" (Ellul's phrase);[12] a faith in a "right" to happiness, defined as self-fulfillment and the growth of collective material wealth; and an unshakable conviction that traditional religion is largely anachronistic in a society that is hurtling inexorably toward an electronic future of unlimited technological possibility and individual choice. (Ellul identifies the techno-optimist Alvin Toffler as one of modernity's high priests.) As Ellul points out, the upbeat mythology of the creed of modernity has little evidentiary basis in the ecological wasteland and

cultural junkyard that is the actual modern world. The modern myth is in many ways as "superstitious" as any ancient faith.

Ellul's theory of the modern myth explains Bultmann's certainty that the invention of the light bulb had made it impossible for anyone to believe in Jesus' resurrection. It also clarifies why two centuries earlier Thomas Chubb, Hermann Reimarus, and Joseph Priestley had similarly ridiculed the idea of miracles. (In 1777, when Gotthold Lessing wrote, "I live in the 18th century, in which miracles no longer happen,"[13] he sounded much like Bultmann in the 20th century.) Finally, it demonstrates that there is a continuum extending from Thomas Chubb and his successors to Rudolf Bultmann and his successors among today's biblical scholars. All share the same mythological presuppositions.

Robert Funk of the Jesus Seminar wrote his doctoral dissertation at Vanderbilt University during the 1960s under Bultmann's disciple (and son-in-law) Kendrick Grobel. When I interviewed Funk in 1994 for a magazine article about the Seminar, he told me that the notion that Jesus was begotten of the Holy Spirit was "a mythological statement that does not belong to the modern age."[14] Like his mentor once-removed Bultmann, Funk was not making a statement of fact, but rather a statement of faith in what Ellul would call a different mythological worldview. Not surprisingly, the Jesus whom the Jesus Seminar has unearthed—a pithy aphorist who said less than 20 percent of the words ascribed to him in the Gospels—bears a striking resemblance to the rationalist-moralist of Chubb and Reimarus and the shadowy existentialist of Bultmann—precisely because they are all products of the same modern mindset. The Jesuses of all of them are stripped of traditional supernatural and divine appurtenances, from virgin birth to resurrection, because only thus are they intelligible to those who subscribe to the mythology of modernity.

This "modern" image of Jesus was not only the result of a change of intellectual mindset that occurred during the 17th and 18th centuries. It was also the consequence of a dramatic change in the way in which most Christians interpreted the Bible, particularly the Gospels.

While all four canonical Gospels purport to tell the life story of Jesus from his youth or early ministry to his death and resurrection, they contradict one another to such an extent that they tend to undermine their own historical credibility. Even Matthew, Mark, and Luke (the first three, or "Synoptic" Gospels, from a Greek verb that means "to see together"), which share a common narrative outline and much common material, are inconsistent in many particulars. Matthew and Luke, for example, recount the tale of Mary's virginal conception of Jesus and his birth in Bethlehem in ways that can be read as contradictory: In Matthew, the infant Jesus and his parents flee to Egypt to escape Herod the Great's murderous wrath over the birth of a putative rival, while in Luke, Jesus is taken peacefully by Mary and her husband, Joseph, to Herod's Jerusalem Temple for a blessing, whereupon the family returns to its home in Nazareth.

The Fourth Gospel, John, is markedly different from the three Synoptics in both story line and content. In the Gospel of John, Jesus does not tell any of his well-known parables, and he works only a handful of miracles. Even the geographical setting of John is dissimilar: Jesus conducts most of his ministry in and around Jerusalem, whereas in the Synoptics he msotly confines himself to Galilee.

All four Gospels contain somewhat comparable versions of Jesus' passion, including his last supper with his disciples, his arrest, trial, and death on the cross, and the discovery of his empty tomb by one or more of his female followers. However, the details are not consistent. According to Matthew, two women went to the tomb, while Mark sets their number at three, Luke at more than three, and John at only one (Mary Magdalene). According to all four Gospels, Jesus tells the apostle Peter at the Last Supper that he will deny him three times before the cock crows twice the next morning. Peter duly denies that he is one of Jesus' followers when queried, but the four retellings of the story record the time and place of these denials in totally disparate ways. Even the date of Jesus' death is a subject of inconsistency. In the three Synoptics, Jesus seems to have died on the first day of Passover, whereas in John he dies on Passover eve.

The discrepancies in the Gospel narratives were not discovered by 18th-century freethinkers such as Reimarus and Chubb. The earliest Christians were quite aware of them. If the canonical Gospels were indeed written between 60 and 100 C.E., as most modern-day scholars hold, it is likely that a great many early Christians were familiar with at least two Gospels, if not more. Within a century of Jesus' death, all four Gospels were in wide circulation, often as a unit. While certain Christian groups—Marcion's followers and the Ebionites—clung to the notion of a single definitive Gospel, most Christians seem to have *wanted* to read several different accounts of Jesus' life.

Letters addressed to Christians in the Eastern Mediterranean by Clement, bishop of Rome at the end of the first century, and Ignatius, bishop of Antioch at approximately the same time, contain what appear to be quotations from Jesus as recorded in Matthew, Mark, and Luke. While it is possible that Clement and Ignatius were drawing on oral tradition or non-Gospel collections of Jesus' sayings, it is also likely that Ignatius had actually read the texts of the three Synoptics. In his treatise called *Expositions of the Sayings of the Lord,* Papias, bishop of Hieropolis in Phrygia, a contemporary of Justin Martyr, noted (according to the fourth-century historian Eusebius) that Matthew had composed the "sayings" of the Lord in a "Hebrew language," and that Mark, who had once served as the apostle Peter's interpreter in Rome, had written his Gospel from what he remembered of Peter's preaching. Although Papias might have been wrong about the circumstances surrounding the composition of Matthew and Mark, the important thing is that like Clement, Ignatius, and Justin, he seems to have known Matthew and Mark's Gospels as separate written documents. Furthermore, none of those early church fathers appears to have been at all perturbed by the differences in narrative detail.

During this early period there was no such thing as a "canon" of the New Testament. As I pointed out earlier, when early Christians referred to "the Scriptures," they meant the Jewish Scriptures, or the Old Testament. In lieu of a Christian Bible, there were only detached copies of the Gospels, the letters of Paul, and a large number of other writings, all in Greek, which were recopied and circulated as small, leather-bound books called codexes. The earliest extant Gospel manuscript, dating from around 125 C.E., is a papyrus fragment containing several verses from the Gospel of John, which was found in faraway Egypt. The second-oldest extant New Testament papyrus, from the late second century, contains the texts of Luke and John.

Today's Christian "canon" of the New Testament (from the Greek word *kanōn* meaning "rule," referring to texts that could be read from in the liturgy) was not the product of church councils, although the rulings of bishops and the opinions of theologians undoubtedly played a role in its formation. By and large, it was created by consensus, or rather by majority consensus, for there were always small groups of Christians who rejected all or part of the canon and maintained their own authoritative books. While the New Testament canon was not officially codified until sometime during the fourth century, as early as 200 C.E. it was more or less in place, and at least one definitive list of canonical books was already in circulation. Within two centuries after Jesus' birth, Christian communities from Britain to Mesopotamia were in relative agreement on the putative shape of the New Testament Scriptures.

The most significant feature of the early canonical literature was the fact that it almost always included the four Gospels of today's New Testament.

Although Christians argued extensively about which other texts should be included (particularly with regard to the Book of Revelation), Matthew and Mark were universally accepted from the very beginning. There was some debate during the second century over the admissibility of Luke's Gospel and the Acts of the Apostles, and as late as 220 C.E. certain fringe groups of Christians refused to accept either John's Gospel or the three New Testament letters attributed to him. Nonetheless, by the year 180, the bishop Irenaeus of Lyons (the successor of the martyred Pothinus), was able to write definitively:

> It is not possible that the Gospels can be either more or fewer in number than they are, since there are four directions of the world in which we are, and four principal winds. . . . The four living creatures [the lion, ox, man, and eagle of Revelation 4:9] symbolize the four Gospels . . . and there are four principal covenants made with humanity, through Noah, Abraham, Moses, and Christ.[15]

The general consensus that there were no *more* than four Gospels led to the elimination of an assortment of other documents that bore the name "gospel." The Ebionites' "gospel" and Marcion's version of the Book of Luke were among the texts rejected. Of the 47 documents associated with second-century Gnosticism that have been unearthed at Nag Hammadi and elsewhere in Egypt, five bear the title "gospel," but not one was accepted into the canon by the Christian majority. Still another second-century text, the Gospel of Peter, features strong anti-Jewish rhetoric, as well as a cross that follows Jesus out of his tomb and speaks. Although popular among certain Eastern Christian communities, it was almost unanimously rejected by the second century's end. The fanciful "apocryphal" gospels, filled with fantastical tales of Jesus' childhood, were similarly banned, even though some of their stories about Mary's life remained staples of popular devotion for centuries to come. The general consensus among the early Christians was that the gospels that had been discarded were not "apostolic"—composed either by Jesus' apostles (Matthew and John) or disciples of the apostles (Mark and Luke, an alleged companion of Paul). Other considerations undoubtedly figured in the process of selection: Most of the rejected gospels, which tended to depict a magical Jesus who was barely human, contained material that was deemed heretical. Furthermore as Irenaeus's statement indicates, the majority of Christians were also certain from the very beginning that there were *no fewer* than four Gospels. They treasured their four stylistically and theologically different narratives of Jesus' life, death, and resurrection.

After Justin Martyr's beheading in 161 C.E., his pupil Tatian left Rome's orthodox Christian community to join a rival sect headed by Valentinus, a brilliant Gnostic intellectual. In 172, Tatian was forced to flee to the East because of his unorthodox views, where he composed an abridgement of the canonical Gospels that he called the *Diatessaron* (from the Greek for "through the four"). Using the Gospel of Matthew as the basis for his narrative, he removed all duplicative passages from the four Gospels, harmonized contradictions, and smoothed out discrepancies of detail in parallel passages.

Despite Tatian's condemnation by Christian officials, his book circulated widely and was extensively imitated. In many Syrian churches it was the only text of the Gospels available for many centuries. It seems to have circulated as far north as Germany and present-day Holland and as far east as China, where there is evidence that Manichean missionaries carried it with them. Such a uniform text would have made it far easier for Christians to evangelize among skeptics, who were always eager to point out the contradictions in the Gospels themselves. Nonetheless, the majority of Christian churches, again affirming their devotion to more than one Gospel, rejected the *Diatessaron,* suppressing it so entirely, even in Syria, that no known copy exists today.

Despite the obstacles to belief raised by the divergent narratives, most Christians agreed with Irenaeus's analogy of the four Gospels and the four winds. In a short poem, the fourth-century church father Gregory of Nanzianzen encapsulated the early Christian affection for Gospel diversity:

Matthew indeed wrote for the Hebrews the wonderful works of Christ,
And Mark for Italy, Luke for Greece,
John, the great preacher, for all, walking in heaven.[16]

Christians of the ancient world and the Middle Ages accepted discrepancies among the Gospels because they did not expect biblical texts to have only one meaning. From earliest times, they tended to read the Scriptures in a complex, multilayered fashion whereby certain passages from the Bible shed light on others. In their minds, stories from the Old Testament, for example, were not only historically accurate, but were also allegorical prefigurations of events in the life of Jesus, or even of Christian teachings developed long afterward. In his *Dialogue with Trypho,* Justin noted that of the two wives of the Hebrew patriarch Jacob, Leah and her younger sister Rachel, Jacob had loved Rachel more. To Justin and other early Christians, the two sisters were historical figures but they also had an allegorical existence, equally real, as prototypes of God's covenants with the Jews and Christians. They contended that the entire Old Testament, although written long before Jesus' birth, looked forward to his arrival as the fulfillment of Judaism. They boldly asserted that the prophets of the Jewish Scriptures had foretold the events of Jesus' life.

The result of such reasoning was a supple, multitextured Christian "hermeneutic," or methodology of interpretation, by which literal, allegorical, and even moral meanings of the Bible complemented one another. In developing this principle, ancient and medieval Christians were essentially imitating the Jews. Beginning in the third century B.C.E., Jewish exegetes had produced a large body of commentaries, imaginatively retold stories, and rabbinic midrash that read layers of mystical meaning and moral directive into the Hebrew Scriptures. Like the canonical Gospels, the Jewish Bible contained its own contradictions and discrepancies. There were two different versions of the creation in Genesis, and two different historical accounts of David's kingdom in Kings and Chronicles. As the scholars James L. Kugel and Rowan A. Greer point out, "Jews and Christians understood and interpreted their Bibles more like one another than either anticipated the standard approach of the modern historical-critical method."[17]

No matter how many interpretations an exegete might have derived from any given scriptural passage, Jews and Christians of ancient and medieval times agreed that its literal meaning was paramount. They read the Bible essentially as realistic narrative, or a series of stories that corresponded to events that had actually taken place. Indeed, as Yale University scholar Hans W. Frei indicated in his 1974 book *The Eclipse of Biblical Narrative,* the multiple layers of meaning were *all part of the story* for both Jews and Christians. Citing Erich Auerbach's seminal work of literary criticism, *Mimesis,* Frei noted that unlike Homer, who had filled the *Iliad* and the *Odyssey* with elaborate and exotic figures of speech, the writers who framed the narratives of the Hebrew Bible and the four Gospels had employed essentially realistic literary techniques.[18] A plain style, careful chronological sequencing, and telling details of geography, clothing, and dialogue were all designed to heighten the reader's awareness of having witnessed an actual event. The biblical authors were not historians in the modern, "critical" sense of attempting to ascertain what had actually happened. Rather, they *assumed* that their stories had in fact occurred, and they narrated them in a straightforward fashion.

There is a pivotal incident in Matthew's Gospel (with parallels in Mark and Luke) in which Jesus reveals to his disciples that he is the Messiah. During a conversation between Jesus and the outspoken apostle Peter, Jesus asks: "But who do you say that I am?"[19] Matthew situates the dialogue at a distinct time, after a sail across the Sea of Galilee, and in a distinct place, Caesarea Philippi, capital of the tetrarch Philip's northern realm. The context of the conversation, the concise limning of a lifelike and impulsive Peter (who blurts out, "You are the Messiah, the Son of the living God"),[20] and the setting in a real place, Caesarea Philippi, all lend the scene a matter-of-fact, novelistic air. There are many things that a medieval Christian might have read into this passage. A Catholic would have interpreted the text as Jesus' investing of Peter, whom Catholics regarded as the first pope, with special authority in the church because of his early recognition of Jesus' divine nature. Alternatively, a medieval Christian might have read the dialogue as an injunction to steadfast faith, even when God seems to be hidden. In any case, however, there was no doubt in their minds that the conversation between Jesus and Peter had actually occurred.

As was the case with early interpretations of Jesus' divinity and humanity, there were also "Alexandrian" and "Antiochene" interpretations of the Christian Scriptures. The Alexandrians, who tended toward allegorical readings, followed the lead of Philo of Alexandria, the Jewish intellectual and contemporary of Jesus. Philo had read Platonic philosophy into the Jewish Scriptures and used allegory to "smooth out" narrative details that appeared trivial or contradictory. In a famous example of Philo's imaginative, even fanciful exegesis, he wrote that the serpent in Genesis's Garden of Eden was a symbol of pleasure, because it crawled on its belly like a voluptuary reclining at table or for sex, and because pleasure, like the snake's venom, had the power to destroy those overcome by it. Philo was a favorite among early Christian writers, especially in Alexandria. The early-third-century Alexandrian Origen identified four different levels of allegorical "figures" or "types" in the Old Testament. In his view, various incidents from the Jewish Scriptures prefigured the coming of Jesus; the Christian church and its sacraments (Moses' parting of the Red Sea symbolized Christian baptism); the last days, which would culminate in Jesus' second coming; and the relationship between God and the soul of man, which resembled his covenantal relationship with the Jews. An Alexandrian bishop named Clement, who lived a generation or two after Origen, held that every Scriptural passage contained at least five meanings: historical, doctrinal, prophetic, philosophical, and mystical.

The Antiochenes, by contrast, proposed a more literal reading of the Scriptures in keeping with their more literal interpretation of Jesus' humanity. One of the leading Antiochene exegetes was Theodore of Mopsuestia, who viewed the Old Testament not as a series of prefigurations of Jesus, but rather as a history of Israel. He insisted that Christians were wrong to assume that certain Old Testament passages were fulfilled in Christ. According to Theodore, even the famous "Suffering Servant" passage from Isaiah that formed the basis for the early hymn cited in my introduction was *not* originally intended as a reference to Jesus' crucifixion. Theodore's methodology was so literalistic that he later became known as a heretic (as did Origen, who was considered overly speculative). However, he did manage to influence several leading theologians of his time, including John Chrysostom, the golden-tongued bishop of Constantinople. Like his dual-nature Christology, explored in the previous chapter, Theodore's emphasis on literal Scriptural meaning was to prevail in the Christian West. Thomas Aquinas followed Theodore's lead in advocating literalism as the primary way of interpreting the Scriptures.

The Western emphasis on the historical truth of every detail in the Gospels led to heroic efforts to harmonize them. The fourth-century church father Augustine, bishop of Hippo in what is now Tunisia, struggled mightily to resolve inconsistencies in the Gospel accounts of Jesus' life. Augustine was particularly stymied by the number of hours that Jesus had hung on the cross before he died. Mark reported that Jesus was crucified six hours before his death (from the third to the ninth hours, or 9 A.M. to 3 P.M.), while the other evangelists recounted that Jesus was on the cross for only about three hours (from the sixth hour, or noon, to 3 P.M.). To make all four accounts agree, Augustine decided that Mark had started the clock running when Jesus was "delivered" to be crucified, and not when he was actually nailed to the cross. As if to acknowledge that this explanation was not entirely convincing, Augustine added:

> For to make a frank acknowledgement, we cannot get over the statement of the sixth hour in John's narrative; and Mark records the third hour; and, therefore, if both of us accept the testimony of those writers, show me any other way in which both these notes of time can be taken as literally correct. If you can do so, I shall most cheerfully acquiesce. . . . Only don't consider it an inevitable conclusion that any one of the four evangelists has stated what is false, or has fallen into error in a position of authority at once so elevated and so holy.[21]

Ancient and medieval efforts to sort out literal from spiritual meanings in the Gospels sometimes produced ludicrous results. In her book *The Study of the Bible in the Middle Ages,* Oxford University scholar Beryl Smalley tells the story of an English monk who was somewhat baffled by an allegorical interpretation of Jesus' raising Lazarus from the dead as a prefigurement of forgiveness of sin in the confessional. He ended up preaching in his sermon that Lazarus had died in mortal sin, which was why his body stank!

The line of demarcation between "Alexandrian" (Eastern) and "Antiochene" (Western) biblical readings was never clearly drawn. The allegorist Origen, for instance, was so concerned about the literal meaning of certain Old Testament passages that he consulted Jewish authorities for help. Eventually, he put together a *Hexapla,* or multicolumned Bible, whose Old Testament contained the Hebrew text in Hebrew letters and Greek transcription, as well as four different Greek translations, including the Septuagint. For their part, the literal-minded Western exegetes adopted wholesale the multilevel hermeneutics of Origen and the other mystical Alexandrians. As a consequence, during the Middle Ages the standard Western approach to reading Scripture—and even secular tales such as Chaucer's—was based on four separate meanings derived from Origen: literal, allegorical, moral (sometimes called "tropological"), and "anagogical," or eschatological. For the most part, ancient and medieval Christians from both East and West were neither crude literalists nor apocalypse-haunted millenarians like some of today's Christians who comb the Book of Revelation for clues to the exact date of Jesus' second coming.

Eastern and Western exegetes continued to consult Jewish scholars even amid the anti-Judaism that evolved into juridical discrimination against Jews once Christianity had become the Roman Empire's official religion. Jerome, a fourth-century church father who produced the Vulgate, the definitive Latin translation of the Bible, convinced of the primacy of the Hebrew texts over Greek translations of the Old Testament, studied Hebrew with a Jewish convert to Christianity and frequently consulted rabbinic works of exegesis.

The Western Christian tradition of using Hebrew texts to redact and interpret biblical manuscripts, which persisted throughout the Middle Ages, promoted astonishingly scientific textual scholarship. During the 12th century, the Abbey of St. Victor in Paris produced several generations of Hebrew-fluent biblical experts who maintained close contact with the Jews of northern France, one of whom was the great rabbi Rashi (1045–1105). Rashi was a religious traditionalist, but his readings emphasized the "literal meaning" *(peshat)* of the Scriptures, and inspired others to do the same.

After consulting with the French rabbis, a Victorine canon named Andrew, who later became prior of an abbey in Herefordshire, England, issued a series of down-to-earth commentaries on the Old Testament books based on their literal meaning, which he assumed were coterminous with the Jewish exegesis of Rashi and his successors. Stephen Langton (1155–1228), a Victorine-influenced scholar, explored the natural world of the Bible's flora and fauna in his scriptural commentaries, and speculated as to what the manna with which God had fed the Israelites might actually have been. The 14th-century Franciscan friar Nicholas of Lyra, who also knew Hebrew thoroughly, studied Rashi's interpretations while preparing a massive Old Testament treatise that was regarded as magisterial for several centuries. Nicholas's scholarship—and that of medieval biblical commentators in general—was so highly sophisticated that it directly influenced the work of the French priest Richard Simon in the late 17th century.

Although Nicholas did not know Greek (which hobbled his studies), certain of his contemporaries were already advocating the same literal approach to the New Testament that scholars had adopted in studying the Old Testament. During the early 14th century, several European universities, including Oxford and the University of Paris, established chairs of Greek, Hebrew, biblical Aramaic, and Arabic. Beginning in the 15th century, there was a surge of interest in Greek, prompted not only by the flight of many Byzantine exegetes to the West after the fall of Constantinople to the Turks in 1453, but also by an intellectual revolt against medieval scholasticism and the Latin language.

This new era came to be known as the "Renaissance," or the "rebirth" of civilization after the millennium of the "dark ages." Although most scholars now agree that the Renaissance was actually a flowering of traditional medieval art and culture brought about by trade-induced European prosperity, there were certain real breaks with the past. Among them was the effort to replace medieval scholasticism with the Greek-language theology of Paul of Tarsus and many of the early church fathers.

Lorenzo Valla, a brash 15th-century Italian monk who was famous for having debunked the so-called "Donation of Constantine," which purported to make the pope the feudal overlord of Europe, was one of this new breed of biblical scholars. Completely fluent in Greek, Valla used his brilliant philological insights to correct variations in the Greek and Latin texts of the New Testament. He also wrote a blistering critique of the ornate phraseology of the Latin Vulgate, which often obscured the plainness of the

Greek original. In the process, he tore to shreds various pious Christian traditions that lacked historical foundation. One of his targets was the Apostles' Creed, which had not been composed by Jesus' 12 apostles, as was commonly accepted in medieval times, but rather by fourth-century ecclesiastics after the Council of Nicea.

During the early 16th century, a group of Spanish scholars at the University of Alcala issued a Polyglot Bible, with texts in Hebrew and Greek. These were arranged in columns alongside the Latin Vulgate. The elaborate manuscript also included an Aramaic "targum," or Jewish paraphrase, of the Pentateuch.

In 1516, the Dutch humanist Erasmus of Rotterdam published the first printed Greek edition of the New Testament on one of the recently invented presses. A compilation of numerous Greek manuscripts, his rendition was considered so authoritative that it became the *textus receptus,* or "received text," until the 19th century (it was also the basis for the original Authorized or "King James" version of the New Testament in English).

The reputation of Erasmus's *textus receptus* is nowadays somewhat tarnished. Not only have new manuscript discoveries produced better readings among text variants; they have also verified that he literally invented certain portions (such as the reverse translation from the Vulgate of a passage in Revelation that he was unable to find in any Greek version). He also included other passages strictly on the basis of personal predilection. Although the authenticity of the well-known story in John's Gospel of Jesus' having saved an adulteress from stoning had been a cause for concern on the part of several early commentators, including Eusebius, John Chrysostom, and Jerome, Erasmus included it in the *textus receptus* anyway, most likely because of its "humanist" theme of forgiveness. Despite its many shortcomings, Erasmus's scholarship marked a breakthrough which, like the 14th-century commentaries of Nicholas of Lyra, paved the way for both Richard Simon's textual criticism and Johann Albrecht Bengel's brilliant classification system of New Testament manuscripts.

Hard on the heels of Erasmus's *textus receptus* came the Protestant Reformation, and with it a revolution in the way in which the Scriptures were read. Martin Luther, a founder of Protestantism, preached that the individual Christian believer, rather than the church, was the final authority in interpreting the Bible. Whereas Catholics had traditionally *emphasized* the literal reading of the Bible, Protestants insisted that it was the *only* possible approach to biblical study. In other words, the Bible was theoretically self-interpreting. (Luther maintained that a seven-year-old child could understand the Scriptures as well as the most learned cleric.)

One of the Reformation's theological pillars was the belief in *sola scriptura*—the notion that every authentic Christian doctrine was based on a specific biblical passage. By contrast, Catholics and Orthodox Christians traced their doctrines to Scripture read through the lens of church tradition. The principle of *sola scriptura* generated a biblical theology that essentially consisted of searching for "proof-texts"—Scriptural passages that could be cited in support of sectarian doctrinal positions.

The Reformers did not entirely practice what they preached. Neither Luther nor the more radical Reformer Jean Calvin a generation later completely eliminated the ancient Christian methodology of finding prefigurings of New Testament events in the Old. Even Paul of Tarsus, in whose writings Luther grounded his theology of justification by faith, had indulged in prefiguration (in his Letter to the Galatians, Paul referred to the patriarch Abraham as a precursor of the faith-filled Christian). Luther also tended to read biblical texts in an idiosyncratic, Christ-centered fashion that sprang from his famous dictum that faith in Christ, rather than good works, was the path to salvation. He went so far as to relegate to a lesser status certain books of the New Testament canon that he regarded as excessively works-oriented (the Letter of James) or insufficiently Christ-centered (Revelation).

The drastic "paradigm shift" away from a belief that biblical texts contained several possible meanings was to have enormous philosophical repercussions. To a certain degree, it resulted from the sudden availability of large numbers of printed Bibles translated into the vernacular, coupled with a sudden rise in the literacy rate of middle-class tradespeople who were not looking for subtlety in the Scriptures. (Luther helped promote both trends by translating Erasmus's *textus receptus* into German for popular consumption and insisting on universal compulsory schooling among Lutherans.) Perhaps, as Marshall McLuhan noted in his visionary book *The Gutenberg Galaxy: The Making of Typographic Man,* the very presence on the printed page of uniformly sized letters set by mechanical type—in contrast to the luminous papyrus or vellum surface of handwritten pages on which every letter was a kind of illustration—spawned a desire for an interpretation of the Bible that was uniform, literal, and mechanical as well.[22]

For Reformation Protestants, as for their ancient and medieval Christian forebears, the literal meaning of Scriptural narratives was coterminous with their historical meaning. While all early Protestants held as absolute truth the supernatural events in the life of Jesus recorded by the Gospels, there would soon be a new generation of Enlightenment-influenced intellectuals and New Testament scholars who did not believe in miracles. Many of them held teaching posts at the great German-Lutheran universities of Jena, Leipzig, Marburg, and Tübingen (the last, where Luther's friend Philip Melanchthon once taught, would figure prominently in the new scholarship).

While those rationalist scholars continued to uphold the Reformation belief that the Gospel texts had a single literal meaning, they eventually divorced that meaning from their interpretation of the historical reality of Jesus' life. For them, there was the authentic "history" of the man Jesus on the one hand, subject to scientific reconstruction, and the supernaturalistic Gospels on the other, subject to literary analysis but not to be taken as historically true. The discrepancies in the Gospel narratives would no longer be harmonized, either in the crude manner of Augustine or in the spiritual manner of Origen. Instead, they were to become the object of ridicule in the style of Hermann Reimarus and his deist contemporaries.

Christians who shared the rationalist/naturalistic assumptions of Reimarus and the deists—Jacques Ellul's mythology of modernity—would have to resort to the demythologizing of Rudolf Bultmann or other mental contortions in order to construct a Christian faith compatible with their faith in science. The assumption of a schism between Jesus (who could be studied historically and scientifically) and Christianity (which shrouded him with the unscientific supernatural content of the New Testament) was at the bottom of the modern search for the historical Jesus.

4

THE TALK OF THE COFFEE HOUSES

The engineer of the paradigm shift that launched the search for the historical Jesus was the brilliant scientist Isaac Newton (1642–1727). As a practicing Christian, he himself did not believe that science and faith in the supernatural were incompatible. However, his scientific theories were steeped in philosophical arguments that made it possible for others to become religious skeptics. Newton the scientist was to become the most influential *philosopher* of the entire 18th century.

For 32 years a professor at Cambridge University, where he invented modern physics, Newton was a master synthesizer and simplifier. His ultimate objective was to apply universal laws to complex natural phenomena such as light, motion, and the decay of matter. Through a series of simple experiments, he discovered that white light contains every color of the rainbow, and conversely, that the rainbow's prism is convertible to white light. He synthesized the law of gravity, which combines principles of physics, mathematics, and astronomy. He also propounded his three laws of thermodynamics, which described the universe as both a perpetual motion machine in which no matter is ever created or destroyed, and a system that is headed inexorably toward dissolution and decay. In other words, the physical world was an intricate mechanism that would eventually break down. His universe was essentially impervious to human or divine manipulation.

In considering God's relation to the universe, Newton envisioned an omnipotent deity who had by and large abandoned his creation after having set it in motion. As he expressed in a letter written in 1693 to his friend the classical scholar Richard Bentley:

> So then Gravity may have put the planets into motion, but without the divine power it could never have put them into such a Circulating motion as they have about the Sun; and therefore for this as well as other reasons, I am compelled to ascribe the frame of this system to an intelligent agent.[1]

Newton's "closed system" of scientific laws that exclude divine intervention still works perfectly in the physics laboratory or on the factory floor. Although the speculative physics of this century has moved beyond his suppositions (Einstein's theory of relativity, for one, negates certain of his theories about light), most of the industrialized world still lives in a mechanistic Newtonian universe.

As already noted, Newton's work also encompassed the realm of scientific philosophy. Earlier scientists, such as his fellow Englishman Francis Bacon (1561–1626), had developed an empirical principle that is now known as the scientific method: All scientific findings must be developed under protocols that allow them to be duplicated, and thus verified or falsified by other scientists. From this basic precept, Bacon developed a grandiose scheme to reform all scholarly pursuits according to scientific principles, calling for "a total reconstruction of sciences, arts, and all human knowledge, raised upon proper foundations."[2] His was indeed a powerful argument. Bacon knew that the results of scientific experiment were potentially *cumulative,* inasmuch as they could lead to more sophisticated, dramatic findings. His conclusions thus incorporated a teleology of progress: the conviction that the human condition would improve as scientific knowledge expanded. This theory was in stark contrast to the traditional view of the human condition: that life is subject to accident and misfortune and always ends sadly.

Bacon's contemporary, the French mathematician and philosopher René Descartes (1596–1650), had developed a similar empirical methodology with an emphasis on deductive logic and mathematical reasoning rather than scientific experimentation. Descartes adopted a fundamental premise of absolute skepticism, theorizing that the only thing that cannot be doubted is doubt itself, as expressed by his famous dictum, *"Cogito, ergo sum"* ("I think, therefore I am"). Based on this principle, he devised proofs of the existence of God and the reality of the physical world: Since human beings are able to conceive of the idea of a "first cause"—a thinking being that set the universe in motion—God therefore must exist, just as man exists in his own mind. Furthermore, as God would not deceive human intellect by creating a web of sensory illusions, the physical world must also be real and amenable to man's understanding.

Descartes's theory, which presupposed a chasm between the human mind and the material world, gave rise to the phrase "Cartesian dualism." In his view of the universe, the abstract God was analogous to human reason. God the Great Mind simply had no place in a corporeal world. In a 1664 textbook on physiology (another of his many passions), Descartes opined that even human emotions such as joy or grief had no connection with the mind, because they expressed themselves through smiles, tears, and other physiological functions.

Newton's genius lay in having combined Bacon's laboratory-centered empiricism with Descartes's philosophical dualism to develop a methodology that held that the only true propositions were those that could be scientifically verified. He went on to predict that the scientific method would lead to limitless progress in the field of ethics as well as science. "And if natural Philosophy in all its Parts, by pursuing this Method, shall at length be perfected, the Bounds of Moral Philosophy will also be enlarged," he wrote optimistically in a treatise on light.[3]

One result of Newton's methodology was to distance God not only from the scientific laboratory but also from intellectual inquiry. During the Middle Ages, theology had been called the "queen of the sciences." After Newton, however, scientists ceased to be involved with theology and metaphysics in general. In Newton's epistemological framework, God was a "God of the gaps," a God responsible only for phenomena that science could not yet explain. With increasing scientific knowledge, these gaps would narrow, as would the role of God. This theological "holding pattern" paved the way for current cosmological theories that preclude divine intervention. Gottfried Leibniz, Newton's German rival (each claimed to be the inventor of calculus) once remarked, "According to [Newton's] doctrine, God Almighty wants to wind up his watch from time to time."[4]

Newton not only limited God's role in the universe; he also portrayed a different kind of God altogether. His was an impersonal, all-powerful monarch who had little interest in the universe he had galvanized. While he would occasionally tinker with the mechanism as a whole, he had no desire to intervene in human affairs. Stripping the physical world of God, who was not only indifferent but irrelevant, was Descartes's dualism writ large. Newton's God was the absolute antithesis of the *personal* God of Jewish and Christian tradition. "You knit me together in my mother's womb," wrote the author of Psalm 139.[5] The Jewish covenant with God was above all one of love. The Christian God cared so passionately for mankind that he had become one of them.

Among the traditional roles of the Scriptures was that of serving as a verbal passageway from the physical to the numinous world. Conservative Jews and Christians alike believed that God manifested his presence not only through signs and miracles, but also through the order of the physical universe he had so lovingly created. Even the "knitting together" of a human being from sperm and egg was considered a divine act of devotion. For traditional Christians, there was a continuum between human conception and the incarnation of God in the flesh of Jesus. The word "nature" itself referred to every aspect of reality, each detail of which was *purposeful* in having been designed by God to be perfect in its own right and also relevant to human destiny.

This persistent belief in divine intervention is the key to the Enlightenment-spawned debate over the existence of "miracles." Before the 18th-century divorce between the natural and the supernatural, the majority of Christians and Jews believed that God regularly interacted with the natural world he had created. In the eyes of Newton, such divine interaction was logically impossible. Instead, all of human history was a series of fortuities, or effects of mechanistic causes. Rather than the story of God's self-revelation in the human world, as Jews and Christians traditionally held, the Scriptures were simply a record of human affairs. Lessing's famous catchphrase—"the ugly, broad ditch" that lay between "the accidental truths of history" and "the necessary truths of reason"[6]—said it all.

Newton himself publicly insisted that the laws he had propounded merely reflected the grandeur of God's creation. Although an avid amateur theologian who became increasingly obsessed with the prophecies of the Book of Revelation, in the end he was affected by his own scientific theories. In his private writings, he confessed that he had stopped believing that Jesus, a mortal man subject to the same physical laws that governed the rest of nature, could possibly have been the son of God. Like Joseph Priestley sometime later, Newton became a Unitarian (or ultra-liberal Protestant who did not accept Jesus' divinity). By the end of the century, when Priestley formally renounced Christianity, Unitarianism had evolved into the West's first full-fledged post-Christian religion.

Newton's principle of universal empiricism—scientific observation as the sole measure of truth—rolled over the intellectual landscape of 18th-century Europe. Pragmatic, easy to understand, and modest in its claims, Newtonianism eventually obliterated the more speculative and metaphysically focused dualism of Descartes, and became the prevailing philosophy of the 18th century.

Ironically, Newton's most vociferous admirers were nonscientists who by and large misunderstood his theories. Foremost among them was Voltaire, who championed the Cambridge physicist as "the greatest man who ever lived" in a letter written in 1736. Forty years later, his enthusiasm for Newton had in no way diminished. "We are all his disciples now," he wrote shortly after the American Revolution.[7] As historian Peter Gay has pointed out, Voltaire and his fellow intellectuals co-opted Newton to fight a polemical battle for their own against traditional religious and political institutions.[8]

Although Voltaire and the wits who frequented the salons of Paris during the mid–18th century called themselves *philosophes,* or "philosophers," they could hardly be considered as such. Rather, they were erudite belletrists and critics, some quite brilliant and amusing like Voltaire himself, whose theories had been borrowed *in toto.* Their aim was not to *do* philosophy, but instead to use it, along with scientific methodology, to dismantle the traditional religious and social orders and build new ones based on "reason." All that was required of them was to strip Newtonianism of its last vestiges of Christianity. As Newton's universe was already desacralized and his God a mere abstraction, their task was effortless.

Peter Gay termed the spread of Newtonianism among lay intellectuals with axes to grind "the philosophes' seizure of science."[9] He wrote: "The philosophes celebrated the scientific revolution, accepted its findings, and imitated its methods. They pushed its philosophical implications far beyond what the scientists themselves would have thought warranted."[10] During the 18th century, all the world wanted to be a scientist. From politics to history to literary criticism to the study of religion itself, each branch of learning was now approached with detachment and objectivity. The words "reason" and "natural" studded contemporary writings.

Militant Newtonianism appealed to the *philosophes* because the teleology of progress implicit in scientific methodology was a powerful ideological weapon. The nonscientists who "seized" Newton's science promised their followers a rosy future in which every form of endeavor would yield tangible improvements in the human condition. However, Newtonianism would not have triumphed so thoroughly had it not been for a different but related intellectual revolution that had taken place in Newton's time in England. Two profoundly influential 17th-century political theorists, Thomas Hobbes (1588–1679) and John Locke (1632–1704), had argued that it was in the best interest of the human race for individuals to substitute their own self-interest for religious passion.

Hobbes is most famous for his aphorism asserting that human life in its natural state is "solitary, poor, nasty, brutish, and short";[11] it appeared in his masterpiece of political and religious cynicism, *Leviathan.* "They that are discontented under *Monarchy,* call it *Tyranny;* and they that are displeased with *Aristocracy* call it *Oligarchy;* so also they which find themselves grieved under a *Democracy,* call it *Anarchy,*" quipped Hobbes about governmental systems.[12] With regard to religion, Hobbes wrote that it consisted of "Opinions of Ghosts, Ignorance of second causes, Devotion toward what men fear, and Taking of things causall for prognostiques."[13] Hobbes was particularly cynical about religion because he had lived through the Thirty Years' War (1618–1648), a protracted conflict that eventually involved nearly every political power in Europe. Most of the hostilities took place in Germany, whose agriculture and commerce were nearly destroyed and whose population drastically declined. It was said that every German peasant family lost at least one son to the war, the original cause of which had been a revolt by Protestant princes against the Catholic king of Bohemia and the Holy Roman Emperor Ferdinand II.

Twentieth-century historians have by and large demolished the notion that religion played the central role in the Thirty Years' War, which was actually a dynastic and territorial struggle among the rising European nation-states (Catholic France aligned itself with the German Protestants, who in turn fought the Protestant Danes). However, the war still figures in the Western imagination as a paradigm of the consequences of taking religion too seriously. The war did, in fact, establish the principle *cuius regio, cuius religio* (he who holds the territory determines the religion), which spawned the brutal persecution of religious dissenters nearly everywhere in Europe.

Like many who followed him, Hobbes was convinced that although organized religion was a force of evil, without some form of authority human beings invariably become selfish, ruthless, and even bloodthirsty. For their own self-protection, he theorized, individuals would do well to surrender their political freedom to a strong, centralized secular government—a leviathan—whose claims to authority would be superior to those of any church, and which would hold a monopoly on violence. By reason of his vision of government as the ultimate caretaker and guarantor of its citizens' safety, Hobbes has been called the father of modern liberalism. More important, however, he encouraged his readers to think of churches as power-hungry, faith as childish (prompted by "fear" of death), religious loyalty as murderous, and the Bible as silly ("opinions of Ghosts").

John Locke was in many ways the philosophical opposite of Hobbes. A part-time statesman and lecturer in Greek and philosophy at Oxford University, who lived through Oliver Cromwell's Puritan revolution, which overturned the monarchy in 1649, the restoration of the monarchy in 1661, and the Glorious Revolution of 1688, which placed the monarchy firmly under the control of Parliament, he eventually became a philosophical hedonist. In equating goodness with pleasure and evil with pain, he characterized human reason as the "star and compass" that would guide mankind in its quest for happiness (or the good life).[14] Whereas Hobbes was suspected of atheism, Locke was a self-proclaimed pious Anglican who spent the last years of his life writing a commentary on Paul's New Testament letters. While Hobbes had an absolutist view of the state, Locke argued for limited governmental intervention. "Man being . . . by nature all free, equal, and independent, no one can be put out of his estate, and subjected to the political power of another, without his own consent," he argued."[15]

Ultimately, however, Locke's vision of a "civil society," or political system of government by consent, represented an even more insidious attack on religion than that of Hobbes. Like his contemporary, Locke believed that all churches should be subject to secular rule. In his diary entries after the Restoration, he championed the complete privatization of religion, opining that churches should be no more than voluntary associations, and that theological concerns had no place in modern civilization. Although an advocate of religious tolerance, he excepted Catholics because they answered to the higher authority of the pope.

Locke was also the philosophical father of capitalism. In his view, the main purpose of government was to protect the right of the individual to acquire unlimited amounts of property, by whatever legal means possible.[16] In a commentary on Locke and other political theorists, the philosophical historian Leo Strauss noted that he proposed "the emancipation of acquisitiveness" from traditional social constraints such as humility, duty toward others, and concern for the less fortunate.[17] He maintained, for example, that giving money to charity was a waste of assets that could be put to better use. Property "is for the benefit and sole advantage of the proprietor," he insisted.[18]

Locke's justification for making a virtue out of the Christian vice of covetousness was essentially utilitarian. He maintained that amassing property through prudence and hard work would *produce more property*—jobs and consumer goods—and thus contribute to the common good. In Strauss's words, "Unlimited appropriation without concern for others [was] true charity."[19] Locke's ideal government, which would be in the business of protecting the "property rights" of the powerful against the powerless, was as coercive a "leviathan" as that of Hobbes. In return, however, government would offer the general public a standard of living that was inconceivable in any other political system. He further advocated that strictly contractual agreements between individuals—even parents and children—would preserve civil liberties, or at least their illusion.

Like those of Newton, the theories of Hobbes and Locke sheared the transcendent away from 18th-century thinking. Newton quietly stopped believing in the divinity of Jesus, which was inconsistent with his view that mankind was completely subject to the mechanistic laws that governed the physical world. Hobbes seldom mentioned Jesus in his writings, openly debunked revelation as "the opinions of Ghosts," and questioned the authenticity of many biblical texts. While maintaining a steadfast belief in Jesus' divinity, Locke devoted himself to "rationalizing" Christianity by attempting to demonstrate that reason and Gospel revelation were in no way incompatible.

In a series of treatises, *Essay Concerning Human Understanding* (1690), *The Reasonableness of Christianity as Delivered in the Scriptures* (1695), and *Discourse on Miracles* (published just after his death in 1702), Locke steered a narrow course between his faith as a Christian and his unshaken confidence in human beings' ability to achieve perfection through the power of reason, which made Christian revelation superfluous. He flatly rejected the traditional Christian doctrine of original sin: A God who would punish all mankind for the transgressions of Adam struck him (and many others of his time) as a being too cruel and arbitrary for "reasonable" belief.

Furthermore, Locke could not bring himself to believe that those who had never heard of Jesus Christ were doomed to eternal damnation. Once again, he argued that the key to salvation lay in obedience to God's moral directives, which were discoverable solely through reason. Before the advent of organized religion, early mankind had practiced "natural religion": a simple acknowledgement of God's sovereignty, coupled with the practice of "virtue" (a favorite 18th-century word). Complex rituals and clerical intermediaries were later corruptions. Like Hobbes before him, Locke was a "sensationalist" who maintained that all intellectual stimuli entered the mind through sensory organs, and that the innate ability to distinguish between right and wrong was reflected in the human heart.

According to Locke's philosophy, goodness was a manifestation of sentimentality and self-regard. For the Christian virtue of charity, he substituted "benevolence," or empathy with one's fellow human beings. In his view, the mind was a "tabula rasa," or blank slate for the inscription of sensory data, which could be trusted to make the proper moral choice if freed of ignorance and unnecessary distractions. In divorcing the mind that processed information from the senses that supplied it, Locke's "sensationalism" applied Newtonian dualism to epistemology.

Although Locke believed that people had a moral obligation to abide by God's law, he was equally convinced that the senses could be easily manipulated by ignorance, foolishness, fear, or the machinations of power-hungry clerics. Those who believed in Jesus, however, could be saved even if they had sinned. "[A]s many of them as would believe Jesus his Son (whom he sent into the world) to be the Messiah, the promised Deliverer; and would receive him for their King and Ruler; should have all their past sins, disobedience, and rebellion forgiven them; and if for the future they lived in sincere obedience to his law, to the utmost of their power; the sins of human frailty for the time to come, as well as all those of their past lives, should, for his Son's sake, because they gave themselves up to him, to be his subjects, be forgiven them . . . ," Lock wrote in the *The Reasonableness of Christianity.*[20]

Locke's theory of "reasonable" Christianity represented telling modifications in traditional Christian doctrine. It compressed Jesus' divine sonship, his atonement on the cross for human sin, and his resurrection from the dead into one simple belief-proposition: Jesus as Messiah. Adherence to that proposition, along with repentance for one's sins and an effort to lead a virtuous life, would guarantee salvation. With his divine attributes theologically minimalized, Locke's Jesus emerged as a moral teacher whose powerful presence had "dissipated" the "darkness" of polytheistic ignorance, freeing mankind to become aware of God's law.

While Locke, unlike many 18th-century rationalists, continued to believe in the miracles of the New Testament, these too had a rationalistic function:

helping humanity to see that Jesus was Messiah and thus to choose right over wrong. Heaven and hell were also useful tools for persuading individuals to shun evil. "Open their eyes upon the endless unspeakable joys of another life; and their hearts will find something solid and powerful to move them," he wrote. "The view of heaven and hell will cast a slight upon the short pleasures and pains of this present state, and give attractions and encouragements to virtue, which reason and interest, and the care of ourselves, cannot but allow and prefer."[21] In reducing Jesus to a crutch for those not intelligent or strong-minded enough to follow the path of goodness on their own, he implied that intelligent, educated adults were scarcely in need of Jesus' guidance.

The rationalizing of Christian faith was not Locke's own invention. There had been a general trend toward the simplification and liberalization of Christian teachings in Protestant Europe as early as the beginning of the Reformation. Soon after Luther broke with Rome in 1521, there arose (to his horror) what has been called the "left wing" of the Reformation: Anabaptists (predecessors of today's Baptists, who rejected the traditional practice of infant baptism), Spiritualists (who rejected the eucharist and all other externals of Christian ritual), Hutterites, Mennonites, and others. This diverse spectrum of "radicals" had in common a minimalist approach to ritual and belief and a militant resistance to secular authority (in contrast to the mainstream Lutherans and Calvinists—as well as Catholics—who readily aligned themselves with regnant political powers).

In addition, many adherents of Lutheranism and Calvinism had come to view their churches as theologically sterile and obsessed with scholastic hyper-refinements of the Protestant doctrines of atonement and grace. Furthermore, the classical Calvinist teaching of strict predestination—that God chooses to redeem only a few and condemns the rest to hell—had begun to strike many 17th- and 18th-century followers as overly harsh. In Germany, Pietism arose as a counterreaction to the dry prevailing Lutheranism. In northern Europe, especially Holland and England, there were formal breaks within Reform Protestantism over the doctrine of predestination. Some liberal northerners even abandoned the cornerstone Protestant doctrine of salvation by faith alone, which was predicated on the notion that human nature was so corrupt that only trust in God's grace could save mankind.

These new Protestants, often called Remonstrants or Arminians (of whom the 18th-century revivalist John Wesley was the most famous), held a more benign view of human nature than many of their forebears. They also attempted to restore the intensity of religious feeling that mainstream Protestantism often lacked. The Arminians taught (like the Catholics) that it was possible to cooperate toward one's own salvation through good works; they also urged their members to cultivate an intense prayer-relationship with Jesus and to beg humbly for God's mercy.

Locke's "reasonable" Christianity was a kind of next-step Arminianism stripped of the emotionalism, the personal relationship with Jesus, and the sinner's pleas for mercy. He was too optimistic about human nature to see much need for prayer, and too intellectually oriented to see much need for direct contact with Jesus. During the 18th century, Locke's brand of rationalist Christianity was extremely popular among educated, science-influenced Protestants (including many clergymen) in England, Germany, Holland, and other northern European countries. When these rationalists read the Bible, they tended to look for natural causes behind Jesus' miracles. Even Wesley, who was generally a strict biblical traditionalist, fell under rationalism's spell when he theorized that the demoniacs whom Jesus cured might well have been epileptics. Certain rationalists, who called themselves "Arians" after the fourth-century heretics, went so far as to deny Jesus' divinity. The Arians (sometimes called Socinians after Lelio Sozzini, a 16th-century liberal Protestant from Italy who had rejected the Trinity), were the precursors of the Unitarians.

As did Locke, the rationalist Protestants of the 17th and 18th centuries viewed Christianity primarily as a system of ethical teachings in which Jesus served as a facilitator. Hugo Grotius (1583–1645), the Dutch theorist who invented modern international law, was one of this new "latitudinarian" breed. After having grown up in a Calvinist household in Delft, he drifted first to Arminianism (for which he was imprisoned by the Netherlands' Calvinist authorities until his wife managed to smuggle him out in a book carton) and then to complete nonsectarianism, although his became fascinated with Catholicism toward the end of his life.

In 1640, Grotius wrote a remarkable series of lengthy annotations to the books of the New Testament that not only paid close attention to their textual variants but also—in a radical departure from traditional biblical scholarship—approached them as ordinary literary works. Grotius considered each New Testament book first and foremost a product of the specific historical period in which it was written. He believed, for example, that the apostle John's primary motive in writing the Fourth Gospel was to refute certain Gnostic opponents of his time, and that the Book of Revelation did not describe calamitous events expected at the end of time but rather political conflicts between Christians and secular authorities that had taken place while Revelation's author was still alive. During the 17th and 18th centuries, the liberal theories of Locke, Grotius, and others—the faith in progress, simplification of beliefs, commitment to tolerance, disavowal of original sin, and "sensible center" mentality—seemed to be the future of Christianity. In England, rationalist faith came to be associated with minimalist "low-church" ritual, sermons that emphasized ethics instead of doctrine, and liberal politics. The vast majority of English rationalist Christians were Whigs who supported the Glorious Revolution of 1688 (which did away with the retrograde Catholic king, James II), parliamentary supremacy, free trade, and nascent industrialism.

The beliefs of the liberal rationalists were to lead to the ultimate question, If Christianity is so "reasonable," why bother with it at all? That was exactly what the English deists began asking in their incendiary pamphlets. As Peter Gay has noted: "Liberal Protestantism was not deism, but it helped to make deism inevitable."[22]

No sooner had Locke published *The Reasonableness of Christianity* (1695) than an admirer named John Toland printed a work of his own titled *Christianity Not Mysterious.* Toland (1670–1722) was an Irishman who had grown up Catholic, converted to Protestantism and studied for the ministry in Glasgow, and then moved south to Oxford, where he was impressed by Locke's empiricism. In *Christianity Not Mysterious* (1696), he carried *The Reasonableness of Christianity* to its ultimate logical conclusion. Whereas Locke had contended that Christianity was an enhanced version of natural religion, Toland argued that *pure* Christianity was *no more than natural religion.* He further maintained that any aspect of Christianity that was not a moral precept—presumed biblical revelation or church doctrine—represented a clerical corruption of pure Christianity.

Locke was willing to believe the Christian creeds and the Gospel stories about Jesus because they struck him as reasonable. Toland was willing to believe *only those portions of the creeds and Gospel stories that could be proved by reason,* thereby making scientific empiricism the sole standard for judging the truth of any religious proposition:

> Whoever reveals any thing, that is, whoever tells us something we did not know before, *his Words must be intelligible, and the Matter possible*. This rule holds good, let *God* or *Man* be the Revealer.[23]

Christianity not Mysterious paved the way for the 18th-century search for the historical Jesus by sharply differentiating the Jesus who taught the precepts of pure Christianity from the Christ of the creeds, who in Toland's view was a fictional concoction of Catholics and others. Furthermore, Toland tried to flesh out his Jesus as a human being, delving into the mind of the man who had founded a "Rational and Intelligible Religion," and not the formal Christianity that bore his name:

> *Jesus* himself appeals to his very Enemies, ready to stone him for pretended Blasphemy, saying, *If I do not the Works of my Father, believe me not: But if I do, believe not me, believe the Works; that you may know, and believe that the Father is in me.* [John 10, 37,38]: That is, believe not rashly on me, and so give a Testimony to my Works; but search the *Scriptures,* which testify of the *Messiah;* consider the Works that I do, whether they be such as become God, and are attributed to him; If they be, then conclude and believe that I am he. . . . [24]

In 1718, Toland published a theological work titled *Nazarenus, or Jewish, Gentile, and Mahometan Christianity,* in which he concluded that the Ebionites, the shadowy second-century heretical sect who did not believe in Jesus' divinity, and who combined Christian and Jewish practices, represented the only group ever to have practiced the "pure Christianity" that Jesus himself had taught. The Ebionites' lost Gospel must therefore have been a compendium of natural religion, "more agreeable to the Law of nature and dictates of Humanity" than the four canonical Gospels.[25] Toland was the first in a long line of amateur and professional biblical scholars (A. N. Wilson is one of the latest) to so theorize. He also maintained that Ebionite doctrine "agrees in every thing almost with the scheme of our modern Unitarianism."[26]

Locke was horrified by Toland's work, especially his jettisoning of the Christian creeds. Although he disavowed any connection between his thinking and that of Toland, it was difficult to deny that his *soi-disant* disciple had merely gone where he had led, and that his own defense of the creeds did not comport logically with his philosophical speculations.

With his belief in the sufficiency of natural religion, his insistence on scientific verifiability as the sole measure of truth, his recasting of Jesus as primarily an ethical teacher, and his use of ridicule to attack formal Christianity as "priestcraft," Toland became the first deist. He had worked out the entire deist creed, whose main proposition was to regard the Christian creed as absurd.

Hard on Toland's heels came Anthony Collins (1676–1729), a confidant of Locke who popularized the word "freethinker" as a synonym for the opponent of organized religion. Collins gave the title *The Discourse of Free Thinking* (1713) to his most famous book, a sarcastic polemic against "superstition" and other traditional Christian teachings. He also belonged to a group called the Freethinkers, which met weekly in a London coffee house, and published a journal called *The Free-Thinker.*

In his celebrated text, Collins defined free thinking as not only desirable but a moral obligation: "Because he who *thinks freely* does his best toward being in the right, and consequently does all that God, who can require nothing more of any Man than that he should do his best, can require of him."[27] Although Collins, like his friend Locke, remained a practicing Anglican, he expressed contempt for those who "take the Opinions they have imbib'd from their Grandmothers, Mothers or Priests."[28] (It was characteristic of deist thinkers to disparage traditional Christianity as a woman's religion.) In another tract, *A Discourse of the Grounds and Reasons of the Christian Religion* (1724), Collins argued that Jesus, his apostles, and the Jews of his time all expected the Messiah to be an earthly deliverer, and that only after Jesus was crucified and resurrected did the apostles decide that he was actually a spiritual savior.

In 1730, Matthew Tindal (1653–1733) published a treatise titled *Christianity As Old As the Creation,* which became known as the "bible of deism." To his mind, Christianity was merely a re-promulgation on Jesus' part of the principles of natural religion, and as such was superfluous. While much of his book was yet another recycling of Locke and Toland, Tindal took the theories of both his mentors one step further. Locke had stated his willingness to accept the Gospel stories about Jesus as "reasonable," while Toland had asserted his belief in only those parts of the Gospel that he considered "rational." Tindal himself counseled his readers to reject *in toto* any Gospel tale that was too miraculous for the 18th century: "To imagine any external Revelation not to depend on the Reason of Things, is to make Things give Place to Words; and implies, that from the Time This Rule commenc'd, we are forbid to act as moral Agents, in judging what is Good or Evil; Fit or Unfit; and that we are to make no other use of our Reason, than to see what is the literal Meaning of Texts; and to admit That only to be the Will of God, tho' ever so inconsistent with the Light of Nature, and the eternal Reason of Things."[29]

Whereas Locke and Toland had struggled mightily to convince their followers to believe in the literalness of Jesus' miracles, Tindal maintained that

Christians—or at least deists—were not obliged to take them literally. To 18th-century Protestant intellectuals who had been conditioned by Luther's dictum that the Scriptures were to be interpreted on a purely literal basis, and who then were influenced by Newton's empiricism, Tindal's directive could have only one meaning: Either find some plausible empirical explanation for the miracles, or disregard them entirely. Toland had attacked the Christian creeds, but Tindal called into question the Bible itself.

Tindal's legitimization of the wholesale debunking of all supernatural material in the Scriptures was not without precedent. Baruch Spinoza (1632–1677), a Dutch contemporary of Locke, had been expelled from the Amsterdam synagogue at age 24 for his unorthodox interpretations of Scripture. In 1670, he published a work entitled *Treatise on Religious and Political Philosophy,* which amounted to a blistering critique of the Bible on what he considered were scientific grounds. A lens-grinder by trade, Spinoza was, like the Newtonians in England, mesmerized by the new science of his era. He concluded that the Bible was no more than a historical artifact representing the primitive views of an ancient culture unacquainted with the new scientific methodology. In one instance, he argued that the famous miracle in the Book of Joshua of the sun's standing still while the Hebrews conquered Jericho could have been devised only by those who did not know that the earth revolved around the sun. Since science potentially offered an explanation for every phenomenon, he maintained that it was impossible for any reasonable person to believe in biblical miracles. Indeed, he maintained that accepting the authority of the Bible—or any divine revelation—would interfere with one's freedom to think for oneself. According to Spinoza, the Bible was no different from any other book. While it contained certain valuable ethical truths (Spinoza believed in natural religion), it was mostly based on "superstition."

In order to "prove" that the Bible's origins were merely human, Spinoza analyzed the Hebrew texts from a philological standpoint. In so doing, he discovered that several of them had more than one literary source and more than one author. For example, Jews and Christians had traditionally ascribed the entire Pentateuch—the first five books of the Hebrew Bible—to the hand of Moses himself. Spinoza pointed out that this was virtually impossible, as the Pentateuch had clearly been the work of a number of authors. It also told the story of Moses' death, which Moses himself could not have written.

In writing his own Old Testament critique in Paris, and apparently unaware of his Dutch contemporary's findings, Richard Simon reached the same conclusion about the Pentateuch's authorship (as had the medieval rabbi Abraham ibn Ezra). Whereas Simon chose not to indulge in polemics, Spinoza insisted that multiple authors and sources *had to mean* that a particular book of the Bible was not divinely inspired. He also called into question the authenticity of the latest authorial redactions of the Scriptures, and emphasized the potential significance of portions of the original sources that had been lost. Using textual analysis to demonstrate his presuppositions about the impossibility of miracles, he devoted part of his *Treatise* to demonstrating how they had been inserted into the Bible.

Although Spinoza wrote in Latin, his *Treatise* became "required reading for radicals in his time," as Peter Gay has commented.[30] Like Hobbes, Spinoza was reputed to be an atheist (which he was not). The English deists, who relished the cheeky, made the *Treatise* their own manifesto. Conyers Middleton (1683–1750), a chief librarian at Cambridge University who became famous for his anti-Catholic tract, *Letter from Rome, Showing an Exact Conformity Between Popery and Paganism,* elaborated on Spinoza's unorthodox theories about miracles in the Hebrew Bible. Middleton theorized that Moses, although a wise lawgiver, had fabricated his miracles in order to impress his primitive audience and did not himself believe they were genuine.

Thomas Woolston (1669–1773), another deist, attacked the New Testament just as Middleton had the Old. After studying at Cambridge and being ordained by the Church of England, Woolston moved to London, where he embarked on a career in journalism. From 1727 to 1730, he published a series of six satirical pamphlets called *Discoures on the Miracles of Our Savior,* which sold for a shilling apiece and were published in numerous editions.

Simply stated, Woolston's theory was that the New Testament miracles had never taken place. Some of them he dismissed as absurdities, such as Jesus' exorcism of the demons by casting them into a herd of swine that rushed headlong over a cliff. If anyone had pulled such a stunt in England, Woolston jeered, the judges "would have made him to swing for it."[31] He characterized Jesus' changing of water into wine as a stock first-century miracle that had also been attributed to the wonder-working philosopher Apollonius of Tyana. Jesus' healings he ascribed to natural processes, portraying the woman he had supposedly cured of a twelve-year hemorrhage as a likely psychosomatic. Finally, the mixture of clay and spittle Jesus had rubbed into a blind man's eyes in Mark's Gospel had probably been a secret medicinal salve.

Woolston's sixth and final pamphlet concerned Jesus' resurrection, which Woolston flatly denounced as a fraud. He supported his theory by suggesting that the disciples had made off with Jesus' body after having sent the Roman guards to "a Gin-shop."[32] Woolston thus completed what Toland had begun and Tindal had continued. For Toland, Jesus had divine attributes and his miracles were real, while the Christian creeds were more or less fictional. In Tindal's view, at least some of the Gospel miracles were as fictional as the creeds. According to Woolston, *all* the Gospel miracles were fictional, and Jesus was no more than an ordinary human being.

Those who did not chuckle at Woolston's pamphlets thought him a lunatic or a blasphemer. After the resurrection pamphlet appeared, he was fined, and then sent to prison for nonpayment, where he died three years later. To the end of his life, he protested that he was a good Christian who happened to be poking fun at a corrupt church that had attributed absurdities and impossibilities to Jesus. He also maintained that *his* Jesus would have been insulted by the church's portrayal of him as a worker of miracles.

Seven years after Woolston's resurrection pamphlet, Chubb's *True Gospel of Jesus Christ Asserted* appeared on the scene. Heavily influenced by Erasmus and Spinoza, *The True Gospel* was an astonishing work that would have made the deists' unwitting godfather, John Locke, turn over in his grave. In *The True Gospel* and his posthumous essay, "Of the Personal Character of Jesus Christ," Chubb made it clear that he did not consider the canonical Gospels authentic—that is, they were probably not written by the evangelists whose names they bore. Furthermore, they were not supernaturally inspired, and their authors were second-rate historians. Taking a leaf from Spinoza's treatment of the Hebrew Bible as a cultural artifact of its period, Chubb averred that the Gospel narratives consisted of "language suitable to the *age* and country in which [Jesus] lived," an age so "generally *distant,* both as to *time* and *place,*" that modern readers should be "very *cautious*" about their historical reliability.[33] Although Christians had traditionally believed that Matthew's Gospel (the favorite of the earliest Christians) was the first to be written, Chubb opined that it was actually Mark, the shortest and most straightforward of the four.

These various theories, all of which are commonplace among many modern biblical scholars, were based solely on Chubb's deistic belief that Jesus was a plain-spoken prophet whose life was later embroidered upon in a series of increasingly unreliable Gospels. Since Mark did not even report Jesus' birth, Chubb believed that his origins must have been obscure. In any case, his one certainty was that the supernatural stories about Jesus' birth recorded in Matthew and Luke—the star of Bethlehem, the Magi, the angels, and above all, Mary's virginal conception—were complete fabrications. As a proper 18th-century rationalist, he refused to admit that such events could ever have taken place.

According to Chubb, Jesus was most likely born in Nazareth, not Bethlehem, and he spent his ministry as an itinerant provincial preacher, not *healing* the sick, but rather caring for them, and sympathizing with the poor. The substance of Jesus' preaching was good deistic "natural religion." Besides morality (simplified to a few general rules that contrasted sharply with what Chubb viewed as the legalisms of Judaism), he preached the coming of his "kingdom," which, as Chubb described it, "laid the foundation for friendly societies or families of love."[34] After three years of wandering and preaching in Galilee, Jesus had a premonition that his life would soon end. Believing that it was a prophet's fate to die in Jerusalem, he ventured south. In Judea, his simple message made him an enemy of the sanctimonious Pharisees (the villains of Chubb's piece), as well as of radical Jewish nationalists who had hoped in vain that he would lead an insurrection. Both factions joined forces to denounce him to a reluctant Pontius Pilate, who eventually bent to the prevailing political winds and ordered him crucified. After Jesus' death, Paul of Tarsus concocted the doctrine of atonement and invented Christianity.

The True Gospel has served as a template for nearly every subsequent reconstruction of the historical Jesus, from Reimarus's seventh *Fragment* of the 1760s to the Jesus Seminars of the 1980s and 1990s. The "historical" Jesus is *almost always* a version of Chubb's: a nonsupernatural ethical teacher born in Nazareth—and not of a virgin—who offended the reigning religious authorities in Jerusalem and found himself in political trouble. Mark's is *almost always* the first Gospel. Paul of Tarsus is *almost always* the real founder of Christianity. Unlike the first generation of English deists, most searchers for the historical Jesus have been professional biblical scholars. As such, they have offered text-based arguments (some quite persuasive) to support, for example, the theory that Mark was the first to write his Gospel. Chubb, who probably knew less about the Bible than the average country vicar of his time, propounded his theories not on the basis of historical evidence—for he conducted no research—but rather on *blind faith* in the power of reason.

By the mid–18th century, English deism was extremely fashionable among the intellectuals on the Continent. In 1701, John Toland had fled to the liberal court of Electress Sophia of Hanover (1630–1714), whose son George would later become King George I of England. Many English Christians regarded Toland as a blasphemer, and the authorities in his native

Dublin ordered the public hangman to burn his *Christianity Not Mysterious.* However, his writings promptly became the rage in Hanover and began circulating elsewhere in Europe.

Voltaire helped to popularize deism in France, where the *philosophes* had their own tradition of using ridicule to battle perceived superstition. In 1697, the skeptic Pierre Bayle (1647–1707) had published a vast *Dictionnaire historique et critique* that combined prodigious learning with dry observations designed to subvert the institutions he described with seeming seriousness. Bayle became a god to the educated circles of 18th-century Europe. He "teaches us so well how to doubt," declared an admiring Paul-Henry Thiry d'Holbach (1723–1789), a German baron who lived most of his life in Paris, socializing with the *philosophes* and promoting the natural religion of the deists until he became an outright atheist in 1750.[35]

Bayle's *Dictionnaire,* which was translated into English during the mid-1730s, undoubtedly influenced deists in England. It also inspired Voltaire to publish his own *Dictionnaire philosophique.* The atheist Denis Diderot (1713–1784), another prominent *philosophe,* later issued his famous *Encyclopédie,* a multi-volume compendium of erudite and irreverent definitions.

Elsewhere on the Continent, the works of the English rationalists were enjoying enormous popularity. Voltaire's *Letters Concerning the English Nation* (1723) were intended to promulgate the writings of Locke, Toland, and Anthony Collins. In 1741, Matthew Tindal's *Christianity As Old As the Creation* was translated into German. Foreign-language editions of Thomas Woolston's notorious pamphlets lampooning Jesus' miracles also circulated freely in Continental salons, where atheism and anticlericalism had become avant-garde fashions.

By the time deism reached its peak on the Continent, it had already run its course in England. Although the Christian divines continued to fulminate against the deists from their pulpits, it was ultimately the satirical writings of several English authors that began to cast serious doubt on the movement as a whole. In 1726, Swift mercilessly lampooned the worship of reason and science in *Gulliver's Travels,* whose high-minded windbags, the Houynyhms, and the mathematics-obsessed denizens of the island of Laputa, were graphic deist parodies. In his mock-epic poem entitled *The Dunciad* (1728), Swift's contemporary Alexander Pope predicted that the triumph of the worldview represented by Locke and the deists would usher in an age of ignorance and vulgarity rather than one of progress and prosperity.

The chief nemesis of English deism was the Scottish philosopher David Hume (1711–1776). A radical skeptic and empiricist like the deists, Hume shared their disbelief in miracles and their sardonic disdain for "priestcraft." However, he rejected entirely the optimistic, Locke-derived assumption that man could achieve wisdom and virtue through his ability to exercise reason. To Hume, the human mind was nothing more than a jumble of sensations, and as such was an *actual* tabula rasa.

Hume characterized the deists' belief in a religion that could be arrived at through reason alone as utter nonsense. In an essay titled "The Natural History of Religion," published in 1757, he argued that polytheism, and not monotheism, was the most "natural," primitive form of religion. In another series of essays, *Dialogues Concerning Natural Religion,* written during the 1750s but not issued until three years after his death, Hume contended that far from being a watchmaker, God was more like a blind organism or an insensate force.

On the other side of the Channel, the sophisticates of the 18th-century intellectual movement that came to be known as the Enlightenment completely ignored Hume's objections. Around 1770, Holbach went so far as to publish a treatise titled *Ecce Homo,* in which he depicted Jesus as a misguided fanatic and his apostles as virtual dunces. While about three-fourths of *Ecce Homo* had actually been plagiarized from an earlier book that had circulated underground, Holbach's embellishments included comments to the effect that Mary was seduced by a sweet-talking young man who told her he was the angel Gabriel, and that Jesus was drunk at the wedding feast of Cana. The Catholic Church placed *Ecco Homo* on its Index of Forbidden Books, but the tract was widely read all over the Continent and translated into English in 1779.

Ironically, deism was to become associated throughout the Continent with the cause of religious freedom. Foremost among its "political martyrs" were Toland, who had been obliged to flee England, Woolston, who had gone to prison for his pamphlets spoofing the Gospels, and Peter Annet (1693–1769), who had been incarcerated for publishing his own series of contradictions in the resurrection narratives. Voltaire himself had been forced to escape several times from France, taking up residence in England, Switzerland, and at the court of Frederick the Great, the "enlightened" despot who ruled Prussia for 46 years.

Voltaire and his salon contemporaries sauced their anti-Christian views with so much wit that they inspired an idiosyncratic revival of English deism in the person of Edward Gibbon (1737–1794), the author of *Decline and Fall of the Roman Empire.* Admitted to Oxford at the precocious age of 15, Gibbon had been so repulsed by one of Conyers Middleton's deist tracts denouncing the miracles of the early Christian saints that he began secretly reading "Popish books" written by Bishop Bossuet and others. The following year, he converted to Roman Catholicism. Since all students at Oxford were required to uphold the Thirty-Nine Articles of the Church of England, he left the university in disgrace, whereupon his father exiled him to Lausanne to lodge with a strict Calvinist pastor. Within months, he abandoned the Catholic Church, which he ridiculed for the rest of his life. Several years later, after having studied the works of Pierre Bayle and John Locke, he rejected Christianity itself.

Gibbon's violent turn against Christianity found its way into *Decline and Fall,* which he wrote during the 1770s and 1780s. Heavily influenced by the political theorist Charles Montesquieu (1689–1755), another *philosophe,* his six-volume tome was partly an imitation of a historical study of Rome that Montesquieu had published in 1734 and, like Montesquieu's book, supposedly reflected the *philosophe*'s "scientific" and "philosophical" approach to historical inquiry. In Gibbon's case, however, scientific detachment was merely a guise for mordant irony. A master of parody and satire, he never failed to poke fun at the various monks and martyrs who had been part of Christianity's epic. Ultimately, Gibbon's *Decline and Fall* was a tribute to human progress, despite the long interlude of Christian "fanaticism" and "superstition" during the Middle Ages which had grossly distorted the teachings of a simple Jewish preacher named Jesus.

Deism and Enlightenment skepticism were as fashionable in Germany as they were in France. Works by Toland, Tindal, Collins, and Woolston circulated in both English and German, gaining converts such as J. Lorenz Schmidt, who published a translation of the Pentateuch together with his own rationalist annotations in 1735, which led to his arrest. The deists generated so much controversy that an entire literature of anti-deist polemic arose among traditionalist Lutherans and proponents of alternative philosophies such as Gottfried Leibniz.

One of Leibniz's disciples was the philosopher Christian Wolff (1670–1754), who was to become a towering presence at several German universities. Although he considered himself an orthodox Christian, like Locke he believed that reason, rather than church authority or tradition, was the final arbiter of truth. Wolff's ultimate objective was to construct a hierarchy of human intellectual pursuit, with philosophy as the supreme discipline, followed by mathematics.

Although Wolff attempted to steer clear of dogmatic disputes, he ran afoul of the influential Pietist theologians at the University of Halle, who accused him of promoting philosophical determinism, a contravention of the Christian doctrine of free will. Halle was part of the Prussian province of Saxony, which was under the rule of Frederick William I, the uncle of Frederick II (the Great). The elder Frederick was a strict Calvinist whose Hohenzollern ancestors had converted from Lutheranism to Reformed Christianity during the early 17th century. In 1723, Frederick I banished Wolff from Halle on pain of death, forcing him to flee to the more tolerant landgraviate of Hesse on the Rhine, where he taught at the University of Marburg for 17 years. When Frederick I died in 1740, his nephew, Frederick the Great, ascended the throne. Fancying himself a philosophical (although not political) liberal, he reinstated Wolff at Halle with great fanfare, and Wolff eventually became chancellor there.

Partly as a result of his persecution, Wolff became an intellectual hero of the late 18th century throughout Europe, especially in his native Germany. One of his acolytes was Immanuel Kant (1724–1804), a life-long resident of the Baltic port of Königsberg in East Prussia (now Kalingrad in Russia). Along with the philosophies of Newton and Hume, Kant immersed himself in Wolff's synthesizing theories. He later devoted his monumental philosophical trilogy, the *Critique of Pure Reason* (1781), the *Critique of Practical Reason* (1788), and the *Critique of Judgment* (1790), to refuting Hume's radical skepticism by establishing a philosophical foundation for the reliability of human reason. It was Kant who invented the word "Enlightenment"—*Aufklärung* in German—as follows:

> Enlightenment is man's emergence from his self-imposed nonage. Nonage is the inability to use one's own understanding without another's guidance.[36]

In Kant's view, the chief nemesis of individual freedom was religious authority, which maintained human beings in a comfortable but stupefying state of "nonage," or mental infancy, by telling them how to act and what to believe. "Above all, nonage in religion is not only the most harmful, but the most dishonorable," he wrote.[37] In voicing this libertarian credo with its optimistic faith in reason, Kant himself was a quintessential Enlightenment figure.

Another avid reader of Christian Wolff and the English deists was Hermann Reimarus. The grandson of a scholarly Lutheran clergyman at Kiel (about 50 miles north of Hamburg), Reimarus studied at Leyden and Oxford and taught philosophy at the University of Wittenberg before assuming a post at the Hamburg Academic Gymnasium in 1727. The son-in-law and former student of Johann Albrecht Fabricius, a renowned Christian apologist, he portrayed himself as a typical 18th-century Lutheran with a liberal bent. In his best-selling book *Die vornehmsten Wahrheiten der natürlichen Religion* (*The Most Elegant Truths of Natural Religion*) (1754), which went through 16 German editions and was translated into English, French, and Dutch, he opined that Christianity and natural religion merely complemented one another. By arguing that Christianity indeed had a place in a scientific world, Reimarus passed himself off as a moderate in his public writings, neither an extreme skeptic nor an anticlerical radical.

Privately, however, Reimarus was virulently anti-Christian, as witnessed by the original version of his rambling two-volume manuscript titled *Apologie oder Schutzschrift für die vernünftigen Verehrer Gottes* (*Apology or Defense of the Rational Worshippers of God*). Reimarus never tried to publish the *Apology* during his lifetime, and the three chapters (or "books") of the *Apology* that Gotthold Lessing published as seven *Fragments* from 1774 to 1778 differ markedly from the copies of Reimarus's complete manuscript now resting on the shelves of archives in Hamburg and Göttingen.

According to Reimarus's 20th-century editor, Charles H. Talbert, his aim in writing the *Apology* was not actually to search for the historical Jesus, in whom he had little or no interest, but rather to plead the case of natural religion as the only means of creating a more civilized society. In Talbert's words, "Like the early church fathers who wrote apologies for Christianity in which attacks on paganism played a large role, Reimarus wrote for natural religion but included in his work attacks on Christianity. He would destroy the one—Christianity or revelation—to make room for the other—natural religion or reason."[38]

Reimarus's real objective explains the peculiar structure (or non-structure) of the *Fragments,* in which bits and pieces of the life of Jesus are interspersed with such seemingly irrelevant material as a plea for toleration of deists and his well-known ridicule of the miracle of the crossing of the Red Sea. Unlike Chubb, he saw no reason to reconstruct a complete "biography" of Jesus in attempting to prove that Christianity and Jesus had no real connection. Reimarus's historical Jesus emerged in bits and pieces. In order to demonstrate that Christian claims about Jesus' place in the Trinity and his atonement for human sin were in no way substantiated by Jesus' own claims, he painted a portrait of a man who had been nothing more than a moral preceptor and political activist:

> Thus the goal of Jesus' sermons and teachings was a proper, active character, a changing of the mind, a sincere love of God and of one's neighbor, humility, gentleness, denial of the self, and the suppression of all evil desires. These are not great mysteries or tenets of the faith that he explains, proves, and preaches; they are nothing other than moral teachings and duties intended to improve man inwardly and with all his heart, whereby Jesus naturally takes for granted a general knowledge of man's soul, of God and his perfections, salvation after this life, etc. But he does not explain these things anew, much less present them in a learned and extravagant way.[39]

In another passage, he wrote: "Jesus taught no new mysteries or articles of faith or undertook to teach them."[40] Reimarus interpreted the passages from the Gospels that referred to Jesus as the "son of God" as meaning that he was beloved by God, and those that recounted the Holy Spirit's descent at the beginning of Jesus' ministry as mere hallucinations of John the Baptist.

According to Reimarus, Jesus thought of himself as a worldly Messiah who mistakenly believed that the end of the world was at hand:

> It was for this reason that [Jesus and John the Baptist] preached repentance, for the Jews believed that if they only repented really and truly, God would allow the Messiah to come and release them from their misery, their bondage, and their oppressors, and would establish among them a magnificent kingdom, like unto David's.[41]

Further, Jesus encouraged his followers to view him as a miracle-worker in the tradition of the great prophets of old, although in fact he worked no miracles.

Reimarus viewed the Christian church as a fraud that had been perpetrated by the apostles, who had been a handful of poor, ignorant laborers bedazzled by Jesus' promise of a better world. After Jesus' death, they achieved wealth and social status by peddling the notion that the second coming of Jesus, or *parousia,* was close at hand. When this prophecy failed to materialize, they maintained instead that the *parousia* would take place the end of time, styling themselves in the meantime as the leaders of a church that Jesus had founded to prepare humanity for his second coming: "Now as the former motives of the apostles invariably and up to the time of the fabrication, had been aimed at worldly wealth and power; it follows with all moral certainty that the possession of worldly wealth and power was also the object of the apostles in the fabrication of their new doctrine."[42]

Most of Reimarus's theories, as well as his sarcastic tone, came straight from the English deists and their Continental admirers. Even his emphasis on Jesus' eschatological fixations, which was so admired by Albert Schweitzer, had been anticipated by a theologian at the University of Halle named Johann Salomo Semler (1725–1791), who held that the preaching of Jesus and the earliest Christians was centered on cataclysmic changes signaling the end of one order and the beginning of another. Nonetheless, Reimarus's writings on Jesus were marked by a scholarly erudition that neither the English deists nor the French *philosophes* possessed. He was familiar enough with biblical texts to be able to place them in historical context, and his knowledge of the Hebrew language allowed him a reasonable understanding of Jewish religious customs and messianic expectations.

Lessing's publication of Reimarus's *Fragments* had an immediate and devastating effect on a German Protestantism that had already been beset by quarrels between liberals and Pietists. As countless young Lutheran seminarians whose faith had been shaken by the writings of the "Unknown" (Reimarus's identity did not emerge until 1814) chose to abandon their ministerial studies, both the author and the publisher were denounced from the pulpit. Although an avowed liberal, Johann Semler of Halle fired the biggest salvo in 1779 when he asserted that ordinary Lutherans and the Christian religion itself were in mortal peril as a result of the *Fragments*.

While attempting to characterize Jesus as first and foremost a Jew, Reimarus managed to convey a profound contempt for the Judaism of the Pharisees, which he denigrated as distorted "ceremoniousness."[43] Whereas the Pharisees were obsessed with legalism, he argued, Jesus preached hope and immortality: "Consequently, his teaching had a considerable advantage not only over that of the Pharisees, but also over that of the Old Testament, where such essential principles of religion were not even considered and where there is mention only of earthly promises and rewards, all hope for man ending with his death."[44] After branding the miracles of the Hebrew Scriptures—the parting of the Red Sea, the sun's standing still for Joshua—as "outrageous and disgusting," he maintained that Jesus' reported miracles were a moral improvement because they mostly dealt with healings.[45]

Reimarus's disdain for Judaism as legalistic and literalistic was partly a holdover from his ancestral Lutheranism (from the beginning, Martin

Luther's theology had contrasted the Christian dispensation of mercy and forgiveness with a Judaism that supposedly emphasized inflexible laws and a stern and distant God) and partly a reaction to the anti-Semitism of the Enlightenment. Whereas persecution of the Jews in the Middle Ages had been based on the Jews' rejection of Jesus as Messiah, the anti-Semitism of the Enlightenment was based on the perception that Jews were backward, legalistic, and avaricious.

In a 1968 study of Enlightenment anti-Semitism, historian Arthur Hertzberg drew upon extensive research to draw an ugly picture of what the *philosophes* of the 18th century really thought of the Jews. Renowned for his public advocacy of religious tolerance, Charles Montesquieu complained in his private papers that the writings of the rabbis represented exercises of "ignorance" and the spirit of slaves.[46] Voltaire, who publicly expressed his disdain for the Jews, noted in his *Essai sur les moeurs* (*Essay on Customs*) that their traditions "were exactly the opposite of all proper social customs," and that the ancient Romans rightly treated Jews "as a people opposed to all others, whom they served, out of greed and hatred; out of fanaticism; they made usury into a sacred duty."[47] Diderot openly mocked the Talmud, while yet another *philosophe,* the Marquis Jean-Baptiste d'Argens, urged the rabbis to devote themselves to writing books of morality rather than the abstruse nonsense of their Scriptural commentaries. He also encouraged Jews in general to become "enlightened" by repudiating their religious and cultural traditions.[48]

Affording Jews full legal and civil rights—one of the first acts of the French Revolution in 1791—was in fact an effort to force them to reject their religion and embrace secularized modernity along with everyone else. Jews were not only forbidden to bury their dead in Jewish cemeteries but they were also warned by a Terrorist proclamation to abandon their traditional occupations of wholesaling and banking ("swindles and extortion") and work with their hands. Otherwise, they would be subjected to "the most severe measures against the detested remnants of a people that has always been both hated and despised."[49] Such disdain for the Jews was bound to seep into the writings of biblical scholars such as Reimarus who considered themselves enlightened.

Enlightenment self-confidence came to an abrupt end in Europe with the mass murders of the French Revolution, and the vision of a time near at hand when reason would triumph over superstition suddenly seemed terribly shallow. In America, however, the movement was at its apogée. The theories of Locke and the *philosophe* Montesquieu found their way into the United States Constitution. Unitarianism also established a firm foothold with the arrival in 1794 of the English chemist Joseph Priestley, who was to found a Unitarian church in Philadelphia and become the group's leading spokesman. During the decades that followed, many of the descendants of New England Puritans joined their growing ranks.

In addition, America spawned a generation of home-grown deists such as Thomas Paine (1737–1809), the English-born radical who had emigrated to the colonies in 1774 to help foment the Revolution. In 1794, he issued a manifesto titled *The Age of Reason,* depicting Jesus as "a virtuous and amiable man" who preached a "system of morality of a most benevolent kind" that resembled the teachings of Confucius and the Greek philosophers." In Paine's view, Christianity was relegated to "little else than the idolatry of the ancient mythologists accommodated to the purpose of power and revenue, and it yet remains to reason and philosophy to abolish the amphibious fraud."[50] Paine was an end-of-century throwback to Thomas Chubb.

The last of the deist searchers for the historical Jesus was the American president Thomas Jefferson (1743–1826), who took up his quest a full century after their heyday in England. Although he had been raised in the Church of England, the established religion of his native Virginia, his philosophical readings led him to espouse natural religion over organized Christianity while he was still in his twenties. The "Nature's God" of the Jefferson-drafted Declaration of Independence is in fact the God of English deism. He also held a typically deist (and Enlightenment) view of Judaism, dismissing the Talmud as insufficiently attentive to morality and obsessed with niggling detail.

Jefferson had little interest in the teachings of Jesus for most of his adult life. As a vociferous advocate of the separation of church and state, he was widely believed to be an atheist. However, when he took office as president in 1801, he realized the importance of creating a moral consensus that would bring together the new republic's violently opposing regional and partisan factions. He eventually seized upon Priestley's Unitarian beliefs, which maintained that one could follow Jesus' precepts without accepting his divinity. In an 1803 pamphlet, *Socrates and Jesus Compared,* Priestley portrayed Jesus as a superior counterpart of the fifth-century B.C.E. Greek philosopher, noting that he had spoken out far more boldly against vice than had his Athenian predecessor. Whereas Jesus had aimed his message of spiritual renewal at all social classes, Socrates had confined his moralizing to the educated aristocracy.

Although Jefferson himself never became a Unitarian, he fully supported their rejection of the creeds he so despised. In 1822, he went so far as to predict that "the present generation will see Unitarianism become the general religion of the United States."[51] Instead, a wave of evangelical Christian revivalism would soon sweep both the United States and Britain.

In the winter of 1804, Jefferson decided to extract from the Gospels what he considered to be the genuine sayings of Jesus. For a man of his intellect and self-assurance, the task must have seemed relatively simple. (The true precepts of Jesus were "as easily distinguishable as diamonds in a dunghill," he wrote enthusiastically to his presidential predecessor, John Adams.)[52] Working by candlelight in the evenings, within little more than a month he sliced the "authentic passages" out of his New Testament and produced a paste-up titled "The Philosophy of Jesus of Nazareth." In 1820, he created a more elaborate polyglot pastiche he called "The Life and Morals of Jesus of Nazareth" from eight different cut-up versions of the New Testament in English, French, Latin, and Greek.

The so-called Jefferson Bibles, neither of which was published during the president's lifetime, make for rather dull reading nearly two centuries later. Jefferson retained a skeletal narrative of Jesus' life in both works, slicing away angels, Christmas stars, dream visions, miracles, proclamations by Jesus of his divinity, and the resurrection. The result in both cases is a long and tedious ramble through Jesus' teachings and parables.

Jefferson's interpretation of the Gospels was no more a work of serious scholarship than were Paine's *Age of Reason,* the pamphlets of the English deists, Holbach's *Ecce Homo,* or even Reimarus's *Fragments.* The rationalists of the 18th and early 19th centuries were merely on an ideological crusade to topple traditional Christianity by focusing on the "historical" Jesus. They were not historians but proselytizers.

5

A GERMAN PHILOSOPHICAL HERO

By the end of the 18th century, many European intellectuals who had tired of deism turned their attention back to Christianity. Although they were unquestionably the heirs to the Age of Enlightenment that the scientific revolution had engendered, they began to view the Christian faith more positively, as a wellspring of deeper philosophical and mythical truths, and Jesus himself as their haunting embodiment. The Middle Ages, which the deists had derided so mercilessly as a dark time of monkish superstition, were consequently transformed a generation or two later into a brilliantly hued epoch of chivalry and courtly love whose folk songs and fairy tales acquired enormous popularity. This new cultural phenomenon, which came to be known as Romanticism, originated around the turn of the century. Its progenitor, however, was a renegade French *philosophe* who had been born in Geneva: Jean-Jacques Rousseau (1712– 1778).

While still in his thirties, the self-taught Rousseau found himself the darling of the Paris salons, contributing articles to Diderot's *Encyclopédie.* In 1749 he won notoriety as the author of a prize-winning essay for the Academy of Dijon that perversely argued, *contra* his fellow *philosophes,* that the progress of science would not improve the human condition. In 1761, he published the hugely successful iconoclastic novel *La Nouvelle Héloïse,* which was to become an ideological blueprint for the French Revolution. The following year, he issued both his famous political treatise, *The Social Contract,* and the most radical of all his novels, *Émile,* which combined ferocious anticlericalism with advocacy of "natural" child-rearing. In the end, it was judged so offensive that it was publicly burnt in both Protestant Geneva and Catholic Paris. *Émile* was more than a standard-issue Enlightenment diatribe against Christianity, however; it also marked another stage in Rousseau's break with the *philosophes.*

Embedded inside *Émile* was a shorter novel, which Rousseau called the "Profession of Faith of the Savoyard Vicar," whose protagonist's distinctly heterodox religious views were those of the writer himself. Besides ridiculing Christianity for having appointed itself as the sole means of salvation, Rousseau's vicar denounced the *philosophes* for their belief that scientific reasoning alone could save the world. "I found them all alike: proud, assertive, dogmatic, professing, even in their so-called skepticism, to know everything, proving nothing, scoffing at each other."[1] Rather than *rejecting* the notion of Jesus as the son of God (as one might expect from an Enlightenment intellectual), the Savoyard proceeded instead to *affirm* the traditional claims of Jesus' divinity, arguing that while they could not satisfy the demands of reason, they satisfied the more important demands of the heart.

Rousseau was in fact convinced that the human heart was the final arbiter of morality. For all his supposed radicalism (including a flamboyant, promiscuous sexual life), he was actually a strict moral (and most likely political) conservative. In *La Nouvelle Héloïse,* which endorsed familial duty while seemingly promoting free love, his wayward heroine, Julie, dies not in the arms of her lover, but of an illness contracted while saving her child from drowning. In so doing, she simultaneously displays maternal magnificence and atones for her carnal sins.

As seen through the eyes of Rousseau's Savoyard vicar, Jesus was so exemplary a moral figure that he truly deserved the appellation "divine." When comparing Jesus to Socrates, Rousseau's heterodox priest depicted him as far more heroic: a man who had lived in a more depraved world than that of the Athenian, and who had died alone and in pain, in contrast to his counterpart, who had been surrounded by his family and friends when he was poisoned. "Yes, if the life and death of Socrates are those of a sage, the life and death of Christ are those of a God," Rousseau concluded.[2] While Jesus did not possess a *supernatural* dimension, he did represent a *metaphysical* dimension that was comprehensible to a philosopher such as Rousseau.

In his study of Rousseau and other proto-Romantics, Vincent A. McCarthy noted: "Against the intolerance of the *philosophes* and their dismissal of everything and everyone in the gospels, Rousseau's is a daring and provocative act, a radical turn in Enlightenment philosophy of religion that heralded and began the philosophical rescue of Jesus, that is, the salvation of Jesus by philosophy, for philosophy, and from the *philosophes.*"[3] Rousseau's revolutionary theory allowed for a reconciliation of philosophy and religion by assigning each to its proper domain: reason to the realm of the mind, and faith to that of the heart.

Although a child of the Age of Reason, Rousseau read the Bible avidly throughout his life. He also admired the simple, unquestioning Christianity of the French peasants. During his bedridden last years, he read and reread Thomas à Kempis's medieval classic, *The Imitation of Christ.*

For more than a century after *Émile*'s publication, theologians, biblical scholars, and lay writers throughout Europe and America produced a steady stream of "lives" of the heroic man of conscience from Nazareth who struggled to enlarge the moral horizons of his fellow human beings. The blueprint for all these works was Rousseau's "Profession of Faith of the Savoyard Vicar," in which he invented what Vincent McCarthy called "a Christianized deism" that persisted throughout the 19th century.[4] In many ways, the Jesus of Rousseau and his followers closely resembled the Jesus of the 18th-century deists. Now, however, the emphasis was not on Jesus' *function* as an explicator of morality, but rather on his *personality* as an *incarnation* of that morality. The deist idea of "natural religion" had fallen by the wayside, replaced by a quasi-Christian code of ethics that Jesus had exemplified and died for in a gesture of magnificent sacrifice.

Rousseau's "Profession of Faith of the Savoyard Vicar" was also to have a profound effect on Kant. Like Rousseau, Kant was a pivotal figure; he had one foot in 18th-century rationalism and the other in 19th-century Romanticism. Despite his faith in reason and his disdain for organized faith, his ideas (and those of many of his German contemporaries) reflected a fundamental religiosity that contrasted sharply with the anti-Christian animus of the English deists and the majority of the French *philosophes.*

The son of devout Pietists, Kant leavened his Enlightenment faith in human reason with an overwhelming sense of human sinfulness, which he defined as "radical evil." While sharing Rousseau's conviction that a life lived morally was the only means of overcoming such evil, he also believed that religion was essentially a *divinely* inspired code of ethics. At the same time, he joined the deists in rejecting the concepts of the power of prayer, the notion of divine intervention in human affairs, and the formal structures of the

Christian church. In a 1793 treatise on Christianity titled *Religion within Limits of Reason Alone,* Kant's criticisms of church dogmatism and hierarchy were so harsh that the Prussian royal censor forbade him to publish any further theological studies.

Kant was equally opposed to the skepticism and materialism that pervaded the thinking of such philosophers as Hume. In his earlier trilogy of "critiques," he had outlined his own "transcendental" or "Idealist" philosophy, based upon the existence of an ultimate ("noumenal") reality that the human mind was unable to penetrate, but that could be deduced from a common human perception of truth and falsehood, and good and evil. His famous "categorical imperative" to the effect that one's actions must take into account the well-being of others was born of this universalist ideology.

In *Religion within the Limits of Reason Alone,* Kant applied his Idealist philosophy to Jesus as well. Although he never actually invoked Jesus' name, he did call him the "envoy from heaven" and the "son of man." As the embodiment of a universal *idea* of goodness, of "humanity in its moral perfection,"[5] Kant's Jesus personified the eternal struggle against the radical evil that is part of human nature. In this respect, Kant's Jesus was much like Rousseau's: a heroic figure who refused to succumb to worldly temptation and pointed the way for others to resist as well. In Kant's view, the essence of Jesus could be found in his teachings, particularly those from the Sermon on the Mount contained in Matthew's Gospel. Indeed, Jesus' Golden Rule, "In everything do to others as you would have them do to you,"[6] was Kant's own categorical imperative.

Kant wrote of Christianity: "Here then is a complete religion, which can be presented to all men comprehensibly and convincingly through their own reason."[7] While touting the Christian faith as superior to all others, he dismissed Judaism as insufficiently universalist, and more politically than morally focused.

For all its strengths, however, for Kant Christianity was only a steppingstone on the path to a universal code of ethics that would no longer require a church or a moral exemplar like Jesus. At some point in a perfect future, he believed (as did the liberal Christian theologian Paul Tillich in this century), Jesus would become obsolete.

Kant's philosophy permeated the German universities, which were the most numerous and academically rigorous in all of Europe in the late 18th and early 19th centuries. His personal search for the historical Jesus would inspire a renewed interest in philology and the classics as well as biblical studies. However, his tendency to construct *theoretial* historical schemes while ignoring *actual* history and archaeology would also have a significant effect on the nature of German biblical scholarship.

The German Jesus-searchers in fact tended to *invent* biblical history, combining careful readings of New Testament texts with adventurous abstract assumptions about the direction they thought early Christian history had taken, or ought to have taken. Few of them actually visited Galilee and Judea, although they wrote about them continually.

Partly because they were Protestants (most Catholics were disinclined to participate in the quest for the historical Jesus, and the writings of Kant and his followers were on the Vatican's Index of Forbidden Books), and partly because they were rationalists, the German biblical scholars propounded various theories that incorporated their Protestant/rationalist/progressivist reading of history. Like Kant, they portrayed Judaism as obsolete and legalistic, Jesus as a "universal" moralizer in the tradition of the great Greek philosophers, and early Christianity as a pristine, "primitive" religion that had been grossly distorted by Catholicism during the second century. While convinced that their research was utterly meticulous, they frequently indulged in historical speculations to fit their philosophical predictions, such as assigning later composition dates (typically in the second century) to nearly every book in the New Testament, almost all of which proved to be wrong. As the intellectual historian J. C. O'Neill has observed, "Nineteenth-century critics of the New Testament worked as they did because of one simple idea: the idea that Catholic Christianity was a late synthesis which more or less seriously misrepresented the historical process that produced it."[8]

Paradoxically, the only 19th-century German biblical scholarship that has withstood the test of time was carried out by theological conservatives. The most brilliant New Testament *textual* critic was the Saxon Konstantin von Tischendorf (1815–1874), who became an instructor at the University of Leipzig at the unheard-of age of 25. An old-fashioned German Protestant, he despised the speculative scholars of his age, steadfastly maintaining, as the early church fathers had, that the entire New Testament had been composed by the end of the first century (later scholarship was to prove him correct).

In 1844, Tischendorf traveled through the desert by camel from Alexandria to the Orthodox monastery of St. Catherine at the foot of Mount Sinai, where he discovered the oldest and least corrupted Greek version of the New Testament, which came to be known as the Codex Sinaiticus. Using the Sinaiticus and a contraband copy of the Codex Vaticanus, another ancient biblical manuscript owned by the Vatican Library, he produced a series of renditions of the Greek New Testament that were far superior to Erasmus's 16th-century *textus receptus.* This monumental work, which included an elaborate critical apparatus, is still the basis for all modern editions.

Such achievements notwithstanding, the majority of German research on the life of Jesus was heavily biased by philosophical theory and nationalistic preenings. Quite simply, the German biblical scholars believed that all intellectual history culminated in themselves. In 1793—the same year in which Kant issued *Religion within the Limits of Reason Alone*—Johann Gottfried Eichhorn (1752–1827) published a review of a German translation of a collection of essays by Conyers Middleton. A philosophy professor and biblical scholar at the University of Göttingen in Hanover, Eichhorn epitomized the chauvinism of his contemporaries:

> This book has taken the reviewer back very pleasantly to the times at first light, just before the dawning of the present day in German theology, when the few bright ideas our compatriots had were gathered from British theologians. Thanks be to the courage and to the German diligence of the immediate past generation! Now the sons of the Britons' grateful German pupils can give back to the Britons the light which was kindled for their fathers—and give it back stronger, purified and clarified.[9]

Such sentiments coincided with the movement for German unification. At the end of the 18th century, most of the German territories remained, if only in name, part of the Holy Roman Empire of the Hapsburgs, although the Austrians' hegemony had been seriously challenged by the Reformation. Composed of a patchwork of kingdoms, principalities, duchies, and free cities spread across central Europe, the German "nation" had yet to be born. Prussia itself was an agglomeration of lands that the Hohenzollern dynasty had annexed during the course of four centuries.

After a decisive victory over the Austrian troops in 1805, Napoleon I dissolved the Holy Roman Empire, forcing the Hapsburg ruler, Francis II, to renounce his centuries-old title and call himself Francis I of Austria. Prussia had joined forces with Austria against Napoleon, and the next year he overran a Prussian army at Jena, a Thuringian university town on the Saale River where the philosopher Georg Wilhelm Friedrich Hegel (1770–1831) happened to be teaching. The humiliating occupation, during which Prussia was obliged to substitute a "modern" bureaucracy for the absolute monarchy of the Hohenzollerns, triggered a nationalistic reaction so violent as to cause

Napoleon's ouster in 1813. The drive for a unified, independent Germany soon became a *cause célèbre* among the intelligentsia, including liberals who approved of Napoleon's "reforms," but who hated being under his thumb.

The unification of Germany came about slowly, as Prussia absorbed all German territory and imposed (with varying degrees of success) its own Protestant, militaristic, authoritarian culture on the rest of the country. By 1871, the "nation" Germany had become an empire (and economic powerhouse as a major center of industrialization) ruled by the firm hand of Chancellor Otto von Bismarck from the old Hohenzollern capital of Berlin.

As early as 1817, the Lutheran and Reformed churches in Prussia had set aside their doctrinal differences to form a unified Protestant "evangelical" church coterminous with the expanding Prussian state, which paid not only the salaries of ordinary clergymen, but also those of university professors of theology, almost all of whom were members of the clergy. The architect of this union was the Prussian monarch Frederick William III (1770–1840), great-nephew of Frederick the Great. In contrast to his great-uncle, Frederick William III was a devout Christian ecumenicist who understood the religious and political importance of reconciling the Reformed Christianity of the Hohenzollerns with the Lutheranism of most of their subjects.

In 1810, Frederick had also founded the University of Berlin, the most aggressively secular institution of higher learning in all of Germany. His minister of education, Karl Wilhelm von Humboldt, was a liberal reformer who intended to implement the most progressive educational policies in Europe. At Humboldt's urging, for the first time *secular,* not religious, instruction became the primary goal of higher education.

Certain of Germany's universities, such as Tübingen and Wittenberg, dated from the late Middle Ages. Others, such as Jena and Marburg, had been established during the Reformation. Whereas their primary purpose had been to educate members of the clergy, Humboldt believed that the future of Germany lay in the cultivation of secular research, and in the training of the new bureaucratic class that had been born of Napoleon's reforms. An heir to the Enlightenment and its abiding faith in *Wissenschaft,* or science, he was convinced that all branches of learning, including theology, were amenable to the scientific method, and as such were to be approached with rigor, detachment, and even methodological atheism. As scholar of religion Daniel L. Pals has noted, "Humboldt made the university a virtual temple to the ideal of *Wissenschaft.*"[10] He also made Berlin the greatest university in Germany and perhaps in all of Europe, a reputation it was to enjoy until

World War II. Among its celebrated teachers and students were Hegel, Ludwig von Feuerbach, Karl Marx, Friedrich Engels, Sören Kierkegaard, Martin Heidegger, and Hannah Arendt.

Berlin was to become the paradigm of the modern Western university, gradually displacing the more genial educational models that prevailed in institutions such as the tutor-centered Oxford and Cambridge. Until after World War I, young German scholars seeking academic careers were required to work as unpaid research assistants for established professors while awaiting the post of "extraordinary" or untenured professor, which afforded them at least a modest salary that enabled them to marry. Known as *Privatdozenten* ("private lecturers"), their only sources of income were informal conferences and tutorials for the benefit of other students. Those who excelled in their chosen fields were eventually named "ordinary" or tenured professors, with a comfortable government-paid sinecure, leisure time in which to hone their lectures, and the services of a new crop of *Privatdozenten* whom they in turn could train as acolytes. This hierarchical, even patriarchal system (students called their thesis adviser *Doktorvater*, or "father professor") transformed the German university into a veritable factory of scholarship. During the early decades of the 19th century, nearly all the older German institutions of higher learning revamped themselves to incorporate the academic ethos of Berlin.

The University of Berlin also incorporated the sacred principle of academic freedom that Eichhorn had praised so highly at Göttingen in 1793. Along with that freedom, however, went the devil's bargain that "enlightened" rulers such as Frederick the Great exacted from intellectuals and academicians: They would think and write whatever they wished about theological and philosophical matters *provided they steered clear of political dissent.* The Prussian authorities, intent on unifying Germany in their own image, ruthlessly suppressed all sentiment favoring a democratic, much less a socialist, pan-German nation.

German theology professors, who were mostly clergymen, had been closely aligned to the German state since the Reformation. Now, the *intelligentsia* was also expected to join hands with the authorities. Hegel, for example, advocated strict loyalty to the state as the embodiment of the divine spirit working through history. Even the theological radical David Friedrich Strauss (1808–1874), who lost his teaching position at Tübingen in 1835 after the publication of his controversial *Life of Jesus Critically Examined,* was in politics a Prussian monarchist of the most bourgeois variety. The quintessential turn-of-the-century liberal theologian (and University of Berlin professor) Adolf von Harnack (1851–1930), whose writing epitomized 19th-century German liberal theories about Jesus, was yet another political authoritarian.

As Eichhorn's paean to the "light" shining from the German academy illustrated, the spirit of *Wissenschaft* had already produced adventurous and unorthodox biblical scholarship. The most famous of the freethinkers was one of Eichhorn's own mentors, Johann Salomo Semler, who taught theology at Halle from 1752 until his death. Although he later became Reimarus's most severe critic, Semler was heavily influenced by his extensive reading of the English deists, and he outraged religious conservatives by contending that the Word of God (which he defined as a code of ethics intended to foster "moral improvement") and the Christian Scriptures were not necessarily the same thing. In his four-volume *Treatise on the Free Investigation of the Canon* (1771–75) Semler argued for the elimination of the Book of Revelation from the New Testament on the grounds that its tone was "unpleasant and repulsive when it speaks of the extermination of the heathen."[11] It was also too "Jewish" (that is, insufficiently concerned with morality) to have been written by its designated author, the apostle John.

Semler was the first in a long line of biblical scholars to divide the early Christian movement into two opposing factions: the Palestinian "Jews," represented by Peter, James, and other apostles, and the foreign "Gentiles," to whom Paul had addressed his letters. If scholars examined the New Testament texts in a careful and detached fashion, Semler believed, they would discover the true history of Jesus and early Christianity that had been deliberately obscured by official Christian tradition, which played down all the factionalism.

In what was then considered a daring move, Johann Jakob Griesbach (1745–1812), who studied with Semler at Halle and later became a professor at Jena, raised the possibility of a literary relationship among the three Synoptic Gospels, suggesting that the evangelists may have actually borrowed material from one another. Traditionalist Christian commentators had generally attributed the parallels in Matthew, Mark, and Luke to the likelihood that all three had drawn from the same eyewitness accounts of Jesus' ministry.

Griesbach pointed out that such a theory was inadequate to explain the striking similarities among the Synoptics, which were not only a matter of nearly identical story material and narrative structure, but also of the words themselves, right down to the Greek verb tenses. He aligned the Gospels in three columns in a "Synopsis" that allowed other scholars to see for the first time how close the texts really were. Griesbach also hypothesized that Mark, traditionally designated the Second Evangelist (after Matthew), had actually been the third evangelist, and that he had written his Gospel with copies of Matthew and Luke in front of him.

The "Griesbach hypothesis," as it came to be known, was followed by an even more audacious theory put forward by Gotthold Ephraim Lessing, the publisher of Reimarus's *Fragments.* In a book issued by his brother after his death in 1781, Lessing contended that all four evangelists had relied upon an *Ur*-Gospel, a long-lost primitive account of Jesus written in Hebrew that had circulated among Jewish Christians in Palestine before the composition of the canonical Gospels in Greek. (Lessing's hypothesis was undoubtedly based on John Toland's *Nazarenus,* which held that the Jewish-leaning Ebionite heretics had been the ones to preserve Jesus' teachings most meticulously.)

The next scholar to propound the idea of an *Ur*-Gospel was Eichhorn, under the influence of Lessing and Johann David Michaelis (1717–1791), a brilliant colleague at Göttingen who had advanced a similar theory. Eichhorn reconstructed a hypothetical version of the *Ur*-Gospel, omitting the miraculous stories of Jesus' birth and childhood found in the Gospels of Matthew and Luke, which he viewed as fictional "sagas" from a later era that provided no reliable information about Jesus. Although an ardent admirer of deism (as revealed by his glowing review of Conyers Middleton's essays), Eichhorn himself was not a deist. He did not believe the Gospels were intentionally fraudulent, as did the deists and Reimarus, whose cynical *Fragments* had so enraged him. In the spirit of Rousseau and Kant, Eichhorn took Christianity seriously. He believed he was simply removing the good-faith but false supernatural accretions with which Christians had covered Jesus. In 1804 he wrote:

> By this freeing [of the Primal Gospel from its accretions] countless doubts with which Jesus, his life and his teaching have been assailed become completely meaningless. . . . By separation of the apostolic from the nonapostolic which higher criticism—if only its gifts be not spurned—recommends for the most important of reasons, the means are found to establish the credibility and truth of the gospel story on unshakable foundations.[12]

Eichhorn was further convinced that the true teachings of Jesus, if properly understood, would survive the mockery of Enlightenment skeptics such as Reimarus.

Semler, Griesbach, and Eichhorn thus encouraged New Testament scholars to disassemble, rearrange, and even cast aside portions of the Scriptures in order to reconstruct a more authentic portrayal of Jesus and early Christianity than the sacred texts provided. They also suggested that scholars ignore long-held Christian traditions such as the order of composition of the Gospels. This "higher criticism" (as Eichhorn called it), or "historical-critical method," in contrast to the "lower" or text-criticism of Tischendorf, Bengel, Simon, and their ilk, was essentially an attempt to rewrite early Christian history through a close reading of literary texts. Its first proponents believed that their new "scientific" accounts of Jesus and his times were far more accurate than the confessional works of church fathers and traditionalists such as Augustine and Eusebius. In point of fact, Semler's and Eichhorn's writings, heavily colored by their own presuppositions, were actually more theological than historical. Eichhorn's theory of the *Ur*-Gospel is regarded today as a mere scholarly curiosity, while Semler's equation of God's word with general moral exhortation is seriously outdated.

Eichhorn and the other German New Testament scholars of the turn of the century were also influenced by novel approaches to the study of mythology and folklore that had been popularized by German universities with the arrival of Romanticism. David Hume's *Natural History of Religion,* which demolished the deist notion that simple monotheism was humankind's earliest faith, was widely read, sparking an interest in "native" polytheism. Another of Eichhorn's colleagues at Göttingen, the classical philologist Christian Gottlob Heyne (1729–1812), used Hume's conclusions to develop an ambitious evolutionary theory of mythology based on his belief in a "childhood of mankind," or primitive mentality, that characterized not only the ancients but the illiterate peasantry of his own time as well. Heyne maintained that because such individuals were incapable of thinking abstractly or discerning cause and effect, they resorted to myth-making to explain the world around them. Significantly, two of his fellow philologists at Göttingen were the brothers Jakob and Wilhelm Grimm, who collected their famous fairy tales from the villages of southern Germany in order to examine the thought patterns of their rural countrymen. The ideas of Heyne and the brothers Grimm presupposed a sharp disjunction—something like Lessing's "ugly ditch"—between the mental processes of prescientific provincials and those of educated sophisticates like themselves.

Heyne's mythological theories attracted the attention of Eichhorn, who applied them to the Old Testament and its miraculous tales of the deliverance of Israel, and then to the New Testament and the miraculous elements in Jesus' birth stories, which he dismissed as "Jewish embellishments."[13]

Johann Philipp Gabler (1753–1826), a student of Eichhorn's at Göttingen who took over Griesbach's chair at Jena on Griesbach's death, went a step further. In a scholarly article published in 1800, Gabler declared that the authors of the New Testament wrote in good faith, but as "primitives" they were *simply incapable of writing true history.* While commenting on the Gospel story of Jesus' temptation by Satan, he presented the following thesis:

> There can be no doubt, I should say, that the evangelists believed they were reporting a true occurrence. The grammatical interpreter has only to concern himself with this, and then his work is finished. But the business of explaining the Bible is by no means over. Indeed his work has only begun, for the fact that the evangelists regarded this as an account of a true occurrence in the world of the senses does not demonstrate by any means that it actually happened in this way. The evangelists, as can be seen from the whole tenor of their narrative, firmly believed in demons and in illnesses caused by demons, but that does not mean that we can regard the insane and epileptic whom Jesus healed as really "possessed." . . . In this instance, then, the explainer of the Bible has the full right and even the duty of investigating further: How did the Evangelists arrive at this belief? Whence did they get this story? And this puts us on the right track: What is it that may really have happened to Jesus to give rise to this story?[14]

Gabler's view of the Gospels was certainly more sympathetic than that of many of the deists, who held that the evangelists had intentionally lied (or reported lies) when they recounted tales of devils, angels, and miracles, or had shaped their supernatural imagery to fit the superstitions prevalent among the uneducated of their time. Gabler believed instead that the evangelists were merely mistaken. Because they were pre-scientific people living in a pre-scientific age, they invented pre-scientific explanations, using stock supernatural figures like the devil, to account for events that had perfectly natural foundations, such as mental illness. In Gabler's view, it was the task of the biblical scholar to *explain* these pre-scientific myths—explain them away, that is—in order to discover what "really . . . happened to Jesus."

Working along the same lines as Gabler, Georg Lorenz Bauer (1755–1806), a professor of Oriental languages at the universities of Altdorf and Heidelberg, developed a comprehensive theory of myth for the purpose of analyzing the contents of the New Testament. Bauer thought that by ascertaining the probability of a given event's having taken place according to the laws of science *or* according to the religious and social customs of the first century, one could arrive at a definite distinction between myth and history. This meant that *any* unusual happening in the Gospels, even a nonsupernatural one such as Jesus' Palm Sunday ride into Jerusalem on a donkey, or his conversation with the despised Samaritan woman at the well, could have been based on myth, not reality.

Wilhelm Martin Leberecht de Wette (1780–1849), a student of Griesbach's and Gabler's at Jena and later a professor at Heidelberg, Berlin, and the University of Basel, propounded the notion that the individual mythic stories in any particular book of the Bible were all part of a mythic whole. The Pentateuch, for example, was a Jewish national epic of theocracy governed by the central myth of the Hebrews' status as God's chosen people. Carried to its logical extreme, de Wette's theory implied that there was no genuine historical material at all in the Pentateuch—or by analogy, in the Gospels—even though many of the narratives read like straightforward and credible history and contained no supernatural material.

Rousseau's heroic "Christianized" deism, Kant's view of Jesus as ideal man, Semler's call for a radical rewriting of New Testament history, and the myth-stripping scholarship of Eichhorn, Gabler, and others set the stage for a century-long spate of "biographies" of Jesus by German philosophers and theologians that were designed to rescue him from skeptics' ridicule. While purporting to be objective depictions of the "historical" man from Nazareth, these sympathetic "liberal lives," as they came to be called, invariably portrayed him as a moral hero of the 19th century who preached a noble 19th-century ethic. Albert Schweitzer derided the Jesus-biographies of the early part of the century for hacking Jesus to bits in an effort to modernize his image:

> The sentimentality of the portraiture is boundless. Boundless, also, and still more objectionable, is the want of respect for the language of Jesus. He must speak in a rational and modern fashion, and accordingly all His utterances are reproduced in a style of the most polite modernity. None of the speeches are allowed to stand as they were spoken; they are taken to pieces, paraphrased, and expanded, and sometimes, with the view of making them really lively, they are recast in the mould of a freely invented dialogue. In all these Lives of Jesus, not a single one of His sayings retains its authentic form.[15]

The original biography of Jesus as moral hero, *History of the Last Three Years of the Life of Jesus,* was published as early as 1768 by the Zurich clergyman Johann Jakob Hess (1741–1828). The "last three years" to which Hess's title referred were those of Jesus' ministry as recounted in John's Gospel. The *History* was reprinted (and revised) a total of seven times over the next half-century. Straddling conventional piety and fashionable rationalism, it was both a traditional harmonizing of the Gospels à la Augustine and a liberal representation of Jesus as an extraordinary man whom God had exalted after his death. Although Hess professed his belief in the virgin birth because it seemed an appropriate way to introduce his heroic Jesus to the world, elsewhere he dismissed many of the Gospel miracles as natural phenomena. The star of Bethlehem, for instance, was actually a meteor, while the devil was not Satan but rather a nameless "tempter" who might have been part of Jesus' subconscious, and supposed demoniacs were merely insane.

In his clumsy way, Hess also pioneered the use of novelistic techniques to humanize Jesus, which meant endowing him with a sugary personality. To illustrate the passage in the Synoptic Gospels in which Jesus told his disciples they must become like little children in order to enter his kingdom, Hess had Jesus take a young boy by the hand, and then embrace him tenderly. Hess's most irritating habit—lampooned by Schweitzer—was his compulsive rewriting of Jesus' Gospel sayings, invariably for the worse. In one of the Beatitudes in Matthew's Gospel, for example, Jesus says: "Blessed are those who mourn, for they will be comforted."[16] In Hess's version, he declares: "Happy are they who amid the adversities of the present make the best of things and submit themselves with patience; for such men, if they do not see better times here, shall certainly elsewhere receive comfort and consolation."[17]

Countless other German "lives" of Jesus were to follow. The publication of Reimarus's *Fragments* in 1774 became the impetus for a number of these biographies, as scholars tried to offer what they hoped would be credible explanations for events that Reimarus had deemed incredible. Some of the "lives," like Hess's, tried to split the difference between reason and faith. Others took the bolder step of doing away with everything in the Gospels that did not strike the 18th-century mind as plausible. Still others, while heavily rationalistic, attempted to create a Jesus with a metaphysical dimension: the Kantian ideal of human perfection. All these late-18th- and early-19th-century biographies, however, had one thing in common: The Jesus they personified preached the Kantian Gospel of universal morality.

The most striking—and inadvertently humorous—of the first German lives of Jesus were those whose authors insisted on finding a natural cause for every supernatural event narrated in the Gospels. Where they could not deduce a rational explanation they felt obliged to invent one. The final products of this sort of "historical" approach were often the most bizarre forms of fiction imaginable.

Over the last eight years of his life, Karl Friedrich Bahrdt (1741–1792), a professor at Leipzig and Halle, composed a rambling 11-volume tome titled *An Explanation of the Plans and Aims of Jesus* that is, quite frankly, a hoot. Out of whole cloth, he ascribed Jesus' mission and miracles to the machinations of the Essenes. In Bahrdt's view, the Essenes had been a first-century secret society along the lines of the Freemasons, who were at the height of their political power and panache as Bahrdt was writing (for example, Mozart composed his Masonic opera, *The Magic Flute,* in 1791).

Bahrdt fabricated scores of new Gospel characters with Hebrew names such as Haram and Schimah, including a cadre of Essenes who kept a watchful eye on Jesus during his boyhood. One of the Essenes, disguised as a shepherd, taught the lad Greek philosophy, laying the foundation for his universalist ethic, and molding a philosophical martyr who longed to die for his beliefs as Socrates had done. A mysterious Persian whom Jesus met in a marketplace gave him two secret potions, one for eye afflictions and the other for nervous disorders. It does not take much imagination to figure out what Jesus did with the medicines, especially after an Essene leader introduced him to Luke the physician.

When Jesus reached adulthood, the Essenes continued to stage-manage his career, organizing his disciples into Masonic-style "orders" reflecting varying degrees of initiation. Luke used his medical training to work whatever healing miracles Jesus could not effect with his secret potions. When Jesus "walked" on water, he was actually on a floating raft that his apostles were unable to see in the dark.

The most dramatic contrivance in Bahrdt's book was Jesus' resurrection. Bahrdt pioneered what came to be called the "two-nails" theory of the crucifixion, an explanation for Jesus' apparent revivification after death that became a staple of nearly all rationalist Jesus-biographies of the early 19th century. Scholars of the time were already questioning the mechanics of Roman crucifixion: Were the condemned fastened to the cross by four nails (one for each limb), or by three (the feet being nailed together), or were only their hands nailed, while their feet were tied to the cross by ropes? Bahrdt and the other rationalists opted for two nails, speculating that Jesus had not died on the cross, but merely swooned, after which he was taken down and revived in his tomb. With unpierced feet, he would have been able to walk with ease after his supposed resurrection.

In Bahrdt's tome, Luke supplied Jesus with drugs to alleviate his pain and induce the requisite deathly faint. The Essenes then spirited him into a cave until he was well enough to "rise" several days later. When Jesus appeared to ascend into heaven from Mount Olivet in front of his apostles (as related in the *Acts of the Apostles*), in actual fact, he merely climbed the mountain until he disappeared into the clouds. From his hiding-place at an Essene lodge, he directed the course of the new Christian church from behind the scenes, occasionally venturing forth as a supposed apparition, such as the one that Paul saw on the road to Damascus, until he died a natural death.

Another two-nail theorist was the clergyman Karl Heinrich Venturini (1768–1849), whose ideas were so radical that he was denied a university post in his native Braunschweig. In his anonymous four-volume *A Non-supernatural History of the Great Prophet of Nazareth* (1800–1802), Venturini equipped Jesus with an entire medicine chest of potions that enabled him, among other things, to raise the dead (who were actually only comatose). The changing of water into wine at Cana, in Venturini's opinion, was simply a matter of misperception: Jesus had brought extra jars of wine to the feast as a wedding gift to the bride, and the apostle John, in all likelihood a little tipsy from sampling the gift vintage misrecorded the incident in his Gospel as a miracle.

Venturini developed the personality of Jesus far more than Bahrdt had done, giving him an intense and conflicted inner life. Like Bahrdt's Jesus, Venturini's was a protégé of the Essenes, but he ultimately outgrew the order and tried to persuade his Jewish followers to exchange their vision of an earthly Messiah for that of a heavenly one. Unlike Bahrdt's Jesus, when Venturini's was arrested and crucified (for his Messianic ambitions), he fully expected to die, and his revival in the tomb was purely accidental: An earthquake and lightning flash jolted him back to consciousness. He borrowed some clothes left behind by a gardener (hence his appearance to Mary Magdalene in gardener's guise in John's Gospel), and lingered in Palestine in frail health for several more weeks before finally expiring for good.

Among the other two-nail biographers were those who argued that Jesus' revival was due to the strong smell of the spices placed in his tomb, or to food that had been left, or even to the balmy weather of the Judean spring.

Philosophers and theologians far more serious than Bahrdt and Venturini offered fanciful naturalistic explanations of Jesus' other miracles.

In 1796 and again in 1797, the philosopher, poet, and literary critic Johann Gottfried von Herder (1744–1803) published treatises delineating his own historical Jesus. In contrast to the semi-fictional concoctions of Bahrdt and Venturini and the tame semi-rationalizations of Hess, his *Redeemer of Mankind According to the Three First Gospels* and *Son of God, the Savior of the World According to the Gospel of John* were startlingly original. After studying with Kant at Königsburg, Herder proposed an evolutionary theory of history in his *Outlines of the Philosophy of Man* (1800) that was redolent of Kant and foreshadowed Hegel. His fellow poet Johann Wolfgang von Goethe, who was then a minister of state for the duchy of Saxe-Weimar in Thuringia, arranged for his appointment as court preacher at Weimar in 1776, and Herder, Goethe, and Friedrich von Schiller (whom Goethe had also brought to the Saxe-Weimar court) became the leading exponents of the explosion of high culture that took place in late-18th-century Weimar.

Like Heyne, Eichhorn, and the brothers Grimm, Herder was fascinated by the myths of "primitive" people. From 1778 to 1790 he published a famous anthology of folk songs. He also speculated that large portions of the Old Testament were actually Hebrew folk-poetry. An ardent admirer of Lessing (Herder, Lessing, and Goethe were the leading lights of the *Sturm und Drang* movement, which combined intense nationalism with bohemian rebellion à la Rousseau), he took up Lessing's idea of the *Ur*-Gospel. However, in a startling departure from Lessing, he proposed that the *Ur*-Gospel had been oral history, not a written document. Furthermore, it was not a single work, but rather a free-floating collection of folk-tales, or pericopes, which had circulated throughout Palestine before being strung together to make up the written Gospels. These short, orally transmitted folk-stories—miracles, parables, sermons, and arguments with the Pharisees—preserved more accurately than any written document the actual words of Jesus.

Herder identified the Gospel of Mark—the shortest, most crudely written, and least "supernatural" of the four Gospels—as the one that was closest in spirit to the *Ur*-Gospel. The Gospel of Matthew, which nearly everyone (including Griesbach) had assumed was written first, was too self-consciously anti-Jewish, with its emphasis on Jesus as the fulfillment of Hebrew prophecies, to be considered authentically primitive in Herder's view. Luke's Gospel, which placed Jesus' life in the context of the Roman Empire and its Caesars, was too Hellenistic. As for the Gospel of John, with its bold declarations of Jesus' divinity and its lack of synchrony with the Synoptics, Herder deemed it a Gnosticism-influenced document written long after Jesus' death.

Unlike Hess and others, Herder believed that it was impossible to reconstruct a harmonized "life of Jesus" from the widely differing portrayals contained in the Gospels: The Jewish Messiah of the Synoptics was utterly incompatible with the Lord of the World shown in the Gospel of John. However, in Herder's view, neither the Synoptics nor John constituted a genuine history of Jesus. Instead, all four were sacred epics of mythology whose authors had embellished Jesus' life and teachings with narrative details designed to portray him as having fulfilled the prophecies of the Old Testament.

Herder, like Semler, posited a theological chasm between the religion *of* Jesus (depicted in Mark and the other two Synoptics) and what he termed "the religion *about* Jesus" (promulgated by John's Gospel, organized religion, and the Christian creeds). It was his hope that just as "the religion about Jesus" had supplanted "the religion of Jesus" during early Christian times, "the religion of Jesus" would inevitably supplant "the religion about Jesus" during the 19th century. He wrote: "Whoever contributes to bringing back the religion of Jesus from a meretricious slavery and from a painful Lord-Lording to that genuine Gospel of friendship and brotherliness, of convinced, spontaneous, free, glad participation in the work of and intent of Jesus as they are clearly set forth in the Gospels he himself has taken part in Christ's work and advanced it."[18]

Although his theories about Gospel composition were ground-breaking, Herder's Jesus was the same one that Bahrdt and Venturini had created, minus the Essenes and medicinal potions. The biblical demoniacs had all been insane, Jesus' transfiguration on the mountain when Moses and Elijah appeared beside him was merely a vision of the apostles, and the heavenly brightness and voice of God that accompanied Jesus' baptism were the effects of a fortuitous thunderstorm. Furthermore, Herder's Jesus had tended to the sick but had worked no miraculous cures, and his resurrection was actually nothing more than his revival in the tomb. (Herder was another two-nails theorist.)

The most aggressive of the turn-of-the-century German rationalists was Heinrich Eberhard Gottlob Paulus (1761–1851), a pastor and professor of Oriental languages who later taught theology at Jena, Würzburg, and Heidelberg. Paulus's father, a deacon in the small town of Leonberg near Stuttgart, was a mystic who was certain that he had witnessed his wife sit up in bed immediately following her death. The elder Paulus was also convinced that he could communicate with departed souls. Eventually he became so preoccupied with spiritualism that he was relieved of his clerical duties when his son Heinrich was ten years old.

In many ways, Paulus's entire career was a violent reaction against his father's obsession with the supernatural. As a student at Tübingen, he immersed himself in the writings of Semler and Michaelis. Later on, he read Kant and Spinoza and prepared a special edition of Spinoza's writings. As he moved from one university post to another, he also came under the influence of Goethe, Schiller, and Herder. Paulus liked to pick fights. A lifelong quarrel with Kant's Idealist disciple Friedrich Wilhelm Joseph von Schelling (1775–1854)—who had been born in the same house as Paulus in Leonberg, had studied at Tübingen, and had even been a colleague at Jena and Würzburg—was also a reflection of his antipathy to mysticism. At the age of 80, Paulus launched a campaign to have Schelling removed from the University of Berlin, where he had been installed by Frederick William III's son, Frederick William IV. The elderly rationalist secured a pirated copy of the notes of Schelling's lectures, which he issued along with a scathing personal commentary highlighting Schelling's logical deficiencies. Schelling sued Paulus for having published his work without his approval, and when he lost his case, he resigned his post in Berlin.

Paulus's *Life of Jesus As the Basis of a Purely Historical Account of Early Christianity* (1828), drawn from a treatise on the Gospels that he had written a generation earlier, was largely a refutation of the theories advanced by Eichhorn and Herder. Paulus discredited both the mythological interpretation of the composition of the Gospels and the authenticity of the *Ur*-Gospel. He also rejected the idea that the Gospel of Mark was the most authoritative of the Synoptics, maintaining instead that all four Gospels had been written shortly after Jesus' death but were tainted by the evangelists' poor memories.

As a Kantian, Paulus believed that natural causes could produce an ideal of human perfection such as Jesus. However, his *Life of Jesus* became famous not for its Kantian theories but for its ingenious (and unintentionally amusing) approach to the Gospel miracles. Most startling of all was Paulus's version of the annunciation in the Gospel of Luke, in which the angel Gabriel informed Mary that she had been chosen to conceive a son by the Holy Spirit. According to Paulus, the "angel" was actually a male friend of her cousin Elizabeth who fathered the child. Paulus's Jesus walked not on the Sea of Galilee, but along its banks, a variation on Bahrdt's raft. The feeding of the five thousand was the result of a spontaneous outburst of generosity, during which members of the crowd shared the contents of their picnic baskets at Jesus' instigation. Jesus cured a blind man not with his own spittle (as reported in Mark's Gospel), but with medicinal clay. Other miraculous healings were more like slow cures than sudden returns to health. Jesus' transfiguration was merely an optical illusion caused by the glare of the sunlight. As for his crucifixion and resurrection, the two-nails theory prevailed: he was nursed back to health by the Essenes, who then arranged his "posthumous" reappearances.

Not all the contemporary Jesus-biographers took such a rationalist stance. Karl August von Hase (1800–1890), a theology professor at Jena, concluded that a few of the Gospel miracles had in fact occurred, including the virgin birth and the resurrection. As for the rest in his *Life of Jesus: A Manual for Academic Study* (1829), Hase adopted his colleague Gabler's theory of primitive myth in stripping away presumably fanciful elements, such as the angels. He also eliminated the star of Bethlehem based on his knowledge of modern astronomy. Finally, he attributed the stories of Jesus' raising of the dead to the ancient Jewish custom of burying people the day they died (or were thought to have died), which resulted in occasional premature burials.

Hase's book was undoubtedly the most elaborate account of Jesus' life to come off the German presses. He liberally indulged in scenic details, for example, such as having Jesus predicting the Temple's destruction "while contemplating its noble architecture."[19] He also described Jesus physically as a good-looking country rabbi (the Gospels say nothing about Jesus' physical appearance). As for why Jesus never married, he concluded that "he . . . found no soul living in his time equal to his own, and capable of such a bond."[20] Most important, Hase described Jesus' ministry in terms of an "early, hopeful cheerfulness" in Galilee, followed by a "year of conflict" in Judea in which he had vivid premonitions of his impending death.[21] In short, Hase's Jesus was a fully developed Romantic hero whose death was a carefully foreshadowed tragedy.

The most celebrated of the early German Jesus-biographers was Friedrich Ernst Daniel Schleiermacher (1768–1834), who has been called the father of modern Protestantism. Schleiermacher's life exemplified the struggle of a well-educated, upwardly mobile Christian to gain the acceptance of a secularized intelligentsia while somehow remaining true to his faith. Schleiermacher was born in the Prussian city of Breslau (now Wroclaw in Poland), which lay due north of the Czech province of Moravia. The son of a

Reformed chaplain in the Prussian army, he was also the descendant of several generations of clergymen on both sides of the family.

The nearby province of Moravia was home to a Pietist sect known as the Moravian Brethren, which traced its lineage to Jan Huss, the Czech priest who had been burnt alive by the Catholics as a heretic in 1415. By the late 18th century, there were numerous Moravian enclaves throughout central Europe. In America, the Brethren had founded the towns of Bethlehem and Nazareth in rural, German-speaking northeastern Pennsylvania.

Although the elder Schleiermacher insisted on sending his son to Moravian schools, Friedrich soon abandoned the Brethren's cultural separatism and biblical literalism for the life of a mainstream intellectual. After a brilliant academic career at the University of Halle, in 1810 he was appointed the first theology professor of the newly established University of Berlin. While his chosen discipline was New Testament scholarship, he also wrote knowledgeably and prolifically on philosophy, culture, psychology, and political theory.

In addition to being an outstanding scholar and lecturer, Schleiermacher was an ordained minister of the Reformed church. As reflected in many of his writings, his was a constant attempt to straddle the opposing worlds of a Christian ministry and a society of well-read and thoroughly jaded agnostics. In fact, his first and most famous book, *On Religion: Speeches to Its Cultured Despisers,* published anonymously in 1799 while he was preaching in Berlin, was a valiant effort to win the secular savants' acceptance of the basic tenets of Christianity. In addressing their Enlightenment skepticism about miracles and the supernatural, he contended that it was a mistake to try to understand religion from an intellectual standpoint, as it would always come up short in a scientific age. The domain of religion, he argued, was not the mind, but rather the heart: One's faith in God depended not on reason, but on an intuitive knowledge of a superior life-force. While Rousseau had based a similar theory on the precognitive beliefs of simple peasants, Schleiermacher maintained that the sophisticated intelligentsia could also feel the power of the divine through an appreciation of higher pursuits, such as music, poetry, and art. Schleiermacher was the first in a long line of 19th-century "mediating" theologians who sought to reconcile Christianity with modern science and philosophy.

From 1819 until his death in 1834, Schleiermacher delivered a series of lectures on the historical Jesus at Berlin. In these lectures, not published in book form until 1864, his attempt to make Jesus intellectually acceptable to "cultured despisers" was essentially a response to Reimarus's sardonic *Fragments,* which were still a topic of discussion among the German intelligentsia.

Like Paulus, Schleiermacher did not subscribe to the fashionable theories of the *Ur*-gospel, or to Herder's "primitive" Gospel of Mark. Nor did he believe, as did Herder and Eichhorn, that the Gospels were examples of early Christian myth-making.

In contrast to the others, Schleiermacher decided that the Gospel of John contained the most accurate history of Jesus' life and times, having been written by the Galilean fisherman who had been one of Jesus' earliest disciples and an eyewitness to his entire ministry. Schleiermacher viewed the Synoptics as crude pastiches that were not historically reliable, in contrast to John's account, which was both realistic and credible. Most important, John contained none of the Synoptic predictions by Jesus of his second coming or other apocalyptic material that the rationalists of the 18th and 19th centuries had regarded with utter disdain.

Jesus' famous declaration, "I am the way, and the truth, and the life; no one comes to the Father except through me,"[22] is only one of several bold assertions found in John of Jesus' awareness of his special status as son of God. Schleiermacher read such statements with a Kantian eye. By promoting the image of Jesus as an individual who embodied a Kantian idea of human perfection ("the way, the truth, and the life"), he hoped to make him more palatable to the 19th century. Consequently, he delineated a Jesus who, despite his exalted status, had no superhuman powers and was unable to predict future events. He affirmed his exalted metaphysical status through his growing consciousness of his special relationship with God. "We can believe, to be sure, that a self-consciousness by which he distinguished himself from all other men can have developed in Christ in a wholly natural way if we presuppose an innate power which was a pure representation of the divine, that is to say, which gave him everywhere the direction to the consciousness of God, so that, as long as the intelligent capacity developed, it became more and more for him a continuum and, as far as this necessarily became consciousness of the divine will, had as a moral power an absolute adequacy," Schleiermacher stated in a lecture that he delivered at Berlin on June 7, 1832.[23]

In the end, Schleiermacher's Berlin lectures reflected his own unresolved intellectual conflicts as he attempted to reconcile the strictly human Jesus he had delineated with the Kantian ideal of the divine. On one hand, he threw out the supernatural stories of Jesus' nativity, since few liberals still believed in them. On the other hand, he wanted desperately to retain other Gospel miracles, such as Jesus' healings. He recast the healings as "moral acts of compassion" that resulted in spontaneous remissions. They were "relative miracles."[24]

In his eagerness to limn a Jesus acceptable to skeptics, Schleiermacher was obliged to make far more intellectual compromises than had the super-rationalist Paulus. Although as a philospher he discredited the literalness of Jesus' resurrection, as a Christian he could not bring himself to disown the doctrine *in toto.* His solution was to say as little as possible about the circumstances of Jesus' death, and to attach no theological significance to the resurrection, which he regarded as irrelevant to his theory of Jesus as the archetype of human perfection. While he rejected the notions of Essene conspiracies as "historical nonsense,"[25] more than once he hinted at the rationalist possibility that Jesus might not have really died on the cross ("We cannot discuss the matter in any further detail, for there is nothing more we know about it," he wrote).[26] He also insisted that after his resurrection, Jesus had continued his ministry in much the same fashion as before his death.

As the story of Jesus' ascension into heaven was too primitive a tale for the post-Copernican era, Schleiermacher hypothesized that he had simply died again, mysteriously, not long after his first death. His "second life . . . had come to an end," he concluded rather flatly.[27] Schleiermacher's philosophical Jesus was so strange a beast—an ordinary human being, the Kantian ideal of perfection, and the Christian son of God, all rolled into one—that he proved to be as susceptible to ridicule as the Jesus of traditional Christianity.

Each in his own way, Schleiermacher, Paulus, Bahrdt, Hase, Kant, and Rousseau had all sought to make Jesus presentable to the modern age by clothing him in philosophical garments. They had believed that by minimizing the supernatural and highlighting the moral, they would be able to rehabilitate his image. Instead, they had produced an entirely fictional character. All their reconstructions of Jesus would soon be rendered obsolete by the theories of a far more influential philosopher—Hegel—whose writings were circulating in Berlin even as Schleiermacher lectured to his audience of cultured skeptics.

6

THE TRIUMPH OF MATERIALISM

Hegel was nearly an exact contemporary of Schleiermacher. He was the son of a minor government official in Stuttgart, the capital of the Lutheran duchy (and future kingdom) of Württemberg, a rural corner of southwest Germany that lay between the Rhine and the Danube. At age 18 he enrolled at the University of Tübingen, which was down the Neckar River from Stuttgart; three years later he received a degree in theology that qualified him for ordination as a Lutheran pastor. Instead, he chose to pursue an academic career, eventually becoming a professor of philosophy at Jena, where he was teaching when Napoleon brought the Prussians to their knees in 1806. Later on, he taught at Heidelberg and then at Berlin, where he remained from 1818 until his death in 1831. When only 37, he published his most ambitious book, *The Phenomenology of Spirit,* in which he set forth the main theories that he would continue to expand upon for the rest of his life. An overnight sensation, this text was to have a profound effect on the way his contemporaries viewed the world around them.

Hegel's philosophy might be described as a unified-field theory of metaphysics, in that he tried to explain the entire universe by means of a few simple principles of motion. Like Kant, Hegel was an Idealist who believed in an ultimate truth that the human mind could only grasp through intuitive thinking. Whereas Kant had theorized that the phenomenal world of the senses and the noumenal world of ultimate reality were completely separate, Hegel postulated that all phenomena were imbued with the noumenal, which he termed *der Geist,* or "the Spirit." A synonym for the presence of God, *der Geist* was not, however, the subjective Holy Spirit *(der heilige Geist)* of Christian theology. Rather, it was an objective Spirit, or life-force, that was constantly embodying itself in new creations through a process of change whereby a given entity (thesis) was inevitably transformed into its opposite (antithesis), after which the combination of the two was resolved into a higher form (synthesis).

In defining change as the product of a constant conflict, or "dialectic," between opposites arising from the internal contradictions inherent in all things, Hegel predicated a universe that was essentially self-creating. The planet Earth had developed from a dialectic between astral bodies, while vegetal life had developed from minerals, animal life from vegetal, and human life from animal. By the same token, contradictions between conflicting forces in primitive societies had resulted in the concept of private property, which in turn had led to the need for laws that would determine a common code of ethics. The growth of civilization was therefore the product of the continuing dynamic interaction of opposing historical forces. Indeed, Hegel's theory of "historicism"—the belief that there are processes at work in history that individuals can do little to alter—was the logical conclusion of his interpretation of reality.

From 1821 to late autumn of 1831, when he died in a cholera epidemic that swept Berlin, Hegel delivered a series of university lectures in which he called upon the dialectical method in order to explain his own religious principles. Like Rousseau and Kant before him, Hegel viewed religion as an inferior form of philosophy. While both embodied the concept of the knowledge of God *(der Begriff),* their use of imagery *(die Vorstellung)* was entirely different. Religion employed an array of myths, creeds, and rituals, in contrast to philosophical abstractions.

However, religion itself had been transformed by the dialectical process over the centuries to arrive at ever higher apprehensions of ultimate truth. Christianity was thus an improvement over animism and Judaism, because its outward manifestations, or *Vorstellungen,* were far less primitive and literalist. Furthermore, the Christian religion itself had reached a higher level of awareness under the influence of the Protestant Reformation. Although Hegel believed that Christianity was the "consummate religion" of his time, inasmuch as God had manifested himself to humankind through Jesus, he was equally convinced that Christian doctrine would eventually be replaced by a superior and more philosophical form of religion as it overcame its own inherent contradictions.

Hegel's avowed faith in Christianity was at least partially an effort to stay in the good graces of Frederick William III, overseer of Berlin. He also believed that a state religion was necessary to imbue the Prussian government with authority. Nonetheless, his theory of constant human improvement by means of dialectical syntheses seriously challenged the Christian doctrine of Jesus' atonement on the cross, which was predicated on persistent human sinfulness. In fact, Hegel's Jesus was not an individual figure but the symbolic embodiment of a moment in history in which mankind was made conscious of its unity with God. As he stated in a lecture delivered at Berlin in 1821, "All are one stem, not this or that single individual . . . and thus one man [Jesus] is humanity as such."[1] Jesus' death was therefore merely a symbol of human alienation, and his resurrection a symbol of reconciliation with God. As Vincent McCarthy wrote: "In other words, Jesus is the man on the scene when it is time for the consummate religion. And one may imagine that, if Jesus of Nazareth had not been there, another would have risen to the task."[2]

During his later years, Hegel enjoyed almost a godlike status at the University of Berlin. In defining all aspects of reality as subject to change, he held forth the promise of a dynamic, evolving, ever-improving society that was immensely attractive to his contemporaries. In tandem with the Industrial Revolution, a time in which machines and mass-production were transforming the way in which Europeans lived and worked, Hegelian historicism represented a teleology of progress and faith in a brighter future.

Charles Darwin's *On the Origin of Species* would not appear until 1859, 28 years after Hegel's death. Well before Darwin, however, Europe abounded with Hegel-inspired theories of human evolution. During the 1830s and early 1840s, the French theorist Auguste Comte (1798–1857), who would later be known as the father of sociology, published a multi-volume work titled *The Course of Positive Philosophy,* which borrowed from Hegel's dialectics in tracing the development of civilization. Comte maintained, for example, that human thought patterns had evolved from the theological (attributing causation to supernatural forces), to the philosophical (attributing causation to metaphysical abstractions), to the scientific (attributing causation to verifiable universal laws). Karl Marx (1818–1883), who studied at Berlin during the 1830s when Hegel's towering presence was still a potent memory, repudiated Hegel's Idealism, and indeed all metaphysics, in arriving at his own interpretation of reality. He did, however, adopt the *metaphor* of Hegel's dialectic to construct a political and economic theory that substituted class struggle for the dynamic role of *der Geist.*

Hegel's philosophy of religion has continued to be the subject of controversy because of its intentional ambiguities. Was Hegel an atheist, a pantheist, or a genuine Christian? In fact, when Frederick William IV succeeded his father on the Prussian throne in 1840, he immediately set out to cleanse the University of Berlin of what he viewed as Hegelian heresies against Christian orthodoxy by granting a teaching post to Schelling, the arch-enemy of the rationalist Jesus-biographer Heinrich Paulus.

Schelling's attempt to rid the university of Hegel's influence by substituting his own Idealist philosophy of religion (based on a theory of the progressive development of God that resembled today's process theology) was an ignominious failure. His series of lectures, delivered from Hegel's old podium in 1841, at first attracted enormous crowds (including the young Friedrich Engels, the young Søren Kierkegaard, and the future Russian anarchist Mikhail Bakunin). However, his audience soon dwindled in light of his obvious eccentricities, and the loss of his case against Paulus over the purloined notes from those lectures was the ultimate humiliation. In 1851, the embittered Schelling returned to Munich, where he died three years later. Hegel's theories had triumphed.

Hegel's disciples split into two violently opposing factions. The "left-wing" faction of atheists and political radicals who used Hegel's historical determinism to further their own theories included Marx, Engels, and Ludwig Feuerbach (1804–1872). In 1841, Feuerbach's *Essence of Christianity* caused a furor by asserting that religious discourse was not about God but about mankind: the projection of human virtues such as wisdom and justice onto an imaginary entity called "God." Marx's own definition of religion as an illusory superstructure whose purpose was to keep the class system in place was derived from Feuerbach.

The most influential of the "right-wing" or more conservative Hegelians was Ferdinand Christian Baur (1792–1860). Like Hegel, Baur had received a degree in theology from the University of Tübingen. After serving briefly as a Lutheran pastor, he taught for nine years at Blaubeuren, a former Cistercian monastery near Tübingen that had been turned into a "lower" theological seminary for boys in the first stage of preparing for the ministry. During his years at Blaubeuren, he immersed himself in the Kantian philosophies of Schleiermacher, the young (and then-Kantian) Schelling, and Johann Gottlieb Fichte (1762–1814), another Kantian acolyte who had been the first rector of the University of Berlin. Baur also became interested in the mythological theories about the Bible propounded by Heyne, Eichhorn, Gabler, and Herder, particularly Herder's belief that the Gospels were merely fairy tales from a childlike era. In 1824 and 1825, he published his *Symbolism and Mythology; or the Nature Religion of Antiquity,* a series of studies that were considered mildly shocking because they treated the Gospels not as history but as religious treatises embellished with mythology.

In 1826 Baur returned to Tübingen as a professor of dogmatics and church history, where he soon achieved celebrity for his mythological approach to the origins and history of Christianity. He became embroiled in a debate with a Catholic theologian at Tübingen named Johann Adam Möhler over the Roman church's claim to represent the earliest and most authentic form of Christianity. Baur, like most Protestants, believed that Catholicism exemplified a relatively late falling-off from a purer, more democratic "primitive Christianity" reflected in the letters of Paul and recaptured by Protestants during the Reformation. To bolster his position that Pauline Christianity and Petrine (that is, Catholic) Christianity had been at odds with one another from the very beginning, in 1831 he published an article titled "The Christ Party in the Corinthian Community," which was to become the single most famous essay in all of New Testament scholarship.

"The Christ Party" was an explication of certain passages in Paul's letters to the Corinthians in which the apostle attempted to reconcile quarrels among various Christian factions. Baur decided that Peter (who had baptized some of the Corinthians) and Paul (who had baptized others) represented two polemically opposed wings of the early church that were reconciled only after the two apostles' deaths. Peter was a proponent of Jewish legalism (the predecessor of the Catholic doctrine of justification by works), while Paul, the apostle to the Gentiles, had promoted the Protestant doctrine of justification by faith and was thus Christianity's real founder. "After this fashion two opposing parties with a very distinct difference of views had come into being as early as those early times in which Christianity had yet hardly begun to break through the narrow bounds of Judaism and to open up for itself a successful field of work in the pagan world," Baur wrote.[3] Baur believed that the early church—and the New Testament writers—had suppressed the full account of the conflict between Petrine and Pauline *Tendenzen* (or "tendencies") in order to present a unified front to unbelievers.

Hegel died the same year in which Baur published "The Christ Party." Some months later, a complete set of his Berlin lectures on religion was published, and they had a riveting effect on Baur, hundreds of miles away in remote and sleepy Tübingen. Hegel's clash-of-opposites theory of history, his profound determinism, and above all, his application of dialectics to the development of Christian doctrine fit perfectly with Baur's own conflict model of the early church. An overnight convert to Hegelianism, he began a lifelong campaign to characterize the events of early Christian history along the lines of Hegel's grand scheme.

Accordingly, Baur heightened the dialectical implications of the Petrine-Pauline conflict he had explored in the "The Christ Party," maintaining not only that the warring factions had continued to battle until the end of the second century, but also that their conflict encompassed differing views of the nature of Jesus as well as of Jewish law. The "judaizing" or "Petrine" Christians did not believe Jesus was divine, he theorized (yet another resurrecting of the Ebionites), whereas the "Pauline" Christians, who believed in Jesus' divinity, were the theological ancestors of the Marcionites and Gnostics.

Baur's theories demanded a radical redacting of the New Testament Scriptures in order to explain why they contained so few references to the Petrine-Pauline skirmishes. He moved the composition dates of nearly all the books out of the first century and into the late second century, including nine of the 13 letters that had been conventionally attributed to Paul (Baur believed that Paul had written only four of the letters bearing his name). Despite their striking stylistic similarities, he also insisted that Luke's Gospel and the Acts of the Apostles (traditionally attributed to Luke) had not been the work of the same author. He further argued that the Gospel of John, written (so he maintained) at the very end of the second century, represented a final Hegelian synthesis of Petrine-Pauline doctrine. "Faith and works are merged in love, their higher unity," he noted in the most ambitious of his books, *The Church History of the First Three Centuries,* published in 1853.[4]

As for Jesus, he was essentially a cipher, or near-abstraction, like Hegel's Jesus, who existed only because the dialectic had created him. Thus, the events of his life, including his crucifixion, held no particular theological meaning. As a rationalist, Baur also dismissed the miraculous aspects of Jesus' life, including his virginal conception, as examples of Christian mythmaking that had no grounding in history.

In Baur's view, Jesus represented another Hegelian synthesis, the synthesis of Jewish religious beliefs and Greek philosophy. He maintained that Jewish "particularism" (the belief that the Jews were the chosen people of God, who would send them a Messiah) and the ethical universalism of the Greeks had been fused in Jesus' teachings, which reflected the best of both ideologies. At the moment in which Jesus uttered the words, "Blessed are the poor in spirit, for theirs is the kingdom of heaven," in the Gospel of Matthew,[5] there was born the "unity of all antitheses," or "the original Christian consciousness." Baur wrote: "In the Sermon on the Mount Jesus insists emphatically on purity and singleness of heart, on a morality which does not consist merely in the outward act, but in the inner disposition."[6] The historical Jesus was thus a universalistic teacher who opposed the empty legalism inherent in Judaism and gainsaid "selfish Jewish particularism" by functioning as a Messiah for all mankind, not just the Jews. However, precisely *because* the Jewish "Messianic idea" had fixed itself on Jesus, he was not simply another philosopher reciting moral maxims.[7] He was bigger than both Judaism and philosophy, exemplifying a consciousness superior to both. Other than as the embodiment of the original Christian consciousness, however, Jesus was of little interest to Baur.

While Baur and his "Tübingen school" were a dominant force among mid-19th century German biblical scholars, other Christian academics, particularly in Britain, gradually tore his Hegelian theories to pieces as new textual evidence emerged—such as the papyrus fragment of John's Gospel discovered in Egypt at century's end, which dated from the early (not the late) second century. Most of today's religious historians are certain that all the books of the New Testament were in fact composed before the end of the first century (not the second century), that the majority of the letters traditionally ascribed to Paul are genuine, and that the author of Luke's Gospel also wrote Acts. It is also clear that Baur made grave mistakes in dating the work of other early Christians writers (he even invented a "Clement" who did not exist but who was useful for his theories).

Even Albrecht Ritschl (1822–1889), Baur's most famous student at Tübingen, ultimately rejected his mentor's theory of two-centuries-long Petrine-Pauline conflict. In 1857, he issued a second edition of his *Origin of the Ancient Catholic Church,* originally published in 1850, in which he maintained that the corruption inherent in Catholic theology had had little to do with Paul, the Jews, or Hegelian metaphysics. Nonetheless, Baur's conflict model of early Christian history—as well as his idea of warring *Tendenzen*—has had remarkable staying power. To this day, many educated people believe that early Christianity consisted of battling sects, that the Gospels were written during the second (or even third) century, that only a few of Paul's letters are genuine, and that Paul was the founder of Christianity.

Baur was eventually overshadowed by another of his students, indeed, his most radical student, David Friedrich Strauss. Strauss's *Life of Jesus Critically Examined,* which appeared in two volumes over the summer and fall of 1835 while Strauss was a 27-year-old seminary tutor at Tübingen, became the most translated, discussed, and debated book about Jesus of the entire 19th century. In one of those strange coincidences of history, the philosopher Hegel and his two most famous theological disciples, Baur on the right and Strauss on the left, were all from the same corner of southern Germany, and all three had intimate connections with Tübingen.

Strauss's father, Johann Friedrich Strauss, was a man of strong Pietistic and mystical leanings who had longed as a youth to become a minister. However, as the eldest son of a tea-and-spice merchant in Ludwigsburg, a former garrison town six miles north of Stuttgart, he was obliged instead to take over the family business, which he ran into the ground, spending most of his time reading Horace, Virgil, and other classical Latin writers, as well as tending to his orchard, keeping bees, and trying his hand at poetry. His practical-minded wife, Christiane, somehow managed to make ends meet. Although a descendant of generations of clergymen, Christiane Strauss had little use for churchgoing. She also taught her children that Jesus was no more than a divinely inspired teacher, and that good deeds were more important than dogma. Young David, who both adored and despised his devout but feckless father, was caught between his parents' conflicting views of faith.

Although he was a prize-winning prodigy at school, especially in languages, as a poor boy Strauss could obtain a university education only by first entering the seminary. He consequently enrolled in Blaubeuren, where Baur was one of his teachers. In 1825, he matriculated at Tübingen, whose faculty Baur joined one year later. While supposedly studying for the Lutheran ministry at Tübingen, Strauss was actually dabbling in mysticism of a decidedly unorthodox nature. He read the writings of Jakob Böhme, a maverick 17th-century visionary who like Spinoza believed that God was present in all things, experimented with fortune-telling and psychic healing, and along with fellow students frequented a female clairvoyant who conducted spiritual sleep-walking sessions in a nearby town.

While Strauss attended a number of Baur's lectures, he was not particularly impressed by his mythological approach, nor was he particularly interested in early Christianity. He did, however, briefly find a spiritual mentor in Schleiermacher, whose "mediating" theology seemed a prudent compromise between the liberalism of certain faculty members and the traditionalist Protestantism that still prevailed in backward-seeming southern Germany.

In 1827, Strauss began meeting with fellow students twice a week to read and discuss Hegel's *Phenomenology of Spirit.* Overwhelmed by a metaphysical system that encompassed every aspect of human experience, he soon abandoned whatever was left of his traditional beliefs in favor of Hegelian dialectics. However, unlike Baur and the other "right-wing" Hegelians, Strauss rejected the notion of Jesus as the sole embodiment of mankind's unity with the divine. He also came to view traditional Christian dogma as colorful detritus left over from a more primitive time.

After graduating first in his class in 1828, Strauss accepted the post of village curate in rural Klein-Ingersheim, not far from Ludwigsburg, where he agonized over the extent to which he should attempt to expose his new parishioners to a more sophisticated interpretation of Christian doctrine. In the end, he decided that it was best to let them cling to their traditional beliefs as simple country folk.

Having completed his doctoral dissertation at Tübingen in 1831, Strauss decided to continue his studies directly under Hegel's tutelage. He arrived in Berlin in November, just after the city's cholera epidemic had reached its peak, and met with his future mentor at the latter's home, where the two men exchanged sallies about the low quality of intellectual life in their native Württemberg. He also attended the first two in a series of lectures on the philosophy of religion that Hegel was scheduled to deliver. Shortly thereafter, on November 15th, Strauss paid a courtesy call on Schleiermacher, who informed him that Hegel had died the previous day. "But it was for his sake that I came here to Berlin," Strauss blurted out, seriously offending Schleiermacher, who took the outburst as a personal affront. Relations between the two men after that were decidedly cool.

Although Hegel himself was dead, Strauss stayed on in Berlin for the duration of the academic year to attend lectures by biblical scholars whose thinking Hegel had influenced. Among these was Wilhelm Vatke, an Old Testament scholar, who later became a close friend of Strauss. According to Vatke's Hegelian revision of sacred Jewish history, the ancient Hebrews had not originally been monotheistic; rather, their god Yahweh was merely a tribal war deity who happened to prevail over the others. Vatke also believed that the composition of the Pentateuch, which showed the influence of the Jewish priestly class, was not even begun until shortly before the Babylonian exile. Above all, he argued that the early priests and prophets had represented antithetical Jewish factions that were ultimately synthesized à la Hegel in post-exilic Judaism.

While studying the notes for a portion of Schleiermacher's long-running lecture series on the life of Jesus, Strauss the Hegelian convert became convinced that the liberal Protestant's "mediating" combination of Enlightenment rationalism, Christian doctrine, and Kantian metaphysics was sadly out of date. "The truth is I found myself repelled by almost every aspect of these lectures," he wrote sometime later.[8] Strauss longed to teach a course on Jesus that would cut through both traditional Christian supernaturalism and liberal rationalism of the sort espoused by Schleiermacher and Paulus. Although the lectures never materialized, he found work as a tutor of philosophy at Tübingen's theological school after returning home the following year. He also set to work on the massive *Life of Jesus* that would finally deliver his message.

Strauss was not an innovator like Baur, who had begun his own Hegelian odyssey while Strauss was working on his *Life.* In fact, Strauss's comprehensive theories about the mythological nature of the Gospel stories are easily traceable to the ideas of Eichhorn, Gabler, Herder, Georg Lorenz Bauer, de Wette, and even Baur himself. In a 1986 monograph on Strauss and his era, Edwina G. Lawler, a New Testament professor at Drew University, examined the various sources that Strauss most likely used, including certain articles from early-19th-century scholarly journals that prefigured many of his ideas about Jesus. As early as the 1790s, there had appeared a series of unsigned essays criticizing the efforts of liberal German theologians to find rational explanations for Gospel miracles, and speculating that the Jesus of the Gospels was in no way connected with historical reality.

Shortly before Strauss started his *Life,* Leonhard Usteri (1799–1833), a Swiss scholar who had studied at Berlin, published an article in which he maintained that the 30 or so years between Jesus' death and the composition of the first Gospel were more than enough time for oral tradition to develop a complete mythology about Jesus. Strauss simply recycled all this mythological theory, from Gabler to Usteri, within a Hegelian framework in order to argue that the Gospels were simply the product of the vivid imaginations of

Jesus' early followers. Jesus himself he viewed as a mere mortal who had nothing to do with supernaturalistic Christianity.

In severing the Gospels from the annals of history and the historical Jesus from the faith that bore his name, Strauss used a double-sided ratchet. His *Life of Jesus,* which ran to more than 1,500 pages in the first German edition, dismissed as legend nearly every Gospel story, leaving the reader with a skeletal outline of the life of a fanatical Jewish preacher who had mistakenly believed that he was the Messiah. While Jesus still represented the Hegelian "idea" of divinity conjoined with humanity, the idea itself had no connection with the deluded Jew who had died so long ago. Moreover, Jesus' mistaken impression that he exemplified the "messianic hope" of the Jews of his day bore no resemblance to the theological beliefs of Christians of any age.[9]

Strauss's version of the Hegelian "thesis" underlying Christianity was exemplified by the richly embroidered but rationally implausible Gospel myths of the early Christian communities. His "antithesis" was personified by the likes of Paulus and Schleiermacher, who tried to find rationalist explanations for those same Gospel stories. Finally, his "synthesis" was represented by his own mythological reinterpretation of the Gospels, which he believed would not only preserve but also enhance their religious significance.

Convinced that he had succeeded in portraying a modern *Vorstellung* of the traditional Christian idea of humanity made divine, Strauss was genuinely surprised when his *Life of Jesus* offended Christians of every stripe, from old-fashioned believers to liberals such as Schleiermacher—and even Baur. Although his *Life of Jesus* sold wildly after a slow start, it cost him both his position at Tübingen and all hope of an academic or ecclesiastical career in the German-speaking world. He spent the rest of his life as an independent scholar, living in lonely comfort while constantly revising his best-selling book. He also worked as a free-lance *littérateur,* penning mediocre poetry and popular biographies of personages he admired, such as Voltaire.

Albert Schweitzer viewed Strauss as a tragic figure. His life certainly bore all the earmarks of such: rugged good looks, a difficult childhood with a failed businessman for a father, a promising career that went seriously awry, and worst of all, a brief, unhappy marriage to a beautiful but just-past-her-prime opera singer in Stuttgart, Agnese Schebest. Flamboyant, prone to a diva's temper tantrums, strikingly nonintellectual, and Catholic, Schebest was the antithesis of Strauss in every way, and his scholarly friends looked down their noses at her.

"In order to understand Strauss, one must love him," Schweitzer wrote.[10] The truth is that Strauss was not very lovable. Moody, egocentric, introverted, stubborn, stingy, and in his own way as much a prima donna as Agnese, he himself was largely responsible for his own martyrdom. Even his closest friends resented the regular bouts of sullenness, during which he refused to speak for days to anyone whose chance remark had irritated him, including his wife.

To a great extent, the furor surrounding Strauss's *Life of Jesus* was a direct result of his talents as a brilliant critic and elegant literary stylist. Above all he was extraordinarily thorough. He brought to his book a restrained but caustic irony that was reminiscent of Hermann Reimarus and Edward Gibbon, irreverently titling a chapter claiming to demythologize Jesus' water miracles "Sea-Stories and Fish-Stories." He was even more scornful of rationalists such as Paulus and Venturini, who had theorized that Jesus was practicing medicine rather than performing miracles when he purported to heal the sick. He particularly enjoyed gibing at Paulus, scoffing at his notion that a skilled physician of the first century—or any century—could restore a blind man's sight by the laying on of hands, even hands containing a powerful Essene-supplied salve:

> For a disease of the eyes, however slight, as it is only engendered gradually by the reiterated action of the disturbing cause, is [unlikely] to disappear on a word or a touch; it requires very complicated treatment, partly surgical, partly medical, and this must be pre-eminently the case with blindness, supposing it to be of a curable kind. How should we represent to ourselves the sudden restoration of vision to a blind eye by a word or a touch? As purely miraculous and magical? That would be to give up thinking on the subject. As magnetic? There is no precedent of magnetism having influence over a disease of this nature. Or, lastly, as psychical? But blindness is something so independent of the mental life, so entirely corporeal, that the idea of its removal at all, still less of its sudden reversal by means of a mental operation, is not to be entertained.[11]

Strauss's favorite technique was that of pitting the rationalists against the supernaturalists, and vice versa. In discussing the miracle of Jesus' feeding a crowd of more than 5,000 with five loaves of bread and two fishes, he first asserted that the meal could not have taken place historically because it contravened the laws of nature. He then proceeded to ridicule Paulus's rationalist argument that Jesus' better-provisioned listeners had spontaneously shared their lunch with those who had nothing to eat. After pointing out that the authors of the Gospels had intended to describe a miracle of multiplication and not an outburst of generosity, he concluded that the tale had to have been a literary invention inspired by the feeding stories in the Hebrew Scriptures: Moses' nourishing Israelites with manna in the Book of Exodus, the prophet Elijah's increasing a widow's supply of flour and oil as a reward for her hospitality in the First Book of Kings, and the prophet Elisha's feeding 100 men with twenty loaves of bread in the Second Book of Kings. "Nothing more is wanting to complete the mythical derivation of this history of the miraculous feeding of the multitude, except the proof, that the later Jews also believed of particularly holy men, that by their means a small amount of provision was made sufficient," he wrote.[12]

With his passion for detail, Strauss cut to shreds the Gospel stories of Jesus' birth, the accounts of his miracles, nearly all of his speeches, and the tales of his death and resurrection, which amounted to more than 90 different New Testament incidents. What was left was the bare Synoptic-derived outline of the life of a man who grew up in Nazareth, was baptized by John the Baptist, traveled throughout Palestine, gathered disciples, opposed the Pharisees, believed himself to be the Messiah and harbinger of God's kingdom, and in the end was crucified. The only narrations that Strauss viewed as historical were several of Jesus' teachings from the Synoptics, as he considered John's Gospel the most mythological and therefore the least reliable.

Strauss's broad-swath methodology of dismissing the stories not only if they contained overtly Christian or supernatural content, but also if they showed parallels with myths and legends from other cultures, has been roundly criticized by later scholars. Even Schweitzer, who thought highly of Strauss, commented astutely:

> For one thing, he overestimates the importance of the Old Testament motives in reference to the creative activity of the legend. He does not see that while in many cases he has shown clearly enough the source of the *form* of the narrative in question, this does not suffice to explain its *origin.* Doubtless, there is mythical material in the story of the feeding of the multitude. But the existence of this story is not explained by referring to the manna in the desert, or the miraculous feeding of a multitude by Elisha. The story in the Gospel has far too much individuality for that, and stands, moreover, in much too closely articulated an historical connexion. It must have as its basis some historical fact.[13]

While possessing the requisite techniques for discrediting the historicity of the Gospels, Strauss never developed a convincing means of identifying authentically historical material. Furthermore (as his 20th-century editor Peter C. Hodgson has noted), although he affected to despise the rationalist Jesus-biographers of his time, in many ways he himself was a kind of super-rationalist. As such, he was not above occasionally joining Paulus's camp and propounding his own naturalistic and psychological explanations for Jesus' miracles. Just like the rationalists, he was certain that those whom the Gospels described as possessed by demons were actually suffering from mental or nervous system disorders amenable to the sort of spontaneous cures that he derided the rationalists for concocting elsewhere.

Strauss's explanation of Jesus' resurrection was the most dramatic example of his willingness to psychologize away the supernatural when it suited his purposes. He was the first in a long line of 19th- and 20th-century scholars to define the resurrection in terms of mass hysteria on the part of the grieving disciples, whom he described as struggling to reconcile their exalted view of Jesus as Messiah with the ignominy of his crucifixion. He contended: "Now there spontaneously arose in them the psychological necessity of solving the contradiction between the ultimate fate of Jesus and their earlier opinion of him." In his view, the resurrection was the result of a psychic phenomenon whereby Jesus' followers, especially the women, experienced "actual visions" of their master.[14]

Despite his rejection of the Christian creeds and nearly the entire New Testament account of Jesus, Strauss still considered himself a Christian, albeit of an advanced sort. Like Hegel, he believed the Christian concept of Jesus as uniting the human and the divine represented an admirable and exalted human idea. Furthermore, he insisted that there was nothing fraudulent about the unconscious mythologizing that he assumed underlay the composition of the Gospels. As Peter Hodgson has pointed out, Strauss was perhaps the original "alienated theologian," an expression coined by Van A. Harvey in 1970 to describe a class of highly educated Christians who are as much doubters as believers.

Strauss fully expected his *Life of Jesus* to be welcomed by other Christian intellectuals yearning to free themselves of superannuated dogmas. He also hoped to promulgate his new form of Christianity, stripped down to its philosophical essence. At the very least, he expected that his work would bring him a full-fledged teaching position at Tübingen. In July of 1835, he was utterly horrified when he was sacked by the university before he had a chance to publish his second volume. Even more humiliating, he was obliged to earn his living teaching at a high school in his home town of Ludwigsburg.

Obviously, Strauss had seriously miscalculated the public's reaction to his *Life*. Not only did it offend traditionalist Christians as had been expected, but it also antagonized liberal Christians of the "mediating" persuasion, several of whom held important positions on the Tübingen faculty. As there was no railroad connection at the time between Ludwigsburg and Tübingen, Strauss's transfer was akin to being banished from academic circles. Although his rationalist mother stood by him, his father, who was to die some six years later, more or less stopped speaking to him. His old teacher, Baur, who had tried to negotiate a settlement between Strauss and his enemies at Tübingen, sought in vain to find an academic post for him at another university. Strauss could easily have transferred from the theology faculty to the philosophy faculty at Tübingen, but as was his nature, he refused to make the compromise.

In the rest of the country *The Life of Jesus* became a bestseller, avidly discussed in the libraries, coffee houses, and study groups where young intellectuals usually gathered. Not only was Strauss the first alienated theologian; he was also one of the first alienated *celebrities* making money from his doubts. At Tübingen, his dismissal had provoked a near-riot among the students. With copies of his book selling as soon as they left the presses, Strauss no longer needed to support himself by teaching. In 1836, he left the high school to bring out (with Baur) a revised edition of *The Life of Jesus*. He then moved to Stuttgart, where he began to indulge his latent artistic yearnings. While working as a drama critic for the liberal newspaper, he came into contact with the city's emancipated intelligentsia and theater-going bohemia, through whom he met Agnese Schebest.

The now-famous Strauss devoted part of his time to responding to a series of broadsides against his book, written by orthodox Christians, "right-wing" Hegelians, and even some of his former teachers at Tübingen (one of them called him "the Antichrist"), all of whom insisted that the Gospels could be read as historically accurate documents. He enjoyed the polemical battles and the opportunities they afforded for needling his theological enemies. He also became the toast of political radicals and "left-wing" Hegelians as far away as Berlin, who interpreted *The Life of Jesus* as a mortal blow to the German alliance of authoritarian state and subservient church. Indeed, it was Strauss himself who invented the phrase "left Hegelians" (with whom he proudly identified) in one of his many pamphlets. Strauss's demolition of the Christ of the Gospels in favor of a messianic—or populist—Jesus seemed a major victory for the left. In 1839, Friedrich Engels declared that he had "sworn loyalty to Strauss's flag,"[15] a position that he reiterated in his famous

1894 treatise, *On the History of Early Christianity,* in which he described the first Christians as a messianic sect of the poor and powerless that defied oppressive Roman rule.

One of Strauss's most fervent admirers was the biblical scholar Bruno Bauer (1809–1882), who was a struggling *Privatdozent* at the University of Berlin and an avowed right-wing Hegelian when *The Life of Jesus* first appeared in print. In one of the first reviews of *The Life,* written in 1835, Bauer upbraided Strauss for rejecting out of hand the miraculous aspect of Christianity. Five years later, however, in the wake of an intellectual crisis, he converted to Strauss's left-wing Hegelianism. By then a professor at the University of Bonn, he took Strauss's mythological theories about the Gospels so seriously that he came to believe that Jesus had never existed and Christianity itself was an invention of the second century. His 1840 treatise averring that the author of John's Gospel had been a disciple of Philo of Alexandria created such controversy that he was obliged to leave the university. He never taught again, retiring instead to a village near Berlin where he became a farmer and amateur pamphleteer.

Bruno Bauer's championing of Strauss's ideas was an academic anomaly. For the most part, the German New Testament scholars set out to prove that Strauss's theories were wrong. In 1837, Johann August Wilhelm Neander (1789–1850), a church historian at the University of Berlin and a leading "mediating" theologian, rushed into print a riposte to Strauss titled *The Life of Jesus Christ.* Born as David Mendel to a Jewish family in Göttingen, at the age of 17 he had read Schleiermacher's *Discourses on Religion,* whereupon he had himself baptized and took the surname "Neander" (the Greek word for "new man"). A devotee of Schleiermacher, he arranged to study with him at the University of Halle as a prelude to joining him on the Berlin faculty in 1813.

Neander's *Life of Jesus Christ,* which went into seven editions, was largely a paraphrase of Schleiermacher's lecture series on Jesus, which was as yet unpublished except in pirated versions such as the one that Strauss had read. Like Schleiermacher, Neander used the Gospel of John as his narrative outline, focusing on Jesus' increasing awareness of his oneness with God. "Jesus at a tender age studied the Old Testament," Neander wrote, but only as an adult did he realize he had a call to the Messiahship that "the limits of his circumstances and his times prevented him from fully comprehending."[16]

In an effort to explain Jesus' miracles, Neander determined upon a semi-rationalism that lay midway between Paulus and Strauss. In Neander's view, although Jesus' cures were genuine, he accomplished them by accelerating the natural process of healing through his unique spiritual powers. He depicted the individuals whom Jesus raised from the dead as having been in a "dormant" state, and Jesus' transfiguration as the hallucinations of his disciples. Most ingenious of all was his quasi-psychic, quasi-alchemistic interpretation of how Jesus had turned water into wine: "By his direct agency, he imputed to [the water] powers capable of producing the same effects [as wine]."[17]

Neander's book (as well as a study of John's Gospel published by the mythologist de Wette) inspired Strauss to moderate his position somewhat in the third edition of his *Life of Jesus.* His decision was also influenced by his good friend Ferdinand Christian Baur, who had become increasingly critical of his dismissal of the Gospels as folklore. Baur saw conscious artistry in the Gospels, especially in the Gospel of John, which he thought Strauss had treated rather cavalierly. Strauss took a more positive historical view of the Fourth Gospel in the third edition of his *Life,* published in 1838. He also dramatically altered his portrait of Jesus, eliminating the imputations of apocalyptic obsession and messianic fanaticism contained in the earlier editions, and at the same time endowing him with an exalted religious consciousness and supernatural healing powers that derived from hypnotism and mental telepathy.

At Baur's urging, Strauss was asked in February 1839 to join the theological faculty at the University of Zurich. Ironically, one of his main supporters was Paulus, the aged rationalist whom he had ridiculed so mercilessly in his *Life of Jesus*. Paulus did not seem to mind, however, and he saw the Zurich offer as a victory for academic freedom. Faculty liberals and progressive-minded burghers in Zurich were also squarely behind Strauss. The city's religious conservatives were outraged, however, and called for a plebiscite on his appointment. The antipathy of both the landed aristocracy and the pious peasantry resulted in a final vote of 39,225 to 1,048 against Strauss.

Although Zurich duly paid him a salary for the rest of his life, the embittered Strauss thereafter forswore any further compromises with traditional Christianity. In the fourth edition of the *The Life of Jesus,* published in 1840, he disposed of the "mediating" material in the third edition, and restored Jesus to his original fanatic status. That same year, he published the first volume of his *The Old Faith and the New,* a lengthy treatise in which he sought to demonstrate that Christian dogmas were historical creations rather than theological truths. He also overtly embraced a kind of pantheism.

In 1846, a young woman named Mary Ann Evans finished an English translation of the fourth edition of Strauss's *Life of Jesus*. Destined to become one of the most celebrated novelists of her time under the *nom de plume* George Eliot (1819–1880), in her early years she was merely a strong-willed, affectionate, earnest, and strikingly erudite young woman who kept house for her father in the Midlands town of Coventry, having left school at age 16 after her mother's death. Her father was a strict evangelical Anglican, and Evans as a teenager had been even stricter, refusing to attend the theater and concerts although she loved music and was herself a talented pianist. Instead, she steeped herself in literature, including the works of 18th-century freethinkers, and she began having doubts about the truth of the Christianity she had once embraced.

When Evans was 22, she announced to her father that she would no longer accompany him to church on Sunday. Deeply hurt, he stopped speaking to her. In the letter she wrote explaining her decision, she evidenced a high moral seriousness that functioned for her (as for many Victorian intellectuals) as a substitute for religious faith:

> I regard [the Gospels] as histories consisting of mingled truth and fiction, and while I admire much of what I believe to have been the moral teachings of Jesus himself, I consider the system of doctrines built upon the facts of his life and drawn as to its materials from Jewish notions to be most dishonorable to God and most pernicious in its influence on individual and social happiness. In thus viewing this important subject I am in unison with some of the finest minds in Christendom in past ages, and with the majority of such in the present (as an instance more familiar to you than any I could name I may mention Dr. [Benjamin] Franklin).[18]

Evans was so attached to her father that she offered to disinherit herself if it would bring about a reconciliation. Her father, for his part, was ready to turn her out of the house until her sister-in-law persuaded him to work out a truce with his freethinking daughter. She agreed to resume her churchgoing with the proviso that she could think as she liked during services.

Evans eventually became part of a local coterie of wealthy dilettantes, tradesmen and professionals and their wives and children, who dabbled in everything from Unitarianism and philanthropy to spiritualism and the brand-new "science" of phrenology (many of the set, including Evans herself, had their skulls measured). These clever, charming people were fascinated by Evans's brilliant, inquiring mind (she was a compulsive autodidact) and her growing theological radicalism. Although they themselves were not particularly accomplished in scholarship or the arts, their cronies included a vast array of 19th-century celebrities, such as Walter Scott, Samuel Taylor Coleridge, Charles Moore, Florence Nightingale, Ralph Waldo Emerson, and even Strauss and Paulus in Germany.

In 1844, one of Evans's new friends, Sara Sophia Hennell, asked her to take over the task of translating the fourth edition of Strauss's *Life of Jesus,* which had been arranged by Sara's brother, Charles Hennell, a prosperous London merchant who had embraced Unitarianism. In 1838, Hennell himself had published a deist-style life of Jesus titled *An Inquiry Into the Origins of Christianity,* which contended that Jesus had preached natural religion, his miracles were mythical, and the Christian creeds were obstacles to free thinking. Hennell had received financing for his book from Joseph Parkes, a Radical-party politician who was married to a granddaughter of the famous chemist-turned-Unitarian Joseph Priestley. Parkes believed that religion and politics were as intertwined in Britain as they were in Germany, and that disseminating Strauss's *Life of Jesus* would undermine both Anglican orthodoxy and landed-class hegemony.

During her teens, Evans had taught herself German and begun reading in the original some of the German "higher criticism" of the Bible. That, along with Hennell's *Inquiry,* had helped shatter her Christian faith. She also revered Strauss as a martyr: Like herself, he had been willing to suffer for his dissident religious views.

At that time, hardly anyone in England outside the high-level Unitarian circles in which Evans moved knew much about German philosophy, theology, or scholarship. The poet Samuel Taylor Coleridge had spent a year in Germany, in 1799, shortly after publishing "The Rime of the Ancient Mariner." He had learned the language and become enthralled with German literary culture, which was then at the height of *Sturm und Drang* Romanticism. When he returned to England, Coleridge became a kind of ambassador of German literature and German philosophy, translating Schiller and promoting the theories of Kant. Emerson also drew on Kantian Idealism to formulate his own version of transcendentalism in America. However Hegel was not translated into English until 1855, 24 years after his death.

Sara Hennell and another young woman, who were among the few English intellectuals fluent in German, had started the Strauss translation but had been daunted by Strauss's tedious methodology. After agreeing to take over the project, Evans spent the next two years working her way through

Strauss's German pages, which were dotted with quotations in Greek, Latin, and Hebrew. They were grueling years. Evans's father's health failed, her own health suffered, and she eventually became "Strauss-sick," as she confided to friends—tired of shredding to demythologized ribbons what she considered beautiful Gospel stories.

Not long after she started the translation, Evans traveled to Germany, where she was able to meet Strauss personally through her English connections. The 23-year-old Evans chuckled over the meeting in a letter back home: "I do not think it was kind to Strauss (I knew he was very handsome) to tell him that a *young lady* was translating his book."[19] When her translation (in supple English prose that still holds up today) appeared in print on June 15, 1846, her name was nowhere to be found and her pay was 20 pounds. Nonetheless, her work was so remarkable that she soon found herself at the center of English intellectual life.

The Life of Jesus was as much a *succès de scandale* in England as it had been in Germany, not only because religious apostasy was fashionable among the English intelligentsia, but also because Strauss's Hegelian theories about Christianity's development fed into a distinctly Victorian fascination with material development and progress. John Chapman, the publisher of Evans's translation, was a tall, handsome young man who lived off his wife's money from the Nottingham lace industry while collecting mistresses, writers, and theological rebels of every sort. In 1851, he bought the *Westminster Review,* a literary quarterly that perennially posted losses (especially under Chapman, a notoriously poor businessman) but was England's most prestigious outlet for progressive writing and positivist philosophy. A typical article was John Stuart Mill's famous essay on the emancipation of women, which was published in 1851, the year that Chapman took over the *Review.*

Chapman persuaded Evans to contribute articles to the *Review.* After her father's death in 1849, he talked her into moving to London, where she boarded with him and his family, and worked for next to nothing doing the lion's share of the editing on the *Review.* Soon after her arrival, Chapman began visiting her in her room to take German lessons at all sorts of odd hours. Although the long-faced Evans was not pretty by anyone's standards, she had a knack for turning intellectual friendships with men into ardent attachments that made wives and mistresses jealous. When she met David Strauss for the second time several years later, he, too, was smitten with her.

At the offices of the *Review,* Evans met the philosopher and *Economist* editor Herbert Spencer (1820–1903), and promptly fell in love with him. Although the two became close (and probably intimate), the eugenics-obsessed Spencer decided that Evans was not good-looking enough for him to marry.

In 1850, Spencer published his *Social Statics,* a philosophically based theory of evolution that predated Darwin's theory of natural selection by a full nine years. For Spencer, a trained scientist as well as a philosopher, evolution was a materialist version of the Hegelian *Geist*—a dynamic force that tied the universe together at every level. He also believed that evolution was the guiding force behind human progress and development. In his *Social Statics,* Spencer wrote, "Progress, therefore, is not an accident, but a necessity. . . . It is part of nature."[20] Darwin borrowed his famous phrase "the survival of the fittest" from an 1862 biology textbook written by Spencer, and inserted it into an 1869 revision of *The Origin of the Species.*

While Spencer's theories of eugenics may have terminated his romance with Evans, the two became close friends. Spencer introduced her to George Henry Lewes, a journalist, amateur zoologist, and free-love enthusiast (until his wife bore two children to the co-owner of his newspaper). As Lewes could not or would not divorce his wife, Evans moved in with him and lived as his surrogate spouse from 1854 until his death in 1878. For several years—until Spencer quarreled with Lewes—he, Evans, and Lewes were a powerful intellectual triumvirate in London. Their ideas resonated against each other, and obliquely worked their way into George Eliot's novels, with their overriding sense of moral purpose and brilliantly imagined world that quivered with spiritual intensity but contained no specific sense of divine presence.

While her father lay dying, Evans had translated Spinoza's *Treatise on Religious and Political Philosophy* from the Latin in order to distract herself. During the mid-1850s, she and Lewes collaborated (with Evans doing most of the work) on a translation of another of Spinoza's treatises titled *Ethics.* Spinoza's pantheism, as well as his skepticism about the historicity of the Bible, meshed with Herbert Spencer's fervor for evolution, Evans's embrace of spirituality without religion, and the scientific positivism that Lewes had taken up while translating Comte's *Philosophy of the Sciences* and pursuing his quintessentially Victorian hobby, dissecting marine fauna. In 1854, Evans translated Feuerbach's *The Essence of Christianity,* which was to be the last of such endeavors before her novels transformed her from underpaid bluestocking into a rich and formidable literary figure. Through Strauss's Jesus and Feuerbach's militant atheism, Evans single-handedly introduced "left-wing" Hegelianism to English-language readers. However, it was left-wing

Hegelianism without Hegel, who was still untranslated as of 1854. It was also intertwined with the thoroughly Victorian fascination with material progress and moral uplift. Toward the end of his life, David Strauss would go down the same path, abandoning his own Hegelian metaphysics in favor of a purely materialistic evolutionary theory that rivaled anything coming out of England. Mary Ann Evans, his translator and worshipper, who was now the far greater intellectual personage George Eliot, had in a certain sense outdone him.

7

A GOOD LIBERAL

Strauss's *Life of Jesus* had virtually no effect on New Testament scholarship in Germany during the 19th century. His portrait of a delusional Jesus was highly disturbing to the liberal Christians who staffed university theology departments. Moreover, Strauss himself no longer had any academic affiliations with which to bolster his stature. By and large, the Jesus-researchers at the German universities ignored Strauss and continued as they had before 1835, finding at least some historical truth in the Gospels and depicting Jesus as a fellow liberal.

Indeed, during the late 1830s, the German "liberal life" of Jesus took on a standard format, invented by Christian Hermann Weisse (1801–1866), a professor at the University of Leipzig, which would survive until the end of the century. In 1838, Weisse and another academic, Christian Gottlob Wilke (1786–1854), published separate books in which they argued that any credible life of Jesus should be based on Mark's Gospel, since it was the first to have been written. Their theory of "Marcan priority" was revolutionary for its time. The poet Herder had considered Mark the most primitive of the canonical Gospels because it most faithfully transmitted the essence of the oral *Ur*-Gospel. Johann Griesbach had argued to the contrary that as a condensation of Matthew and Luke, Mark was the third of the Gospels. Schleiermacher had maintained that John was the most accurate of the Gospels. Baur and Strauss had held to the traditional position that Matthew's Gospel was the first to have been composed.

Christian Wilke, a onetime Lutheran pastor who converted to Catholicism in 1846, was more theologically conservative than Weisse. He devoted his 1838 book, *The Ur-Evangelist,* to an attack on both Herder's and Griesbach's theories. He contended that the Gospel of Mark, which displayed considerable thematic organization and artistic unity, was itself the *Ur*-Gospel, and that an oral version had never existed. He also noted that Matthew and Luke generally followed Mark's narrative outline when they used material that also appeared in Mark, which for him was evidence that Mark had been written first.

Weisse shared neither Wilke's theological conservatism nor his modesty of aim. He had been trained in philosophy rather than theology and was an avowed "right-wing" Hegelian. His *Gospel History Treated Critically and Philosophically,* which was the result of research carried out when he left Leipzig after having been denied a promotion (he later returned and became a full professor in 1845), was not simply an argument for Marcan priority. Unlike Wilke, Weisse did not believe that Mark's Gospel displayed any particular artistic sophistication. On the contrary, it was relatively short (just over half the length of Matthew and Luke), written in rough-and-ready Greek, and far less literary than the other two Synoptic Gospels. Weisse believed that Mark's Gospel had come first because it was the least literary and the most primitive in style. He also invented what has come to be known as the "two-document hypothesis" of Synoptic composition, theorizing that Luke and Matthew, who shared about one-fifth of their non-Marcan material, had relied not only on Mark but on a second written source that had become lost.

Besides trying to refute Herder and Griesbach, Weisse also attempted to reconstruct a more coherent historical Jesus than that of Strauss. Although he believed, like Strauss, that all the Gospels contained mythical material, he also maintained that Mark's composition reflected a reliable historical tradition. For one thing, Mark usually referred to Jesus as a "teacher" rather than as "lord," indicating perhaps that he had a less exalted and mythical view of Jesus than the other three evangelists. Furthermore, the oldest texts of Mark contained no stories of Jesus' post-resurrection appearances, but only the tale of his empty tomb.

Weisse's Jesus, as portrayed in both the *Gospel History* and in his *Present Position of the Problem of the Gospels,* which was published in 1856, was a visionary who personified the Hegelian ideal of the God-man without being embarrassingly supernatural. To counter Strauss's contention that Jesus was fanatically obsessed with visions of the end of time, Weisse argued that Jesus' many references in the Synoptics to judgment and God's kingdom did not refer to a coming supernatural event, but rather to his own spiritual transformation and possibly that of his followers.

Although Weisse used the time-tested liberal technique of rationalizing away the miracles reported in Mark and the other Synoptics, he did so in a far more sophisticated fashion than Paulus and his ilk. Furthermore, unlike Strauss, he treated the miracles as myths with kernels of historical truth, such as the story of the loaves and fishes, which he contended had possibly grown out of sayings of Jesus that alluded to miraculous feedings. Most notable was Weisse's interpretation of Jesus' resurrection. Paulus had maintained that Jesus had not died, and that his rising was a trick of two nails and two Essenes, while Strauss had argued that Jesus had died, and that his resurrection was a myth that had developed from the disciples' grieving. Weisse believed instead that Jesus' disciples had actually seen their resurrected master, but the question of whether their visions were founded on reality or illusion was "beyond the confines of purely historical criticism." He added: "[T]he resurrection of Jesus is a fact which belongs to the domain of the spiritual and psychic life, and which is not related to outward corporeal existence in such a way that the body which was laid in the grave could have shared therein."[1] Weisse thus sailed skillfully between Paulus and Strauss, turning Jesus' resurrection, like his messianic status and his "kingdom," into a strictly spiritual phenomenon.

Weisse's theories carried the day in 19th-century German New Testament scholarship. In 1863, Heinrich Julius Holtzmann (1832–1910), a professor of theology at Heidelberg, published a massive treatise titled *The Synoptic Gospels* that used detailed linguistic analysis to support both Marcan priority and the two-document hypothesis. With Mark in ascendancy, the Gospel of John was banished to the sidelines of irrelevancy as a source of historical information about Jesus and his time. The Gospel of Matthew retained its primacy only among tradition-bound Catholic scholars, a handful of Protestant academics, and the thinning ranks of Ferdinand Christian Baur's Tübingen school. In fact, Marcan priority and the two-document hypothesis are still the regnant theories of Synoptic composition to this very day.

Holtzmann gave a crisply defined, Mark-derived "plot" to Weisse's looser psychological portrait of Jesus, going so far as to break down Jesus' ministry into seven separate stages during which the revelation of his messianic nature, at first a secret among the disciples, became ever more clear as he journeyed through Galilee. Like Weisse, Holtzmann took pains to demonstrate that contrary to what Strauss had argued, Jesus' growing self-awareness had nothing to do with any apocalyptic expectations of cataclysm or his own second coming. In his view, the "kingdom" to which Jesus alluded was an ideal human society, and not a vision of God's rule. "To wish to found a theocracy in the midst of the Roman Empire would have been the fantasy of a fanatic," Holtzmann wrote.[2]

According to Holtzmann, the Synoptic Gospels described "a manifold and progressive development of a life whose driving principle is shaped by the religio-moral factor that operates with a power that completely divests itself of all the theological disputations and scholastic opinions of his day."[3] While Weisse's Jesus had retained some traces of the Hegelian God-man, Holtzmann's was a plain theological liberal who preached a universal moral code that transcended any particular religious dogma. His divinity was attenuated to a mere consciousness of a divine mission to improve the human race.

After Holtzmann, "liberal lives" of Jesus continued to flow from the German academic presses up to the turn of the century. These "biographies" were all more or less similar in content and form to that of their predecessor. Using the Gospel of Mark as their narrative skeleton, they portrayed Jesus as a man of humble origins who discovered only in adulthood that he had a divine calling, which he gradually revealed to his disciples with the instruction that they keep it secret. While his miracles were mostly psychic phenomena, his teachings bore a close resemblance to the "fatherhood-of-God–brotherhood-of-men" message of the deist Jesus of the 18th century. Indeed, Jesus' messianic aims were so "spiritualized" that they amounted to little more than a sense of ethical mission. One of the Jesus-biographers, Gustav Volkmar of the University of Zurich (1809–1893), went so far as to theorize in his *Jesus of Nazareth and the Origins of Christianity* (1882) that Jesus had never made any claims to be the Messiah, and was only attempting to reform the legalistic Judaism of his time. All the apocalyptic language in the Gospels was toned down to the point where it pertained merely to the community of selflessness and tolerance that Jesus hoped to see realized on earth. In an 1864 book titled *Jesus Christ and the Messianic Beliefs of His Time,* another of the biographers, Timothée Colani of the University of Strasbourg (1824–1880), argued that Jesus had never even uttered most of the apocalyptic statements attributed to him in the Gospels. Once again in the tradition of Weisse, Jesus' resurrection was treated as a spiritual experience on the part of his disciples that could not be proved or disproved historically. In the end, the Jesus of the liberal lives was so *un*-fanatical that Albert Schweitzer dubbed him the "bourgeois Messiah."[4]

Some of the liberal lives were far more imaginative than others. Theodor Keim (1825–1878), a theology professor at Zurich, made a trip to Nazareth to conduct field research for his 1,700-page *History of Jesus of Nazara,* which appeared in three volumes from 1867 to 1872. He used his observations of 19th-century Nazarenes (mostly Maronite Christians), whose "beauty," "cleanliness," "courtesy," and "toleration" had greatly impressed him, to speculate about the village's formative influence on Jesus' psyche nearly two millennia earlier.[5] In so doing, Keim depicted the early months of Jesus' ministry as a "Galilean springtime," which was followed by a "Galilean storm" as his enemies gathered strength, and culminated in a very bad last winter in Jerusalem. Good liberal that he was, Keim characterized Jesus' message in generalized, anti-dogmatic terms as "the religion of humility, of freedom, of humanity."[6]

Underlying all the biographies was a universal condemnation of the Jews. In the minds of the liberal Protestants, first-century Judaism was a stand-in for Catholicism and other forms of orthodox religion. Ritualistic, legalistic, and censorious, it had been based on the doctrine of justification by works (obedience to Torah) à la Catholicism, in contrast to the Protestant doctrine of justification by faith.

By the end of the century, the theories about the historical development of Judaism propounded by David Strauss's old friend Wilhelm Vatke at the University of Berlin had become deeply entrenched in German scholarship. The reigning Old Testament scholar was Julius Wellhausen (1844–1918), a former Lutheran pastor who had broken with Christian orthodoxy and become a theology professor at the universities of Marburg and Göttingen. A formidable text analyst and creative theoretician, he adopted Vatke's position that the Pentateuch was the last section of the Hebrew Scriptures to have been composed, arguing that it displayed such an overwhelming obsession with rules of behavior that it had to have represented a late and decadent stage of Judaism. Wellhausen believed that the ancient Hebrews had been far more free-spirited and genuinely religious than the Second Temple Jews.

As I pointed out in a previous chapter, secularized European intellectuals had been denigrating Judaism as retrograde since Enlightenment times, and Wellhausen's ideas about the Old Testament only strengthened their convictions. In his article on "Israel" for the ninth edition of the *Encyclopaedia Britannica,* he characterized Judaism as a pathological religious system founded on invented history, and Jesus' message as a "protest against the ruling tendency of Judaism" in the name of "another principle of morality, that of the service of one's neighbor."[7] As Wellhausen's comments indicate, implicit anti-Semitism was often built into the liberal portrait of Jesus.

As the notion of the liberal Jesus took hold in German academia, David Strauss found himself on the intellectual sidelines. As early as 1840, he was quarreling with other left-wing Hegelians, especially the Marx-Engels faction, and he was particularly annoyed that Bruno Bauer, who now claimed that Jesus had never existed, was becoming the new darling of the political left. Strauss was further alienated by the political turmoil of the 1840s in Germany and elsewhere in Europe, which was marked by rioting in the streets and a growing nationalistic fervor. While Strauss's theological views were unconventional, his political sympathies lay with the order-obsessed Prussian monarchy in Berlin, even though he loathed the reigning king, Frederick William IV. His own vision of a united Germany was that of an expanded Prussia. When an anti-Prussian, anti-Austrian, socialism-fueled rebellion swept southern Germany in 1848, Strauss had been elected to represent his home town of Ludwigsburg in the Württemberg assembly. He infuriated the pro-democracy majority by supporting the use of troops to quell the 1848 riots. He also disquieted his rightist allies by picking unnecessary fights with the radicals. He resigned ignominiously within months of taking his seat.

At the same time, Strauss had become wealthy from the royalties from *The Life of Jesus,* which he had invested with his younger brother, Wilhelm, who had a head for business (unlike their father) and a thriving sugar refinery in Cologne. He had married Agnese Schebest in 1842, she enchanted by his celebrity and he by her looks. Five years, two children, and countless quarrels later, the mismatched couple separated, but the Catholic Schebest refused to agree to a divorce. Strauss was too prudish to take a mistress and too self-absorbed to endure his marital woes stoically, so he sulked in self-pity.

He spent the 1850s roaming restlessly from one German city to another, including Munich, Weimar, Cologne, Heidelberg, Berlin, Heilbronn, and Darmstadt, while writing biographies of nonconformists whom he viewed as fellow victims of religious and political obscurantism. Finally, he enmeshed himself in the cause of pro-Prussian nationalism to the point of obsession, even turning against his native Württemberg for refusing to ally itself with Bismarck's Berlin-based German-unification strategy.

Strauss did not return to New Testament theology until the 1860s, when his publisher suggested that he produce an updated version of *The Life of Jesus* to mark the 30th anniversary of the original. In 1864, he issued his *Life of Jesus for the German People,* whose very title (translated into English as *A New Life of Jesus*) reflected the spirit of nationalism that had become Strauss's new faith. Intended to be a "popular" book that would appeal to educated lay people rather than professional biblical scholars, it was dedicated to his businessman-brother Wilhelm. "I consider him as a representative of the people, believing that among the German people, for whom the book is destined, there are many like himself, many who find their best solace after a day of toil in serious reading," Strauss wrote.[8]

As a book designed for a general readership, the *New Life of Jesus* widely missed its mark. Of its nearly 900 pages (not counting several lengthy prefaces), he devoted more than 200 to an explanation of his own critical methodology, and over 400 to a highly technical elucidation of what he viewed as mythical material in the Gospels. Nor did the *New Life of Jesus* go down well with biblical scholars. Strauss had not kept up with the new trends that had taken hold since his original *Life* had appeared in 1835. Most significantly, he refused to give credence to the theory of Marcan priority, which by 1864 was Holy Writ in German theological circles. He maintained that the proponents of Marcan priority advocated a return to the supernaturalistic interpretation of the Gospels. He continued to insist that Matthew's Gospel had been the first to be composed, a position that the academic world ridiculed as amateurish and even crankish.

Furthermore, Strauss's view of Christianity had changed. No longer did he see himself as an alienated theologian with a mission to reform the faith. He now considered Christianity as a "crutch" for the feeble-minded and looked forward to the day when "the public mind" would be "emancipated from superstition, and initiated into a purely human culture."[9] Strauss had supplanted his youthful Hegelianism with Darwinism, or, more precisely, Herbert Spencer's social Darwinism, which dovetailed perfectly with his certainty that the German people exemplified the highest development of the human race.

Accordingly, Strauss eliminated his earlier Jesus who had believed himself to be the Jewish Messiah, and replaced him with a Jesus characterized by a "Hellenic element," with a "beautiful nature from the first which had only to develop itself out of itself."[10] Moreover, Strauss's new Jesus was now a stellar example of the "purely human culture" that Strauss hoped would supersede religion: "While Jesus was forming within himself this cheerful tone of mind, identical with that of God, comprehending all men as brothers, he had realized in himself the prophetic ideal of a new covenant with the law written in the heart."[11] With his belief in the brotherhood of man and his advocacy of a universal moral code—and even his opposition to Judaism—Strauss's Jesus was not very different from the Jesus of the "liberal lives" that his scholarly contemporaries were writing, or the philosophical hero of Rousseau and Kant, or the preacher of natural religion of the deists. Strauss's new Jesus for the German people was yet another liberal.

The year 1864 also marked the publication of the lectures on the life of Jesus that Friedrich Schleiermacher had delivered so long ago at the University of Berlin (as well as at least 25 other Jesus-biographies, as Albert Schweitzer noted). By the mid-1860s, Schleiermacher's literalistic rationalizing of Jesus' miracles was hopelessly outdated, but his genial "mediating" theology was back in fashion. The following year Strauss, who had always found Schleiermacher's theology contemptible, dashed off a scathing critique titled *The Christ of Faith and the Jesus of History,* in which he reiterated his original thesis that it was impossible for a historical figure to embody the ideal of humanity at one with God. "The ideal of the dogmatic Christ on the one hand and the historical Jesus on the other are separated forever," Strauss argued, adding that Schleiermacher's Christ of faith was "only a memory from a long-forgotten time, like the light of a distant star which still strikes the eye today although the body from which it shone has been out for years."[12] However, his new Jesus, the moral hero of unbelievers, was not so very different from Schleiermacher's moral hero of Christians.

In 1872, the year before he died, Strauss published a tract called *The Old Faith and the New,* in which he openly embraced Darwin's principle of natural selection as a substitute for a personal God, speculating that Christianity would soon be replaced by the worship of the ever-evolving and ever-improving "All," as he called the universe. Written just after the double Bismarckian triumph of German unification and the humbling of France in the Franco-Prussian war of 1870–71, Strauss's last religious manifesto was a paean not only to Darwinian progressivism but also to the new Germany, which he depicted as a kind of Periclean utopia wherein every man was a philosopher. No longer was there a need for the consolation of Christianity, as the German people now could find spiritual sustenance in their literature and music, Strauss wrote.

In a chapter titled "Are We Still Christians?" (the answer was no), Strauss once again altered his portrait of the historical Jesus, maintaining now that he was *not* the moral leader he had delineated in his 1864 book, but rather the fanatic figure he had portrayed in 1835: "The word long ago ceased to have the disparaging and derisive connotation which it had in the last century; there have been noble and ingenious fanatics; a fanatic can stimulate, can improve things; the result of his actions can be quite long-lasting; but we would not choose such a man to be our guide in life."[13]

One of the most trenchant critics of *The Old Faith and the New* was Friedrich Nietzsche (1844–1900). The one thing that could be said about Nietzsche was that he was not a liberal. At age 20, as a theology student at the University of Bonn, he had read Strauss's 1864 *Life of Jesus,* whose debunking of the Gospels had so overwhelmed him that he refused to take communion the following Easter, abandoned his ministerial studies, and transferred to the University of Leipzig, where he became a classicist and philosopher.

The New Faith and the Old repelled Nietzsche, who viewed Strauss's self-satisfied accolade to the new German bourgeoisie as a repudiation of the tragic sense of life, which Nietzsche as a classicist considered an integral and ennobling part of human experience. In an 1873 essay that was perhaps instigated by his friend Richard Wagner, whose music Strauss openly disliked, Nietzsche derided Strauss as a "philistine," and a poor German stylist to boot.

The 20th-century Swiss theologian Karl Barth, another severe critic of German liberal theology, perhaps had the final say on Strauss: "And almost the last thing there is to be said about the nontragic quality of his general attitude . . . is that he did not even have the qualifications of a true evil heretic. It is that the result of all his negations was by no means an appalling Promethean uproar, but for all his attempted flat denials of God always only this self-conscious intellectual bourgeois quality, which was always morose, without the slightest notion of all the true heights and depths of life, the bourgeois quality in its specific national German form at the sunset hour of the age of Goethe, upon which Nietzsche then poured such cruel scorn as the embodiment of the 'philistine of culture!'"[14]

Although Strauss's final work went through six editions, it, like all the others, had little effect on the German New Testament academy. As the 19th century drew to a close, the liberal historical Jesus had triumphed. In fact, he had become the Christ of liberal faith. If liberal Christians could not believe in creeds or doctrine, they could believe in a man of exemplary character. Wilhelm Hermann (1848–1922), a theology professor at the University of Marburg, summed up the new liberal Christianity as one that focused on the supposed "inner life" of the historical Jesus rather than the dogmatic propositions about him that traditional Christianity had later devised. "We, for our part, become conscious of God's communion with us most distinctly by the fact that the Person of Jesus reveals itself to us through the power of his inner life," Hermann wrote.[15] Liberal Christians were inspired by Jesus, but they did not worship him as traditionalist Christians had. Instead they prided themselves on worshipping God the father *with* Jesus through the Lord's Prayer that he had composed.

At century's end, the dean of liberal German biblical scholarship was Adolf von Harnack (1851–1930), a Lutheran pastor and church historian on the faculty of the University of Berlin. Harnack was a student of Albrecht Ritschl, the former disciple of Ferdinand Christian Baur, through whom he imbibed something of Baur's (and Hegel's) deterministic view of historical forces. Harnack was the personification of a 19th-century German scholar. He was a fervent Prussian (and German) patriot who served as director of the Prussian State Library from 1905 to 1921 and from 1911 until his death as president of the Kaiser Wilhelm Society for the Advancement of Science (now known as the Max Planck Institute), the research foundation that, together with many charitable activities, financed the development of poison gas during World War I. Harnack believed unequivocally in the sacred cause of the German military effort. He was at the same time a quintessential theological latitudinarian who told his students that he wished the Lutherans would abandon the Apostles' Creed with its old-fashioned supernaturalistic dogmas and focus instead on Jesus' inner life and teachings.

During the academic year 1899–1900, Harnack delivered an enormously popular lecture series called "The Essence of Christianity" (the same as Feuerbach's famous book, coincidentally), whose published version (*What Is Christianity?* in English) sold 73,000 copies during the first year, eventually going into 14 editions. According to Harnack, "the whole of Jesus' message"[16] consisted of trust in a benevolent God coupled with love of one's fellow man. True Christianity, the Christianity that Jesus preached, "contains no statutory or particularistic elements; . . . *it is, therefore, religion itself.*"[17]

Harnack also maintained that the second-century heretic Marcion, who had tried to eliminate the Old Testament from the Christian Bible, was actually a great reformer along the lines of Martin Luther, who had also founded his theology on the letters of Paul. Marcion had merely sought to reinstate the original message of Jesus and Paul: that the God of love had no real interest in legal or doctrinal niceties. It was perhaps fitting that the culmination of 19th-century German academic theology was the attempted reinstatement of an anti-Jewish polemicist by a fervent German nationalist.

In 1905, the German novelist Gustav Frenssen (1863–1945), a former Lutheran pastor in Schleswig-Holstein, published a novel called *Holyland,* a turgid fictionalization of stifling daily life on the bleak North Sea. Its hero is a theology student and intellectual at the University of Berlin named Kai Jans. After a local beauty breaks his heart, Jans sails for the African colonies, leaving behind a manuscript of the life of Jesus that he has written "in accordance with the results of German research" and "entirely from the historical point of view."[18] However, Jan's manuscript is not really about Jesus, but about Germany. For Jans (and probably for his creator as well), the life of Jesus is no more than a nationalistic allegory, a literary effort to "weld together the discordant elements, Christianity and the German race," as a "foundation of the German Renascence."[19] David Strauss and Adolph von Harnack would have approved.

As the examples of Harnack and Frenssen illustrate, Jesus scholarship in Germany was inextricably linked to nationalism, imperialism, and local culture. However, given the prestige of German universities and philosophical ideologies throughout the Western world, the countless German "lives of Jesus" were soon being read by the rest of Europe and the mainline Protestant churches of North America. Even certain Catholics who wanted to be thought forward-looking endorsed liberal Protestant theories. Alfred Loisy (1857–1940), a priest and theology professor at the Collège de France who was excommunicated by the Vatican for "Modernist" heresy in 1908, repudiated the entire Nicene Creed except for the statement that Jesus was crucified under Pontius Pilate. In a book published shortly before his death, Loisy characterized Jesus' resurrection in good liberal Protestant style as a delusion of his disciples brought on by an intense belief in him that could not be shaken by his death: "[F]aith declared him living forever, because faith itself was determined never to die."[20]

In Britain, George Eliot and her set were not the only intellectuals to be bowled over by the "higher biblical criticism" emanating from Germany. In 1865, Matthew Arnold (1822–1888) argued in his *Essays in Criticism* that it was impossible for German scholars to be anything other than strictly objective because "there is a great force of critical opinion controlling a learned man's vagaries and keeping him straight."[21] However, German biblical scholarship had far less effect on academic and ecclesiastical circles in Victorian Britain than it did elsewhere, since the country's leading theologians tended to be conservatives. Among them was Joseph Barber Lightfoot (1828–1889) of Cambridge University, who helped to destroy many of the factual underpinnings of Baur's Hegelian account of early Christian history. Moreover, the "Broad Church" Anglican movement, based on a rationalistic version of Christianity that stressed the ethical teachings of Jesus rather than creeds and rituals, was never highly popular.

While the Victorian age produced numerous "lives of Jesus," most were conventionally devotional. One notable exception was *Ecce Homo: A Survey of the Life and Works of Jesus Christ,* published in 1865 by John Robert Seeley, a Latin professor at University College in London who undertook a psychological portrait of Jesus as a teacher, in a cautious version of the German "liberal lives." Another was *The Jesus of History* by Richard Davies Hanson (1869), who borrowed certain of Strauss's theories in depicting a Jesus whose concerns were "self-respect" rather than traditional Christian "humility," and "self-assertion" rather than Christian "self-denial."[22]

By the early 20th century, however, the tenets of German historical criticism had established a firm foothold in England. The theory that Mark's Gospel was the first to be written had gained almost universal acceptance, as had the notion that Matthew and Luke had used a second source, which the German scholars now called "Q" from *die Quelle,* the German word for "source" (Harnack had even "reconstructed" the text of Q in 1907). During the years between the World Wars, a group of Oxford University scholars led by divinity professor William Sanday made their own foray into "source criticism," as the new German discipline devoted to the literary origins of the Gospels had come to be called. Among them was Burnett Hillman Streeter (1874–1937), a fellow of Queen's College and a famously liberal churchman eager to reconcile religion and modernity. In 1924, he published a 600-page book titled *The Four Gospels: A Study of Origins,* which summarized the results of scientific study of the New Testament in both Germany and England. Many of Streeter's conclusions came straight from Germany, including his theories that Mark's Gospel was the most historically reliable, that the text of Q could in fact be reconstructed (which he himself attempted), and that John's Fourth Gospel was a devotional work influenced by Hellenistic philosophy rather than a credible narration of the life of Jesus. However, he went

Perhaps the oldest surviving "portrait" of Jesus is this third-century graffito from an imperial building on Rome's Palatine Hill, probably scrawled by a soldier in the Roman army. Underneath the crude drawing of a crucified figure with an ass's head, before which a man stands in prayer, the amateur artist wrote a wisecrack in Greek: "Alexamenos worships God." Throughout the Roman Empire, aristocrats and common folk alike found the Christian deification of a condemned man disgusting.

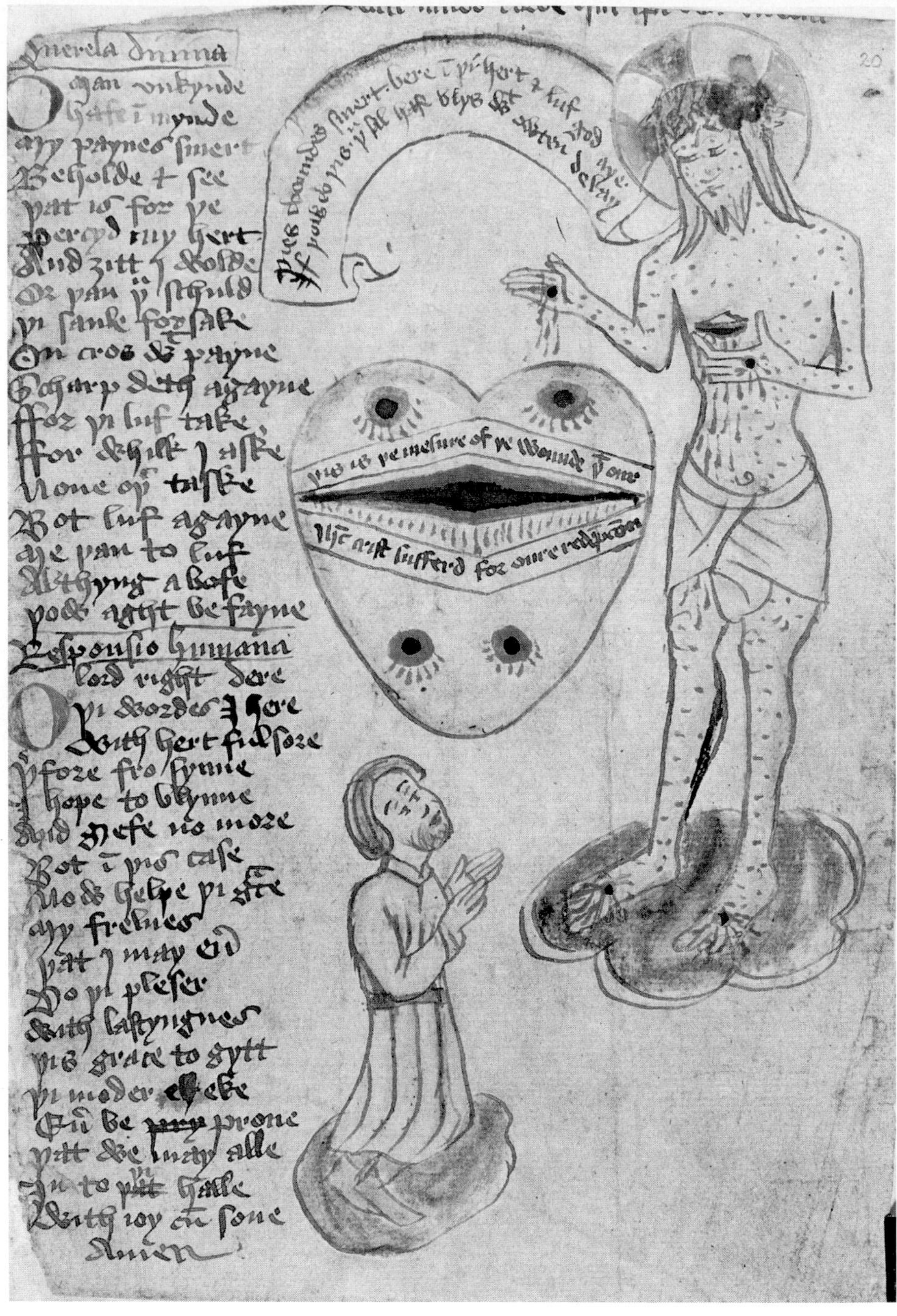

This illustration from a 14th-century manuscript of English religious poetry is also probably the work of an amateur. The figure of Jesus, crowned with thorns and covered from head to foot with the wounds of the passion, offers his heart like a valentine to the kneeling figure below: "Behold & see / that is for thee / piercéd my heart." In contemplating the human sufferings of Jesus on the cross and the divine love they represented, medieval Europeans came to terms with the central theological paradox of Christianity—that God had become a human being like themselves.

Thanks to Napoleon's conquest of Egypt in 1798, the Near East became easily accessible to Western travelers; numerous 19th-century artists and writers went to the Holy Land and incorporated the exotica they found there into their versions of Jesus' life. Among them was the French painter James Joseph Jacques Tissot (1836–1902), whose hyperrealistic "Sojourn in Egypt," depicting Mary and the boy Jesus at an Egyptian harbor, was one of a series of paintings growing out of his 11 months of travel and research in Palestine, Syria, Lebanon, and Egypt. Like others of his era, Tissot succumbed to the myth of the "timeless Orient" and assumed that little had changed in the Near East since Jesus' day, including the kind of clothes people wore.

The questers for the historical Jesus have tended to find a Jesus exactly like themselves. The Jesus of the Boston art-photographer F. Holland Day *was* Day himself. In the summer of 1898 he starved himself to emaciation, grew his hair to shoulder length, and had himself "nailed" (tied with leather thongs, actually) to a large wooden cross, holding a shutter bulb in one of his outstretched hands to take the above picture and others, while a supporting cast of friends and professional actors posed at his feet in "authentic" costumes made in Egypt.

The photographs Day took of himself as Jesus on the cross included a montage of close-ups titled *The Seven Last Words*. In "Father, Forgive Them, For They Know Not What They Do" (Luke 23:34), Day in his crown of thorns rolls his eyes heavenward. The series, though derided by critics, had a cinematic freeze-frame look that prefigured the biblical movies soon to flow from the studios of the nascent film industry.

The first Hollywood version of the life of Jesus, Cecil B. DeMille's *King of Kings* (1927), continued a 19th-century tradition, invented by Ernest Renan in his *Vie de Jésus*, of using the figure of Mary Magdalene to infuse the story of Jesus with eroticism. The Magdalene of DeMille's film, played by Jacqueline Logan (top of page), is a scantily clad harlot encrusted with art deco jewels. Even after she forsakes her life of sin, her raven tresses cascade fetchingly over Jesus' feet as she anoints them (below).

In Hollywood's most recent (to date) version of the life of Jesus, Martin Scorsese's *The Last Temptation of Christ* (1988), eroticism has become explicit. Barbara Hershey as Mary Magdalene, resplendent in eighties glitter as pictured above, has turned to prostitution out of frustrated love for Jesus, and she tortures him by taking her clothes off in front of him and trying to lure him to her bed. Scorsese's Jesus (played by Willem Dafoe, right) reflects the view of Jesus presented in Nikos Kazantzakis' novel *The Last Temptation*: a tormented 20th-century artist much like Kazantzakis himself.

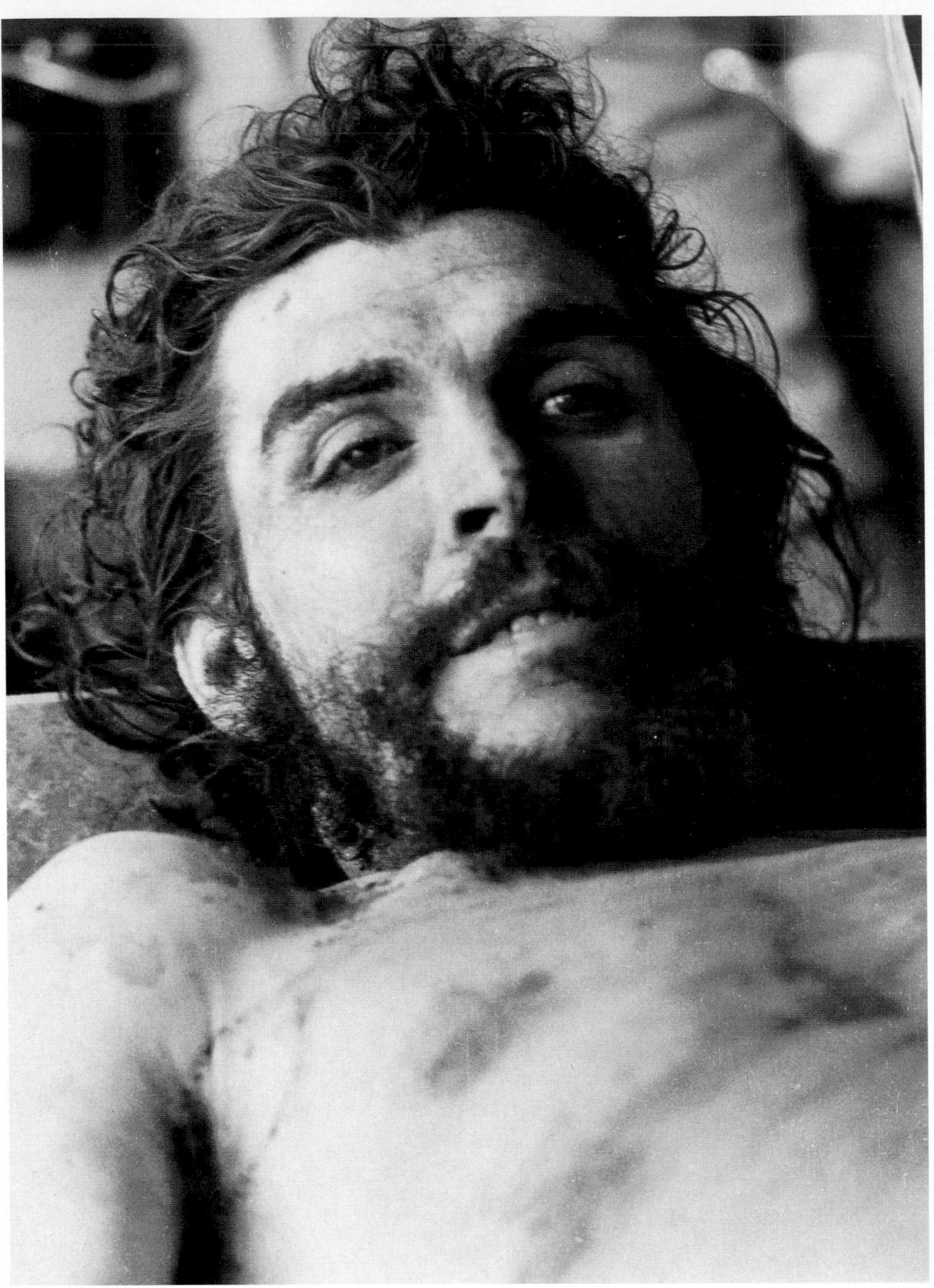

This famous close-up of the corpse of Che Guevara, taken by the photographer Freddy Alborta a few hours after his execution by the Bolivian military in 1967, endowed the dead Cuban revolutionary with a Christlike aura. Guevara's death coincided with the rise of liberation theology in Latin America, a fusion of Christian and Marxist principles that tended to view "direct action" (often interpreted as revolutionary action) on behalf of the poor as more important than Christian belief. In the eyes of many liberation theologians, "the historical Jesus" was a Che-like antiestablishment figure who preached class struggle.

even further than his German contemporaries in hypothesizing the sources of the Synoptics. While most Germans subscribed to the "two-document" theory (Mark plus Q) to account for the composition of the Gospels of Matthew and Luke, Streeter thought he had found traces of at least four written sources for the Synoptics, as well as strands of oral tradition, which could be traced to Caesarea, Antioch (where he surmised that Q had been written), Corinth, and Rome. The three Synoptic Gospels were thus conflations of seven different documents, including a "proto-Luke" that was markedly different from the canonical Gospel of Luke, Streeter theorized.

German biblical criticism arrived relatively early in America. In 1844, a newly ordained Reformed minister named Philip Schaff (1819–1893), who had received a doctorate in church history from the University of Berlin, accepted a professorship at a tiny German Reformed seminary in Mercersberg, in the Allegheny Mountains of western Pennsylvania. Born out of wedlock in the Swiss village of Chur, he had been sent to boarding school near Stuttgart under the sponsorship of his hometown minister, who had recognized his scholastic abilities. Schaff enrolled in the divinity school at the nearby University of Tübingen in 1837, two years after Strauss's *Life of Jesus* had occasioned its author's highly publicized dismissal from the faculty.

Schaff was not a theological radical like Strauss, nor was he a "right-wing" Hegelian like Baur, who was then Tübingen's most famous faculty member. However, from Baur's teachings he did adopt a Hegelian faith in historical progress and development, which he tried to combine with his orthodox Christian beliefs. As Schaff moved up academically from Tübingen to Halle to Berlin, his heroes were to become Schleiermacher, Neander, and August Tholuck (whose assistant he was in Berlin), the "mediating" theologians of the mid–19th century who sought to define a truce between science and piety. Although he had no use for either "higher criticism" or the rationalized Jesus that Schleiermacher, Neander, and Tholuck had reconstructed in their "lives," Schaff carried to America the notion of ecumenical mediation among the various Christian churches.

Schaff believed that the Hegelian *Geist,* or World-Spirit, was working through him personally to bring German theology to a nation that was just over 50 years old. As his reputation among leading American church historians continued to grow in stature, he believed it was time to leave the tiny, highly sectarian seminary at Mercersberg in favor of a more progressive environment. In 1863, in the middle of the Civil War, he accepted a teaching post at the prestigious Union Theological Seminary in New York City, which was already the flagship of liberal Protestantism and advanced theological scholarship in the United States.

While Schaff's lifelong cause of Christian ecumenism was ultimately doomed to failure (indeed, the rift between the evangelical and liberal wings of Protestantism has only widened with the years), he never abandoned his basic optimism. In 1893, he attended the famous Chicago meeting of the World Parliament of Religions, where he not only gave his blessing to the first gathering of the world's major faiths, but also embraced Darwin's theory of evolution, which he believed was the scientific counterpart of the Hegelian theory of historic development.

Schaff's towering presence paved the way for other American Protestants who looked to Germany for the most advanced trends in scholarship. Shailer Mathews (1863–1941), who was born in Portland, Maine, obtained a doctorate in theology from the University of Berlin in 1887, after which he returned to America to reconstruct his own historical Jesus with a distinctly American flavor. Following a seven-year teaching stint at his alma mater, Colby College in Waterville, Maine, Mathews accepted a position at the University of Chicago's divinity school, where he taught the New Testament, and later comparative theology. For 25 years he also served as dean of the faculty at Chicago, during which time he was elected president of the Federal Council of Churches of Christ in America, the predecessor of today's National Council of Churches.

Like his fellow liberal Protestants, Mathews was convinced that the days of Christian creed and dogma were over. "[I]nherited orthodoxy is so colored by outgrown philosophies, pre-scientific conceptions, outgrown political ideals and prejudices, as to be unusable by many an earnest man and woman," he noted in *The Gospel and Modern Man,* the most famous of his publications.[23] Inspired by the German theologians who were seeking to reconstruct *Urchristentum*—"primitive Christianity"—in their churches, he called for "a return to the primitive gospel itself" and the "original gospel of Jesus."[24]

Mathews was equally fascinated by the new field of sociology. His contemporary Émile Durkheim (1858–1917), the father of modern sociology, published his most important studies at the turn of the century, including a seminal investigation into religion's function in society titled *The Elementary Forms of the Religious Life* (1915). (Durkheim's functionalism dovetailed with the optimistic pragmatism that another of Mathews's academic colleagues, the philosopher John Dewey [1859–1952], was promoting at Columbia

University.) As a pragmatist himself and a political progressive, Mathews tended to confuse sociology with social work and socialism, although his version of the last was a benign, middle-of-the-road ideology whose hallmark was human solidarity.

Mathews loved the very word "social." In *The Social Teaching of Jesus: An Essay in Christian Sociology* (1897), he depicted Jesus as a reformer whose major objective was the betterment of human society. "By the kingdom of God Jesus meant *an ideal social order in which the relation of men to God is that of sons and* (therefore) *to each other, that of brothers,*" he wrote (the italics are his).[25] However, he regretted the fact that Jesus had not devoted more attention to the practical details of shoring up the family (which was then under severe stress from urbanization) by giving parents specific advice about how to raise their children. In a later work titled *The Gospel and the Modern Man,* Mathews described Jesus as "a person of moral perfection, possessed of remarkable powers to work cures through the evoking of faith on the part of others, a teacher who [embodied] the religious and ethical possibilities and conception of humanity; a religious master whose very life was an imperative call to trust in the fatherly love of God."[26]

Mathews's "social gospel" had many devotees, including Walter Rauschenbusch (1861–1918), a Baptist minister who had worked with German immigrants in New York City before accepting a teaching post in church history at the Rochester Theological Seminary. In 1916, he published *The Social Principles of Jesus,* which depicted Jesus as a proto–social worker, labor advocate, and even early feminist (as evidence, Rauschenbusch pointed to Jesus' gentlemanly treatment of the woman taken in adultery in John's Gospel). His book, distributed by the temperance-promoting YMCA, noted that Jesus and his disciples drank wine, but it advised present-day Christians to abstain from alcohol because "modern life demands an undrugged nervous system for quick and steady reactions."[27]

In *The Man and the Master* (1906), James E. Freeman portrayed Jesus as a "strong and masculine" teacher and reformer.[28] (Freeman was much taken with the "muscular Christianity" that flourished in Britain and America at century's end, inspiring such works as *The Manliness of Christ,* an 1879 book by Thomas Hughes, the author of *Tom Brown's Schooldays*). In Bruce Barton's *The Man Nobody Knows* (1924), Jesus was taken to perhaps the ultimate pragmatic extreme, a super-salesman, as exemplified by his rapid organization of his new social-change movement.

The most sophisticated life of Jesus to emerge from the social gospel movement was *Jesus: A New Biography,* written in 1927 by a colleague of Mathews on the Chicago divinity faculty named Shirley Jackson Case. Combining the social visionary portrait of Jesus that Mathews had painted in *The Social Teachings of Jesus* with the latest results of higher critical thinking in Germany, Case reconstructed the inner life and psychological development of a Jesus who was a mystic, prophet, and "Nazarene reformer."[29] While he did not consider himself the Messiah, nor did he found a religious movement, Case's Jesus "felt himself wholly in the grip of the Almighty," and "aimed to transform the character of his hearers."[30] Case also re-created the social environment of first-century Palestine in great detail.

The American version of the liberal Jesus was congenial to the temperament of most native churchgoers, who, as Alexis de Tocqueville famously observed, were characteristically less interested in doctrine than in moral principles that transcended sectarian differences. Focusing on a Jesus who was merely a lofty personality enabled the numerous Christian denominations to downplay their theological disagreements during a time when the divisions between mainline and "fundamentalist" churches were not so deep as they are today. The Jesus of the Golden Rule and the Sermon on the Mount served as a religious lowest common denominator that united Americans culturally. The American lives of Jesus were also remarkably free of the anti-Judaism that pervaded those of the Germans, most likely because many Protestant churches saw themselves as the new Israel.

The Jesus of American popular culture was thus always studiously nondenominational. In the first American novel based on Jesus and his times, *The Prince of the House of David, or Three Years in the Holy City,* published in 1859 by Joseph Holt Ingraham (1809–1860)—a dime-novelist turned Episcopal priest who accidentally shot himself to death with his own gun—a lovely Jewish maiden named Adina becomes a follower of the handsome young prophet from Galilee who tells his listeners to love one another and changes water into wine. However, Ingraham's long-winded tome, which served as a literary model for *Ben-Hur,* focused more closely on the harsh Roman treatment of Palestinian Jews and on Adina's romance with a gallant centurion who converts to Judaism than on Jesus or early Christianity.

Twenty-one years later, in the bestselling (and meticulously researched) novel *Ben-Hur: A Tale of the Christ* (1880), the onetime Hoosier newspaperman, lawyer, and Civil War general Lew Wallace (1827–1905) constructed a Jesus compatible with the Gilded Age's obsession with the amassing of wealth and power. In a plot twist that does not appear in the well-known

1959 film version, Judah, the novel's protagonist, becomes super-rich: the sole heir not only of the princely Hur family, but also of the Roman commander Arrius, who conveniently dies a natural death shortly after Judah saves him in battle. (In the movie, Charlton Heston's Judah turns down Arrius's fortune in order to embrace his Jewish identity. Director William Wyler also eliminated Iras, the vampish daughter of one of the three wise men, who has her eye on Judah.)

In bestowing not one but two heaps of gold on his protagonist, Wallace seemed to be saying that one can do good and do well at the same time. Furthermore, in the novel it is Judah who cuts the spokes of his rival Massala's chariot wheel, and not the other way around as portrayed in the film, an apparent benediction on Wallace's part of cutthroat competition. Finally, his Judah does hear of Jesus and his message of love and forgiveness, but it is almost as an afterthought.

The gospel that seemed to move Wallace most was that of Henry Ward Beecher (1813–1887), the eloquent Brooklyn preacher (as well as brother of Harriet Beecher Stowe and author of his own "liberal life" of Jesus in 1871). Besides the abolition of slavery, Stowe extolled the accumulation of a large fortune as part of one's Christian duty. Wallace, who actually had no religious beliefs, was inspired to write *Ben-Hur* only after hearing the celebrated agnostic Robert G. Ingersoll (1833–1899), like himself a veteran of the battle of Shiloh, scoff at Jesus' divinity in an 1876 speech, which provoked Wallace's contrarian urges. Consequently, he ignored theology and depicted Jesus in the vaguest possible terms. That pleased American readers. By 1912, *Ben-Hur* had sold one million copies, and the next year Sears Roebuck & Co. ordered a second million to vend to its own customers. Wallace's Jesus was so nonsectarian that his novel attracted, besides mainstream Protestants, hordes of Catholics, Baptists and Methodists who disapproved of fiction, and Jews who resonated strongly to the author's sympathetic portrayal of Jewish characters. They did not seem to mind that he had subtitled his book *A Tale of the Christ.*

Ben-Hur inspired numerous imitations, including Sholem Asch's *The Nazarene* (1939), Fulton Oursler's *The Greatest Story Ever Told* (1949), Thomas Costain's *The Silver Chalice* (1952), and Pär Lagerkvist's *Barabbas* (1950). The most successful of Wallace's 20th-century epigones was Lloyd C. Douglas (1877–1951), a clergyman and sometime University of Illinois chaplain who had retired from the ministry when his first novel, *Magnificent Obsession* (1929), which had a religious motif, became a best-seller. A native Indianan like Wallace, Douglas as a boy had listened to his father read *Ben-Hur* aloud to the family. Douglas's venture into a fictionalized life of Jesus, *The Robe,* published in 1942, sold more copies than any American novel except *Ben-Hur,* and was made in 1955 into the first Hollywood movie to employ the wide-screen technique of CinemaScope. Douglas imitated many of Wallace's literary techniques, including his careful historical research and his portrayal of Jesus through the eyes of one of his followers, in this case a young Roman tribune named Marcellus Gallio, who oversees Jesus' crucifixion and then wins his seamless robe in a drunken gamble at the foot of the cross.

In many ways, *The Robe* was a fictionalization of Shailer Mathews's social gospel, with the teachings of Jesus reduced to expostulations on kindness to one's neighbor and the building of a more just political order. After Marcellus touches Jesus' robe and is cured of a deep depression brought on by his ugly task in Jerusalem, he becomes what amounts to a labor leader, taking a job on a melon plantation, where he persuades the owner to give the workers a raise and build them a swimming pool. Marcellus and his bride, Diana, are eventually executed by the emperor Gaius, a raving tyrant whose real-life model was undoubtedly Hitler, but they are political rather than religious martyrs. "I have no wish to live another hour in an Empire so far along the road to ruin that it would consent to be governed by one who has no interest in the welfare of his people," Diana declares in a brave but thoroughly secular speech at the novel's end.[31] In *The Robe,* the gospel of social meliorism and liberal democracy have completely displaced the transcendent as the religion of Jesus—a quintessentially American development.

8

SEX AND DEATH FOR THE CINEMA

In 1863, a 40-year-old Breton intellectual named Joseph Ernest Renan (1823–1892), who had made his living by his wits for nearly two decades after leaving a Catholic seminary, published his *La Vie de Jésus* (*The Life of Jesus*), which rapidly became one of the best-selling books of the 19th century. Renan depicted Jesus as a "beautiful young man" who roamed the byways of Galilee on the back of a gentle donkey, attracting crowds of dreamy young followers.[1] The following year, Renan's *Life* was translated into nearly every other European language. There were five different German versions alone.

Renan reconstructed Jesus as a mystic who taught a doctrine of universal brotherhood but worked no miracles. In Renan's view, the reconstruction was strictly scientific. He had received a doctorate in Semitic languages from the University of Paris in 1852. He had lost his Catholic faith several years earlier. An admirer of David Friedrich Strauss and his demythologizing of the Gospels, Renan wanted his own book to be as thorough and intellectually rigorous. "[T]here is no room for belief in a thing of which the world can offer no experimental trace," he wrote in the preface.[2]

Renan's *Life* was actually nothing like that of Strauss. In the spring of 1861, he had retraced what he was certain were the very steps of Jesus in the Gospels during a month-long side trip to the Holy Land while he was overseeing an archaeological excavation at Byblos (modern Jbail), an ancient Phoenician port city north of Beirut. As a consequence, his narrative was steeped in the sights, sounds, and smells of 19th-century Palestine, which to his mind were the same as those of the first-century Palestine in which Jesus had lived. Unlike Strauss's book, Renan's read like a sort of autobiographical novel in which Jesus the martyr-reformer and persecuted genius was a stand-in for Renan himself. Far from "demythologizing" the Gospels as Strauss had done, Renan used them to create a mythical Jesus who was actually a self-portrait.

The Life of Jesus made Ernest Renan (he had dropped the "Joseph" from his pen name) an instant celebrity who now had entree into the best—and most louche—drawing rooms in the Paris of the Second Empire. He soon became an intimate of Gustave Flaubert (1821–1880), who was quickly dissipating, in brothels and elsewhere, the considerable fortune he had made from his novels *Madame Bovary* (1856) and *Salammbô* (1862). While Flaubert was handsome and sexually extroverted to the point of monomania, Renan was squat and unprepossessing with a bulbous head and a voyeuristic reticence that attracted him to nuns. He also enjoyed a relationship with his domineering older sister, Henriette, which was at least as intense as that with his wife, Cornélie.

Although Renan had doffed his soutane in 1845 and stopped attending Mass in 1848, he still reminded nearly everyone of a priest. Nonetheless, the prim Renan and the lubricious Flaubert attended the same dinner parties, flirted with the same demimondaines and well-born matrons, wrote admiringly of each other's works, and influenced each other's literary styles. Renan even autographed a copy of his *Life of Jesus* for Jane de Tourbey, Flaubert's confidante and (probably) off-again-on-again mistress, a washerwoman's daughter who by her early twenties had become the most beautiful, fashionable, and intelligent of the grandes cocottes of the Second Empire.

Between them, Renan and Flaubert wrote some of the most graceful French prose of the century. They shared a taste for religious and Orientalist exotica that found its way into most of Flaubert's novels and also Renan's *Life of Jesus,* along with six sequels published by Renan over the next 18 years that carried Christian history through the reign of Marcus Aurelius. In these seven volumes, which he collectively titled *The History of the Origins of Christianity,* he served up a colorful mix of doctrinal disputes, ancient debaucheries, imperial tortures, and naked virgin martyrs torn apart by lions in the arena.

Before his *Life of Jesus,* Renan had supported himself variously for 18 years by serving as a librarian of antiquities at the Bibliothèque Nationale in Paris, classifying library manuscripts in Rome, and supervising the Byblos dig on appointment from the reigning French emperor, Napoleon III. A gifted philologist whose specialty was Hebrew, in 1847 he had written an essay on Semitic languages that won him the coveted Prix de Volney, in honor of Constantin François de Volney (1757–1820), a scholar and traveler whose Near Eastern journals had helped Napoleon Bonaparte (Napoleon III's uncle) conquer Egypt in 1798. As a result, he became a doctoral candidate at the University of Paris, where he wrote his thesis on medieval Islamic philosophy.

In late 1861, after traveling to the Holy Land and writing the first draft of his *Life of Jesus,* Renan was elected to the long-coveted chair in Hebrew at the Collège de France. That position lasted only a few months. During his inaugural lecture in February 1862, while not exactly denying Jesus' divinity, he called him an "incomparable man" whose achievements entitled him to be thought of as God,[3] a characterization Renan viewed as a fair compromise between Catholic orthodoxy and his own scientific positivism. However, Napoleon III's empress, Eugénie, who had surrounded herself with a powerful clique of Parisian clerics, was so offended at the secularist implications of Renan's words that the government suspended his lectures at the Collège.

When *The Life of Jesus* appeared in 1864, the French government canceled Renan's appointment at the Collège altogether, which nettled his pride but did him no financial harm. Following the disastrous Franco-Prussian War and Napoleon's death in 1873, the anticlerical Third Republic reinstated Renan, who returned in triumph as the Collège's director (and a member of the French Academy). Ironically, his dismissal from his teaching post had left him free for the nonce to become what he really was: not a scholar (although he certainly had the qualifications), but a littérateur of the highest order.

Not only did Renan's *Life of Jesus* enjoy enormous popularity; it was also the most influential study of Jesus ever written outside of the canonical Gospels. As such, it left its literary imprint even on pious lives of Christ written by Catholic and Protestant clergymen during the late 19th and early 20th centuries. Renan had made it de rigeur for any author contemplating a book about Jesus to visit the Holy Land firsthand (or at least consult a good map). Moreover, his work spawned an entire generation of religious fiction: Flaubert's "Herodias" (published in 1877 as one of his *Three Tales*), a fictionalized account of the Gospel story of the beheading of John the Baptist; Oscar Wilde's play *Salome* (1893), whose plot Wilde lifted from "Herodias"; Henryk Sienkiewicz's early Christian epic *Quo Vadis* (1895); and Nikos Kazantzakis's *The Last Temptation of Christ* (1952) are all literary offspring of Renan.

Renan's lush descriptions of the Near East, especially those of Near Eastern women, fed into a 19th-century craze for "realistic" and subtly sexual literary and visual depictions of biblical themes. They inspired the imagery of the biblical episodes in D. W. Griffith's movie *Intolerance,* released in 1916, which in turn inspired Cecil B. DeMille's *King of Kings* in 1927. The first feature-length film ever made about Jesus, *King of Kings* was a heady combination of silver-screen glamour, conventional Christian reverence, and lavish interior decoration. (Griffith, who happened to be visiting DeMille's location in San Pedro, California, even guest-directed a portion of Jesus' crucifixion.)

DeMille's vampish Mary Magdalene, played by the raven-tressed Jacqueline Logan, sported high-heeled sandals, a brassiere forged of two brass coils, a pet leopard, and a Grecian-columned palace that looked exactly like a Los Angeles mansion of the 1920s until Jesus (portrayed by the rugged H. B. Warner) forgave her her sins. The sequences involving Jesus and the Magdalene were so intimate in tone that DeMille trimmed them at the last minute in order not to offend the Prohibition-era churchgoers who were the film's target audience. Indeed, DeMille made Mary the real star of his film, conducting a well-publicized "casting search" for the right actress to portray her. When Logan accepted the Magdalene role (Gloria Swanson had turned it down), she told DeMille, "I don't want to play her as a bad woman, but as a woman who doesn't know the difference between right and wrong."[4] As for Warner, a hard drinker, DeMille had him followed home every night to ensure that he would not stop off at speakeasies or otherwise engage in activities considered inappropriate for the King of Kings.

DeMille's Mary Magdalene—passionate, emotional, and subliminally in love with Jesus (the cinematic forerunner of the harlots who figure prominently at Jesus' side in Andrew Lloyd Weber's musical *Jesus Christ, Superstar* and Martin Scorsese's 1987 film version of *The Last Temptation of Christ*)—was essentially the creation of Renan. In the Gospels, Mary of Magdala is a tantalizing minor figure. Although Jesus was reported to have exorcised seven devils from her, the Evangelists do not describe her as a prostitute. (Later

Christian tradition identified her with the female "sinner" in Luke's Gospel who washed Jesus' feet with her tears at a Pharisee's banquet and dried them with her hair, and in the Middle Ages she became the patron saint of reformed streetwalkers.) In John's Gospel, Mary Magdalene is the first to witness the risen Jesus, and she tries to embrace him until he bids her not to touch him.

Renan placed Mary Magdalene in the very center of his *Life of Jesus,* as the woman who "remained faithful to [Jesus], even to Golgotha."[5] Afterwards, she was able to fantasize Jesus back to life—and persuade his disciples that he lived again—through the sheer force of what can only be described as a romantic crush. "Divine power of love!" wrote Renan at the end of his *Life of Jesus.* "Sacred moments in which the passion of one possessed gave to the world a resuscitated God!"[6]

While Renan's Jesus was never sexually active, he was always the center of adoring female attention:

> The women, in fact, received him very gladly. He had in their society those reserved manners which render a very agreeable union of ideas between the two sexes possible. . . . Three or four devoted Galilean women always accompanied the young Master, and disputed among themselves for the pleasure of listening to him and of attending on him in turn. . . . Some of them were rich, and, placing their fortunes at the disposal of the young Prophet, put him in a position to live without having to follow the occupation to which he had been brought up.[7]

Renan's Jesus was in short a matinee idol: handsome and languorous, with perfect manners and winning ways, whose attractiveness to women added a sexual frisson to the traditional Gospel stories. There is a direct line of descent from Renan's *Life of Jesus* to DeMille's *King of Kings,* for Renan had invented the cinematic Jesus.

Renan's book also conveyed the look and feel of the Holy Land. Archaeology, which was then a young science, was by and large ignored by the academic biblical scholars of the century. For the great German exegetes of the era—Paulus, Schleiermacher, Strauss, Neander, Weisse, Holtzmann, Harnack, and even Wellhausen—a voyage to Palestine was beside the point, as the life of the historical Jesus was for them solely a matter of interpreting texts. In 1838, three years after Strauss had published the first edition of his own *Life of Jesus,* a newly appointed professor at Union Theological Seminary named Edward Robinson tried to assemble an up-to-date biblical atlas but discovered that no one had done enough field work to make such a project possible. Robinson solved the problem himself by making the first scholarly exploration of the Holy Land later that year.

In contrast to the German scholars, Renan wrote his *Life of Jesus* from his own experiences in Palestine. In April 1861, accompanied by his wife and sister (the latter acting as his secretary), he took a 34-day vacation from the Byblos excavation he was supervising to wend his way south by mule through Galilee, Samaria, and Judea. The trip was not easy on either of the women. Henriette was physically unwell, and Cornélie was feeling guilty about having left the Renans' four-year-old son behind in Paris. Furthermore, the two women could scarcely abide each other. Renan, who was famous for his indefatigable physical energy and indifference to other people's problems, flogged on the little caravan to cover a huge amount of ground in hardly more than a month. However, it was spring, wildflowers were blooming everywhere, and Palestine was a primitive and picturesque backwater of the Ottoman Empire. Even the humblest Galilean village probably seemed like a rural idyll. Stopping at the places where the Gospels said Jesus had stopped, Renan began to imagine the stories taking place before his very eyes.

In Nazareth, which had a substantial Maronite Christian population, he marveled at the courtesy of the inhabitants, the beauty of the veiled women, the stony paths, and the rude one-room houses, asking himself if he might be looking at the actual well where Jesus' mother had drawn her water, or the same kind of windowless shop where Jesus' father had done his carpentry. On the dirt roads he traversed, Renan saw in his mind Jesus walking with his disciples. He stopped at the very well where, according to John's Gospel and Christian tradition, Jesus had asked for water from a Samaritan woman. He lay on his back in a boat floating on the Sea of Galilee. He was reliving Jesus' life—or at least the life he fancied Jesus had led. It is not surprising that Renan put Jesus on the back of a mule, since that was his own mode of transportation in the Holy Land.

When Renan returned to Lebanon in July, he wrote almost the entire first draft of his *Life of Jesus* in a feverish three months, with the devoted Henriette copying out each page (Cornélie had returned to France to be with her son, who had fallen ill). On September 19th, as Renan was about to set to work on the Last Supper, both he and Henriette came down with a virulent case of malaria. They were staying in a remote mountain village called Amschid in order to avoid the searing summer heat of the Levantine coastal plain, and by the time a doctor arrived with quinine injections, it was too late for Henriette, who died on September 24th. As he himself fought the ravaging fever, Renan had a vision of his sister calling to him from the grave. He confused her with both Jesus and the demigod Adonis (who was said to have been gored to death by a boar but resurrected by Zeus for six months out of every year). Byblos had been the center of an ancient cult of Adonis; the Adonis River near Byblos was said to have been reddened annually by his blood. Between bouts of fever, Renan forced himself to finish the manuscript, constantly reminded of Henriette's death and his own brush with mortality as he wrote about the crucifixion.

Unlike the ponderous German "liberal lives" of Jesus that were coming off the scholarly presses during the 1860s, Renan's book was relatively short. (The English translation was only 343 pages long, plus a 40-page appendix.) Not surprisingly, few of the German texts had many readers outside the New Testament academy. By contrast, Renan had the ability to combine his vast erudition with a poetic imagination and fluid, concise literary style. Indeed, he was the first master of what the French call "haute vulgarisation"—popularized renditions of serious subjects for the enjoyment and edification of the lay reader.

Renan was quite conscious that he was producing literature as well as scholarship. He boasted in a letter to his lifelong friend, the chemist Pierre Eugène Berthelot (1827–1907), just before being stricken with malaria: "I have succeeded in giving all these events an ordered sequence which is completely lacking in the gospels. I believe that this time one will have before his eyes living beings, and not these pale, lifeless phantoms—Jesus, Mary, Peter, etc., considered as abstract beings, and only typified."[8] He called his *Life of Jesus* a "fifth Gospel," which he viewed as the basis for the canonical four, and which he himself would bring to life.[9]

Renan's Jesus is a young Galilean rabbi preaching love under a brilliant blue sky, leading his gaggle of fishermen, attending weddings, and sharing his meals with the dregs of society. Later on, the scene darkens dramatically in Renan's book when he travels to Jerusalem for Passover. After his message of love is denounced by the Temple, he abandons his Jewish faith in favor of a new "kingdom" of universal brotherhood that will topple all religions.[10] While he performs no actual wonders, he uses his intuitiveness to let people *think* he can cast out their demons, heal their sick, and even raise their dead.

Renan's Jesus lets himself be called "Messiah" and even "Son of God," although he regards his kinship with God as metaphorical and his Messiahship as nonexistent. As time passes, however, he grows cranky and paranoid and begins to yearn for martyrdom, setting out once again for Jerusalem. His disciples quarrel, one of them betrays him, and his enemies plot against him. In the end, his crucifixion is an act of ultimate self-transcendence: He must die by the hand of his inferiors in order to be worshipped as a god.

Renan leavened his tragedy with any number of idyllic set pieces:

> The beautiful climate of Galilee rendered the existence of these honest fishermen a perpetual enjoyment. They were a true prelude to the kingdom of God—simple, good, happy—rocked gently on their charming little lake, or sleeping at night on its banks. . . . The clear and mild eyes of those simple souls contemplated the universe in its mythic origin. . . . Sometimes he sat upon the mountains which skirted the lake, where the air was so pure and the sky so luminous. The faithful band led thus a gay and roaming life, receiving the inspirations of the Master fresh from his lips.[11]
>
> . . . .
>
> His preaching was unimpassioned and pleasing, redolent of nature, and of the perfume of the fields. He loved the flowers, and drew from them the most charming lessons. The birds of the air, the sea, the mountains, the frolics of children, were introduced by turn into his discourses.[12]
>
> . . . .
>
> He thus traversed Galilee in the midst of a continual feast. He rode on a mule (which in the East is a good and safe mode of traveling), whose large black eyes, shaded by long eye-lashes, give it an expression of gentleness. His disciples sometimes disposed themselves around him with a kind of rustic pomp, at the expense of their garments, which they used as carpets. . . . Women came to pour oil upon his head, and perfumes on his feet.[13]

Among the Germans, the only who came close to Renan in literary effect was Theodor Keim, who also went to the Holy Land, and worked a "Galilean springtime" and "darkening storm" into his narrative. However, Keim's multi-volume, 1,700-page *Jesus of Nazara* was hardly popular literature.

Renan had tried to make his book academically respectable, peppering it with learned footnotes that cited the Gospels, other early Christian writings, rabbinical literature, and Josephus. He put his vast Hebrew erudition to work as well, giving some of the Gospel characters their names in Hebrew instead of the Gospels' Greek. (In poking fun at this practice, an Irish critic noted: "Annas and Caiaphas, Judas Iscariot, Bartholomew, Joseph of Aramathea—we have known them from our childhood; but they have quite a new look as Hanan and Kaiapha, Judas of Kerioth, Nathaniel Bar-Tolmai, and Joseph of Haramathaim.")[14] Moreover, Renan's sentimental allusions to nature, small children, and the ministrations of women recapitulated material that was actually contained in the Gospels, if in less hothouse form.

However, Renan's portrait of Jesus as a man too great for this world was nowhere to be found in the Gospels. The brilliant, fastidious, grossly misunderstood Jesus with a vision of superior political and religious order was more like Renan himself, who had been living the life of Jesus inside his head long before he made his trip to the Holy Land. When he became engaged to Cornélie in 1856, Henriette had gone wild with jealousy, consenting to the marriage only if she could share their living quarters. Renan was clearly thinking of his wife and sister when he wrote about the women who "disputed among themselves" for the privilege of waiting on the Master.

A photographer assigned to the Byblos archaeological dig reported that the two women were open rivals for Renan's attention, vying with each other to tie his tie, brush his clothes, and accompany him to sites. Renan also relished being in charge of a crew of grateful Lebanese underlings whose job it was to cater to his every whim. In one of his letters to Berthelot, in February 1861, Renan described the archaeological site as "my kingdom of Byblos."[15] He further confided: "During two months I have reigned supreme; I have seen a corner of the world wholly attentive to my service, eager to obtain my smile and anticipate my desires."[16]

One of the most arresting passages in Renan's *Life* is the depiction of Jesus hanging on the cross as he awaits his death. Renan narrates the scene from Jesus' point of view as he looks down from the gibbet onto the swarming mob below:

> Jesus had before him only the spectacle of the baseness or stupidity of humanity. The passers-by insulted him. He heard around him foolish scoffs, and his greatest cries of pain turned into odious jests; "He trusted in God; let him deliver him now, if he will have him: for he said, I am the Son of God." . . . The sky was dark; and the earth, as in all the environs of Jerusalem, dry and gloomy. For a moment, according to certain narratives, his heart failed him; a cloud hid from him the face of his Father; he experienced an agony of despair a thousand times more acute than all his tortures. He saw only the ingratitude of men. Repenting perhaps in suffering for a vile race, he exclaimed: "My God, my God, why hast thou forsaken me?"[17]

For orthodox Christians, Jesus' lament (drawn from Psalm 22) bespeaks profound sorrow and suffering. Coming from Renan's Jesus, it sounds rather like the writer himself: overly impressed with his own importance and contemptuous of the mass of ordinary people blind to his merits.

Renan's poetic, essentially sympathetic portraits of Jesus, Mary Magdalene, the apostles, and other Gospel characters sprang from his lifelong love-hate relationship with the Catholic Church. During his crisis of faith, at the seminary of St. Sulpice in 1845, he wrote a "psychological essay on Jesus Christ," which was actually a letter begging Jesus to tell him something that would allay his doubts about his divinity. When Jesus remained silent, Renan walked out of the seminary and took a train to Paris, where Henriette, who had already lost her own faith, was waiting for him to join her.

In 1849, Renan went to Rome to work on a manuscript cataloguing project, where he was at first appalled by the filth, poverty, and (to his mind) superstition rampant in the Eternal City, which housed at least 400 churches and hundreds of barefoot begging friars. At that time, Rome was still papal territory and in many ways a medieval city. As a political progressive, Renan was flabbergasted when the tattered Romans supported the reactionary Pope Pius IX against the republican troops of Giuseppe Garibaldi (1807–1882), who were supposed to be liberating them. However, when French troops routed Garibaldi and escorted Pio Nono back to the Vatican, and the Romans went into a frenzy of joy, with three days of festivities that included strolling musicians, singers, and general merriment, Renan concluded that what the masses really needed—and wanted—from their rulers was a combination of repression and entertainment.

Although he detested Catholic dogma, Renan came to love the folk Catholicism—the processions and streetcorner shrines—of the Roman tenement dwellers. As he wrote in *Patrice,* a semi-autobiographical novel from that period, he also discovered a strong sexual attraction for pious young women, whether clad in nuns' veils, kneeling in church, or embracing the crucifix. They presented a vision of chastity that in his mind begged for violation.[18] This paradox of purity and cruelty, which he called the "aesthetic of Christianity,"[19] remained with him for the rest of his life. In fact, one of his last literary works was a play titled *The Abbess of Jouarre* (1886), in which a beautiful nun imprisoned during the French Revolution is seduced—and also ravished of her faith—by an aristocratic former suitor while they are both awaiting death by the guillotine.

While living in Paris in the mid-1840s, the young Renan had published two anonymous essays touting the virtues of Strauss and other radical German New Testament scholars. In an 1848 tract, *The Arrival of Science,* he also espoused Hegel's "developmental" theories on history and religion. Convinced that science would eventually replace religion, in the preface to the 13th edition of his *Life of Jesus* he wrote, "Science alone seeks after pure truth."[20] On an 1864 trip to Egypt, Renan found another hero in Ferdinand de Lesseps (1805–94), the French diplomat/engineer who was supervising the construction of the Suez Canal through a combination of charisma and force of will. To Renan, Lesseps embodied the ideal combination of authoritarianism and intellectual curiosity that characterized the modern man of science.

Nonetheless, like his Romantic predecessor Rousseau, Renan also believed that religion bespoke truth, a spiritual truth that was more accessible to the uneducated and naive than to the sophisticated intelligentsia. Although he worshipped science, Renan despised scientific reductionism, and he had no use for Feuerbach's theory that religion was merely a projection of social reality. "The greatest simpleton, provided he practices the worship of the heart, is more enlightened as to the reality of things than the materialist who thinks he explains everything by accident, and leaves it there," Renan wrote in the preface to his *Life of Jesus.*[21]

The German New Testament scholars, who viewed Renan's interpretation of the Gospels as far too literalistic and his fondness for the Gospel of John as completely outdated, did not return Renan's admiration of them in kind. Renan paid no attention to their theory of "Marcan priority," and continued to insist on the historical accuracy of John's Gospel. The Germans wrote Renan off as a frivolous Frenchman who had no business tampering with serious subjects like the Bible. Speaking for his colleagues at Strasbourg, Timothée Colani remarked: "We opened Mr. Renan's book with sympathetic interest; we closed it with deep disappointment."[22]

As for Renan's hero David Friedrich Strauss, his admirers were convinced that Renan had tried to upstage him by publishing his book while Strauss was still completing his *New Life of Jesus.* At the outbreak of the Franco-Prussian War, Renan sided with the Prussian Protestants against the Catholic French. Having already written several fawning letters to Strauss, whom he had never met, Renan wrote again, appealing to him to promote a truce by suggesting that Prussia give Alsace-Lorraine back to France. A staunch Prussophile who had little use for Renan's more literalistic interpretation of the Gospels, Strauss replied with a blast of withering sarcasm published in a Prussian newspaper. That terminated any possibility of a literary friendship between the two men. Eventually Renan came to loathe both him and Bismarck.

Although officially denounced by the Catholic Church, Renan's *Life of Jesus* attracted countless Catholic readers, who were drawn to its soft-edged portrait of the savior, its gracefully presented erudition, and its enchanting details of Near Eastern life. They most likely chose to skim over the parts of the book that debunked miracles and to focus on the sections that struck them as conventionally devotional. (Taken out of context, the passage quoted earlier describing Jesus' feelings while hanging on the cross could have passed for a Good Friday reading in a 19th-century cloister.) Albert Schweitzer, on the other hand, found Renan's book repellently sugary (although gripping), and as mawkish as a plaster statue of Our Lady of Lourdes. "The gentle Jesus, the beautiful Mary, the fair Galileans who formed the retinue of the 'amiable carpenter,' might have been taken over in a body from the shop window of an ecclesiastical art emporium in the Place St. Sulpice," he noted.[23]

Renan spent almost his entire adult life thumbing his nose at the Catholic Church. (While even Voltaire had called in a priest on his deathbed, Renan held out until the very end.) Nonetheless, he wrote in a specifically Catholic devotional tradition, alternately sentimental and lurid, that harked back to the Middle Ages and was especially popular after the Enlightenment, when intellectually besieged Catholics took refuge in their faith's aesthetic and emotional components. The constant interplay of sensationalism and violence in Catholic art, both high and popular, focused on the gory details of Jesus' passion, the beauty and tenderness of his mother, and the torments of the martyrs and other saints. It revealed a distinctly Catholic imagery that often contained an implicitly erotic element as well. Extreme examples of this tendency included a perennial fascination with St. Sebastian pierced by arrows, St. George rescuing the chained maiden from a dragon, and the ecstasy of St. Teresa in Bernini's famous sculpture.

Camille Paglia described this particular aspect of popular Catholicism (which she termed Italian, although it was actually universal in the West) as a holdover from ancient paganism:

> Paganism is eye-intense. It is based on cultic exhibitionism, in which sex and sadomasochism are joined. The ancient chthonian mysteries have never disappeared from the Italian church. Waxed saints' corpses under glass. Tattered armbones in gold reliquaries. Half-nude St. Sebastian pierced by arrows. St. Lucy holding her eyeballs out on a platter. Blood, torture, ecstasy, and tears. Its

> lurid sensationalism makes Italian Catholicism the emotionally most complete cosmology in religious history. Italy added pagan sex and violence to the ascetic Palestinian creed. And so to Hollywood, the modern Rome: it is pagan sex and violence that have flowered so vividly in our mass media.[24]

Renan's "cinematic Jesus" was hardly a modern concept. Rather, he was heir to a Catholic iconography that had existed for over a thousand years.

In *Madame Bovary,* Flaubert portrays the maudlin Catholic culture at young Emma's convent school as a saturation of the senses at the expense of the intellect, blurring the line between the mystical and the sexual:

> As she continued to live uninterruptedly in the insipid atmosphere of the classrooms, among the white-faced women with their brass crucifixes dangling from their rosaries, she gently succumbed to the mystical languor induced by the perfumes of the altar, the coolness of the holy-water fonts, the gleaming of the candles. Instead of following the Mass she kept her prayer book open at the holy pictures with their sky-blue borders; and she loved the Good Shepherd, the Sacred Heart pierced by sharp arrows, and poor Jesus stumbling and falling under his cross. . . . The metaphors constantly used in sermons—"betrothed," "spouse," "heavenly lover," "mystical marriage,"—excited her in a thrilling new way.[25]

The nuns in Flaubert's novel encourage their teenage charges to view Jesus as a semi-erotic figure with wounds to be nursed (by a devoted female) and a burning, bleeding heart. Just before she dies, Emma Bovary kisses a crucifix with a passion that borders on the blasphemous.

It was Renan, however, who was the first to transport the implicit eroticism of certain aspects of mainstream Catholicism into the realm of the explicit. Indeed, his *Life of Jesus* was the inspiration for the long looks that pass between Jesus and Mary Magdalene in DeMille's *King of Kings,* and the scene in Scorsese's *Last Temptation of Christ* in which the Magdalene takes off her clothes in front of Jesus and tries to lure him into her bed. Renan was also the first to use Jesus as a vehicle for narcissistic fantasies that purported to be historical.

Meditation on the sufferings of Jesus and the martyrs is one of the oldest of Christian traditions. As I pointed out earlier, the Passion was the matrix by which members of the faith, especially in the West, were able to come to terms with the doctrine of the humanity of God. Beginning with the letters of Paul of Tarsus, who averred that he bore the wounds of Christ—the stigmata—on his body, the fascination with those who had undergone torture and execution rather than deny their faith was to become an integral part of Christian iconography. In one of his letters, the first-century bishop Clement of Rome called his readers' attention to the female victims of Domitian's persecutions, who were sometimes forced to reenact in the arena the fates of mythological heroines such as Dirce, tied to the horns of a bull and gored to death for offending the nymph Antiope. These martyrs, whom Clement called the "Dirceads," "endured fearful and diabolical tortures; yet in spite of their bodily frailty they finished the race of faith unshaken."[26]

From earliest days, the Christians martyrs were viewed as symbols of the suffering Christ. The chronicler of the tale of the victims of Marcus Aurelius's persecutions in 177 C.E. in Lyons described as a living crucifix the young slave woman Blandina, who had been hung on a post for wild animals to devour: "She looked as if she was hanging in the form of a cross, and through her ardent prayers she stimulated great enthusiasm in those undergoing their ordeal, who in their agony saw with their outward eyes in the person of their sister the One who was crucified for them."[27]

Female victims like Blandina made a striking impression on the authors of these early martyrologies, perhaps because condemned women symbolized the passivity of the suffering Jesus, as well as the heroism implicit in the theology of his atonement. The agonies of women praying on the blood-soaked sands of a Roman amphitheater were arresting and touching spectacles. During the early third century in Carthage, a pair of young mothers, 22-year-old Vibia Perpetua and her slave Felicitas, who had given birth only a few days before, were brought into the stadium with other Christians to wrestle a leopard, a bear, a boar, and a wild cow as part of a birthday celebration for the emperor Septimius Severus. The sight of them stripped naked, especially Felicitas, whose breasts were dripping with milk, moved the crowd to pity, a rare occurrence at such events. The guard quickly removed the pair, put clothes back on them, and sent them out again, where they died in one another's arms.

The stories of the Dirceads, Blandina and the other Lyons martyrs, and Felicitas and Perpetua by and large were historically accurate (Perpetua, who came from a good family and was literate in Latin and Greek, wrote part of her own tale). As time went on, however, readers of martyrologies demanded even more melodramatic flourishes. Later chronicles of the victims of Diocletian's persecutions at the beginning of the fourth century transformed many of the female martyrs into lovely, nubile young women whose modesty was sometimes fetchingly sheathed by their knee-length hair. Some were pursued by handsome suitors who asked for their hands in marriage, and others were condemned to brothels, where angels or various wild animals would intervene to save their honor.

Behind these embellishments often lay the body of a genuine martyr, interred in the Catacombs or another Christian burial place. St. Agnes, one of the most famous of the early Roman martyrs, was a girl of perhaps 13 who was killed by a sword driven into her throat, a common form of Roman execution. Around Agnes's remains, which were buried along the Via Nomentana in Rome, numerous legendary accretions arose, such as a wicked prefect's placing her in a house of ill repute, where she converted his son to Christianity when he came to have his way with her.

The name of St. Sebastian is another of the best known among the early martyrs, in part because of his popularity as a subject of Renaissance paintings. Although almost nothing certain is known about him, he is a classic example of the workings of Christian legend-making. Supposedly an officer of the imperial guard in Rome under Diocletian, when it was discovered that he was a Christian, he was sentenced to be shot to death with arrows. Sebastian recovered, confronted the emperor, and was beaten to death by clubs.

During the mid–13th century, a Dominican friar named Jacopo (1220–1298) who was born in the seaside town of Varazze on the Italian Riviera, wrote a Latin compendium of nearly 200 lives of the saints (along with a synopsis of the life of Jesus), which he arranged according to the liturgical calendar of the Middle Ages. Named archbishop of Genoa several years before his death, Jacopo of Varazze (whose Latin name was Jacobus de Voragine), called his book a "saints' legend," although it later became known as the *Legenda Aurea,* or *Golden Legend.* It was filled with titillating tales of martyrdom. Although Jacopo's main sources were the works of ancient historians and church fathers, including Josephus and Eusebius, he also resorted to scattered chronicles that reflected more than 1,000 years of Christian folklore in the West.

Within a matter of years, the *Golden Legend,* which was translated into nearly every European vernacular language, became the most widely read medieval book after the Bible. When the printing press was invented about a century and a half after Jacopo's death, the *Golden Legend* was one of the first books to be issued in print. Jacopo's lives found their way into medieval mystery and miracle plays and onto church altarpieces and stained-glass windows, and they were almost certainly read by Dante and Chaucer. Chaucer's *Clerk's Tale,* whose heroine, the patient Griselda, undergoes an improbable series of mental tortures at the hands of her husband as a test of her holiness, undoubtedly had as its literary model some of the saints' lives in the *Golden Legend.*

The individual tales in the *Golden Legend,* which are only a few pages long on average, make entertaining reading even today, although their historical value is generally negligible. Primarily a devotional writer with little interest in scientific fact, Jacopo focused on a number of saints, including Christopher, Valentine, and the Seven Sleepers (who fell asleep during the emperor Decius's persecution and woke up, Rip Van Winkle–style, nearly two centuries later), whose names were stricken from the Catholic calendar after the Second Vatican Council for want of evidence that they had ever existed.

The stories in the *Golden Legend* are remarkable for the extent and variety of tortures that their protagonists endured, reflecting their readers' taste for such bloodthirsty detail, as well as for romance and recondite Eastern locales. In one of the best-loved tales, the lovely, high-born Margaret of Antioch (another martyr whose historical existence is doubtful) spurns a marriage offer from Diocletian's prefect Olybrius because she has dedicated her chastity to Christ, whereupon he has her hung from a rack, beaten with rods, and lacerated with iron rakes until her flesh hangs from her bones. The following day she is stripped of her clothes, burnt with torches, submerged under water, and finally beheaded. During intervals between torments, Margaret wrestles with Satan, who first assumes the shape of a dragon (who swallows her and bursts asunder) and then that of a man (whom she pushes to the ground before planting her foot victoriously on his neck). Margaret was an especially popular saint among medieval wives, who prayed to her to ease their labor pains.

During the 19th-century, the *Legend*'s fantastical narratives appealed to Romanticism's interest in folklore and fairy tales and its exaltation of sentiment and primitive sensibility. Flaubert based his novella "Saint Julian the Hospitaller" (another of his *Three Tales*) on Jacopo's account of a young man who mistakenly kills his parents and spends the rest of his life doing penance by ferrying people across a dangerous river. Julian's story had also been set (by a 13th-century artisan probably familiar with the *Golden Legend*) into a stained-glass window gracing the Gothic cathedral in Flaubert's native Rouen, the cathedral that Claude Monet painted so many times.

The *Legend* also served as a literary source for the pioneer of French Romanticism, the aristocrat and belletrist François-René de Chateaubriand (1768–1848). Chateaubriand was a Breton like Renan. Both were born in storm-lashed English Channel towns, the former in the port of Saint-Malo and the latter in Tréguier, a destitute former cathedral town to the west of Saint-Malo where the chief economic activities were begging and prostitution. Both were short, heavy-set Celts with large heads that squatted on their shoulders.

Chateaubriand, who bore the title of viscount, was born into a noble family that traced its ancestry to a baron named Brian (or Briant), who had ridden beside William the Conqueror at the Battle of Hastings. By the 18th century, however, they were left with little else besides their glorious name and their moldering castle at Combourg. As for Renan, when he was only five years old the body of his father, a merchant seaman, had washed up not far from Tréguier under circumstances that bespoke either accident or suicide. His mother struggled to support Ernest, Henriette, and an older brother as the owner of a tiny, failing grocery shop on a narrow Tréguier street.

Brittany made up for the hard life it afforded its inhabitants with the unearthly beauty of its terrain. The gnarled and misty landscapes of the Côtes du Nord were a wellspring of Celtic folklore, intertwining Christian and pre-Christian motifs, such as the enchanted forest of Brocéliande, the cave where Merlin sleeps to this day, and the sunken city of Is whose churchbells ring underneath the sea. The edge of the known world—Finistère—was only a few miles west on the Atlantic coast. In 1859, the year before he left for Byblos, Renan had published an essay titled "The Poetry of the Celtic Races," an idealization of the homeland whose proud and independent ways he viewed as a repudiation of the bourgeois barbarities of industrialized Europe. In celebrating the fairy lore, bards, and saints of the Bretons and Gaels, Renan essentially created the "Celtic twilight" school of literature and criticism that would influence Matthew Arnold and William Butler Yeats.

Chateaubriand's Romanticism was to take a far more flamboyant turn. Like Rousseau, his favorite writer as a young man, he was a royalist. A naval officer for the king, when the French monarchy fell in 1791 he fled to America, where he wrote a possibly fictitious travel memoir. Five months later, after Louis XIV's arrest, he returned to France to place his sword at the king's service, which nearly cost him his life. Wounded and left for dead in a counterrevolutionary skirmish in Lorraine, he managed to escape to England in 1793, and when he returned to France in 1800 he thought it advisable to use an assumed name for a time.

Upon the death of his devoutly Catholic mother in 1798, Chateaubriand experienced an emotional reconversion to his childhood faith, which he had abandoned not long after making his First Communion as a boy. In 1802, he published his most famous book, *The Genius of Christianity,* which combined a Rousseauian celebration of feeling with an impassioned apologia for all that was beautiful in Catholic civilization. His glorification of medieval art, music, and architecture was particularly well timed. The bloodbath of the French Revolution had cast a pall on the Enlightenment's worship of reason, and religion and medievalism were acquiring a new vogue and glamor among the Romantics.

The Genius of Christianity brought Chateaubriand fame and fortune. Even Napoleon Bonaparte, whom he despised, made overtures in his direction, appointing him to several embassy posts. The French Academy offered him a seat. However, when he refused to endorse the Revolution as required, he had to wait until after Waterloo for actual acceptance into the circle of immortals.

The Catholic Church was of two minds about *The Genius of Christianity.* Chateaubriand had turned Catholicism into a kind of grand opera, with an enormous amount of spectacle and tears but not much intellectually coherent substance. "I wept, and I believed," he had declared in his preface.[28] On the other hand, the priests and prelates who read his text must have privately condoned it as an important counterthrust to Gibbon's *Decline and Fall of the Roman Empire,* which had identified Christianity as a major cause of Roman civilization's decay. Although under a vague cloud of clerical disapproval, *The Genius of Christianity* soon enough became virtually required reading for all French Catholics. (In *Madame Bovary,* a passage from Chateaubriand is read aloud to the girls at the convent school every Sunday for entertainment.)

In 1806, Chateaubriand made a trip—unprecedented for its time—to the Holy Land and other Near Eastern sites for the purpose of gathering material for a historical novel about early Christianity. He ended up writing the novel, *The Martyrs,* while still on his travels, using his observations of 19th-century life in the Levant to give it local color and some degree of accuracy. Chateaubriand was the pioneer of what might be called travel as pseudo-research, travel as a mode of self-exploration that passed as historical insight. He noted that he had visited the Near East in order to "mingle" his "tears with those of the Magdalen."[29] His sojourn, whose notes he later published, combined religious sentiment and egotism in equal measure. During a stopover in Egypt he had his name inscribed on one of the Pyramids.

Chateaubriand borrowed freely from the *Golden Legend* for the plot of *The Martyrs.* One of Jacopo's most melodramatic and fanciful stories concerned Chrysanthus and Daria, two young people who had died in Rome during Septimius Severus's early-third-century persecutions. By the Middle Ages, Chrysanthus, of whom little is actually known, had evolved into a young Alexandrian aristocrat in Rome, whose father tried to lure him away from Christianity through the persuasive powers of Daria, a vestal virgin of great beauty. Instead, Chrysanthus converts her, and they enter into a kind of spiritual marriage that combines passionate love with vows of chastity. After their arrest, Daria is consigned to the usual brothel, where a lion that has escaped from the amphitheater protects her virginity by standing guard at her door. She and Chrysanthus are martyred after numerous tortures by being buried alive in a sand-pit on the Salarian Way.

Out of this material Chateaubriand crafted a full-blown love story. *The Martyrs* was the first historical novel of the 19th century, and the first to use early Christian history as its theme. Chateaubriand set his story in the reign of Diocletian in order to include such fourth-century historical figures as the future emperor Constantine, the philosopher Porphyry, the tyrant Galerius (a thinly veiled portrait of Napoleon), and Jerome, the compiler of the Latin Vulgate Bible. Chrysanthus becomes Eudorus, a young soldier from a Christian family; and Daria, Cymodoce, a 16-year-old priestess of the Muses.

Moreover, a number of scenes from the novel were precise transcriptions of Chateaubriand's own boyhood surroundings as well as the various sites he had visited in the Near East. Eudorus is promoted to commandant of Armorica (the Roman name for Brittany), and Cymodoce accompanies Constantine's mother, Helena, to Palestine, where she finds the True Cross, and Cymodoce is baptized in the Jordan by Jerome. Elsewhere in *The Martyrs,* Chateaubriand reveled in detailing the decadence of the ancient world, with its gladiators, prostitutes, bacchanalians, and wild beasts in the arena. His description of a glittering, Alma-Tádema-esque Roman banquet could have applied to Mary Magdalene's feasts in DeMille's *King of Kings.*

> With hands filled with branches of dill, and brow crowned with chaplets of roses and violets, each guest abandoned himself to transports of joy. Fluteplayers, skilled in the arts of Terpsichore, inflamed the passions by effeminate dances and voluptuous songs. . . . Marble, crystal, silver, gold, and precious stones reflected and multiplied the blaze of torches, while the odors of the perfumes of Arabia mingled with those of the wines of Greece.[30]

Chateaubriand also described in detail Cymodoce's numerous costumes, including the helmet and armor she dons when she disguises herself as a soldier and flees from the dungeon where she has been thrown by a jealous suitor named Hierocles (a real historical figure). She manages to escape just in time to watch Eudorus, after having his flesh torn apart by hooks and burnt with pitch, being marched through the streets of Rome to the Coliseum while onlookers pelt him with stones and broken pottery.

Eudorus the martyr becomes an image of Jesus in his sufferings: "[H]e was treated as if he had been the Christ for whom these wretches had so much horror."[31] When Cymodoce jumps down to the floor of the arena to kiss his feet and embrace his lacerated chest and arms, the mob, most likely modeled on the crowds who flocked to the guillotines of the French Revolution, screams for both their deaths. In an improbable but affecting scene, the pair exchange marriage vows in front of the roaring spectators, and Eudorus tears off his cloak to protect Cymodoce's modesty before the two of them are devoured by a tiger.

Renan, who had read *The Martyrs,* worked a reference to Cymodoce into *Antichrist,* the fourth volume of his *History of the Origins of Christianity,* which dealt with Nero's persecutions of Christians, especially (as Renan imagined) good-looking young maidens. Flaubert, who as a youth had memorized certain passages from *The Martyrs,* undoubtedly used Eudorus's ordeal as a model for the scene in his novel *Salammbô* in which his hero undergoes similar tortures before his equally horrible death. Many other of Chateaubriand's literary touches appeared in *Salammbô* and in "Herodias."

As popular among 19th-century readers as *The Genius of Christianity, The Martyrs* became a template for overdramatized Christian history. Its offspring was the Hollywood Bible movie, with its share of wreathed heads, marble palaces, flickering torches, orgies, spectacles of brutality, and lovely females in décolletage or less. Chateaubriand was also widely imitated in his own day by others besides his French contemporaries. In 1821, John Gibson Lockhart (1794–1854), the son-in-law of Walter Scott and a pioneer of the costume novel in Britain, published his *Valerius,* in which a young Roman of the emperor Trajan's time falls in love with the Christian maiden Athanasia and converts to her faith. Edward Bulwer-Lytton (1803–1873) followed suit in 1834 with his own Christian-pagan melodrama, *The Last Days of Pompeii.*

The most flamboyant of these early-19th-century Christian productions was not a historical novel in the strictest sense. Rather, it was a life of Jesus, nearly 2,000 pages long, which was the result of a seven-year collaboration between Anna Katharina Emmerich (1774–1824), a German housemaid-turned-nun who claimed to have the stigmata, and Clemens Brentano (1778–1842), a German Romantic poet. Brentano maintained that he had transcribed a series of visions experienced by Emmerich while she lay in bed in the Westphalian town of Dülmen suffering from her wounds and receiving an ever-increasing number of pilgrims. In 1833 he published part of his account in a book titled *The Dolorous Passion of Our Lord Jesus Christ.* After Brentano's death, a Redemptorist priest named Carl E. Schmöger sifted through the poet's journals and issued two more collections of Emmerich's visions, *The Life of the Blessed Virgin Mary* in 1852, and *The Life of Our Lord and Savior Jesus Christ,* a conflation of the first two books that appeared in both German and French in 1858.

Although the books received little official fanfare, they quietly began to sell, and went into one edition after another. Even the Protestant Albert Schweitzer, writing at the turn of the century, knew the Emmerich-Brentano corpus well, and summarized it in his *Quest of the Historical Jesus. The Life of Our Lord and Saviour Jesus Christ* (which is still in print at Catholic presses) was in some ways a riposte to Strauss's *Life of Jesus,* painstakingly retelling the Gospel stories—along with some material from the second-century apocryphal gospels—that Strauss had dismissed as wholly mythical and imaginary.

Emmerich did not have the typical mystic's preoccupation with the intensity of her own religious experiences. Her forte was an abundance of meticulous detail. She told her readers what Jesus and his disciples wore—sometimes down to their undergarments—on every single occasion. She explained how the houses of Gospel personages were laid out architecturally, and what sort of music they played at their feasts. She gave names, ages, and personalities to various anonymous figures in the New Testament, and added dozens more. She assessed their characters' faults and virtues, described what they ate for dinner, and told whom they had married.

Everyone in the Gospels came alive: Judas, with a red beard and a dancing-girl mother who had borne him out of wedlock; Peter, who owned no fewer than three fishing boats; and the bride at the marriage feast at Cana, a special friend of Jesus' mother, Mary, who had helped her choose her wedding ring. Mary Magdalene, who had a huge wardrobe of silk veils and embroidered dresses, quarreled off and on with her sister, Martha of Bethany. Jesus traveled extensively outside Palestine, visiting Cyprus, the Chaldean home of the Three Kings, and Salamis, where he dined at the proconsul's table. As intrigued by marriages, engagements, family ties, and household arrangements as was her English contemporary Jane Austen, Emmerich reported numerous weddings, births, and reconciliations between estranged spouses that were nowhere to be found in the Gospels.

Whether Anna Katharina Emmerich was a saint, a fraud, or simply a hysteric is a debate that continues to this day. In any case, her visions appealed immensely to Catholics of little or no education who felt besieged by a secular world they could not understand. Emmerich herself was born to peasant parents who were poor but deeply devout. She started working at the age of 12, first on a farm, then with her needle, and finally as the unpaid servant of an impoverished organist and his family in order to be able to take music lessons. Her mother would bring her food, which she would share with her famished employers.

At age 28, Emmerich entered a convent of Augustinian nuns at Dülmen, where she annoyed the other sisters with her frail health, her frequent ecstatic trances, and her desire to be treated as the lowliest of the lowly. After Napoleon Bonaparte conquered Prussia in 1806, his brother Jerome, whom he had set up as king of Westphalia, went on an anticlerical rampage. When he secularized Emmerich's convent in 1812, she took a room in the home of a priest.

The following year, she began experiencing the stigmata, which caused her such terrible pain that she remained bedridden for the rest of her life. She suffered not only the four nail wounds in her hands and feet but also the marks of the crown of thorns and two crosses imprinted on her chest. As the wounds continued to bleed intermittently, especially on Good Friday, she tried to keep them a secret, but eventually her bandaged hands and feet attracted attention. After being forced to undergo grueling interrogations, first from the church and then from civil authorities, she was not pronounced an impostor, but neither did she receive official ecclesiastical recognition.

Nonetheless, for the smallholders, day-laborers, and kitchen maids of Westphalia, the suffering but always cheerful Emmerich was a holy hermit and her bedside a shrine. Every day she received visitors who came to confide their sorrows and their sins. She listened to their woes with sympathy and often dispensed her own home remedies for their ailments. By the time of her death, she was known far and wide as the Beguine of Dülmen, and there was an immediate movement to canonize her that has recently been revived.

Katharina Emmerich was a powerful symbol of defiance toward modernity, and also of a masochism that seemed to border on the sexually perverse. In the mid–20th century, the French literary critic Jean Paulhan, in his preface to *The Story of O,* which his mistress had written under a pseudonym, made reference to the nun of Dülmen, comparing her to Justine, the Marquis de Sade's masochistic heroine. In fact, there was an ambiguous element of barely sublimated eroticism in both Emmerich's fascination with the suffering Jesus (whom she called her "bridegroom") and her extraordinary passivity. When Flaubert gently caricatured this aspect of 19th-century Catholicism in the convent school passages of his *Madame Bovary,* he might well have had Katharina Emmerich in mind.

By 1818, the year in which Clemens Brentano arrived in Dülmen and installed himself at her bedside, Emmerich was already famous throughout Germany for her bleeding stigmata. Brentano himself was a prosperous Frankfurt merchant's son who had studied for years at Jean, Halle, and Göttingen without ever taking a degree. Eventually, he began writing poetry and collecting German folk-songs and fairy tales. The three-volume compilation of old ballads titled *Des Knaben Wunderhorn* ("The Boy's Magical Horn"), which he and his brother-in-law, the novelist Achim von Arnim, published from 1805 to 1808, was to exert a powerful influence on poetry and music both in Germany and abroad. Heinrich Heine, the brothers Grimm, Henry Wadsworth Longfellow, and Gustav Mahler were only a few of Brentano and Arnim's artistic debtors. Brentano's sister, Bettina von Arnim, was a well-known poet in her own right, who carried on a regular correspondence with Beethoven.

After the success of *Des Knaben Wunderhorn,* Brentano suffered a decade of disillusionment and despair marked by the death of his first wife and a failed second marriage. During this time of emotional stress, he rediscovered the Catholic faith of his youth, and the experience riveted his creativity. When he first met Emmerich, he was stunned when she told him that she already knew who he was and that God had sent him to help her write down her revelations. In Katharina Emmerich, Brentano found what he had been looking for all his life.

At first glance, the relationship between these two entirely different middle-aged personalities—the world-weary poet who had traveled all over Germany, and the semi-literate "victim soul" who had never been outside Westphalia—would perhaps strike one as odd. In any case, it reflected an extraordinary singlemindedness of purpose: When reading the text, it is virtually impossible to separate Emmerich's raw visionary material from the shaping Brentano gave to it. While Brentano undoubtedly supplied much of the literary flair, elaborating on the visions as he recrafted them, Emmerich herself was clearly endowed with a vivid imagination. Above all, *The Life of Our Lord* evokes a series of wide-angle photographs, or perhaps movie stills, with a cast of thousands. Emmerich's description of Jesus carrying his cross through Jerusalem to Calvary is a graphic example of her talent for setting the scene:

> The procession of the Crucifixion was headed by a trumpeter, who sounded his trumpet at every street corner and proclaimed the execution. Some paces behind him came a crowd of boys and other rude fellows, carrying drink, cords, nails, wedges, and baskets of tools of all kinds, while sturdy servant-men bore poles, ladders, and trunks belonging to the crosses of the thieves. The ladders consisted of mere poles, through which long wooden pegs were run. Then followed some of the mounted Pharisees, after whom came a lad bearing on his breast the inscription Pilate had written for the cross. The crown of thorns, which it was impossible to leave on during the carriage of the cross, was taken from Christ's head and placed on the end of a pole, which this lad now carried over his shoulder. This boy was not very wicked.
>
> And next came Our Lord and Redeemer bowed down under the heavy weight of the cross, bruised, torn with scourges, exhausted, and tottering. Since the Last Supper of the preceding evening without food, drink, and sleep, under continual ill-treatment that might of itself have ended in death, consumed by loss of blood, wounds, fever, thirst, and unutterable interior pain and horror, Jesus walked with tottering steps, His back bent low, his feet naked and bleeding. With His right hand He grasped the heavy load on His right shoulder, and with the left He wearily tried to raise the flowing garment constantly impeding His uncertain steps. The four executioners held at some distance the cords fastened to His fetter-girdle. The two in front dragged Him forward, while the two behind urged Him on. In this way he was not sure of one step, and the tugging cords constantly prevented His lifting His robe.[32]

The Emmerich-Brentano version of Jesus' passion, which takes up a full quarter of the book, is indeed harrowing. While the Gospel accounts are laconic and matter-of-fact, Emmerich's narrative piles on excruciating details: Jesus is not just nailed to the cross, but his bones are brutally torn from their joints as the executioners pull his hands and feet to fit the holes made by the nails.

The Life of Our Lord is hardly without artistic flaws. Emmerich frequently arranged chance meetings between Jesus and certain New Testament characters—the Good Thief, for example—long before their dramatic encounters in the Gospels, thereby diluting narrative suspense. She also could not resist bringing Jesus' mother, Mary, into almost every episode of his life. Moreover, the staggering amount of detail gives the book a suffocating quality that leaves nothing to the reader's imagination. Worst of all, Emmerich often slipped into bathos during the passages that were intended to be most reverent. In her description of Jesus' being stripped of his garments before his crucifixion, while Mary wrings her hands over her son's nakedness and considers passing him her veil, a long-lost nephew of Joseph named Jonadab suddenly emerges from the crowd to hand Jesus a piece of linen cloth. As Emmerich digresses to explain that Joseph had pawned his donkey with Jonadab after returning from his flight into Egypt, the reader can scarcely refrain from chuckling.

Much of the geography in Emmerich's book was uncannily accurate for a woman who had scarcely been to school. The 19th-century Swiss New Testament scholar Johann Leonhard Hug was astonished that her topography of Jerusalem in *The Dolorous Passion* matched Josephus's own descriptions of the city. In other places, however, her depiction of Holy Land locations was completely mistaken.

While *The Life of Our Lord* had literary precedents in medieval and Counter-Reformation devotional writings, one of its primary sources undoubtedly was *The Martyrs,* which Brentano had likely read. There are many features of *The Martyrs* in Emmerich's book, including costumes, travelogues, banquets, young lovers, and a *via dolorosa* that might well have been modeled on Eudorus's march to the Coliseum.

It is also entirely possible that Ernest Renan came across a copy of *The Life of Our Lord* before he began working on his own *Life of Jesus.* Emmerich's Mary Magdalene, for example, had the same impulsive, passionate nature that had led Renan to imagine her fantasizing Jesus' resurrection. At the cross, Emmerich's Magdalene "was like one out of her mind. She tore her face with her finger nails, till her eyes and cheeks were covered with blood."[33]

Both Renan and Chateaubriand had Napoleon Bonaparte to thank for their visits to the Holy Land. In 1798, he had invaded Egypt, which like Palestine at the time was part of the Ottoman Empire. The Egyptian incursion was a strategic move against England, designed to block its trade routes and to detach India from British rule. What Napoleon actually accomplished was a penetration of the seemingly invincible frontier of the Ottoman Turks, who had controlled the Near East since the 15th century, thereby allowing

Western scholars to explore previously forbidden territory. Napoleon made his Egyptian military campaign a scholarly one as well, enlisting the aid of a team of several dozen linguists and Quranic experts. His troops' discovery of the Rosetta Stone—the key to the hieroglyphics of the Pharaohs' tombs—on the Nile delta in 1799 was his crowning achievement.

In the late 17th century, the Turkish empire had stretched from Budapest to Persia, and from Syria to the entire northern coast of Africa. In 1683, the Turkish grand vizier Kara Mustafa had besieged and nearly conquered Vienna, the capital of the Holy Roman Empire. Over the centuries, only a handful of travelers, traders, and religious pilgrims (mostly from Eastern Christendom) had ventured into the Near East. Volney, the scholar who gave his name to the prize that Renan won in 1847, was one of the few Westerners to conduct scientific research behind Ottoman lines. Napoleon's conquest suddenly made the Near East easily accessible to the West.

In 1805, the Turks and the British joined forces to drive out Napoleon's army, resulting in England's total control over Egypt and its environs. The following year, Turkey and Britain signed the Treaty of Chanak, which assured unofficial British hegemony throughout the entire Mediterranean. Although short-lived, the French regime in Cairo (marked by a brief foray into Syria) had spawned a fascination with all things Egyptian, and a passion for visiting the Near East. In 1800, the philosopher Friedrich von Schlegel declared in a lecture, "It is in the Orient that we must search for the highest Romanticism."[34] Chateaubriand was the first in a long line of Western writers of the 19th and 20th centuries to use their Near East travels as a stage for dramatizing their own idiosyncratic interest in the outlandish, the peculiar, and the religious. As Edward Said once noted: "After Chateaubriand, pilgrims rewrote him."[35]

Among the various historians, artists, and literati fascinated by the region were Lord Byron (1788–1824); Alphonse Lamartine (1790–1869); Gérard de Nerval (1808–1855); Richard Burton (1821–1890), the translator of the *Arabian Nights,* who disguised himself as a Muslim pilgrim so as to sneak into Mecca; Alexander Kinglake (1809–1891); E. M. Forster (1879–1970); and T. E. Lawrence (1888–1935), who like Burton donned Arab clothing and passed himself off as a Muslim. In general these Orientalists were to find the decaying Ottoman Empire both wondrously exotic and woefully backward—the "sick man of Europe" limping along in a losing cultural race with the West.

From 1849 to 1851, Flaubert traveled to Egypt, Syria, Lebanon, Turkey, and Greece. Especially in Egypt, when not indulging his satyriasis (whereby he caught several venereal diseases), he was observing and recording in detail the physically and sexually grotesque: belly dancers, transvestites, advanced-stage syphilitics, and cadavers under dissection. From Lebanon he rode south to Jerusalem, thinking about Chateaubriand and his visit to the Holy Land and imagining Jesus walking barefoot along the very same roads. Just outside the city, he had a vision—probably brought on by one of his chronic epileptic seizures—of Jesus dressed in blue and surrounded by a crowd as he set out to climb the Mount of Olives. In Nazareth, he stared hungrily at the Arab women, and concluded that they had not changed since biblical times. Their robes, gathered at the waist with tight sashes, gave their bodies what he called a "biblical" movement that emphasized their hips and buttocks and reminded him of the Song of Solomon.[36] When the French Romantic poet and novelist Lamartine had visited the Holy Land in 1833, he had also claimed that the landscape itself afforded him spiritual insights into Jesus, whose spurning by the priests and Pharisees in Jerusalem called to Lamartine's mind Rousseau's ostracism from Geneva.

That same year, the French painter Horace Vernet traveled to Algeria and Syria, where he fancied that the Arabs lived, dressed, and even looked exactly like the Hebrews and Egyptians of biblical days. From Damascus he wrote: "This country has no epochs. Transport yourself a few thousand years back, it is always the same physiognomy. . . . The Arabs have not changed."[37] After Vernet started painting biblical scenes—Rebecca with her pitcher, Hagar driven out into the desert by Abraham—in which the characters wore the Arab garb of the 19th century, other French artists followed suit, drawing on the supposed "timelessness" of the Near East for the Bedouin costumes of their scriptural subjects.

Holman Hunt (1827–1910), one of the founders of the Pre-Raphaelite movement in England, made three prolonged voyages to Palestine and Syria from the 1850s to the 1880s. Hunt's intention was to "Orientalize" biblical art, liberating it from the Renaissance and Baroque traditions that had dominated Western religious art for hundreds of years. Accordingly, he sought out models from the Jewish population of Jerusalem, and consulted with rabbis on how to depict the rituals of scriptural times. Hunt boldly painted Jesus' mother not in the traditional red and blue of the Renaissance, but in an embroidered Palestinian robe and carrying a sheaf of wheat on her head. In 1864, the year after Renan's *Life of Jesus* appeared, the French art critic Thoré-Bürger advised: "Instead of coldly inventing in a Paris studio the scene of Rachel at the well, or the Samaritan woman conversing with Jesus, go and paint in the desert some fountain in the middle of an oasis, with the Arab girls drawing water."[38]

In 1886, yet another French painter, James Joseph Jacques Tissot (1836–1902), spent seven months in Palestine, returning for another four-month stay in 1888, when he also visited Egypt, Syria, and Lebanon. From various sketches, notes, and photographs, over the next six years he produced an array of 365 watercolors and pen drawings of the life of Jesus, the largest biblical series ever created in the Orientalist mode. Years before, Tissot had become famous for his carefully crafted, painstakingly realistic depictions of high society in Paris and again in London, where he had lived for ten years after the Franco-Prussian War. In all his paintings, he had paid particular attention to the dresses of the strikingly beautiful women who posed for him, sometimes showing more of their calves and petticoats than art critics deemed strictly necessary.

In 1882, while Tissot was still living in London, his mistress and favorite model, Kathleen Newton, died of tuberculosis at age 28. A convent-educated Irishwoman whose husband had divorced her because of an adulterous affair that resulted in the birth of a child, she was taken in by Tissot, who became not only her lover but her only friend. Beside himself with grief at her death, he returned to Paris and dabbled for a while in spiritualism, hoping to contact her beyond the grave. In 1885, while sketching nuns at the Church of St. Sulpice for one of his genre paintings, he had a vision of Jesus covered with blood and crowned with thorns, which resulted in his decision to return to Catholicism and devote the rest of his life to illustrating the Bible. For a society painter of the militantly anticlerical Third Republic, it was not an easy choice. In fact, a number of his irreligious artist friends, including Edgar Degas, never stopped mocking him as an exploiter of the commercial possibilities of faith.

Tissot prepared himself for his Holy Land voyages by reading the Gospels, the Talmud, early Christian apocrypha, and Josephus's Jewish histories, as well as speaking with archaeologists and rabbis. He read also Katharina Emmerich's *Life of Our Lord and Savior Jesus Christ,* and was struck by the photographic quality of her visions. The paintings that came out of his travels and research, 270 of which he exhibited in Paris in 1894 together with appropriate scriptural passages, combined the mystical and the hyper-realistic, including such subjects as the boy Jesus with his mother at an Egyptian harbor filled with old boats, and the crowds around the cross as seen from Jesus' perspective. Encapsulated in a book of the Gospel illustrations titled *The Life of Our Savior, Jesus Christ* that Tissot published in 1896 and 1897, the exhibit was immensely popular with Catholics and Protestants alike. Like Emmerich, Tissot had provided an answer to skeptics like Renan, "proving" in concrete terms that the events reported in the Gospels had really taken place.

Tissot turned next to a series of illustrations of Old Testament episodes that were less mystical and more openly narrative, and thus more successful as works of art. Again, he studied archaeology and ethnography in an effort to make his paintings historically accurate. In August of 1897, some peasants in the southeastern Spanish town of Elche, near Alicante, had dug up a life-size stone bust of a woman wearing a diadem flanked by huge wheels that framed her face and covered her ears. Known as the Dama de Elche, the sculpture was thought to be the work of an artist from the ancient Iberian civilization that had dominated Spain before the Roman invasion. The parallels between her ornaments and those depicted in ancient Assyrian art led archeologists to speculate further that the bust had come to Spain with the Phoenicians, who had been trading with the Iberians around Elche since the days of King Solomon. After the Louvre acquired the Dama, Tissot sketched her numerous times, concluding that her huge ear-wheels must have been common among ancient Israelite women as well as Phoenicians. He therefore hung them on the ears of many of the Hebrew beauties in his Old Testament illustrations, including Sarah, the wife of Abraham.

Many contemporary art historians believe that the Dama (who resembles no other work of Iberian art) was actually a late-19th-century forgery. Indeed, her ear-wheels and languid facial expression look more art nouveau than Near Eastern. Despite such historical faux pas, because of his attention to detail, his flair for dramatic composition, and his extraordinary commercial success, Tissot became the artist who most influenced 20th-century biblical movie-making. In 1912, the French studio Pathé used his illustrations as models for set decorations in the first film ever made on the life of Jesus. Four years later, D. W. Griffith drew on Tissot's Old Testament paintings for his *Intolerance.* DeMille used the Pathé movie, the biblical sequences in *Intolerance,* reproductions of Tissot's illustrations, and the engravings of Gustave Doré to create *King of Kings.*

All those 19th-century Orientalist artists and scholars, Renan included, completely ignored the fact that nearly two millennia had passed and several empires had risen and fallen between their time and that of Jesus. While the modes of agricultural production and many of the foodstuffs of the Near East were much the same as those recorded in the Bible, the topography, economy, clothing, religion, language, and even ethnicity of the Holy Land's inhabitants had changed beyond recognition. Most of the thriving cities described by the ancients were gone or reduced to villages. The population of Palestine had fallen from around two million in Jesus' day to half a million, only one-fifth of which was Christian and Jewish, by the end of the 19th century. The rural idyll of sleepy towns, picturesque wells, flowing robes, and meandering donkeys encountered by the Orientalists in Galilee and Judea bore little resemblance to the bustling, densely populated, polyglot world of Jesus, crisscrossed by busy trade routes and crowded with a hodgepodge of cultures, architectural styles, and wares of every kind.

With the literary and artistic travelers to the Holy Land came the archaeologists, and later the tourists. The first of the scientific explorers was Edward Robinson from Auburn Seminary, who published a three-volume topographical survey of Palestine in 1841. Next came Titus Tobler, a German-Swiss physician whose hobby was biblical topography. For several decades, Robinson, Tobler, and their colleagues mapped numerous places mentioned in the Bible. Under Queen Victoria's patronage, the Palestine Exploration Society was launched in 1865 as the first permanent body to fund long-term archaeological projects.

Robinson, Tobler, and the other early explorers brought with them a Protestant skepticism regarding the authenticity of many of the shrines that were traditionally associated with Jesus and venerated by Catholic and Eastern Christian pilgrims. These included numerous historically dubious sites such as the room where the Last Supper was held, the impression made by Jesus' knees as he prayed in the Garden of Gethsemane, and the exact spot where the cock crowed after the apostle Peter betrayed Jesus. None of these holy places predated the fourth-century reign of the emperor Constantine, who had transformed Jerusalem from a pagan Roman city into an attraction for Christian pilgrims. The Protestant archaeologists also harbored a revulsion at the swarthy, smelly foreigners who flocked to the sites mumbling rituals, peddling religious trinkets, and squabbling over which among the Catholic, Greek Orthodox, and Armenian churches had right of possession over the shrines.

The main target of Protestant skepticism (and disgust) was the Church of the Holy Sepulcher, a cavernous basilica that was supposed to have been built over the site of Calvary and Jesus' tomb. Aided by his court historian Eusebius and a body of Christian oral tradition about Jerusalem's holy places,

Constantine had personally selected the location, north of the remains of Herod the Great's palace and west of the Temple Mount. By the 19th century, the church was a dank, dimly lit, earthquake-damaged ruin of an edifice that had replaced Constantine's original church after its destruction by the Caliph of Cairo's army in 1099. It also stank of incense and candle fumes, and ugly girders covered its walls because the various monks and priests could not agree on repairs.

Tobler determined that the basilica could not have been the site of Jesus' death and burial, since it lay inside the ancient walls of Jerusalem (Jewish purity laws at the time of the Second Temple banned tombs within the city limits). In Jesus' day, Jerusalem was surrounded by two walls (a third was built shortly after his death), and traces of both had virtually disappeared during the intervening centuries. Although it was possible to hypothesize a city wall between the church and Herod's palace, Calvary was traditionally supposed to have been a hill (although the Gospels do not describe it as such), and Tobler surmised that no one would erect a line of fortification next to a high point from which enemies could attack.

Tobler's views on Calvary, which generally prevailed among his contemporaries received a boost when the British general Charles Gordon (1833–1885), nicknamed "Chinese" Gordon for having suppressed the Taiping Rebellion against the Manchu dynasty (and also for his fondness for Chinese costumes), arrived in Jerusalem in 1883 armed with a Bible and his own ideas about New Testament sites. Gordon concluded that the real Calvary was a high point well north of Jerusalem, which was known as Skull Hill because it had the shape of a human skull. His theory took into account the fact that the word Calvary (Golgotha in Hebrew) was derived from the Latin *calvaria,* meaning skull. Adjacent to Skull Hill was a garden with an old tomb cut into sheer rock that had been discovered in 1867 while the property owner was removing refuse. Both the tomb and Skull Hill were some distance north of the walls that the Turks had built around Jerusalem.

Devoid of tawdry icons and squabbling monks, Gordon's "Garden Tomb" satisfied Protestant notions of a suitable burial place for Jesus. After the site was purchased by the British and endorsed by the Archbishop of Canterbury in 1893, it became a Protestant shrine. Although many evangelical Protestants still venerate the Garden Tomb as Jesus' burial place, few archaeologists nowadays give Gordon's theory much credence. While there is evidence that it was used as a tomb in the Iron Age and again during Byzantine times, the gravesite has no features of a first-century Jewish burial place. Moreover, Skull Hill received its name (and probably its shape) long after Jesus' day. The Church of the Holy Sepulcher has also gained new archaeological respectability as a likely site for Calvary and the tomb. Recent excavations near the church have revealed that it was built not on a hilltop, but adjacent to an ancient quarry filled with rubble from the first century and before, which would definitely have lain outside city walls.

The story of the Garden Tomb illustrates how readily 19th-century visitors to the Holy Land refashioned New Testament history from impressions gained during a few months or even weeks of travel. The English novelist Anthony Trollope (1813–1882) gave this tendency a delicious sendup in his 1859 novel, *The Bertrams,* which he based in part on a tour of Palestine he had made in the spring of 1858 while on a business trip to Alexandria on behalf of the British Post Office. *The Bertrams* satirized the hordes of middle-class English and American tourists who were flooding the Holy Land during the 1840s and 1850s, flush with the new prosperity brought by the Industrial Revolution. Trollope's fictional tourists are outrageously Anglo-Saxon: They gad about in native costume, complain about the unfamiliar food at their Jerusalem hotel, barge into religious services, and hold a picnic (complete with a ham!) in the Valley of Jehoshaphat, the sacred resting place of Jewish kings. Finally, Trollope's hero, George Bertram, who has been planning on a clerical career, takes one look at the fleabag basilica of the Holy Sepulcher packed with grubby Holy Week pilgrims and promptly loses his faith. He thereupon returns to England and writes a skeptical book called *The Romance of the Gospels* (a spoof of Strauss's *Life of Jesus*) that bars him forever from the cloth.

By the latter part of the century, the Holy Land was a grid on which Western writers, artists, archaeologists, and well-heeled tourists alike worked out their fantasies, religious or otherwise, about who Jesus really was. Ernest Renan was the most spectacular example. No sooner had his *Life of Jesus* appeared than he began working on a sequel. With Henriette dead, Cornélie took over her role of amanuensis, manager, and chief guardian of the Renan shrine. On the 1864 trip that took him to Egypt to meet Lesseps, Renan also visited Damascus, Antioch, and parts of Greece, attempting to retrace the voyages of Paul as narrated in the Acts of the Apostles.

Renan's next two books, *The Apostles* (1866) and *Saint Paul* (1869), bore the mark of his new friendship with Flaubert. *Salammbô* was based on Flaubert's extensive Near Eastern travels. Since Carthage had been founded by the Phoenicians, Flaubert decided that whatever could be said about the ancient Levant could also be said about Carthage. He used his 19th-century Near Eastern impressions to transport his readers to the Carthaginian court of Hamilcar Barca, father of Hannibal, 250 years before Jesus' birth. His protagonist, Salammbô, Hamilcar's daughter and a priestess of the fertility goddess Tanit, was modeled at least in part on a celebrated dancer-courtesan named Kuchuk Hannem with whom Flaubert had slept many years before in Cairo. As a sign of her virginity, she wears a thin gold chain that loosely binds her ankles together. The chain breaks during the novel's erotic climax, when she spends the night in the tent of her lover, the mercenary Mâtho. Salammbô's hieratic, pornographic "period" clothes, tight along the hips and exposing the breasts, drew denunciations from French pulpits. The Catholic Church also placed both *Salammbô* and *Madame Bovary* (for which Flaubert had been tried and acquitted on charges of corrupting public morals) on its Index of Forbidden Books.

Salammbô was a tour de force of costumes, scenery, sensuality, and above all brutality, with its almost clinically detached descriptions of appalling barbarities, including crucifixions, floggings, tortured prisoners, mistreated animals, mutilated corpses, cannibalism, the burning alive of children in sacrifice to the god Moloch, and the final ordeal of Mâtho, which occupies a full five pages of the book. The infuriated crowd whips Mâtho to ribbons, rips the flesh off his bones, sticks him with needles, douses him with boiling oil, and burns him with red-hot irons. Finally, a priest of the sun god splits open his chest and tears out his heart as an offering, in front of the swooning Salammbô, who is sitting on the sidelines trussed in her jewels.

Flaubert's latest creation was rivaled only by Victor Hugo's *Les Misérables* as the most talked-about French novel of 1862. The Empress Eugénie wanted to dress up as Salammbô for a masked ball, except that Jane de Tourbey, Madame Rimsky-Korsakov, and Queen Isabella II of Spain had already beaten her to it. There was even talk of a Salammbô opera, and Giuseppe Verdi and Hector Berlioz both offered to write the music. Despite its huge popular success, however, *Salammbô* received a number of unfavorable reviews as a sensationalistic knock-off of *The Martyrs.* When Charles-Augustin Sainte-Beuve (1804–1869), France's most famous literary critic, called attention to Flaubert's fascination with cruelty, the author feared that he might be arrested and prosecuted as another Marquis de Sade.

Salammbô, which fused religion, sex, cruelty, and Orientalia as no other book ever had, found an immediate convert in Renan, who was fascinated with punishment and spectacle as instruments of social control. (He would later publish his theories in a collection of essays that looked forward to a world governed by an oligarchy of intellectuals who possessed unlimited power and used torture and terror to keep the rest of humanity in line.) Beginning with *The Apostles,* he began embellishing his narratives of Christian origins with orgiastic panoramas that could only have been borrowed from Flaubert—and probably from *The Martyrs* as well. His debauchery-sotted picture of Antioch in the time of Paul of Tarsus resembled Flaubert's Carthage:

> [It was] an inconceivable medley of merry-andrews, quacks, buffoons, magicians, miracle-mongers, sorcerers, priests, impostors, a city of races, games, dances, processions, fetes, debauches, of unbridled luxury, of all the follies of the East, of the most unhealthy superstitions, and of the fanaticism of the orgy. By turns servile and ungrateful, cowardly and insolent, the people of Antioch were the perfect model of those crowds devoted to Caesarism, without country, without nationality, without family honor, without a name to keep. . . . The great Corso which traversed the city was like a theatre, where rolled, day after day, the waves of a trifling, light-headed, changeable, insurrection-loving population. . . . The sights were strange; there were some games in which bands of naked girls took part in all the exercises with a mere fillet around them; at the celebrated festival of Naiouma, troupes of courtesans swarmed in public in basins filled with limpid water.[39]

The fourth volume, titled *Antichrist* (1873), covered the reign of Nero, whom Renan considered a Hegelian antithesis of Jesus (and hence an "antichrist"). As he had previously done with Jesus, Renan portrayed the degenerate emperor as a version of himself, projecting not only his power fantasies but also the pleasure he derived from the violation of young and virtuous female martyrs:

> Living flesh quivering in a wild beast's jaw, or a poor shrinking girl, screening herself by a modest gesture, then tossed by a bull and cast in lifeless fragments on the gravel of the arena, must exhibit a play of form and color worthy of an artist-sense like his. Here [Nero] was, in the front row, on a low balcony, in a group of vestals and curule magistrates—with his ill-favored countenance, his short sight, his blue eyes, his curled light-brown hair, his cruel mouth, his air like a big sulky baby, at once cross and droll, open-mouthed, swollen with vanity, while brazen music throbbed in the air, turned to a bloody mist. He would,

> no doubt, inspect with a critic's eye the shrinking attitudes of these new Dirces, and I imagine he found a charm he had never known before in the air of resignation with which these pure-hearted girls faced their hideous death.
>
> . . . .
>
> It was an hour registered in heaven when womanly purity, till now so scrupulously hidden from the world's eye, appeared in open daylight before fifty thousand spectators, unashamed as the marble figure in a sculptor's studio, in the form of a maiden about to die. . . . When with brutal hand the jaded world tore away the veil of Christian modesty, that it might find a new sensation in the martyr's agony, the poor child might think of herself, "I, too, am beautiful."[40]

This sort of algolagnia, which was nowhere to be found in Renan's ancient Roman sources, had more than enough parallels in *Salammbô.* From Flaubert, Renan had learned how to rewrite the history of Christian origins as erotic fiction. In return, Flaubert borrowed from Renan's superior scholarship. While writing "Herodias" during the mid-1870s, he consulted *The Life of Jesus* and *The Apostles,* and also used Renan's personal library.

Besides their common taste for literary sadism, Renan and Flaubert shared a complex attitude toward Catholicism. In some ways, Flaubert was more sympathetic than Renan toward the Catholic aesthetic and simple piety, and he lacked Renan's terrible bitterness toward the church. Although Flaubert despised theology and did not believe in metaphysics, he soaked up Catholicism's theatricality, which appealed to his artistic eye. His *Temptation of Saint Anthony,* which he started as a young man and rewrote many times, was inspired by a puppet show (one of the last medieval miracle plays) about the hermit and his pet pig that was staged annually in front of the Rouen cathedral on Anthony's feast day. He was also delighted when his *Three Tales* ("Herodias," "St. Julian the Hospitaller," and "A Simple Heart," the story of a servant girl who confuses her mistress's stuffed parrot with the Holy Spirit) found its way onto lists of recommended reading for Catholics. By the end of his life, he even attended Mass every now and then, although he could never quite overcome his religious skepticism. When he died in 1880—penniless and possibly of tertiary syphilis—his friends managed to secure him a Catholic funeral.

Flaubert based his "Herodias" on his Near Eastern tour of nearly thirty years before, and on another stained-glass window from Rouen cathedral, this one depicting Salome, Herod Antipas's teenage stepdaughter, dancing on her hands. In combining Salome's acrobatics from Rouen with memories of Kuchuk Hannem's dancing the "Bee," during which she would slowly remove one garment at a time to the accompaniment of a flute, "Herodias" was a New Testament reworking of *Salammbô.* Salome's performance takes place at Antipas's birthday party, a Chateaubriandesque orgy where the beautiful, the ugly, and the epicene meet in a riveting panoply:

> Aulus wore his robe of violet silk interwoven with silver thread with the sleeves tied together to keep them out of the way. His hair was dressed in tiered rolls, and a sapphire necklace sparkled on his bosom, plump and white as a woman's. Beside him, sitting cross-legged on the mat, was a very beautiful boy, with a fixed smile. Aulus had seen him in the kitchens, could no longer do without him, and as he found it hard to remember his Chaldean name, simply called him "the Asiatic." From time to time he stretched out on the triclinium. Then his bare feet dominated the assembly.
>
> On that side were the priests and Antipas's officials, citizens of Jerusalem, leading men from the Greek towns, and, beneath the Proconsul, Marcellus with the publicans, friends of the Tetrarch, the notables of Cana, Ptolemais, Jericho; then, all mixed together, men from the mountains of Lebanon and Herod's old soldiers: a dozen Thracians, a Gaul, two Germans, gazelle hunters, Idumean herdsmen, the sultan of Palmyra, sailors from Eziongaber. Each one of them had in front of him a cake of soft dough to wipe his fingers and their arms reached out like vultures' necks to pick out olives, pistachios, almonds. Every face was joyful beneath a garland of flowers.[41]

Flaubert, who had seen plenty of homosexual prostitution in Egypt, transposed it across the Suez and backward some 2,000 years.

In 1893, Flaubert's "Herodias" became the source for *Salomé,* a play in French by Oscar Wilde (1854–1900), which his lover, Lord Alfred Douglas (an aspiring poet who coined the phrase "the love that dares not speak its name"), then translated into ponderous English. Although Wilde retained the Hebrew name "Jokanaan," that Flaubert had given to John the Baptist in "Herodias," he reworked the plot somewhat, making Salome the villainess instead of her mother. A sexual predator who is literally consumed with desire for the Baptist, when Salome realizes she cannot have him, she performs the Dance of the Seven Veils (Wilde's version of the "Bee") for Antipas in order to secure the prophet's death. As the executioner offers her his head on a shield, she lifts it up and kisses its mouth. Douglas's 1894 translation was famous for its morbid illustrations by the Decadent artist Aubrey Beardsley (1872–1898), who depicted Salome as an adolescent virago and John's head as a phallic symbol. In the hands of Wilde (and Flaubert), Salome had become another Mary Magdalene, a sexually charged Gospel figure.

Wilde's own version of the historical Jesus was modeled after Renan's *Life of Jesus,* which he had read and greatly admired. Although Wilde, like Renan, came to view himself as Jesus, the context in which he came to do so was very different. During two years of imprisonment (1895 to 1897) for sodomy, the result of a criminal trial that followed the foolhardy libel suit he had brought against Douglas's father, the Marquess of Queensbury (of prize-fighting fame), for calling public attention to the love affair with his son, the humiliation he suffered during his confinement as a common criminal was almost unendurable. Moreover, he had been at the height of his fame as a playwright when the Douglas scandal disgraced him and forced him to declare bankruptcy.

In his prison cell, Wilde began reading the Gospels in Greek. He also wrote a 60,000-word letter of reproach to Douglas, who had made himself scarce after the trials; it was published in 1905 under the title *De Profundis,* five years after Wilde's death. *De Profundis* was a mixture of lugubrious self-pity (besides deserting his lover, Douglas had been a world-class sponger who treated himself to Savile Row suits and imported pâté on Wilde's literary earnings), heartbreaking loneliness (after his conviction, his wife had made sure that he would never see their two young sons again), and Romantic railings against the respectability-obsessed plutocracy of fin-de-siècle Britain, whose chilly philanthropy Wilde viewed as a substitute for genuine Christian charity toward sinners and outcasts like himself. With his theatrical temperament, it is not surprising that he saw himself as Christ on the cross, and the Jewish priests who sought Christ's death as the vulgar, self-satisfied Philistines who had made their fortunes from the British Empire and then hounded him in the name of morality.

In rapturous language suffused with allusions to Dante, Wilde transformed Jesus into a fellow aesthete:

> Those whom he saved from their sins are saved simply for beautiful moments in their lives. Mary Magdalen, when she sees Christ, breaks the rich vase of alabaster that one of her seven lovers had given her and spills the odorous spices over his tired, dusty feet, and for that one moment sits for ever with Ruth and Beatrice in the tresses of the snow-white Rose of Paradise. All that Christ says

> to us by way of a little warning is that every moment should be beautiful, that the soul should always be ready for the coming of the Bridegroom, always waiting for the voice of the Lover.[42]

Besides Mary Magdalene (whose "seven lovers," like Salome's seven veils, are Wilde's inventions), the adulteress whom Jesus saved from being stoned by hypocrites figures prominently in *De Profundis.*

Whereas Renan's Jesus was fundamentally cold-hearted, Wilde imbued his Jesus with a selfless, passionate love for all mankind, which he combined with an extraordinarily Romantic sensibility. "I see in Christ not merely the essentials of the supreme romantic type, but all the accidents, the willfulnesses even, of the romantic temperament also," Wilde wrote. "Christ, like all fascinating personalities, had the power not merely of saying beautiful things but of making other people say beautiful things to him."[43]

In *De Profundis,* Wilde resolved that his next work would be a study of Jesus as the precursor of the Romantic movement. After his release from prison, however, he left England for Paris, where he was plagued by illnesses (including syphilis), overindulgence in absinthe, near-penury, and the reappearance of Douglas, who spent what little money Wilde had. Just before his death three years later, Wilde was baptized into the Catholic church. As his biographer Richard Ellman has speculated, his embrace of Catholicism might well have been yet another of his affectations, like the wearing of green carnations—but it might also have sprung from his broken heart. Although he maintained to nearly the end that he did not believe in Jesus' divinity, as he lay on his deathbed in a cheap hotel, half-conscious from morphine and swollen with infection, he wore a rosary around his neck, its crucifix on his chest, which undoubtedly gave him the most intense pleasure.

Wilde's aesthetic fascination with Jesus was part of a larger literary and artistic movement that revolved around the hermetic and occultic societies that flourished among intellectuals at the end of the century. In rebelling against the Darwinist scientific reductionism that had become fashionable, the occultists blended elements of Christian religiosity, Gnosticism, Indian philosophy, Buddhism, Neoplatonism, cabalism, spirit-raising, and magic. The devotees of occultism were essentially educated individuals who could no longer believe in Christianity, but who were nonetheless certain that there was a spiritual reality.

The best-known of these groups was the Theosophical Society, founded in 1875 by Helena Petrovna Blavatsky (1831–1891), a Russian woman of vague aristocratic connections who claimed to have lived in Tibet for seven years, after which she was able to work miracles. Until certain of her former acolytes charged her with fraud shortly before her death, Blavatsky had an enormous worldwide following.

The occult societies were usually esoteric, restricting membership, requiring initiation, and demanding strict secrecy. At least one of the groups, the Order of the Hermetic Students of the Golden Dawn, used symbolic crucifixion as a hazing ritual, during which the initiate was bound to a "cross of suffering" by ropes so tight that they cut into the flesh. William Butler Yeats, who belonged to several secret societies including Blavatsky's, underwent the Golden Dawn initiation, as did Oscar Wilde's wife, Constance.

Like many of today's New Agers, the occultists attempted to incorporate Jesus into the Eastern spirituality that so intrigued them. In 1894, Nicolas Notovitch published his *Unknown Life of Jesus Christ,* in which he speculated that Jesus had traveled to India and Tibet, and that his preaching of voluntary poverty was a result of his exposure to Buddhist monasteries. It was the first of a long line of books to postulate that Jesus had visited Tibet before beginning his ministry. In a 1902 biography of Jesus, Ernest Bosc, a French Theosophist, former secretary to Blavatsky, and author of 11 treaties on topics as diverse as hashish, cannabis, and Celtic lore, contended that Jesus himself was an occultist, and was therefore able to raise the dead. He also resurrected the Essenes as Jesus' mentors, Buddhist monks with paranormal powers. In the tradition of Renan, he made Mary Magdalene a tall blonde in a silk turban and red kidskin sandals who was hopelessly in love with Jesus.

In 1903, Émilie Lerou, who wrote under the male pen name Pierre Lahor, published a novelistic life of Jesus that was filled with occultic Flaubert-derived set pieces. Lerou's Jesus, who had been a hypnotist since childhood, fell in with a Brahmin who took him to Egypt to learn the healing arts, while her Mary Magdalene, the illegitimate daughter of a Roman sailor, was a wealthy prostitute in Tiberias. In both Bosc and Lerou, Jesus survived his crucifixion, and was rescued by friends (in Bosc's book, he settled in Alexandria, where he lived for another 30 years). Such theories of Jesus' Eastern travels are by no means passé. In 1996, the novelist Paul Parks published *The Gospel of Corax,* in which Jeshua of Nazareth goes to the foothills of the Himalayas to acquire wisdom in the company of an escaped catamite slave and a Cynic philosopher.

The most bizarre fin-de-siècle re-creation of Jesus was the work of a Boston photographer named F. Holland Day (1864–1933). Born to a wealthy industrialist family in Norwood, Massachusetts, Day became infatuated early on with the Decadent movement of Wilde and Beardsley. After traveling to London in 1890, where he ingratiated himself with Wilde, Yeats, and others, three years later he set up a publishing firm in his native Boston with Herbert Copeland, a former schoolmate who had helped him form a homegrown occult group called the Visionists (Copeland was Exarch, and Day was High Priest of Isis). Once incorporated as Copeland and Day, the two men were determined to import Decadence to stodgy America. The following year, they obtained the American rights to Wilde's *Salomé,* along with a book of his poetry and *The Yellow Book,* the scandalous quarterly that published Beardsley's hermaphroditic drawings. Day's closest friend was a Catholic poet of some repute named Louise Guiney, who advised him where to draw the line between shocking proper Bostonians and inviting criminal prosecution. Thereafter, the firm alternated its Decadent-theme books with the works of obscure Catholic writers whom Guiney had discovered.

Along with Alfred Stieglitz, Day pioneered the genre of "art" photography, in which the subject was posed, often in costume, as if for a painting. Using a platinum nitrate film process that was prohibitively expensive but produced pictures of exquisitely soft and refined shading, he once portrayed Louise Guiney in a laurel wreath as St. Barbara. Most of his models, however, were teenage boys or slightly younger, preferably dark-complexioned—Italians, Greeks, and Levantine immigrants or American blacks, whom he would dress in Oriental or African costumes, or bind with ropes to depict St. Sebastian, or pose naked as young gods or fauns, with laurel wreaths and pipes of Pan. Day found his models by volunteering as a tutor in the settlement houses that high-minded Boston ladies operated as a way of Americanizing new immigrants. One of his discoveries was the adolescent Khalil Gibran (1883–1931), who would later write *The Prophet* (1923) and a mystical life of Jesus called *Jesus, Son of Man* (1928). Day made numerous photographs of the Syrian-born Gibran in Arab dress, and eventually became his literary patron.

In July 1898, when Day's photographic career was at its height, he shot a series of pictures on a hill outside Norwood that reenacted Jesus' crucifixion. He patterned the pictures on photographs taken at Oberammergau, Germany, in which local residents staged a set of *tableaux vivants* depicting Jesus' suffering and death. He decided that he would play the role of Jesus himself. He secluded himself for several months, grew a beard and shoulder-length hair, and starved himself so that he would have the emaciated look of

Jesus in a famous crucifixion painting by Velázquez. For his cast of supporting characters, portrayed by professional Boston actors and Norwood residents, he ordered robes from Egypt that were supposed to be historically accurate, but were suffocatingly hot for the humid New England summer. He also imported a huge wooden cross from Syria.

As both protagonist and photographer, Day had himself tied to the cross wearing an enormous crown of thorns and holding a shutter bulb in one of his outstretched hands, with the camera pointed at him from a tripod. The series included Jesus' seven last words (Day in his crown of thorns with seven different facial expressions), Jesus' entombment (Day lying supine, complete with halo, while Mary Magdalene wept at his feet), and Jesus' resurrection (Day in a robe standing in front of something that vaguely resembled a tomb).

Later that year, Day exhibited a number of the pictures in montages that included shots of his boy-models in mythological poses. The critics' reactions ranged from derision to scandalized horror to complaints by other art-photographers that it was improper to pose in a halo for one's own portrait. What they did not realize, however, was that in imagining himself as Jesus, Day had merely taken up where Renan had left off some 30 years earlier. In fact, his crucifixion series was a still-photography bridge between Renan and cinematography.

Toward the end of his life, Day's existence increasingly reflected a self-imposed martyrdom. As a result of a quarrel, and perhaps because of his outré subject matter, Stieglitz omitted Day from a definitive anthology of modern photographers that he was preparing. After that, Day gradually abandoned photography. In 1917, he took to his bed for good in a room on the third floor of the family mansion in Norwood. His widowed mother, who was also bedridden, lived on the second floor. The two of them communicated by notes, his mother sometimes complaining about the stream of large-nosed, foreign-looking male visitors he continued to receive.

The literary bridge between Renan and the cinema was the novel *Quo Vadis,* published in 1896 by Nobel Prize–winning Polish nationalist Henryk Sienkiewicz (1846–1916). Set during the time of Nero's persecution of the Christians, *Quo Vadis* did not deal directly with Jesus, although the apostles Peter and Paul were major characters. However, Sienkiewicz drew extensively on Renan's *Antichrist* and Chateaubriand's *Martyrs* for his plot and juicy subject matter. From Chateaubriand, he derived the ideas of centering early Christian history on a love story and working his own country into a tale of ancient Rome. Ligia, his heroine, is the daughter of the chief of the Lugii tribe, who in Nero's day occupied part of what is now Poland.

From Renan, Sienkiewicz came up with the notion of spicing his story with nudity, sadism, and pagan debauchery. Although a devout Christian whose virtue is impeccable, Ligia is a lithe 18-year-old blonde whose clothes come off rather often. Her beauty inflames the young Roman commander Marcus Vinicius, who eventually learns to love her chastely and becomes a Christian himself. In the denouement, Ligia barely escapes martyrdom after being tied naked to the horns of a raging bull as part of a spectacle in the amphitheater.

To this day the best-selling novel of all time, *Quo Vadis* was a masterpiece of intricately plotted and thoroughly researched second-rate fiction. Sienkiewicz, who had been educated in the classics, visited Rome to master the topography, and he incorporated many historical characters into his narrative. In the end, Sienkiewicz's mix of religion and sex proved irresistible even to the Catholic Church. Bishops recommended the book for seminary reading, as long as certain of the orgy scenes were cropped. In 1951, when Hollywood director Mervyn LeRoy shot *Quo Vadis* on location in Rome, Pope Pius XII blessed the script. Polish-born Pope John Paul II spoke fondly of Sienkiewicz's novel in his inaugural address of 1978.

The year of *Quo Vadis*'s publication also witnessed the invention of the movie camera. Some 30 years later, in 1928, when it was still possible to serve up a Renan-style (and Sienkiewicz-style) mix of sex, sadism, revealing costumes, and Christianity without getting into trouble with churches and censors, Cecil B. DeMille directed his *King of Kings,* with its cast of 3,000 actors and 1,500 animals. Still considered the best biblical movie ever made, *King of Kings* was DeMille's own favorite. Although he was not at all religious, he would watch the film over and over in his private screening room and weep.

Five years after his *King of Kings,* DeMille filmed a knock-off of *Quo Vadis* called *The Sign of the Cross,* which featured crocodiles devouring naked maidens, lions devouring Christians, the empress Poppaea (played by Claudette Colbert) bathing in asses' milk, and an attempted lesbian seduction. It was too much for the times, at least in America, and it was also the Depression, when movie attendance had already dropped precipitously. The following year, Hollywood tightened the Hays Code to ensure that all future biblical movies would remain within the bounds of early-20th-century decency. In

William Dieterle's 1951 film *Salome,* for example, Rita Hayworth played her as a wholesome princess who listens reverently to Jesus' sermons.

However, literary artists were still free to follow Renan. In 1925, the Greek writer Nikos Kazantzakis (1883–1927) sailed to Palestine, where he imagined Jesus amidst a landscape that seemed as timeless to him as it had to Renan in 1861 and to dozens of other Orientalists in the decades that followed:

> We followed His shadow through the souks sweet with the scent of cinnamon, as mysterious as the veiled countenances, as fresh as the desert wells. We saw Him crouching by the fire, on the edges of the Sea of Galilee, sharing the meal of the fishermen. We scrutinized His multiple metamorphoses. At times we felt as if we were being sucked up by the cyclone of His gentle blue-green eyes, as blue-green as the eye of the Dead Sea. We murmured funeral laments over His tombstone, and summoned Him triumphantly with the muezzin, our necks bent back and our palms over our ears.[44]

Kazantzakis's *Last Temptation of Christ,* written in 1951 from these Palestinian impressions, was Renan's *Life of Jesus* for the 20th century. In calling his novel a distillation of the "essence" of Jesus, Kazantzakis believed he had conveyed what the evangelists would have written had they not been in thrall to the Christian church, echoing Renan's desire to create a "fifth gospel" that would have been the basis for the canonical four. Like Renan, Kazantzakis portrayed Jesus as an intellectual, a superhuman, and the object of Mary Magdalene's unrequited love. Jesus' "last temptation," in fact, was his yearning to be an ordinary man. Again like Renan, Kazantzakis was certain that the Jesus he had portrayed was none other than himself. As he wrote to a friend, "I became Christ."[45]

9

THE LIBERAL CHURCH CRUMBLES

By the turn of the 20th century, the religion of most educated Christians in Northern Europe and America was a doctrinally easygoing liberal Protestantism. David Friedrich Strauss had drawn a distinction between the Jesus of history and the Christ of faith. However, for liberal Christians of the 19th century, the Jesus of history—as they understood him—*was* the Christ of their faith. Traditional creeds and dogmas were outmoded in favor of Adolf von Harnack and Shailer Mathews's view that Jesus preached merely the creation of a just society, based on his desire that people share his sense of unity with God and treat their fellow human beings like brothers. Other than that, the "historical Jesus" had no connection with the traditional precepts of organized Christianity.

Even Germany's humiliating defeat in World War I put no dent in Harnack's liberal armor. In fact, he continued to teach the theories he had expressed in *What Is Christianity?* until his retirement in 1929. One of his very last students at Berlin was Dietrich Bonhoeffer, who would be imprisoned and hanged for plotting to assassinate Hitler.

However, even in the early part of the century, there were cracks in the liberal wall. One of Harnack's critics, Albert Kalthoff, a cynic who did not believe that Jesus had ever existed, dismissed Harnack's faith in the historical Jesus as a sort of universalized Judaism that Kalthoff called "Jesusism."[1]

Kalthoff argued instead that biblical scholars should have gone all the way and eliminated Jesus from their theology altogether. "The critical knife was . . . brought into requisition, and everything was cut out of the Gospels that referred to the Christ of the centralized Roman system," he wrote in 1902 in his *Rise of Christianity.* "But as liberalism lacked the force and courage of real religious independence, it had to find a new authority for the faith in the historical Jesus; and so, while crying energetically for 'separation from Rome,' it bound its followers all the more to Jerusalem."[2] Moreover, Kalthoff accused liberal Christians of reading the 19th-century cult of the individual into the historical Jesus, viewing him as nothing more than a great man with a powerful will. Kalthoff also faulted them for imagining that early, or "primitive," Christianity resembled contemporary liberal Protestantism. "Liberal Christianity needs to recognize itself in primitive Christianity," he scoffed.[3]

Kalthoff was not the first to pick up a wrecker's ball and aim it at the liberal church. In 1892, Martin Kähler, a much-admired theology professor at the University of Halle, had published a critique of the gross sentimentality of liberal theologian Wilhelm Hermann's inner-life-of-Jesus conception of Christianity. Kähler's *So-Called Historical Jesus and the Historic Biblical Christ* also attacked what he viewed as the hidden agenda of the liberal biographers of Jesus. "Today everyone is on guard when a dogma is frankly presented as such," he noted. "But when Christology appears in the form of a 'Life of Jesus,' there are not many who will perceive the stage manager behind the scenes, manipulating according to his own dogmatic script, the fascinating spectacle of a colorful biography."[4] He added: "What is usually happening is that the image of Jesus is being refracted through the spirit of these gentlemen themselves."[5]

Kähler pointed out that for all their detailed exegesis, the stalwarts of the 19th-century life-of-Jesus movement had contributed next to nothing in the way of undisputed new historical knowledge about him. The "liberal-life" chroniclers had not even been able to agree on the actual sayings of Jesus, which vary in wording from Gospel to Gospel. "People like to speak of the 'assured' words of the Savior; it is a fact, however, that the exact wording of his sayings has gone undisputed only when there is but one account of his saying," he observed.[6]

Kähler further contended that it was impossible to winnow the grains of historical truth in the Gospels from the chaff of theological speculation: One could not arbitrarily eliminate certain events, such as the supernaturalistic infancy narratives or the accounts of post-resurrection appearances, because every event narrated in the Gospels was a testimonial to the early Christians' holistic faith in Jesus as risen lord and Messiah. The Gospels could not be read in a "historical" or "biographical" way that was different from the way one read the theology-saturated New Testament letters of Paul and the other apostles. "The New Testament presentations were not written for the purpose of showing how Jesus developed," he commented scathingly.[7] In contrast to the "liberal lives," which treated Jesus' passion and death as footnotes to his exemplary life, Kähler noted that the Gospels made the crucifixion and resurrection the whole point of their narrative: "To state the matter somewhat provocatively, one could call the Gospels passion narratives with extended introductions."[8] Finally, the Gospels depicted a Jesus who had abrogated to himself an authority that would have been obnoxious had he not been divine as well as human. In short, Kähler accused the liberal scholars of substituting the worship of Christ enshrined in traditional dogma with a pseudo-scientific hero-worship of Jesus that had no textual or genuinely scientific foundation.

The So-Called Historical Jesus effectively "deprivileged" (to borrow a bit of contemporary jargon) New Testament scholars' claim (which is still very much in evidence) that they were the only ones competent to interpret the Bible and the life of Jesus. Carl E. Braaten, who translated Kähler's book into English, summed up Kähler's aims succinctly:

> He was moved by a deep apologetic concern to preserve the Christian laity from the papacy of scholarship. If faith is made dependent upon the methods or results of historical scholarship, then the historian becomes the priest of Protestantism. To equate the results of research with the facts of faith implies that the believer is dependent upon the oscillating opinions of historians. Faith is made to rest upon a great uncertainty, and in relation to Christ the learned man is given a place of privilege over the ordinary Christian.[9]

Kähler himself was by no means a traditional Christian. Like the liberals, he dismissed the creeds as products of a Byzantine mindset, which he rejected as thoroughly as did his liberal contemporaries. In his view, the risen Christ was merely a metaphor for the Jesus whom the apostles joyfully preached after his death. Moreover, the discrepancies among the canonical Gospels indicated to Kähler that none of the evangelists had had any interest in historical accuracy. However, as a theologian he argued that Christians should ignore such uncertainties and embrace the "historic Christ" that the Bible so beautifully revealed. There was a disturbing paradox in Kähler's reasoning: The "historic Christ" was to be found in the Bible, but the Bible was in many places historically wrong. Although Kähler wrote about the Gospels with moving eloquence, he was really asking his students and readers to hold a faith that was at heart irrational.

As might be expected, the liberal Jesus-scholars did not take kindly to Kähler's deconstruction of the historical figure they had so painstakingly created. Willibald Beyschlag (1823–1900), a colleague of Kähler at Halle, devoted the preface of an 1893 edition of his own biography to blasting *The So-Called Historical Jesus.* Another liberal, Otto Ritschl, the son of Albrecht Ritschl, protested that if Jesus had actually existed, he was subject to historical investigation by professionals like anyone else.

The same year that Kähler published his book, an associate professor of New Testament at the University of Göttingen named Johannes Weiss (1863–1914) issued a short tract titled *Jesus' Proclamation of the Kingdom of God,* in which he used the latest tools of historical-critical scholarship to dissect the Gospels. However, his Jesus was not the congenial, dogma-eschewing, universalistic egalitarian of the liberals, but rather a figure who was utterly alien to the modern age. Weiss's portrait of Jesus was that of a first-century Jew steeped in the Judaism of his time, especially the apocalyptic literature that spoke of a great battle that would lay waste to the entire world. When Jesus referred to his "kingdom," he was not talking about spiritual regeneration, much less the liberal "social gospel." Instead, he was alluding to the messianic era, or "eschaton," which would take place at the end of time. When he purported to exorcise demons, he was not curing mental illness, but pitting the power of God against that of Satan. His ethical teachings were merely an "interim" system designed to tide his followers over until he returned from the dead as judge and son of man—although not the Messiah, in Weiss's view. Finally, while Jesus himself could do nothing to bring about the eschaton, he urged others to pray to God ("thy kingdom come!") and repent of their sins, for repentance would hasten the kingdom's arrival:

> The actualization of the Kingdom of God is not a matter for human initiative, but entirely a matter of God's initiative. The only thing man can do about it is to perform the conditions required by God. The Kingdom of God, in Jesus' view, is never an ethical ideal, but is nothing other than the highest religious Good.[10]

In the end, Weiss believed that the notion that Christians could re-create the kingdom of God on earth by good deeds or better government was "thoroughly unbiblical and un-Jewish, inasmuch as the notion of an 'actualization of the Rule of God' by human ethical activity is completely contrary to the transcendentalism of Jesus' idea."[11] While it was impossible for contemporary Christians to comprehend such an alien Jesus, Weiss concluded, they should at least try to imitate his loving relationship with God the father.

Unlike Kähler's book, which had annoyed the liberal Protestants, Weiss's generated a theological crisis. Although only 67 pages in length, his *Proclamation* had used the very tools of liberal methodology (including the theory of the priority of Mark's Gospel) to reconstruct a Jesus who was far more faithful than the conventional liberal Jesus to the Gospel depictions of him (especially those of the Synoptics, where eschatology is a major component). Moreover, Jesus' disturbing references to the end-time, or the coming of the son of man in judgment, did not have to be drastically reinterpreted to fit into the liberals' middle-class Christianity.

Weiss's *Proclamation* was partially the result of a theological "generation gap." Much of his early training had consisted of conventional Synoptic studies (he was the first to give the name "Q" to the hypothetical sayings-source on which Matthew and Luke were thought to have relied). In 1882, his father, Bernhard Weiss (1827–1918), a New Testament professor at the universities of Kiel and Berlin, had authored one of the "liberal lives" that Kähler denounced by name in his *So-Called Historical Jesus.* Weiss's father-in-law was Albrecht Ritschl, a leading promoter of the liberal notion of Jesus' new kingdom on earth. Out of respect for Ritschl, Weiss refrained from publishing his treatise until three years after his death in 1889.

Weiss's portrait of Jesus as an eschatological insect-in-amber who had little relevance to the present time had its roots in the theories of a group of young Göttingen scholars who were exploring various depictions of early Christianity that were radically different from the liberal Protestant utopia. Just as Weiss viewed Jesus as a remote Jewish figure, the Göttingen circle held that early Christianity was a remote Hellenistic creation that was equally irrelevent to modernity. The aim of the group, which soon acquired the name "history-of-religions school" (or *Religionsgeschichteschule*), was to approach the origins of Christianity as a historical phenomenon by comparing its beliefs, symbols, and rituals to those of other Hellenistic religions, on the theory that early Christians had borrowed their rites and theology from Greek and Eastern cults. What the history-of-religions school was promoting was comparative religion.

In 1870, a German-born philologist named Max Müller (1821–1900), who was teaching at Oxford University, had delivered a series of lectures at London's Royal Institution in which he argued that it was possible to examine world religions scientifically, and to develop general theories concerning similarities in mythologies and motifs. Müller, whose own specialty was ancient Hindu texts, called this new field of study *Religionswissenschaft,* or "the science of religion."

One of the first fruits of *Religionswissenschaft* was James George Frazer's *The Golden Bough* (1890–1915), a monumental work in which Frazer (1850–1941) compared strands of folklore, magic, mythology, and ritual from an enormous array of ancient cultures. In discussing the death and rebirth of vegetation gods such as Adonis, Osiris, and Tammuz, who were associated with fertility and the annual cycle of growth, harvest, and death in Mediterranean agrarian cultures, Frazer pointed out the obvious parallels with the accounts of Jesus' crucifixion and resurrection enshrined in Paul's letters and in the Gospels. He also related the Christian doctrine of Jesus' atonement on the cross to ancient Celtic, Roman, and Scandinavian myths of young rulers or gods who died on or near a sacred tree (the "golden bough") in order that others might live. Many of those cultures reenacted the saving death of the god with human sacrifices at planting and harvest times. In Frazer's view, all the Christian and non-Christian stories, including those that undoubtedly underlay the ancient Hebrew ritual of the scapegoat connected with Yom Kippur, were essentially the same story of blood atonement and fertility.

To this very day, it is impossible to underestimate the appeal of Frazer's theories. Joseph Campell's *Hero with a Thousand Faces* and his popular television series on comparative religion essentially recycled Frazer's ideas, together with the archetypal psychology of Carl Jung. In 1946, the English poet Robert Graves (1895–1985), who had a lifelong interest in mythology, published a novel titled *King Jesus,* in which he made Jesus the ritualistic leader of a fertility-linked cult that antedated Hebrew monotheism in the Holy Land. The following year, Graves's *White Goddess* expanded upon these themes to reconstruct a cult of the mother-goddess that he believed had flourished throughout Europe and the Near East in prehistoric times.

In regarding early Christianity as only one of the countless myth- and ritual-laden cultic systems of the ancient Hellenistic world, the history-of-religions school was somewhat of a throwback to Ferdinand Christian Baur's theory of Christianity as a fusion of Judaism and Hellenism. Like Baur, many history-of-religionists believed that Paul of Tarsus had founded Christianity after having imbibed pagan mythology and ritual—including the legend of the dying and rising god—from his native city in Anatolia and the Gentile lands he had visited as a missionary. Others maintained that these myths had most likely been incorporated into Christianity *before* Paul's time in Antioch, which was thought to have swarmed with bizarre cults during the first century.

The godfather of the history-of-religions school was a theology professor at the University of Berlin named Otto Pfleiderer (1839–1908). In an 1887 treatise on early Christianity, Pfleiderer theorized that Paul had derived the Christian sacraments of baptism and the eucharist from the Eleusinian mysteries, the secret rites in honor of the Greek earth goddess Demeter that included an initiation ceremony and a sacrificial meal. Paul had even used the word "mystery" (*mystērion*) several times in his letters, a word that Pfleiderer believed sprang from Greek rather than Jewish theology.

The publication of Pfleiderer's text coincided with the first meetings of a circle of upstart young scholars at Göttingen, whose leader was a young pastor named Albert Eichhorn (1856–1926), who was studying for a doctorate in early church history. He had gathered together his group of young radicals—including Weiss—with the specific purpose of undermining Albrecht Ritschl, the reigning theologian at Göttingen and one of the paladins of Christian liberalism. Eichhorn contended that Ritschl and his confreres had invented a spurious history of the origins of Christianity predicated on their notion that creeds and dogmas represented a decadent phase in the development of the early church, a corruption of the pure and rationalistic religion that Jesus had preached and his apostles had disseminated. Eichhorn and his coterie believed instead that far from being pure and rationalistic, the earliest Christianity was a fantastic hodgepodge of borrowed myths and rituals.

Although Eichhorn's interest in comparative religion was sweeping, extending to the Mayans of Mesoamerica, his health was not good, and his scholarly output was meager. His only major work was an 1898 study of the Last Supper, in which he argued that the Gospel accounts of Jesus' Passover meal with his disciples did not seem to have any connection with the sacramental eucharist described by Paul in his first letter to the Corinthians. While his own conclusions about the origins of the eucharist were somewhat tentative and reserved, another member of the group named Wilhelm Heitmüller (1869–1926) boldly asserted in a 1903 publication that Paul's eucharist had been derived from a cultic ritual observed throughout the Hellenistic world that involved the symbolic consumption of the body of a particular deity. Moreover, Jesus could not have instituted the eucharist because his gospel was strictly spiritual, Heitmüller concluded. Finally, Roman

Catholicism was not a decadent version of an earlier, Protestant-style Christianity. By introducing pagan rites into the church, Paul himself had been the very first "Catholic," said Heitmüller.

A third member of the Eichhorn circle, Richard Reitzenstein (1861–1931), whose specialty was classical philology, published an ambitious study in 1910 in which he attempted to demonstrate that in his capacity as a Christian missionary, Paul had consciously adapted his native Judaism to the mentality, speech patterns, and forms of worship of the pagan Gentiles he sought to convert. Paul was "the bearer of the strongest influence that Hellenism ever exerted on Christianity," Reitzenstein concluded.[12] Furthermore, the origins of Christian motifs lay as far east as Persia, Mesopotamia, and even India according to Reitzenstein.

In 1913, Wilhelm Bousset (1861–1920), yet another member of the Eichhorn group and a lifelong friend of Heitmüller, published *Kyrios Christos,* the literary masterpiece of the history-of-religions movement. Earlier on, he had written a book titled *Jesus,* which was by and large a conventional German liberal life. However, in *Kyrios Christos,* Bousset tried to explain the process by which the historical Jesus, whose central message was faith in God and who at most considered himself to be the son of man, a figure of Jewish apocalyptic, became the Hellenistic "kyrios Christos," or "Lord Christ," a cult figure to be worshipped as divine.

According to Bousset, the very earliest Christians viewed Jesus strictly as a non-divine eschatological figure who would return at the end of time to establish the kingdom of God. However, the drama of his death, resurrection, and hoped-for second coming, which the first Christians reenacted every Sunday in their liturgies, was so emotionally overwhelming that they began imagining him as a sacramental personage who was alive in their midst, in whose name they exorcised demons and whose body and blood they consumed in communion. In support of his theory, Bousset marshalled a brilliant array of religious practices that had flourished throughout the Mediterranean world during the first two centuries of Christianity: the cults of Attis and Serapis, where the central figure was sometimes addressed as "lord"; the rites of the goddess Isis, who like the Virgin Mary radiated holiness and power; prayers addressed to Hermes containing mystical language that linked divinity and humanity in much the same way as John's Gospel; and the ritualistic branding of the initiate in the cult of the bull-slaying god Mithra, which may have served as a model for baptism and the sign of the cross.

Nearly alone among the history-of-religionists, Bousset did not believe that Paul had invented the "kyrios cult," as he called it. Instead, Paul had adopted it from the early Gentile Christian communities, all of whom were former mystery-worshippers who simply changed the name of their god to Jesus of Nazareth when they converted to Christianity. None of them, Paul included, had any interest in Jesus as a historical figure or in preserving his authentic teachings. "Paul does not proclaim the faith of Jesus, but faith in Jesus," Bousset wrote.[13] The early Christians lived in an eternal religious present in which a Jesus infused with mystery and magic died and rose many times over.

The theories of the German history-of-religionists—and of a Belgian fellow traveler named Franz Cumont (1868–1947), who wrote an important 1899 study of parallels between Mithraism and early Christianity—were a welcome antidote to the liberal theologians. Not only did they credit the first Christians with a vivid liturgical and sacramental life that the liberals had ignored; they also documented the powerful role that polytheism played in the Hellenistic world. Religion—and magic—saturated the lives of the ancients, even in Rome itself, where the remains of a temple to Mithra underlie the ancient Christian church of San Clemente. It was impossible for some of the mystery motifs not to work themselves into Christianity, just as the history-of-religionists surmised.

However, much of the history-of-religions scholarship consisted of compiling—and misinterpreting—exotic Hellenistic data. The majority of theories assumed, for example, that the Mithraic rituals of the second century and the reference to "the table of our Lord Serapis" in a third-century papyrus reflected far older pagan traditions that influenced *first*-century Christianity. They never considered that the influence might have been the other way around.

Heitmüller and Reitzenstein made their worst mistakes when they tried to correlate early Christian imagery with that of Gnosticism. The pair hypothesized that a Gnostic story of a savior who descended from heaven to liberate the human race, which they called the "pre-Christian redeemer myth," had eventually found its way into the theology of Paul (who Reitzenstein was certain was a Gnostic) and the Gospel of John, where God sends the Logos to enlighten those in darkness. However, the only evidence for the existence of a pre-Christian redeemer myth during the first century consists of the letters of Paul and the Gospel of John themselves—both Christian texts.

Between them, Johannes Weiss and the history-of-religionists more or less fulfilled Eichhorn's dream of undermining the liberals. The final blow was dealt by Wilhelm Wrede (1859–1906), another veteran of Eichhorn's coterie. A Privatdozent at Göttingen during the early 1890s and later a professor at the University of Breslau, Wrede took to heart the history-of-religions axiom that the first Christians had no interest in the historical Jesus. If Bousset and the others were correct, he reasoned, the only conclusion to draw was that none of the four canonical Gospels, not even the Gospel of Mark, could be trusted to provide reliable information about Jesus. While certain of Wrede's theories resembled those of Kähler, the latter was a theological conservative who believed that the Bible accurately presented the "historic Christ," while the radical Wrede maintained that the historic Christ was a Christian fiction and the historical Jesus was fundamentally unknowable.

In 1901, Wrede published his *Messianic Secret,* whose title referred to the incident at Caesarea Philippi recorded in the Synoptic Gospels in which Jesus confides to his disciples that he is the Messiah. For many of the liberals—Hermann Christian Weisse, Heinrich Julius Holtzmann, David Friedrich Strauss (in his 1864 *New Life of Jesus*), Bernhard Weiss, and even Bousset—the messianic secret had marked the end of the historical Jesus' Galilean springtime and the beginning of the road to his death. Wrede argued instead that the incident did not pertain to an event in the historical Jesus' life and had been invented by the first Christians after they had persuaded themselves that Jesus had risen from the dead. In his view, most of the events recounted in the Gospels were similarly heavily colored by early Christianity's post-Easter faith. "The extent to which the Resurrection is the focus of the entire presentation of the Gospels becomes particularly clear," he noted.[14]

After Wrede finished tearing the Gospels to shreds, a number of his contemporaries—including Albert Kalthoff—concluded that there never had been a Jesus. (Bruno Bauer was back in style). In 1903, George Robert Stow Mead (1863–1933), a Cambridge University graduate, amateur Gnosticism expert, and leading Theosophist who had served for a time as Helena Blavatsky's personal secretary, published *Did Jesus Live 100 B.C.?* Mead's book contended that the Gospels were merely a collection of Jewish folk-tales that presented a garbled version of the life of a renegade rabbi named Jeschu mentioned in the Talmud who had lived during the reign of the Jewish king Alexander Jannaeus, nearly a century before Jesus Christ's supposed birth. All the Gospel stories, as well as the disparaging accounts of his life in the Talmud and medieval Jewish literature, were not about a man from Nazareth, but rather about his namesake of a century earlier, who had been excommunicated from Judaism, possibly for dabbling in magic while living in Egypt. Mead also maintained that the Gospels were relatively late rehashings of the Jeschu tales, and that none had been written during the first century. Another scholar, Arthur Drews, theorized that Jesus was a fictional creation of the Gnostics, who had conflated passages from the Book of Isaiah, the Psalms, and the Wisdom of Solomon (as apocryphal Jewish text) to patch together a mythical redeemer-figure.

Five years after Wrede's book, Albert Schweitzer's *Quest of the Historical Jesus* dealt the coup de grace to the comfortable liberal image of Jesus. An early-blooming polymath of prodigious energy and talent, Schweitzer was only 26 years old when he started writing his famous tome. In 1905, the year in which he finished the manuscript, he published two other books of religious scholarship and a study of the music of Bach, while serving as a Lutheran minister in Strasbourg. He also decided that year to abandon intellectual life, enroll in medical school, and become a medical missionary in Africa.

Schweitzer's father was a Lutheran pastor in the town of Kaysersberg in Alsace, newly Prussianized although it had been part of France since the days of Louis XIV. An accomplished organist from early childhood, in 1893 young Albert enrolled as both an arts and a theology student at the University of Strasbourg. One of his professors was Heinrich Holtzmann, whose theories he would later critique mercilessly in *The Quest*.

At age 24, Schweitzer wrote his first book, *The Secret of the Messiahship and Passion of Jesus,* while in the process of completing his doctoral thesis on the Last Supper. The following year, he was ordained as a Lutheran curate, obtained a licentiate in theology that enabled him to give lectures as a Privatdozent, and published his doctoral thesis under the title of *The Mystery of the Kingdom of God.* Three years later, he was appointed principal of the theological seminary in Strasbourg.

After *The Quest* came off the presses in 1906, Schweitzer spent the next several years studying medicine, conducting research for a book on the apostle Paul, and preparing a massive guide to the building and playing of organs. After passing the state medical examination in 1911 (he financed the fee with an organ performance at the Munich Festival of French Music), he oversaw the publication of his Paul book, *Paul and His Interpreters.* Two years later, he completed his medical internship, issued an enlarged second edition of *The*

Quest and a six-volume critical edition of the music of Bach, and left for Africa as planned. Sponsored by the Paris Evangelical Missionary Society, he set up a hospital near Lambaréné, a remote village on the Ogooué River in what was then French Equatorial Africa and is now Gabon. He spent the rest of his life there.

The Quest of the Historical Jesus was a survey of more than 200 books about Jesus, from Reimarus's *Fragments* to *The Messianic Secret.* Schweitzer had borrowed the books from Strasbourg theology professors, the Strasbourg university library, and the private libraries of Edward Reuss (1804–1891), an early champion of the theory of Marcan priority. He then arranged the books in stacks, in his rented room, each stack representing a separate chapter. When he finished a chapter, he would return the books. His methodology helps explain *The Quest*'s strengths and weaknesses. The main strength of his book lay in his witty dispatching of the most idiosyncratic of the Jesus-theorists, including Bahrdt, Venturini, Paulus, and Renan. His sendup of Holtzmann and the other liberals was withering, he had no truck with the history-of-religions school as exemplified by Heitmüller and Reitzenstein, and he found Wrede's arch skepticism irritating. *The Quest*'s major weakness was its tendency to read like a compilation of book reports (more than 400 pages of them in English translation) without much overall structure.

Schweitzer's overarching theory was that the liberal scholars who had devoted more than a century to making Jesus a modern like themselves had got the "true historical Jesus,"[15] as he called him, all wrong. His own Jesus, whom he dramatically unveiled at the book's very end, was the culturally remote, eschatology-obsessed first-century Jew whom Johannes Weiss had limned in *Jesus' Proclamation of the Kingdom of God.* Moreover, Schweitzer, unlike the history-of-religionists, saw no theological disjunction between Jesus and Paul, who were both Jewish mystics fixated on the end of the world. He also maintained that Jesus himself, not Paul, had instituted the Christian sacraments of baptism and eucharist, and also the doctrine of atonement, as part of his eschatological preoccupation.

Whereas Weiss's Jesus had rather passively hoped to return as the son of man, Schweitzer's was a heroic, almost Nietzschean figure, who thought—mistakenly but magnificently—that he was already the son of man as well as the Messiah. Through his voluntary death as atonement, or "ransom for many,"[16] he believed that he could change the course of history by bringing about God's glorious intervention in human affairs, which he called "the kingdom of heaven." Like Weiss, Schweitzer contended that Jesus' moral teachings were a mere "interim ethic" to be observed until the final days that Jesus himself would instigate with his atoning death. Furthermore, Schweitzer averred that the Synoptic Gospels narrated a life of Jesus that was essentially historical, including the "messianic secret," which Judas betrayed by informing the Temple priests of Jesus' aspirations, thereby provoking the blasphemy trial that led to his crucifixion.

Schweitzer's portrayal of Jesus was that of a worldly and religious failure whose death did not trigger the coming of God's Kingdom as he had envisioned. Nonetheless, he was a failure of dazzling proportions:

> There is silence all around. The Baptist appears, and cries: "Repent, for the Kingdom of Heaven is at hand." Soon after that comes Jesus, and in the knowledge that He is the coming Son of Man lays hold of the wheel of the world to set it moving on that last revolution which is to bring all ordinary history to a close. It refuses to turn, and He throws Himself upon it. Then it does turn; and it crushes Him. Instead of bringing in the eschatological conditions, He has destroyed them. The wheel rolls onward, and the mangled body of the one immeasurably great Man, who was strong enough to think of Himself as the spiritual ruler of mankind and to bend history to His purpose, is hanging upon it still. That is His victory and His reign.[17]

The image of Jesus' mangled body, the metaphoric crucifix (which Schweitzer might have derived from memories of the Catholic altars he saw as a boy in Catholic Alsace) remained with him for the rest of his life. Like many of the biblical scholars he criticized, Schweitzer himself wanted to *be* Jesus, in making an existential sacrifice on behalf of others. It was hardly coincidental that the day Schweitzer set sail for Lambaréné, a punishingly hot, tropical disease-beset outpost near the Atlantic coast of central Africa, was Good Friday. The break with his past, however, was never quite as dramatic as he liked to think. In fact, he returned to Europe for extended periods every few years to lecture, teach, and hold organ concerts, and he continued to publish theological and philosophical books throughout his life. As he became increasingly famous (he won the Nobel Peace Prize in 1952), he hobnobbed with aristocrats and literati who came as pilgrims to Lambaréné and regarded him as a saint.

It goes without saying that Schweitzer's *Quest,* although an immediate best-seller (especially in England, where a translation appeared in 1910), met with enormous hostility in liberal German circles. Adolf Jülicher (1857–1938), a New Testament professor at Marburg, wrote a scathing review for a scholarly journal, while Ernst von Dobschütz (1870–1934), who taught at Strasbourg, Breslau, and Halle, delivered a series of lectures at Oxford in 1909 devoted to trying to disprove Schweitzer's eschatological theories. Schweitzer had to find a French missionary society to act as patron of his jungle hospital because no German Protestant organization would sponsor him.

Schweitzer's conception of Jesus was indeed problematic. In objective terms, the hero he depicted was insane, a victim of delusions of grandeur. Schweitzer argued that the miraculous feeding of the five thousand was actually a symbolic ritual, wherein each participant received only a crumb of bread, a ritual that was freighted with private meaning for his eschatologically fixated Jesus. However, if the "feeding" took place the way Schweitzer described it, it (and Jesus himself) surely must have seemed bizarre to the hungry crowd. Although he continued to write books about Jesus and Paul for the remainder of his life, Schweitzer stopped paying attention to New Testament scholarship after his arrival in Africa. He was essentially unable to deal with mid-20th-century interpretations that pushed his historical Jesus to the sidelines.

Over time, Schweitzer's bush hospital at Lambaréné, where his wife served as anesthetist, became a medical anachronism. At best a mediocre physician, he had also developed a "reverence for life" philosophy that led him to ban meat, clocks, flush toilets, and even electricity and insecticides from his clinic for fear of harming other creatures. After Gabon won independence from France in 1957, the shambling Lambaréné clinic, where farm animals wandered freely among the patients and a white-haired European with a Nobel Prize played the genial tyrant, must have embarrassed the new country's leaders, who wanted the world to view Gabon as a cutting-edge "developing" nation with the latest in medical technology.

In Germany, however, there were more attacks to come on the liberal Jesus-searchers of the 19th century. Ernst Troeltsch (1865–1923), another veteran of Eichhorn's circle, published an essay in 1911 whose thesis was that Christian communities throughout the course of history had fashioned Jesus according to their own social and psychological needs. Although a student of Ritschl when the latter was at the height of his fame, he had eventually rejected liberalism, becoming first a history-of-religions enthusiast and then a thoroughgoing historicist. While he himself was a theology professor at the universities of Heidelberg and Berlin, he was convinced that only the objectivity of the secular historian, not the theologian, could possibly present a reasonably accurate picture of the historical Jesus.

Three years after Troeltsch's essay appeared, liberal Christianity in Germany collapsed entirely with the outbreak of World War I on August 1, 1914. A mere three days later, 93 German intellectuals signed a manifesto drafted by Harnack urging support for Kaiser Wilhelm II's policies. Among the numerous liberal theologians who lent their names was Wilhelm Hermann. Whether Germany was indeed responsible for the devastation that reached every corner of Europe and left 10 million dead is still a matter of intense debate. Britain and France certainly had their scores to settle. In the end, however, the vaunted German war machine, together with its economy, was in tatters. The country's boundaries were truncated, its empire gone, and its citizens shamed and demoralized by ruinous reparation payments and the knowledge that so much blood had been shed for nothing.

In the wake of so much destruction, the younger biblical scholars in Germany longed for a theology that was neither liberal nor historical. The most prominent of these was Rudolf Bultmann (1884–1976), who was to leave his mark on New Testament studies for the rest of the 20th century. Like so many of his predecessors, Bultmann was the son of a Lutheran pastor. In his case, both grandfathers had been Lutheran ministers as well (his paternal grandfather had served as a missionary in Sierra Leone). He, too, decided to enter the ministry, studying theology at Tübingen and Berlin, and finally at Marburg, the old Protestant university on the Lahn River in Hesse, where he also grounded himself thoroughly in the Greek and Latin classics. Among his professors at Marburg were Wilhelm Hermann and Johannes Weiss. The latter urged him to pursue an academic career instead of a pastoral one, assigning him a doctoral dissertation comparing Paul's letters to the diatribes of the Stoic and Cynic philosophers. When Weiss moved to Heidelberg in 1908, Bultmann finished his thesis under the supervision of the history-of-religionist Wilhelm Heitmüller.

The teachings of his three renowned mentors were to become an integral part of Bultmann's own theology. From Hermann, he learned that it was no longer possible for a modern to believe in the orthodox Christian creeds. From Weiss, he learned that the first Christians had transformed Jesus the proclaimer of an end-of-the-world kingdom into Jesus the proclaimed (the *kerygma* in Greek), endowing him with divine titles that reflected a worldview as distant from modernity as it was from Jesus himself. From Heitmüller, he learned that early Christianity had woven Jesus' name into a congeries of Hellenistic myths, including that of the pre-Christian redeemer. (Bultmann later incorporated the pre-Christian redeemer myth into a major study of John's Gospel that he published from the years 1937 to 1941, hypothesizing that Gnostic texts were among John's sources.)

While writing his dissertation on Paul and the philosophers, Bultmann also absorbed the sad-edged iron determinism of the Roman Stoic Epictetus, who was born some 25 years after Jesus' death. Epictetus's theory of a closed-system universe in which no laws governed except those of science informed Bultmann's famous 1941 declaration (quoted earlier in this book) that it was impossible for anyone who used electricity to believe in the supernatural. Bultmann took teaching positions at Breslau and the University of Giessen before moving back to Marburg in 1920 to fill the chair of the retiring Heitmüller. He lived in Marburg until the day he died. He was also an active pastor, preaching—most eloquently—all the orthodox Lutheran doctrines about Jesus from his pulpit, but in his heart, his classroom, and his books holding to something very different.

During his early days at Tübingen, Bultmann had become a favorite of Hermann Gunkel (1862–1932), another alumnus of the immensely talented circle of young academics that Eichhorn had gathered around him at Göttingen. As a scholar of the Old Testament, Gunkel was less interested in its theology than in the specific function that the Scriptures' component parts had played in the religious life of the early Hebrews. Gunkel viewed the books of the Bible not as conscious literary compositions, but rather as freeze-frames of a living religion. As such, they reflected ancient folk-myths and customs (with roots as far away as Babylon) far more than the theological preoccupations of the writers whose names they bore.

In conceiving of the books of the Old Testament as amalgams of Hebrew folklore, Gunkel revived the 18th-century ideas of Johann Gottfried Eichhorn and Johann Gottfried Herder, who had also interpreted the Bible as a folk-collection, as well as those of David Friedrich Strauss, who had theorized in his 1835 *Life of Jesus* that the Gospels were collections of primitive myths. With specific regard to the Psalms, Gunkel noted that they could be classified into certain "forms"[18]—lamentations, hymns of thanksgiving, celebrations of God's enthronement, and so forth—each of which served a different religious or social purpose.

In 1919, Martin Dibelius (1883–1947), a Semiticist at Berlin, published a book titled *From Tradition to Gospel,* in which he applied the "form criticism" invented by Gunkel to a study of the New Testament evangelists. In his view, the Gospels were not connected narratives that told Jesus' life story as a biography, but rather grab-bags of folk-tales. In attempting to sort out their origins, he devised a form-criticism vocabulary for the various types of recurring incidents and sayings: aretalogy (miraculous action), chria (epigragm), paradigm (illustrative story), and so forth. He also used the phrase *Sitz im*

Leben ("life-situation") to describe the particular social or religious function that each Gospel tale (pericope) served, and the word *Gattung* to identify the literary genre into which each of the Gospels and its sources fell.

Dibelius believed that Jesus himself was probably responsible for the sayings and parables attributed to him in the Gospels, but that the narratives about him were most likely inventions of his disciples, whether expansions of his sayings or pagan miracle-stories borrowed from the early Christians' neighbors. Only the Gospel passion stories were complete narratives that had developed as a whole, which Dibelius believed were derived from a single story composed of strands of Old Testament prophecy that the early Christians had woven into a largely fictional account of Jesus' crucifixion.

In his first major book, *The History of the Synoptic Tradition* (1921), Bultmann expanded on Dibelius's theories, contriving more detailed classifications of the forms and more exhaustive speculations on the histories of the Christian communities that had retold the Gospel stories. His ideas about the composition of the individual Gospel tales were also more mechanistic and schematic than Dibelius's. Indeed he contended, unlike Dibelius, that it was highly improbable that the Gospels reflected many of Jesus' actual words, much less his deeds. Rather, they had developed from simple core aphorisms (perhaps reflecting Jesus' actual sayings) into longer, contextualized discourses and narratives.

Bultmann believed it was possible to engage in a kind of textual archaeology whereby one could peel off layers of elaboration in the Gospel stories in the hope of reaching a primal stratum that reflected the earliest theology of the community that had composed the story. While he readily admitted that there was something circular about the layering approach—using a particular text to reconstruct the community that had written it, and then using the reconstructed community's "needs" and "history" to determine what parts of the text were most ancient—he persisted nonetheless. In his monumental study of the layers of tradition in John's Gospel, which was marked by similar schematicism and circular reasoning, Bultmann concluded that John's sources had included the "pre-Christian redeemer myth," which actually existed only in Christian writings, and a hypothetical "signs source" that did not exist in any extant text.

Bultmann embraced form criticism, with its implication that the Gospels were almost entirely fictional, because he, like Schweitzer, had transformed his Christian faith into a kind of existentialism. One of his closest friends was the existentialist philosopher Martin Heidegger (1889–1976), who taught at

Marburg from 1923 to 1928. Bultmann and Heidegger attended each other's classes, and in the summer of 1927, they jointly taught a seminar on the subject of Luther's commentary on Paul's letter to the Galatians. Although an atheist, Heidegger admired the Christian theology of Søren Kierkegaard, who had emphasized a tension between temporal existence and eternal truth that could generate both deep despair and a feeling of closeness to God. Heidegger turned Kierkegaard's theology into secular existentialism, postulating that one could achieve an authentic mode of being through choosing to act, even if blindly, which was the equivalent of faith.

Another of Bultmann's colleagues was the Swiss theologian Karl Barth (1886–1968). Born in Basel to a family of Calvinist ministers of Pietist leanings, Barth was a conventional liberal Protestant until 1914. He had persuaded his traditionalist father to allow him to enroll in the University of Marburg in 1908 in order to study with Wilhelm Hermann. However, the appalling calamity of the war, with its trenches and poison gas, which had been endorsed by most German liberal theologians, led him to abandon the notion that Christianity consisted merely of feeling at one with Jesus and working toward an ethical goal of improving the human race. He became liberal Protestantism's most sustained and merciless critic (his 1946 book, *Protestant Theology in the Nineteenth Century,* would scornfully dismiss all forms of bourgeois Christianity).

In a commentary on Paul's letter to the Romans published in 1918, Barth depicted a God who, far from being the genial father of liberal theology, was so utterly remote that human beings could know him only through radical faith in Jesus Christ. Moreover, any effort to understand God or Jesus, especially by means of historical inquiry, was not faith, but rather the "works" that Luther had classically condemned. The bleakness of Barth's view was a theological encapsulation of the cultural despair that permeated Europe after the war. (The year 1918 also saw the publication of Oswald Spengler's *Decline of the West,* followed in 1920 by J. B. Bury's *Idea of Progress,* which openly mocked the 19th-century belief in the betterment of human civilization.) In passionate language, Barth bade his readers to contemplate instead the cross of Christ, the miraculous gift of God that bridged the chasm between human and divine and assured that all mankind would be saved.

Bultmann read the second edition of Barth's commentary on Romans, and wrote an enthusiastic review of the book. He and Barth became lifelong correspondents, and together they established what they called "dialectical theology," which focused on the confrontation between human beings and the unknowable God. Although the theological alliance did not last long, the friendship did. Barth eventually championed what he termed "neo-orthodoxy," which was based paradoxically on the theory that the Bible, as God's revelation, was beyond the bounds of history, and as such, should be accepted as absolute truth, even though very few of the events it narrated had likely taken place. He took a perverse delight in encouraging skeptics' efforts to undermine the historicity of the Bible, which simply made Christian faith all the more independent of history.

Barth's position infuriated Bultmann, who deemed his neo-orthodoxy both religiously and philosophically dishonest. His own attempt to reconcile Christian faith with scientific determinism was grounded in form criticism and history-of-religions theory. Bultmann's studies had taught him that the New Testament was a collection of myths—a fusion of Jewish apocalypticism and Gnostic redeemer tales—from which it was impossible to learn anything about the historical Jesus. In his opinion, the atonement doctrine reflected primitive notions of blood-guilt, Jesus' ascension into heaven depended on pre-Copernican cosmology, and the eucharist as earthly food—bread—could not feed the soul. Furthermore, the historical Jesus was irrelevant to Christian faith, which depended instead on the reality of the proclamation of Christ as living savior, the *kerygma* that the New Testament embodied in its myths. The Gospels had taken on a mythical form because they were composed in the first century, a naive time when people could still believe that supernatural events such as Jesus' healings and resurrection had actually occurred.

While the New Testament *kerygma* was relevant to the 20th century because it invited Christians to believe in a living Jesus Christ, it was pointless to sift through the Gospels looking for Jesus as a historical reality. All that anyone could know with certainty about Jesus was that he had died on a cross; Bultmann called this core fact the *Dass,* from the German word for the conjunction "that." In an essay titled "The Significance of the Historical Jesus," written in 1929, he concluded:

> Therefore the kerygma is neither a vehicle for timeless ideas nor the mediator of historical information: what is of decisive importance is that the kerygma is Christ's "that" *(Dass),* his "here and now," which becomes present in the address itself.
>
> One cannot therefore go behind the kerygma, using it as a "source" *(Quelle)*, in order to reconstruct an "historical Jesus" with his "messianic con-

> sciousness," his "inner life," or his "heroism." That would merely be "Christ according to the flesh," who no longer exists. It is not the historical *(historisch)* Jesus, but Jesus Christ, the one who is preached, who is the Lord.[19]

In Bultmann's view, it was the task of the 20th-century New Testament scholar to strip away the layers of myth-saturated accretion from the Gospel stories to find their core message, a process that he called "demythologizing." In the same 1941 treatise in which he had deemed science and supernaturalism irreconcilable, he explained demythologization as follows: "Demythologizing seeks to bring out the real intention of myth, namely its intention to talk about human existence as grounded in and limited by a transcendent, unworldly power, which is not visible to objectifying thinking."[20]

Bultmann contended that the central proposition of Christianity was the revelation of God's boundless love, which had been revealed through the historical existence of a man named Jesus. Only through complete submission to God could humankind free itself from the anxiety inherent in the human condition. Christianity and existentialism were thus the same thing. According to Bultmann, the entire Christian *kerygma,* once demythologized, could be boiled down to a single sentence in Paul's second letter to the Corinthians: "So, if anyone is in Christ, there is a new creation: everything old has passed away; see, everything has become new!"[21]

Bultmann's existential Christianity was genuine and powerful, but it was difficult for most of his contemporaries not to view his theology as scientific reductionism with a vaguely religious gloss. For example, he maintained that while Jesus' crucifixion had actually occurred as a historical event (the *Dass*), his resurrection had not, leading many of his critics to charge that he did not believe in the resurrection. Bultmann radiated susceptibility to misunderstanding: a lanky, impassive figure with a brush mustache and sunken eyes limned in intelligence and sorrow, he had lost one brother in France in 1917, and the other was to die in a Nazi concentration camp. He seemed to feel trapped by history.

When Adolf Hitler took office as German chancellor in 1933, among his first acts was the removal of all non-Aryans from government positions, including university teaching posts. One of Bultmann's favorite students, the Jewish scholar of Gnosticism Hans Jonas, decided to leave Germany immediately. Bultmann invited Jonas to his home for lunch before he left, and was deeply pained by his plight, but he did nothing to contest it. (He wrote a foreword to one of Jonas's books in 1934, however, which took genuine courage.) His friend Heidegger, who initially supported Hitler (he later become disillusioned), was appointed rector of the University of Freiburg, where he delivered an inaugural speech glorifying the concept of "struggle" (*Kampf*) and the historical destiny of the German people. Bultmann defended the speech in his classroom at Marburg. He was genuinely ambivalent: He detested the racial fixations and posturing of Nazism, but like many middle-class Germans of the early 1930s, he also despised the Weimar Republic as feckless and decadent, and longed for the return of the Bismarckian values of hard work and respect for authority that Hitler seemed to promise.

The Nazi party seized control of the Protestant ecclesiastical establishment, set up a quasi-governmental organization called the German Christian Church, and extended its purge of non-Aryans from the civil service to the church, which was ordered to remove all clergy of Jewish descent from the pulpit. Karl Barth helped found a counter-organization called the Confessing Church, which Bultmann joined. In 1934, Barth drafted a document known as the Barmen Declaration, in which all signatories pledged their loyalty to Jesus Christ above any government authority. The Barmen Declaration was a line drawn in the sand against Hitler. Barth was severely punished the following year when he was relieved of his post at the University of Bonn and stripped of an honorary degree he had received from Freiburg. He returned to Basel and accepted a teaching position there. Although Bultmann signed and supported the Barmen Declaration, he made it clear that in his view it applied only to the realm of the church and not to government-subsidized secular institutions.

Bultmann's proposal in 1941 to demythologize the New Testament could not have been more poorly timed. The Second World War was in full swing, and the Confessing Church had been forced to go underground. Nonetheless, its signatories continued to hold conferences, at two of which Bultmann delivered his paper. His aim was to correct what he saw as theological narrow-mindedness on the part of many Confessing Church ministers. However, his theory that traditional Christian orthodoxy was not suitable for the 20th century deeply shocked his colleagues instead. Only one step ahead of the Gestapo, they did not think that the middle of Hitler's war was an appropriate time for religious iconoclasm. In his treatise, Bultmann rather tendentiously maintained that a literalistic interpretation of the events narrated in the Gospels required a belief in an archaic physical universe, a three-decker structure with heaven on top, earth in the middle, and hell below. In so doing, he seemed to be making fun of the New Testament mindset at a time when faith in the Christ of the New Testament was for many the only locus of hope in a world that had turned into a nightmare. Bultmann became an embarrassment to the Confessing Church.

The controversy over Bultmann's demythologizing polemics continued to rage in academic and clerical circles even after the end of the war. In 1952, the United Lutheran Church of Germany issued a pastoral letter that condemned demythologizing without mentioning Bultmann by name. Karl Jaspers (1883–1969), a leading non-Christian existentialist, openly questioned why Bultmann did not carry his demythologizing all the way and jettison the *Dass*—the historicity of Jesus' crucifixion. In a 1958 debate with Bultmann, Jaspers contended that Bultmann was trying to interject a supposedly objective fact into an existential event—God's intervention in the world—that had no boundaries of time or place.

Throughout the war, Bultmann had doggedly worked on his massive study of John's Gospel. Toward the war's end, when he was already in his sixties, he also assumed pastoral duties in Marburg, where every man of fighting age, including the clergy, had been called to the front. When the war was finally over, it must have been devastating for him to have been on the losing side twice in his lifetime. Yet he had also won an important victory: His academic reputation was so awe-inspiring both in Germany and abroad that he succeeded in halting the search for the historical Jesus for three full decades.

Even in America, where the historical Jesus had had a longer life than in Europe, existentialism gradually replaced liberalism as the theology of avant-garde Protestants. When Paul Tillich (1886–1965), a leading German existentialist, Lutheran pastor, and former colleague of Bultmann at Marburg, lost his teaching post at the University of Frankfurt in 1935 because of his vocal opposition to the Nazis, Reinhold Niebuhr (1902–1971), America's most famous Protestant theologian, welcomed him at Union Theological Seminary, where Niebuhr reigned as dean of American religious liberalism. After Union, Tillich moved to the Harvard Divinity School, and ultimately the University of Chicago. Tillich, Bultmann, and Barth were the triumvirate of Christian existentialism and their theories dominated academic thinking in Europe and America until well into the 1960s.

Ironically, for all his insistence that the historical Jesus was unknowable and irrelevant, Bultmann had actually formulated a rather clear idea of who he was. In 1926, while he, Barth, and several others were hammering out the principles of dialectical theology, he published a small book titled *Jesus* (*Jesus and the Word,* in the English translation). Drawn from the Synoptic Gospels, Bultmann's portrait of Jesus was not unlike that of Johannes Weiss and Albert Schweitzer: A Jewish figure who breathed the apocalypticism of his time, he was born in Nazareth of human parents, was baptized by John the Baptist, and briefly belonged to the Baptist's ascetic sect. Later he broke with John and disavowed his asceticism. He ate with outcasts and, like a rabbi, he gathered disciples around him. He believed that he could work miracles, and he did things the people attributed to a miraculous agency: healing the sick and exorcising reputed demons. He recited something akin to the Lord's Prayer, and talked of the coming of the "son of man," although not in reference to himself. He was crucified by the Romans as a would-be Messiah, although he probably did not consider himself the Messiah.

Like Schweitzer's Jesus, Bultmann's mistakenly expected the world to come to an end during his own lifetime. However, when properly "demythologized," Jesus' allusions to "the kingdom" and "the final hour" actually related to an existential reality in which every hour is final and the world is always about to pass away. Consequently, his teachings were not an "interim ethic," as Weiss and Schweitzer had contended, but rather a permanent code of morals that stressed "radical obedience," or total submission to God. Above all, Bultmann's Jesus was a messenger of God: "By tradition Jesus is named as the bearer of the message; according to overwhelming probability he was."[22]

Bultmann heavily qualified his reconstruction of Jesus, insisting that it actually represented not Jesus himself but merely the bottom, or "Palestinian," layer of certain accounts in the Synoptic Gospels. He also argued that the Jesus he had uncovered might have been no more then an image of Jesus that his disciples carried around in their heads. "Whoever prefers to put the name of Jesus always in quotation marks and let it stand as an abbreviation for the historical phenomenon with which we are concerned, is free to do so," he hedged.[23] What is most interesting about Bultmann's Jesus (or "Jesus") was that he was a teacher of a timeless ethic. In that respect, he bore a striking resemblance to the old liberal Jesus that Bultmann himself had helped to destroy. Buried deep beneath Bultmann's existentialist theology, the liberal Jesus seemed to be waiting to rise again.

10

AVANT-GARDE FASHIONS

Within a decade after the war, the search for the historical Jesus resumed, as surely as if there had never been a Rudolf Bultmann. For more than a generation, Bultmann's theories had dominated German New Testament scholarship, as biblical experts carried on his demythologizing project, stripping away layers of supposedly mythical material in the Gospel stories and reinterpreting them in up-to-date language—a science they called "the new hermeneutics." His existentialist philosophy (which he had borrowed to some extent from Martin Heidegger) had also become the reigning intellectual fashion, reaching its zenith in the writings of Jean-Paul Sartre (1905–1980) and Albert Camus (1913–1960) in the days of the French Resistance. In the aftermath of the war, Bultmann's dark theology mirrored the nihilistic despair of the European intelligentsia.

In the 1950s, as memories of the war's horrors dimmed and the aging Bultmann was less formidable a presence, existentialism underwent a radical change. Under the influence of Sartre and Camus, who had joined the Communist Party during their Resistance years, the existentialist movement became synonymous with radical political action, usually of a Marxist bent. In time, the two philosophies became virtually synonymous, and Marxism—or something close to it—gradually replaced existentialism. It was therefore not surprising that the younger biblical experts found Bultmann's dimly perceived existentialist Jesus unsatisfying, and yearned for a more solid figure whose teachings were relevant to political action.

The revolt against Bultmann came from his own former students. By the early 1950s, many of the bright young scholars who had written their doctoral dissertations at Marburg during the 1920s and 1930s were distinguished New Testament professors in their own right. With the postwar division of Germany, the West German universities where Bultmann's protégés taught—Tübingen, Göttingen, Münster, and Marburg—became centers of avant-garde intellectualism. At a 1953 gathering of the *alte Marburger,* or "Old Marburgers," as Bultmann's former acolytes called themselves, Ernst Käsemann (1906–1998), a New Testament professor at Tübingen, read a paper titled "The Problem of the Historical Jesus," in which he took issue with Bultmann's central proposition that there was an impassable gulf between the human Jesus who had lived in Palestine and the divine Jesus Christ proclaimed in the Christian *kerygma* of the New Testament. Käsemann agreed with Bultmann and other form critics that the Gospels were not "biographies" in any conventional sense, and that it was impossible to re-create the sort of chronologically precise "life of Jesus" that the 19th-century liberals had attempted. However, he believed that it was possible to get beneath the *kerygma,* so to speak—to piece together from the Gospels (or at least the three Synoptics) a true portrait of the historical Jesus. After all the early-church accretions were stripped away, the bedrock layer revealed Jesus himself, and not just a few tantalizing quotations, he argued. In contrast to Bultmann, Käsemann maintained that the early Christians had not turned Jesus into a wholly mythological figure, and that the Gospels had preserved a certain amount of historical memory.

As it turned out, Käsemann's historical Jesus was a replica of Bultmann's as presented in his 1926 book, minus his qualifications and quotation marks. Like Bultmann, Käsemann maintained that Jesus had primarily been a teacher, which meant that the surest clues to his historical identity lay in his teachings, not in his reputed deeds. The scholar's task should therefore be to pick the authentic sayings of Jesus out of the morass of words attributed to him in the Gospels for the purpose of lending authority to early Christian beliefs and practices. One way to accomplish this was to look for statements that could not have been made by any first-century Jew or early Christian. For example, Mark's Gospel has Jesus saying, "[T]here is nothing outside a person that by going in can defile, but the things that come out are what defile."[1] As such brazen defiance of Jewish food laws would have been unthinkable for all first-century Jews and almost all Jewish-born Christians, the statement must have truly come from Jesus.

Käsemann's paper provoked other former students to rise in revolt against their *Doktorvater.* Three years later, another "old Marburger," Günther Bornkamm of the University of Heidelberg, published the first "life of Jesus" to emerge from the German academy since the beginning of World War I. In contrast to the ponderous biographies of the 19th century, Bornkamm's *Jesus of Nazareth* was a slender, elegantly written volume. Like Käsemann, Bornkamm assumed that the real Jesus was to be found in the bottom, aphoristic layer of his sayings that Bultmann and the other form critics had isolated. He also adopted Käsemann's methodology of isolating (and attributing to Jesus himself) statements that could not have come from Jesus' Jewish or Christian contemporaries. Bornkamm's was a Jesus of "originality."[2] The "words of Jesus in their concreteness have nothing to do with the casuistry of Jewish legalism," he wrote.[3] Nor did they have anything to do with material "which on very good grounds can be shown to have sprung from the faith of the later Church."[4]

Once again, Bornkamm's Jesus, derived from the three Synoptic Gospels, was a version of Bultmann's. However, Bornkamm's narrative limited itself to the barest of details, including the fact that Jesus had had a human father and numerous siblings, had once followed John the Baptist, and had spent most of his life in Galilee until his fatal trip to Jerusalem. He had not claimed to be the Messiah (messianic material in the Gospels represented Jewish and Christian overlay), or the son of man, or the coming judge of the world. While Bornkamm accepted Bultmann's theory that Jesus was talking about the future reign of God when he referred to his "kingdom," he also believed that Jesus was talking about a present reality, conflating the future and the present. Bornkamm thus agreed with Bultmann that Jesus had taught a "timeless" rather than an "interim" ethic as Albert Schweitzer had contended. In line with his emphasis on Jesus' role as a teacher, he devoted nearly half of his book to explaining what he viewed as his "authentic" teachings, devoting hardly any space to his reported miracles.

Käsemann and Bornkamm launched what came to be known as the "New Quest" for the historical Jesus, in contrast to the "Old Quest" of the 19th century. There were similarities between the quests. For both schools, Jesus was primarily a preacher of a new ethic that stood in stark contrast to the decadent, "legalistic" morality of the Judaism of his time. (Even though the new-questers had lived through the near-annihilation of European Jewry under Hitler, they largely maintained the anti-Judaic theology of their predecessors.) They also shared the old-questers' view that the "kingdom" Jesus promised was a purely spiritual phenomenon. However, whereas the old school had identified Jesus' kingdom with human progress, the new school identified it with existential freedom.

In defining Jesus exclusively in terms of his sayings, the new-questers deemed nearly all his actions—from his healings to his resurrection—as purely mythical, with the exception of those that amounted to practicing what he preached. "Just as he faced up to his opponents, so he had to prepare his own for the struggle which lay ahead of them, too," wrote Ernst Fuchs (1903–1983), another Bultmann protégé, who had assumed his *Doktorvater*'s chair at Marburg.[5] Beyond the fact that Jesus had been a religious and social radical whose observance of poverty, trust in God, healing of the sick, and exorcising demons had served as examples for his disciples, there was little else to say about his life.

Finally, the new Jesus of history was the same old Christ of faith. "The so-called Christ of faith is none other than the historical Jesus," Fuchs noted, adding that "what is much more important is the statement that God wants to be encountered by us in the historical Jesus."[6] Yet another New Quest scholar, Gerhard Ebeling, defined the true Jesus "as he comes to be known by strictly historical methods, in contrast to any alteration and touching up to which he has been subjected in the traditional Jesus picture. Hence the 'historical Jesus' as good as means the true Jesus."[7] According to Ebeling, the historical Jesus was a corrective to the traditional, creed-oriented faith, and Christians should alter their theology and even their dogmas to conform to the reality of the historical Jesus. "Jesus is therefore not an object of faith in the sense in which we are accustomed to speak of objects of faith," he wrote. "Rather, he is the ground of faith."[8]

The New Quest was such a successful phenomenon in German academia that by the early 1960s there was not a single faithful adherent left among Bultmann's crop of brilliant protégés. Although he never wavered in his insistence that the New Quest was pointless, his former students had reason to believe that they could reconstruct a more credible historical Jesus. Already in the 1950s, most of them had moved beyond the rigid form criticism that Bultmann and Martin Dibelius had pioneered, which viewed the Gospels strictly as collections of folk-anecdotes about Jesus whose authors were mere conduits for the Jesus-traditions of their communities. Bultmann believed, for example, that the evangelist Mark, whose Greek was extremely uncultivated, was neither mentally bright nor theologically deep. "Mark is not sufficiently master of his material to be able to venture on a systematic construction himself," he wrote in his *History of the Synoptic Tradition.*[9] He also tended not to distinguish theologically or stylistically among the three Synoptic Gospels. As the title of his book indicates, he viewed all three as representing a single, undifferentiated "tradition."

His students, by contrast, developed a technique called "redaction criticism," which focused on the individual evangelist's creative role as editor in arranging and compiling the stories in his Gospel. Actually, this approach to the New Testament was not entirely new. Among several British researchers of the interwar period, R. H. Lightfoot (1883–1953), son of the 19th-century scholar J. B. Lightfoot, had traveled to Germany after World War I to study form criticism. He had written several studies examining the ways in which the evangelists had interpreted traditional material to reflect their own concerns. As World War II had interrupted scholarly lines of communication, the Germans essentially reinvented Lightfoot's methodology after the war.

The first German scholar to experiment with redaction criticism was Bornkamm. In a 1948 article on Matthew's Gospel, he explored the way in which the evangelist had reinterpreted Jesus' calming a storm at sea, one of the stories he had borrowed from Mark (the relevant passages are Matthew 8:23–27 and Mark 4:34–41). Bornkamm noted that Matthew had reworked Mark's tale to emphasize a theme of faith and discipleship that was not in Mark's version. With the help of two of his students, in 1954 Bornkamm expanded his article into a book titled *Tradition and Interpretation in Matthew,* which interpreted Matthew's Gospel not as a narrative about Jesus but as a theological exploration of Matthew's understanding of the Christian church.

Two years later, Willi Marxsen (1919–1987), another Bultmann protégé who taught New Testament studies at the University of Münster, published *Mark the Evangelist,* a dramatic reexamination of the evangelist's writing that turned Bultmann's old conception of Mark as a semi-literate naif on its head. Marxsen (who actually invented the phrase "redaction criticism") presented Mark as a sophisticated theologian who had skillfully selected and arranged every narrative detail of his Gospel in order to present his own idiosyncratic interpretation of Jesus' teachings. According to Marxsen, Mark was not writing a biography of Jesus, but rather exploring certain theological topics connected with Jesus that he found particularly compelling: his resurrection, second coming, great battle against Satan, and "messianic secret," which

Marxsen viewed not as a real secret but as a way of talking about the hiddenness of God. Even the geographical setting of Mark's Gospel—mostly Galilee—was strictly symbolic, and thus had nothing to do with Jesus' actual life or travels.

The most radical of the redaction treatments of the Gospels came from Hans Conzelmann, a former student of Bultmann's at Göttingen, who maintained that when Jesus used the phrase "son of man," rather than referring to the apocalyptic figure mentioned in the Book of Daniel, he was only using an Aramaic idiom synonymous with "human being." In his *Theology of St. Luke,* published in 1954, Conzelmann examined both Luke's Gospel and his Acts of the Apostles. From earliest Christian times, Luke had been regarded as the true "historian" of the four evangelists. Unlike the others, he had taken pains to place Jesus' birth and ministry during specific years of the reigns of Roman emperors and governors, thereby moving his life into the larger tableau of human history. In the Acts of the Apostles, numerous well-documented historical personages of Jesus' day—Jewish royalty, Roman procurators, and local officials—have colorful walk-on roles.

Although David Friedrich Strauss and various other skeptics had scoffed at Luke for having possibly mistaken the date of the Roman census that was supposed to have coincided with Jesus' birth, his accounts had otherwise appeared amazingly accurate, including the arcane titles of minor provincial officials. He had also displayed a firm grasp of ancient geography, politics, and weather conditions as he traced Paul of Tarsus's journeys. Certain parts of Acts seem eerily to track Josephus's later-written Jewish histories. Conzelmann contended that Luke's historical detail was not history in the secular sense at all, but rather pure theology. As an example, he pointed to Luke's situating Jesus' post-resurrection appearances in or near Jerusalem, whereas the other evangelists had seemed to place them in Galilee. Conzelmann theorized that Luke had relocated the sightings to Jerusalem in order to emphasize the city's central role in an elaborate but artificial scheme of "salvation-history" that had moved from Galilee to Jerusalem to Rome.

Conzelmann's revisionist approach to Acts was especially devastating to those who had relied on the book as a fairly authentic historical record. In recasting Luke's second book as pure theology, Conzelmann rendered Acts useless as a historical source for documenting the spread of early Christianity or dating other New Testament literature such as Paul's letters. After Conzelmann finished with Luke, earliest Christianity *had* no history, except such "history" as he and other scholars could uncover (or invent) from the close reading of other New Testament texts.

At first glance, it might seem as though form criticism and redaction criticism were antithetical New Testament disciplines. The former supposed that the Gospels were naively assembled collections of folk-tales, while the latter contended that they were carefully crafted literary creations whose every word-placement was as freighted with significance as a poet's choice of a simile in a sonnet. In reality, however, the redactionists believed that they were taking up where the form critics had left off. According to Conzelmann, Marxsen, Bornkamm, and others, the redactionary reshaping of traditional material on the part of the evangelists was simply another layer of development as the Gospel stories grew from aphorisms to complete narratives.

Moreover, the evangelists' distinctive theologies were not their own but those of their communities. The very fact that the religious concerns of each of the Synoptics were so distinctive—Matthew's fascination with discipleship, Mark's with divine conflict, and Luke's with "salvation history"—indicated to the redaction critics how widely divergent, and even sectarian, the various early Christians' perceptions of Jesus really were. Because the evangelists had essentially functioned as scribes, not creative inventors, the redaction critics were as confident as the form critics had been that by peeling off one textual layer at a time they could trace the historical development of the Christian community that had produced each of the Gospels.

The entire form-redaction movement was based on the assumption that people simply cannot transmit a lengthy story with any reasonable degree of accuracy, and therefore none of the layers above the bedrock aphorisms reflected genuine memories of Jesus. While those who study the telling of folk-tales and folk-epics in living oral cultures might beg to differ, the redactionists insisted that the Gospels were entirely fictional, with the exception of a few sayings of Jesus that revealed his historical personality. They thus anticipated the structuralist and deconstructionist New Testament interpretations of the 1980s and 1990s, which view the Gospels as mere "texts" bearing no relation to reality (because there is no such thing) and whose narrative voice fractures into a kaleidoscope of identities.

The New Quest and the rise of redaction criticism coincided with the rediscovery of a 1934 book, *Orthodoxy and Heresy in Earliest Christianity,* that was to spark a revolution in academic thinking about Christian origins. Its author, Walter Bauer (1877–1960), a New Testament professor at Göttingen, had been known primarily as a Greek lexicographer. His life's masterpiece was an authoritative dictionary of New Testament and early Christian Greek that is still in use today. However, Bauer also delved into history-of-religions theory. In 1925 he had published a monograph on John's Gospel that explored thematic parallels between John's theology and that of the Mandaeans, an obscure but still-extant sect in southern Iran that combines Parsi rites, Gnostic-like spirituality, and devotion to John the Baptist. Although the extant Mandaean holy books date no further back than the eighth century C.E. (and were probably influenced by medieval Christianity, Manicheism, and other eighth-century religions), Bauer hypothesized that Mandaeanism actually began soon after Jesus' death as a kind of analogous religion to Christianity that also incorporated elements of Gnostic theology. Bauer believed, in fact, that the evangelist John had been a Gnostic, and that his Gospel reflected Mandaean parallels. In short, both Christianity and Mandaeanism grew out of Gnosticism, but in different ways.

Bauer's speculations about the relation between Mandaeanism and Christianity relied heavily on circular reasoning. Not only did he assume that eighth-century texts were actually written in the first century because they contained parallels to John's Gospel; he also used that very assumption to "prove" that John's Gospel must have relied on the same pre-Christian Gnostic "sources" employed by the Mandaeans (of course, there is no evidence for the existence of such sources).

In *Orthodoxy and Heresy,* Bauer broadened the speculations he had explored in his book about John, contending that all branches of early Christianity, from the most orthodox to the most heterodox, represented independent developments of certain pre-Christian religious themes that were already circulating in the first-century Hellenistic world. For more than half a century, the standard German Protestant version of early church history, exemplified in the works of Adolf von Harnack, had been grounded in the theory that earliest Christianity had been uniform of faith, widespread throughout the ancient world, and as yet unspoiled by Catholic frippery such as popes and veneration of the Virgin Mary. Heresies had come later, according to conventional scholarly wisdom. In *Orthodoxy and Heresy,* Bauer argued instead that from its very beginnings, Christianity had exhibited an extraordinary theological diversity that amounted to bickering sectarianism.

With regard to the supposed heresies, Bauer maintained that they were mere geographic variants of the faith that dated back to the days of Paul, who had spoken of those "false apostles, deceitful workers, disguising themselves as the apostles of Christ."[10] Gnosticism, for example, was the only variety of Christianity available in Egypt until the third century, Bauer maintained. In Edessa, Mesopotamia (now Urfa in Turkey), the earliest Christians were Marcionites, while in Palestine they were the Ebionites, or "Jewish Christians," who did not believe that Jesus was divine. In Asia Minor, the first Christians were members of that eclectic, Mandaean-like Gnostic sect of which Bauer believed the evangelist John had been a member. (John had an "extremely confused religious outlook," he added drily.)[11] Most significant of all was the fact that all these supposedly heretical groups regarded themselves as the true orthodox Christians, and their theological and ethnic opponents as heretics.

In Bauer's view, the only community of Christians whose theology would be regarded as orthodox today was the Roman church. Using a combination of well-placed polemic and institutional innovations (such as bishops, who ruled their dioceses like kings), the highly centralized church of Rome eventually imposed its theology on the heterodox majority of the rest of the Christian world. However, in the early decades before Rome flexed its muscles, even Paul himself, in whose letters Bauer saw many of the same "pre-Christian Gnostic" features that he had identified in John's Gospel, was a heretic by Roman standards. He further theorized that at a later date, the Catholics had rehabilitated Paul by attributing to him several spurious but theologically "orthodox" New Testament letters.

Bauer also rejected the idea that the canonical New Testament reflected mainstream Christianity, maintaining instead that any book written by early Christians—or even non-Christians like the Mandaeans—was as important as any other in understanding the origins of Christianity. In fact, certain of the canonicals, such as Paul's letters and the Gospels of Luke and John, displayed a theology that Roman Christians would have regarded as highly unorthodox. In *Orthodoxy and Heresy,* Bauer single-handedly revived the "conflict model" that Ferdinand Christian Baur of Tübingen had proposed a century before. However, in contrast to Baur's tidy, neatly resolved Hegelian dialectic between Jewish and Hellenistic Christianity, Bauer's model of Christian origins was a free-for-all that the Roman church succeeded in controlling to some extent but could not eradicate entirely.

The tone of *Orthodoxy and Heresy* was snide, and when the book was reviewed (by many of the great names in interwar German scholarship, including Martin Dibelius), few had much good to say about it. Bauer drew criticism for his overbroad assumptions, his unsubstantiated hypotheses, his arguments from silence (there are almost no extant records of first-century ecclesial organization), and his interpretation of unclear documents in tendentious ways that served his own arguments. His sections on Egypt and Edessa were considered especially weak. Indeed, the majority of scholars nowadays believe that non-Gnostic Christians actually outnumbered Gnostics in Egypt, and that the Syrians, rather than the Marcionites, brought Christianity to Edessa.

Despite Bauer's shortcomings, there was general agreement (and there still is) that he had made an important point about the variety of expressions of Christianity during its earliest years, at a time when no formal creeds and hardly any centralized authority obtained. Bauer even gained the sneaking admiration of some Catholic reviewers, who appreciated his casting the Roman church as a bulwark of orthodoxy.

The year in which *Orthodoxy and Heresy* was published also witnessed the Barmen Declaration. Beleaguered Protestant churchmen, intent upon forging a unified front against Hitler, had no use for a scholar who contended that the Christian "orthodoxy" on which they had based their anti-Nazi stand was merely the theology of the victors in a prolonged ecclesial power struggle. To make matters worse, in 1927 Bauer had published an essay titled "Jesus the Galilean," suggesting that since Galilee had been conquered and reconquered by Hellenistic warlords many times over before Jesus' birth, its inhabitants (including Jesus) were an ethnic mix that felt no particular loyalty toward Jerusalem, the center of Jewish religion and culture. Although Bauer himself was not anti-Semitic and never intended "Jesus the Galilean" as a racial polemic, the article lent credence to Nazi wartime propaganda promoting the notion that Jesus was not really a Jew.

Rudolf Bultmann, who found many of Bauer's theories intriguing, informed him in a letter written in February 1935 that he had "learned much"[13] from *Orthodoxy and Heresy.* He also cited Bauer in his monumental *Theology of the New Testament.* Both men were convinced that early Christianity—especially as portrayed in John's Gospels and Paul's letters—had been heavily influenced by Gnosticism. Furthermore, Bauer's conclusions about the diversity among the first Christians dovetailed with Bultmann's belief that the various Christian communities who transmitted the Gospel stories had developed their theologies and shaped their narratives in ways that were often antagonistic. Given Bultmann's towering reputation, it was only a matter of time before *Orthodoxy and Heresy* enjoyed a postwar revival. In 1964, when the New Quest was at its height, Bauer's book was republished in West Germany to much scholarly fanfare.

The following year, another of Bultmann's former students, a New Testament professor at the University of Frankfurt am Main named Dieter Georgi, published a lengthy monograph about the "false apostles" to whom Paul had referred in his second letter to the Corinthians. Extrapolating from those scanty allusions, Georgi fleshed out not only a complete theology for Paul's opponents, but also a lengthy history of their religious community, which he believed had survived well into the second century and had influenced Luke's Gospel. Like Bauer, Georgi contended that neither Paul's theology nor that of the "false apostles" necessarily reflected what Jesus had taught or how he had acted. Furthermore, Georgi moved Bauer's conflict model of early Christianity from the late first century to the time immediately following Jesus' death. Georgi declined to refer to the early strains of Jesus-belief as specifically "Christian." He instead described them as components of a hydra-headed "Jesus tradition" that included Gnostics, proto-Marcionites, proto-Ebionites, and others who would later be condemned as heretics. The term "Jesus movement" is now the preferred locution for early Christianity among avant-garde scholars.

The move to rewrite early Christian history gained momentum from the fact that beginning in the 1880s, explorers, archaeologists, and even local peasants had been stumbling across ancient manuscripts that had lain buried for centuries, suddenly providing scholars with far more information about early Christianity than they had ever possessed. Most of the discoveries were made in the harsh deserts of Upper Egypt, where the dry air acted as a preservative, the searing heat deterred tourism and economic activity, and the remoteness of the villages ensured that burial sites would remain undisturbed. In 1886, an extensive fragment of the Gospel of Peter—censured as heretical by the early church but otherwise completely lost—was discovered in an eighth-century Egyptian tomb. Two smaller fragments turned up around 1900 in a cache of second-century Greek papyruses unearthed in the ruins of the ancient Hellenistic town of Oxyrhynchus, west of the Nile. The Oxyrhynchus collection also included parts of the Gospel of Thomas, another missing ancient text that had been associated with the Gnostics and Manicheans.

The most dramatic Egyptian discovery, a library of 12 fourth-century papyrus books written in Coptic and 18 pages from a 13th book, was made in 1945 at the village of Nag Hammadi. Among the 52 different texts in the

Nag Hammadi corpus, many of which incorporated Gnostic religious themes, was a complete Coptic version of the Gospel of Thomas that matched the second-century Greek fragments found at Oxyrhynchus. Comprising 114 different aphorisms, it began with the words, "These are the secret sayings which the living Jesus spoke and which Didymos Judas Thomas wrote down,"[13] and ended with, "The Gospel According to Thomas."[14] While many of the sayings paralleled statements of Jesus in the four canonical Gospels, others were entirely idiosyncratic.

While none of the Egyptian manuscripts dated to anywhere near the time of Jesus, certain critics were convinced that they could reach a first-century compositional stratum in them. In Dibelius's view, for example, the primal layer of the Gospel of Peter preserved an authentic passion story that was independent of the four canonicals. Others thought it possible that the Gospel of Thomas contained authentic sayings of Jesus omitted by the evangelists because their theologies differed from those of Thomas's community. In the manner of Bauer on the Mandaeans, they were using later texts to make assumptions about an earlier period.

The majority of New Testament scholars in Germany and elsewhere did not sign on to the Walter Bauer revival, or to the notion that fourth-century Coptic texts had much to say about the historical Jesus. On the contrary, they regarded the Gospels of Peter and Thomas as mid-second-century creations that were literarily dependent on the canonicals (there is a growing consensus, however, that a few of Thomas's sayings may reflect the actual words of Jesus). Moreover, Gnosticism itself postdated Jesus' time.

As European biblical scholarship grew increasingly conservative in this regard, the vacuum in avant-garde New Testament studies began to be filled by Americans. Starting in the 1950s, American universities began offering teaching posts to disciples and admirers of Bultmann. Harvard Divinity School acquired Helmut Koester, one of the last Marburgers to write a doctoral dissertation for Bultmann, as well as Dieter Georgi. Another radical, Hans Dieter Betz, who had received his doctorate in theology from the University of Mainz, emigrated to America, where he joined the faculties of Claremont Graduate School and the School of Theology at Claremont in 1957, moving to the University of Chicago's divinity school in 1978. Vanderbilt University's divinity school welcomed Robert Funk's mentor, Kendrick Grobel, an American who had studied with Bultmann at Marburg and married one of Bultmann's daughters, and later Gerd Lüdemann, a former student of Hans Conzelmann at Göttingen. All these scholars imbibed Walter

Bauer's theories of Christian diversity and passed them on to their American students.

The pivotal figure of avant-garde German New Testament studies in America was James M. Robinson. Born in 1924, Robinson was the son of a theologically conservative evangelical pastor who taught at the Columbia Theological Seminary in Georgia, where Robinson himself trained for the ministry. Intrigued by the existentialist neo-orthodoxy of Karl Barth, he set off for Basel in the late 1940s to study with him personally. While in Europe, he took a summer course from Bultmann at Marburg and converted from Barth's existentialism to Bultmann's, becoming a tireless promoter of the "new hermeneutics," the New Quest, and Walter Bauer.

Robinson returned to the United States in 1952 to teach at Emory University's Candler School of Theology. In 1957, he moved to Claremont, where Betz was to set up a research center at the graduate school known as the Institute for Antiquity and Christianity, which was devoted to exploring pluralistic explanations for Christian origins. During the 1960s, Robinson became head of the institute, a position he still holds today.

In a short book titled *A New Quest of the Historical Jesus* (1959), Robinson introduced American readers to New Quest theories and the post-Bultmannian worldview. Robinson went even further than the Germans had ventured: While Käsemann, Bornkamm, and others had emphasized a continuity between the historical Jesus and the New Testament *kerygma,* Robinson contended that historical methods provided an *independent* means of access to Jesus that could supplement the *kerygma*. In other words, professional scholars could come to know more about Jesus than any Christian believer. Robinson wrote: "These two avenues of access to the same person create a situation which has not existed in the Church since the time of the original disciples, who had both their Easter faith and their factual memory of Jesus."[15] In language reminiscent of the historicist Ernst Troeltsch, he went so far as to declare that only professionally trained academicians were competent to find the real Jesus, deriding as amateurish Robert Graves's fanciful reconstruction of the first century in *King Jesus.* "For specialization has advanced to the point where membership in the intelligentsia no longer qualifies for participation in the quest for the historical Jesus," Robinson declared.[16]

During the 1970s, under the auspices of the United Nations Educational, Scientific and Cultural Organization, Robinson persuaded the Egyptian government to break a monopoly held by German and French scholars and permit the first facsimile publication of the Nag Hammadi manuscripts, copies of which had been languishing unpublished in university archives since the 1950s. The result was a 1978 English translation of the Coptic texts, overseen by Robinson, which to this day remains the only complete translation of those ancient religious manuscripts. Robinson's massive (and impressive) feat of text assembly provided historians with yet another avenue of independent, non-New-Testament-linked access to Jesus and the origins of Christianity.

Robinson and Helmut Koester worked in tandem to persuade their graduate students at Claremont and Harvard to learn Coptic along with Greek, Aramaic, and Hebrew as a prelude to the study of Christian origins. In 1971, the same year in which Fortress Press published an English translation of Bauer's *Orthodoxy and Heresy,* Koester and Robinson issued a collection of essays, *Trajectories through Early Christianity,* which used Bauer's methodology to contend that any arguably Christian text from any century could be used to plot a trajectory, backward or forward, of the thinking of early Christian groups. It was thus possible to take two thematically related texts from different periods and trace the history and evolution of the community that was presumably responsible for both. Underlying their arguments, however, was the assumption, certainly debatable, that each early Christian community read only a single text at any given time.

Koester and Robinson inspired an entire generation of trajectorists among their students and admirers. The most famous scholar to be influenced by trajectory theory was Elaine Pagels, who wrote her doctoral dissertation for Koester during the late 1960s. In her best-selling *The Gnostic Gospels* (1979), Pagels maintained that far from being a heresy, Gnosticism was simply a Christian variant that happened to be out of favor with the more politically powerful orthodox Christianity.

Another active promoter of the new methodology was Norman Perrin (1920–1976), whose own quest in many ways resembled that of Robinson. Born in England, Perrin had been a conservative Baptist minister before enrolling at age 36 in a doctoral program at Göttingen, where Robinson was a visiting professor. Under the latter's influence, Perrin threw aside his earlier religious conservatism and embraced the then-brand-new redaction criticism as well as Bultmann's demythologization program. He followed Robinson to Emory, and later joined Chicago's divinity school faculty.

Not only was Perrin filled with a convert's enthusiasm for the new German biblical analysis, but he was eager to make up for the time he had lost by beginning his academic career when nearly 40. In the 17 years between 1959 and his death from cancer at age 56, he published seven books and approximately 30 articles. An eighth book, dealing with the Synoptic Gospels' treatment of Jesus' resurrection, appeared the year after his death.

Perrin publicized the New Quest and redaction criticism in a didactic, absolutist fashion that received a great deal of attention from American scholars. Whereas the first generation of German new-questers had attempted to establish continuity between the historical Jesus and the Christ proclaimed in the *kerygma* of Christian faith, and Robinson had proposed supplementing the *kerygma* by providing an alternative flow of information about Jesus and Christian origins, Perrin argued that the historical Jesus was a completely different person from the Christ of faith that the Christian *kerygma* proclaimed. "The Christ present in the *kerygma* is necessarily distinct from the historical Jesus," he stated in a book published in 1967.[17] In Perrin's view the New Testament was practically irrelevant to understanding the historical Jesus.

Perrin believed that research on the historical Jesus had the potential to reshape the traditional *kerygma* so as to bring Christian faith more in line with the real Jesus. "Knowledge of the historical Jesus is, then, important in that it can contribute positively to the formation of the faith-image, i.e. it can help to provide faith with its necessary *content,* and in that it can act negatively on false or inappropriate faith-images,"[18] he wrote. Indeed, he was convinced that Christian faith had an obligation to redefine itself according to what he called "historical knowledge of Jesus."[19] Moreover, he took the position that the professional historian (and not the Christian theologian) was the only qualified interpreter of Jesus: "[W]e may and we must use such historical knowledge of Jesus as we possess to test the validity of the claim of any given form of the Church's proclamation to be Christian proclamation."[20] In other words, biblical scholars had the right to tell Christians what to believe.

Perrin's approach to redaction criticism, encapsulated in a catechismal 1969 monograph, was equally absolutist. Käsemann and Bornkamm had established a test for identifying authentic sayings of Jesus: their distinctiveness from either the Judaism of his time or early Christianity. Perrin elevated this "criterion of dissimilarity" to top priority. "[M]aterial may be ascribed to Jesus only if it can be shown to be distinctive of him, which usually will mean dissimilar to known tendencies in Judaism before him or the church after him," he noted, adding, "An example of this would be the address to God, 'Abba' (Father), in the Lucan version of the Lord's Prayer."[21] Perrin established two other standards for defining a Gospel saying as authentic. The first was the "criterion of multiple attestation," meaning that at least two Gospel sources (such as Mark and Q) or independent pre-Gospel traditions had ascribed the saying to Jesus—unless it pertained to a church practice such as the eucharist, in which case it was inauthentic despite multiple attestation. The second, which Perrin called the "criterion of coherence," was roughly equivalent to the "That's Jesus!" standard that the Jesus Seminar uses in deciding whether he actually uttered a certain phrase. A particular saying had to be consistent in tone and subject matter with those already attributed to Jesus.[22]

Even if a given saying met all three stringent criteria, Perrin nonetheless deemed it inauthentic if it seemed to originate from Greek or from the Aramaic of the early Palestinian church. Accordingly, he placed every "son of man" saying that referred to the Second Coming in the latter category. Like Bultmann and his German disciples, he also maintained that no part of the Gospel of John, not even material that paralleled the Synoptics, could be ascribed to Jesus. As can easily be seen, Perrin's draconian standards amounted to an ironclad guarantee that there would be little left of Jesus once the historical critic had winnowed from the Gospels all "inauthentic" statements. "From this moment Life of Jesus research must proceed in this way and use this kind of methodology," he pronounced.[23] "The impact of form and redaction criticism is such that nothing less than this kind of stringency is possible."[24]

In the meantime, existentialism had gone out of fashion during the late 1960s. The tumultuous 1968 student riots at universities all over Europe and America, as well as Mao Tse-tung's Cultural Revolution in China, had made out-and-out Marxists out of many Western intellectuals who had once been merely existentialists of a leftist bent. In the realm of theology, the distant God of Christian existentialism could no longer be accessed by a leap of Barthian or Bultmannian faith. The notion arose that God had died, and that Christianity was in a terminal decline. The American theologian Thomas J. Altizer promoted what he called "Christian atheism," a kind of religionless religion that was as stark and gray as the unadorned concrete churches of the 1960s, and in which the deity, if he existed at all, never intervened in human affairs. A 1966 *Time* magazine cover declaring, "God Is Dead" found its way into Roman Polanski's 1967 movie *Rosemary's Baby,* whose theme was the dawn of the reign of Satan after the deity's death.

Death-of-God theology inevitably affected the search for the historical Jesus. Stripped of even his existential significance, Jesus had become an ordinary, error-prone human being. Depicting Jesus as a divine idiot savant who had no sense whatsoever of his mission, British author J. A. Baker contended that Jesus bumbled through his ministry "mistaken about the programme which God planned to follow."[25] *The Myth of God Incarnate,* a widely read collection of essays published in 1977 by a coterie of young theologians who were mostly from Birmingham University, toyed with the idea of fashioning a New Quest Christianity centered on a historical Jesus who had no special connection to God. Frances Young, a New Testament lecturer, declared that "modern knowledge of genetics and reproduction"[26] made it impossible for her to believe in the virgin birth. Michael Goulder, a theology tutor and convert to trajectory theory, opined that the doctrine of the incarnation was an invention of the Samaritans. Don Cupitt, dean of Emmanuel College at Cambridge University, concluded that the incarnation was a pernicious teaching because it had inspired Christians to conceive of Jesus as an emperor and God the father as a pope. Dennis Nineham, warden of Oxford University's Keble College, suggested that instead of focusing on Jesus, Christians should change their central myth into "a story in which the protagonist's role belongs undividedly to God."[27] Moreover, by eliminating Jesus as the dominant male figure of Christianity, Christians would make it easier for feminists to conceive of an androgynous God.

Other scholars of the New Quest took up Norman Perrin's position that the historical Jesus was a countercultural figure and reconstructed a countercultural Jesus who thumbed his nose at authority. The most arresting such portrait of Jesus was that of Morton Smith, a history professor at Columbia University who had read *Trajectories through Earliest Christianity.* In 1973, Smith published a startling monograph titled *The Secret Gospel,* which recast Jesus as a kind of bathhouse shaman who had initiated his (mostly male) disciples by means of late-night baptismal rituals featuring nudity and most probably sex. To support his unusual hypothesis, Smith relied heavily on trajectory theory, contending that the church fathers had suppressed nearly all documents relating to this particular strand of Jesus-tradition.

In the 1950s, during a visit to the Mar Saba monastery near Jerusalem, Smith had discovered an 18th-century copy of a fragment from a hitherto-unknown letter written by Clement of Alexandria, one of the church fathers who had lived around 200 C.E. While complaining about the licentious activities of the Carpocratians, a sect of Egyptian Gnostics who believed that committing sins of the flesh guaranteed them eternal salvation, Clement stated that the evangelist Mark, after writing the "public" version of his Gospel, created a "secret" version for an inner circle of spiritually advanced Christians in Alexandria. According to Clement, the Carpocratians had adopted the "Secret Mark" and reinterpreted it as a justification for their libertinism.

During the course of his diatribe against the Carpocratians, Clement quoted approximately 20 lines of Greek that he claimed had come from the "Secret Mark." The passage which elaborated the identity of a mysterious "young man . . . wearing nothing but a linen cloth,"[28] who was with Jesus in the Garden of Gethsemane at the time of his arrest in Mark's account of the passion. When a soldier grabbed the young man, he ran off naked, leaving his linen cloth behind. In the "Secret Mark" fragment, the young man, whom Jesus had earlier raised from the dead, visited him by night wearing nothing but his piece of linen to receive esoteric instruction.

Smith believed that the "Secret Mark" presented a truer picture of the historical Jesus than that of any of the canonical Gospels. He argued that Jesus' main message had been "freedom from the law," which meant flouting Jewish ritualistic and moral conventions. He further speculated that Jesus had been the leader of a gay Judean underground, as evidenced by Mark's New Testament reference to a "man carrying a jug of water,"[29] who had to have been a drag queen, in Smith's view, since lugging water was considered women's work. The young man who fled Gethsemane on the night of Jesus' arrest had been hoping to be baptized into Jesus' inner circle in the Kidron brook, which adjoined the garden. Smith described the ritual in lurid detail:

> It was a water baptism administered by Jesus to chosen disciples, singly and by night. The costume of the disciple was a linen cloth worn over the naked body. The cloth was probably removed for the baptism proper, the immersion in water, which was now reduced to a preparatory purification. After that, by unknown ceremonies, the disciple was possessed by Jesus' spirit and so united with Jesus. One with him, he participated by hallucination in Jesus' ascent into the heavens, he entered into the kingdom of God, and was thereby set free from the laws ordained for men and women in the lower world. Freedom from the law may have resulted in completion of the spiritual union by physical union. This certainly occurred in many forms of gnostic Christianity; how early it began there is no telling.[30]

Not surprisingly, Smith's theories were controversial. For one thing, no other Western scholar has ever seen the Mar Saba manuscript, which has led many experts to question whether it represents a genuine letter from Clement of Alexandria or simply a later forgery. However, Helmut Koester gave the "Secret Mark" his trajectorist blessing, concluding that the quoted fragment reflected an authentic strand of tradition about Jesus that dated to the first century. Koester further contended that the "Secret Mark" story of Jesus' raising the young man from the dead might have been an independent version of the one used by the evangelist John in his narrative of the raising of Lazarus.

In 1978, Smith expanded his theories in *Jesus the Magician,* maintaining that the negative references to Jesus and Christianity in ancient pagan and Jewish texts portrayed a more accurate picture of him than did the New Testament. Smith in fact believed that Jesus' career had resembled that of the late-first-century philosopher Appolonius of Tyana, who had studied magic in Babylonia, asceticism in Egypt, and Brahmin mysticism in India before gathering a circle of disciples. Three years after vanishing from a Roman courtroom where he was on trial for sacrificing a young boy in order to read his entrails to learn more about a conspiracy to kill the emperor Domitian, Appolonius was said to have ascended into heaven.

Smith also contended, as had many of the ancients, that Jesus was illegitimate, citing the 1859 discovery near Mainz of the tombstone of an Aramaic-speaking Roman soldier from Tiberius's time named Pantera, which was part of Jesus' patronymic in certain rabbinic texts. Combining the tombstone and the rabbinic references, he suggested that Jesus' real father lay buried in the German grave.

Smith's Jesus not only flouted the Jewish law, but he also let people think he was a god and a king. When he spoke of "love," in all likelihood he meant sexual promiscuity. The eucharist itself was an orgiastic rite with overtones of cannibalism, in which Jesus united his followers to himself by the consumption of his body and blood. Instead of mythicizing Jesus, Smith believed that early Christianity was actually more rationalist than the original Jesus movement, concluding that the "lower-middle-class respectability"[31] of the merchants and craftsmen who composed the first Christian communities under Paul had gradually toned down a bizarre personality cult.

Morton Smith was hardly a mainstream new-quester. In basing his historical Jesus on the partial historicity of all four canonicals, he actually took the Gospel stories much more seriously than many of his colleagues. He was convinced that the Gospel accounts of Jesus' scandal-surrounded conception, his miracles, his institution of the eucharist, and his founding of a community bearing his name were essentially true, even if his own interpretations of those accounts ran counter to traditionalist Christian thought.

By the 1970s, thanks to the proselytizing efforts of Robinson and Perrin, the New Quest for the historical Jesus was largely centered in North America. Like their German predecessors, its participants focused on what Jesus had said in contrast to the Gospel accounts of his deeds. Many of them were drawn to Q, the hypothetical source of some 200 parallel verses in the Gospels of Matthew and Luke. Q consisted almost entirely of Jesus' sayings, among which were the Lord's Prayer, the Golden Rule, the Sermon on the Mount, the Beatitudes, and the famous admonition, "You cannot serve God and Mammon."[32] Furthermore, as much of the Q material had no narrative context, layering theory held that some of it must have represented bedrock aphorisms going all the way back to Jesus. The Q partisans also maintained that many Q sayings seemed to pass the stringent test of Perrin's criterion of dissimilarity in that they were neither overtly Christian nor overtly Jewish in theology. For a considerable number of new-questers, Q became what the Gospel of Mark had been for the old-questers: the matrix of the historical Jesus.

As there exists no separate text of Q, it is impossible to determine what the original manuscript contained besides the Matthew-Luke parallels, or even whether it was based on a single source. Moreover, a significant minority of scholars continue to believe that there never was a Q, arguing that Luke might have derived his Q passages from Matthew, for example. Still others question the theory of Marcan priority on which the entire Q hypothesis hinges.

Nonetheless, for many of the new-questers, Q quickly took on a palpable reality as a complete first-century document that both Matthew and Luke had preserved intact in their Gospels. On the theory that it represented layers of composition like the other New Testament texts, they subjected it to form and redaction criticism. During the late 1960s, no fewer than three young German scholars submitted doctoral dissertations that purported to analyze the "layers" of Q. Other experts, particularly in America, began building up Q by adding material from Matthew and Luke, and even Mark, that seemed to convey a similar tone, thereby expanding the Q text to as many as 250 verses.

In *Trajectories through Early Christianity,* Robinson had devoted one of his essays to identifying the *Gattung,* or literary genre, of Q, describing it as a collection of *logoi sophōn,* or "sayings of the wise," a type of literature that was well known in the ancient world. In another *Trajectories* essay, Koester took Robinson one step further in designating Q as a "wisdom gospel" with its own "wisdom theology," a theory that Robinson later came to adopt as well, noting that Q itself referred to bringing the "gospel," or "good news," to the poor.[33] As additional proof that a collection of sayings could qualify as a gospel, Koester, Robinson, and others pointed to the Gospel of Thomas discovered at Nag Hammadi, many of whose 114 sayings of Jesus are also found in Q (or at least in Matthew and Luke). Robinson and Koester, who had already concluded that the oldest layers of Thomas dated to the first century, within striking distance of Q, reasoned that a sayings collection was already a well-established gospel format by then.

Using Thomas to prove the existence and gospel status of Q, and Q in turn to substantiate an early date for Thomas, was more of the circular reasoning that had always dogged form and redaction criticism of the New Testament. Furthermore, Robinson's designation of Q's genre as a collection of wisdom sayings was a bit of a stretch: There are several significant narrative passages in Q, including the complete story of John the Baptist except for his birth and beheading, as well as the story of Jesus' temptation by Satan. There are also two miracle accounts: Jesus' healing the Roman centurion's slave and his exorcism of a mute demoniac. Even among the sayings, many are not references to wisdom or ethical precepts, but rather to Jesus' relation to his father and the Holy Spirit, the Second Coming, the last judgment, and other material with distinct apocalyptic overtones.

Nonetheless, Robinson's genre-designation was widely accepted. In 1981, he established the International Q Project, under the auspices of the Society of Biblical Literature, the leading American organization of biblical scholars, whose purpose was to reconstruct and publish the original version of Q. John S. Kloppenborg, a young professor at the University of Windsor in Ontario who had joined Robinson as co-editor of the Project, published *The Formation of Q: Trajectories in Ancient Wisdom Collections* in 1987 as one of a series of studies for Robinson's Institute of Antiquity and Christianity at Claremont. He contended that because Q represented a particular genre, it was "genre-bound" with respect to meaning. Anything in Q that did not reflect a "wisdom" theology was therefore an addition to the original text on the part of later editors.

Kloppenborg broke Q down into three layers to illustrate its growth and development over the life of the community that had created it: a primal "sapiental" stratum of Jesus' teachings; a "polemic" stratum with apocalyptic overtones reflecting the group's increasing awareness of the threat posed by its orthodox Christian competitors; and finally a narrative stratum prefiguring the group's absorption by the orthodox, who preferred gospels like

Mark's that told stories. In Kloppenborg's opinion (as well as Robinson's and Koester's), the earliest Q layer portrayed Jesus as an emissary of God's wisdom, but not primarily as an apocalyptic figure, much less the divinely sent one who appears in Matthew and Luke. Moreover, even in its final version, Q contained no account of Jesus' death and resurrection, and no reference to him as the Messiah or Christ. Consequently, the individuals who composed and read Q were either unaware of or uninterested in how and why Jesus had died. "Q represents a theologically autonomous sphere of Christian theology," Kloppenborg wrote,[34] thus defining the Q community as a branch of the Jesus movement that could not really be called Christian in any traditional sense.

Kloppenborg's most significant contribution to the New Quest for Jesus was his placement of the eschatological material in the second layer of Q, which represented a time well after Jesus' death. This was a dramatic departure from the Jesus of Bultmann and most of his New Quest successors. The Jesus of Bultmann and his immediate followers had been certain (albeit mistakenly) that the end of the world, the arrival of the son of man, and the cataclysmic intervention of God were events that would occur soon after his death. Bultmann had thought that Jesus' references to the "kingdom" had an existential meaning that could be discerned via demythologizing, while Käsemann, Bornkamm, and others tended to conflate the "kingdom"'s future significance to Jesus with its present existential meaning. They all agreed, however, that Jesus was referring to an imminent supernatural event when he used the word "kingdom." Indeed, one of Bornkamm's students had published a 1963 treatise wondering whether Jesus was talking about himself or someone else when he used the phrase "son of man." Only Norman Perrin had dissented, arguing that Jesus had never used the phrase "son of man" in a futuristic sense. After Kloppenborg's book, the American New Quest by and large become a search for a non-eschatological Jesus whose "kingdom" was an ideal system of social and ethical organization in contrast to a reality-altering event.

Eliminating eschatology had a special cultural significance for the American new-questers. Many of them, including Perrin and Robinson, had grown up in fundamentalist Christian families for whom the Book of Revelation and other visionary material in the Bible held a special meaning. During the 1970s and 1980s, such highly publicized evangelical groups as the Moral Majority, which also emphasized (often in literal-minded fashion) the apocalyptic struggles in Revelation, began to play key roles in American political life. Beginning in the 1970s, the word "apocalypse" had also become associated in the public mind with the violent rhetoric of the religious and quasi-religious outer fringe, exemplified by Charles Manson, Jonestown, Waco, and most recently, the Heaven's Gate mass suicide

In 1975, Paul Hanson, a professor at the Harvard Divinity School, published *The Dawn of Apocalyptic,* in which he theorized that the Jewish apocalypticism of Jesus' time was a paranoid sociological phenomenon in which certain Jews who felt ostracized by the worldly Hasmonean monarchy retreated into isolated sects such as the community at Qumran that produced the Dead Sea Scrolls. According to Hanson, they then produced a morbid polemical literature whose theme was God's eventual vindication of their beliefs and his destruction of their enemies. In stating his position that apocalypticism equaled bottled-up frustration that led to cults, Hanson pointed to the Hare Krishna street people of the 1970s as a possible example of rampant apocalypticism reborn in soul-alienating urbanized America.

Hanson's study of ancient Judaism dovetailed with the heyday of televangelism and the undoubtedly embarrassed awareness on the part of many new-questers that the Religious Right was part of their own backgrounds. Since the days of H. L. Mencken, Christian fundamentalism has been a pundits' bogeyman, standing for a combination of puritanism, fanaticism, and not knowing which fork to use. Besides Perrin and Robinson, a number of new-questers have followed up-from-the-Bible-Belt career paths. Robert Funk, the founder of the Jesus Seminar, Marcus J. Borg of Oregon State University, a Jesus Seminar activist, and John Shelby Spong, the headline-making Episcopal bishop of Newark who has written several books promoting a stripped-down Jesus, are all proud of their break from religious conservatism. Burton L. Mack, a recently retired New Testament professor at the School of Theology at Claremont who promotes a theory of Jesus as a Hellenistic authority questioner, was a Nazarene minister before enrolling at Göttingen during the 1970s to study with Conzelmann.

If one consults the biographical appendix to *The Five Gospels,* the Jesus Seminar's slangy 1993 translation of Matthew, Mark, Luke, John, and Thomas, one can spot a similar pattern: an undergraduate degree from an obscure Christian college followed by graduate work at a more sophisticated institution. The non-eschatological Jesus of the American New Quest is a congenial figure for many American academics who associate eschatology with snake-handling and polyester blends, or who fear that putting apocalyptic sayings into Jesus' mouth supports the political goals of the Christian Coalition.

The bottom, or "Jesus," layer that Kloppenborg and others have found in Q is exceedingly brief, comprising two dozen or so short passages incorporating about 70 Gospel verses, including the Golden Rule, several parables, a few Beatitudes, a truncated Lord's Prayer, instructions to love one's enemies and turn the other cheek, and a number of aphorisms that, when taken out of their Gospel context, lend Jesus a distinctly subversive air. The verse from Luke's Gospel, "Whoever comes to me and does not hate father and mother, wife and children, brothers and sisters, yes and even life itself, cannot be my disciple,"[35] is considered to derive from bedrock Q, as is Jesus' famous "mission speech," also found in Mark, in which he bids his disciples to "carry no purse, no bag, no sandals"[36] when they are on the road, but to depend on the hospitality of strangers. Indeed, the Jesus of the lowest Q stratum, taken out of the Gospel context, is a sixties hippie—and also a thoroughly secular figure who has no interest in anything beyond the grave and never makes any divine claims for himself. As such, he is an oddity in purely historical terms. Although the Holy Land of the first century, as described by Josephus, abounded with prophets, baptizers, Torah-revering Pharisees, Qumran-style ascetics, and would-be Messiahs, there were no other known Jewish teachers of so nonreligious a brand of wisdom.

In the absence of historical data supporting the theory that Jesus was a wisdom-teacher, a number of new-questers began looking for *theoretical* models that might provide him with such a context. They moved from history to the social sciences. In 1966, the sociologist Gerhard Lenski had written a study titled *Power and Privilege: A Theory of Social Stratification,* setting forth a universal model for defining ancient and modern societies according to their class systems. "Social stratification," usually with a Marxist spin derived from his theory of class warfare, was a hotly debated issue among sociologists during the 1960s. Earlier, C. Wright Mills, the intellectual godfather of the New Left, had rattled his idealistic sociological compatriots by revealing in his *Power Elite* that even egalitarian America possessed a class system.

Lenski's class-struggle motif in *Power and Privilege* displayed the influence of Eric Hobsbawm, the Marxist social historian whose career reached its apogee in the 1960s. In examining what he called "agrarian" societies like those of Jesus' time, which had developed sophisticated metallurgy and commerce but were definitely pre-industrial, Lenski analyzed their social structure as a tiny elite of rulers, bureaucrats, military brass, merchants, and priests who exploited the stoop-labor of huge numbers of illiterate, semi-starving peasants. Even lower in status were the artisans, who were essentially peasants dispossessed of their land who had to live by the tools of their trade. Lenski's theories were extremely popular during the 1970s and 1980s, when the Marxist revolutionary movements in Central America began styling themselves as agrarian uprisings despite the fact that their leaders were mostly university-trained intellectuals. Moreover, Lenski's analytical model provided a new way of looking at Jesus: As a carpenter, he would have belonged to the illiterate, dispossessed peasant class. He might also have despised organized religion as a tool of the oppressors, and regarded his ministry primarily as a social revolution.

Furthermore, beginning in the late 1970s, a group of anthropologists influenced by Fernand Braudel's sweeping studies of Mediterranean social history developed another theoretical model that entailed examining the different rural cultures that had ringed the Mediterranean for thousands of years to establish what they had in common. In 1982, David Gilmore, the most enthusiastic of the cross-cultural pan-Mediterraneanists, went so far as to make a list of the "universals" of Mediterranean village life: gregariousness, parochialism, patriarchy, authoritarian child-rearing, disdain for manual labor, belief in the evil eye, the immediate family as the chief locus of loyalty, reliance on personal patronage rather than formal institutions, a strong role for religion, and an "honor-shame syndrome which defines both sexuality and personal reputation."[37] Many pan-Mediterraneanists believed that these "universals" applied equally in the mountains of Andalusia during the 1950s, in the land of Canaan during the time of the Hebrew patriarchs, and in Galilee during Jesus' day.

One might point out that Gilmore's checklist sounded less like anthropological research than the observations of northern European tourists piqued by erratic service at an Aegean hotel. Nonetheless, pan-Mediterraneanism has taken so firm a hold on American New Testament studies that it is nearly impossible to attend a Society of Biblical Literature meeting these days without hearing a panelist discourse generically about "the village" or "honor and shame" in relation to Jesus and his teachings. One New Testament pan-Mediterraneanist, Bruce J. Malina, a theology professor at Creighton University in Omaha, recently advised the readers of one of his books to view such "Mediterranean" films as the *Godfather* series, *Prizzi's Honor,* and *Lawrence of Arabia* as a way of getting a better feel for the social interactions in Jesus' time.[38]

The most influential biblical scholar to incorporate sociological theories into Jesus research was Gerd Theissen, a New Testament professor at the University of Heidelberg, and most likely the last of the truly innovative German scholars working in the Bultmann tradition. The model that Theissen used had been developed by the most famous of all Heidelbergers, Max Weber. In a 1922 study titled *The Sociology of Religion,* Weber had theorized that every religion began as a free-form association around an autonomous prophet, or "bearer of charisma," such as Jesus, Buddha, or Muhammad. Later, the religions settled into more orderly or authoritarian "bourgeois"[39] structures.

In 1977, Theissen published a treatise in which he determined that Jesus' first followers had been "wandering charismatics"—individuals who had forsaken their homes, families, and possessions to travel from place to place preaching, healing, and relying for support on the rural communities they visited. Theissen further maintained that Jesus himself, who was homeless and socially rootless, had "called into being" the wandering-charismatics movement.[40] As evidence, he pointed to Jesus' "mission speech" and other material that happened to be in Kloppenborg's bedrock layer of Q. In 1986, Theissen worked his theories into *The Shadow of the Galilean,* a novel about a young Jew from Sepphoris who never meets Jesus, but is so overwhelmed by the impression that his personality has made on others that he starts composing a gospel about him.

In a series of essays written during the 1970s and early 1980s, Theissen focused intently on these "wandering charismatics" of Galilee and the Jesus who had initiated their life-style. One of the essays, "Wandering Radicals," derived from a lecture delivered in 1972 at the University of Bonn, identified another group of despised outsiders who might have been in Galilee during Jesus' time: Cynic philosophers. The Cynics were nothing if not countercultural. They begged for their bread and flicked pithy aphorisms at anyone who gave them a handout or tried to strike up a conversation. Their founder was Diogenes, the Athenian who had carried a lamp in broad daylight in search of an honest man nearly 400 years before Jesus' birth. Diogenes' disciples reveled in flouting convention. Hipparchia, the one known female Cynic, was said to have consummated her marriage to Diogenes' protégé Crates outdoors in full view of the public. Like their epigones in Woodstock Nation, many Cynics undoubtedly abandoned such a life after a brief period of time. The movement died out, but during the latter half of the first century C.E., it enjoyed a revival throughout the Roman Empire, and numerous self-styled philosophers roamed the Hellenistic world with their distinctive walking sticks and begging-bags. One off-again-on-again Cynic site was the city of Gadara east of the Jordan River, which produced several famous Cynic writers before and after Jesus' time. Indeed, as Theissen and others have noted,

Jesus' "mission speech" in Q, with its instructions to take up a life of vagabondage and its mention of a Cynic-like "bag," contains definite parallels with the Cynic credo.

After reading Theissen, certain North American new-questers similarly wove the Cynics into their reconstructions of Jesus. Leif E. Vaage of the Toronto School of Theology, who had studied with Robinson at Claremont, theorized in his 1986 doctoral dissertation that Jesus' first followers actually lived like Cynics, possibly because Jesus was exposed to their philosophy while visiting Gadara. In Vaage's view, the aphorisms in Q that Christians came to associate with selflessness, including "Love your enemies"[41] and "If anyone strikes you on the cheek, offer the other also,"[42] in reality were clever survival strategies for unpopular Cynics in strange places. Vaage's Jesus was also a thoroughgoing individualist who disdained any form of work, thumbed his nose at such pieties as respect for one's parents, and reveled in unconventionality for its own sake. His original acolytes, who later became the Q community, were proto-beatniks encamped along the Sea of Galilee who recorded his teachings during spare moments in their wanderings.

If one combines the trends in avant-garde American Jesus research of the past 20 years—the New Quest, layering analysis, trajectory theory, Norman Perrin's authenticity criteria (especially that of dissimilarity), Q studies, "peasant" sociology, pan-Mediterraneanism, the rediscovery of the Cynics, and most important, the jettisoning of eschatology—one arrives at the ultra-minimalist Jesus of the Jesus Seminar. Set up in 1985 by Robert Funk to vote on the historicity of the Gospels, the Seminar is known for its startling negative pronunciamentos (such as the fact that Jesus did not compose the Lord's Prayer), which the Seminar issues to the tune of maximum media coverage. It also claims (see the preface to *The Five Gospels*) implicitly to represent a consensus of current New Testament scholarship, even though no more than 35 or 40 scholars (out of over 6,000 biblical specialists in the United States alone) show up on average at its semi-annual meetings.

In *The Real Jesus,* a 1996 critique of the Seminar and related phenomena, Luke Timothy Johnson, a professor of New Testament and Christian origins at Emory, pointed to the lackluster *curricula vitae* of many of the Seminar's participants, noting that of the leading American graduate faculties in New Testament studies, only Claremont was represented. Indeed, the roster appendixed to *The Five Gospels* listed two members whose place of employment was the Westar Institute in Sonoma, California, the foundation that Funk himself established to operate the Seminar; another who worked for the

"People's Church"; and a fourth who gave "the Double Bar A Ranch" as his professional address—not to mention film director Paul Verhoeven of *Robocop* and *Basic Instinct* fame, who had been attending meetings in preparation for a movie about Jesus.

While the Jesus Seminar may not represent the majority of New Testament scholars or even the mainstream, it definitely reflects the consensus of a New Quest faction with a specific Jesus in mind: a peasant "sage" of subversive wisdom with Cynic overtones who totally shunned eschatology. Indeed, the Seminar made the non-eschatological Jesus one of its "seven pillars of scholarly wisdom" in *The Five Gospels,* a standard for automatically rejecting any sayings of Jesus that refer to God's judgment or the Second Coming. Many of the leading scholars associated with Q or the New Quest, such as James Robinson, John Kloppenborg, Burton Mack, and Leif Vaage, have participated at one time or another in the Jesus Seminar. The large proportion of Claremont graduates is not coincidental.

The results of the Seminar's votes on Jesus' sayings, as chronicled in *The Five Gospels,* indicate that of the 1,500-odd statements attributed to Jesus by early Christian texts, a mere 18 percent (or 90 sayings, mostly from Q) were actually made by him, a conclusion that comports with Kloppenborg's Q stratification as well as Perrin's criterion of dissimilarity. In accordance with form criticism's assumption that the Gospel stories developed from aphorisms into longer discourses and narratives, the Seminar also contends that Jesus spoke *only* in aphorisms. Moreover, in his role as sage, he seldom initiated a conversation:

> Like the cowboy of the American West exemplified by Gary Cooper, the sage of the ancient Near East was laconic, slow to speech, a person of few words. The sage does not provoke encounters. . . . The sage is self-effacing, modest, unostentatious.[43]

To lend credibility to the notion that "sages" abounded in the ancient Mediterranean world, *The Five Gospels* also defines Moses, the Hebrew prophets, the author of the Psalms, Job, Socrates, and Aesop as sages, or at least as "people with important things to say."[44] Finally, although no one, including Vaage, has said that there were actually Cynics in first-century Palestine (there is no evidence that they ever ventured west of the Jordan), *The Five Gospels* declares boldly that "the Cynic philosophers . . . plied their trade in Galilee in Jesus' day."[45]

In their literature as well as in numerous press interviews, Funk and others have made it clear that in addition to its scholarly mission, the Jesus Seminar has a polemic mission: battling Christian fundamentalism. I myself attended a session of the Seminar as a member of the press in October 1994, at which time Funk expounded an agenda that could only be called theological. He seethed visibly when the assembled participants, who were voting on the historicity of the Gospel's infancy narratives, declined to reject explicitly the traditional Christian proposition that Mary conceived Jesus of the Holy Spirit. "I think they're a bunch of cowards," Funk told me in an interview after the vote: "Scholars believe that Jesus had a human father."[46]

Whereas most New Testament scholars avoid the issue of Jesus' resurrection as historically unprovable, the Seminar voted at its March 1995 session that it had never occurred, later issuing a press release asserting that Jesus' crucified corpse probably "rotted in some unknown grave," and quoting a statement by Seminar activist Marcus Borg, a professor of religion at Oregon State University, to the effect that "a video camera present at one of Jesus' [post-resurrection] appearances would not have recorded anything on tape."[47] The Seminar has also publicized the scholarship of Gerd Lüdemann, a New Testament professor at Vanderbilt and Göttingen (where he is also director of the Institute of Early Christian Studies), who uses depth psychology to argue that Jesus' post-resurrection appearances in the Gospels were instances of mass hallucination.

Recently, Funk has moved his theological preoccupations to the foreground, and seems to be intent on forming his own branch of Christianity. In a high-blood-pressure book published in 1996 titled *Honest to Jesus,* which rails against a spectrum of conservative Christian functionaries ranging from the Vatican Curia to the Southern Baptists, Funk outlines a 21-point program for reinventing Christianity in order to make it truer to the historical Jesus and also more compatible with the needs of the 21st century. One of his proposals is to demote Jesus from the son of God to a "secular sage" conceived out of wedlock and with a subversive sense of humor.[48] Funk's retooled Christianity would certainly be more fun than the traditionalist version: As part of his back-to-Jesus movement, he endorses "responsible, protected, recreational sex between consenting adults."[49]

Other scholars who have participated in the Jesus Seminar over the years have similarly promoted the theory of Jesus as a secular sage. Burton Mack, who dropped out of the Seminar after several sessions in order to concentrate on early Christianity, also argues in favor of the Cynics' influence on Jesus. After meeting with Vaage at Claremont, he began working the Cynics into his theories in his *Myth of Innocence* (1988), which contended that the evangelist Mark had been the founder of Christianity, by inventing (nearly out of whole cloth) the story of Jesus' ministry and crucifixion, which became Christians' definitive social myth. According to Mack, Jesus himself had a "Cynic's self-understanding,"[50] specialized in "social critique,"[51] and was "no doubt from a Jewish family,"[52] which was his only apparent connection to Judaism or any other religion. Mack also adopted Walter Bauer's theory that the Galileans were more Greek than Jewish. "Jesus Jewishness is . . . not self-evident from the nature of his discourse," he wrote. "His discourse reveals a remarkable openness to Hellenistic culture at a popular level, a stance that makes Galilean provenance quite possible."[53]

By 1993, when Mack published *The Lost Gospel,* a commentary on Q that featured his own reconstruction and translation into breezy, "demythologized" language, Galilee had grown into a full-blown multicultural mosaic, its inhabitants "a mixed people" with no "specific ethnic identity"[54] who probably paid some attention to the Jewish religious laws, but were not particularly Jewish in culture. Mack's Jesus had become a guru of diversity, encouraging his Galilean followers to "experiment with novel social notions and life-styles," to "question taboos on intercourse with people of different ethnic roots," and to "free themselves from traditional social constraints and think of themselves as belonging to a larger human family."[55]

In 1995, Mack crystalized his secularized Jesus in *Who Wrote the New Testament?,* characterizing him as a "bright enough" fellow, "something of an intellectual," who spoke in "pithy aphorisms" that communicated "a playful, edgy challenge to take up a countercultural lifestyle," and who was apparently attracted to Cynic philosophy "as a way for individuals to keep their integrity in a compromising world."[56] Convinced that no one really knows how Jesus died, Mack has been putting together a scholarly consortium that would "redescribe" Christian origins by some other means than the Gospel narratives and their "crucifixion drama," as he calls it, thus exploding even Bultmann's *Dass*.[57]

A co-chairman of the Jesus Seminar, John Dominic Crossan, a recently retired New Testament professor at Chicago's De Paul University, has formulated a Jesus who is an eclectic combination of every American New Quest trend. A former Catholic priest of Irish birth who is best known for his theory that Jesus' crucified body was eaten by wild dogs, Crossan is an engaging and eloquent writer whose books weave Q layering, peasants, pan-Mediterraneanism, honor and shame, the Cynics, and a de-eschatologized

Jesus into a seamless web. His *Essential Jesus* (1994) boils Jesus' sayings down to 93 haiku-like verses. Essential to Crossan's methodology is the principle that any of the noncanonical gospels—Thomas, Peter, the Secret Gospel of Mark, and so forth—is likely to contain earlier and more authentic Jesus traditions than the canonical four.

In his books, Crossan paints a melodramatic but engrossing Gerhard Lenski–influenced picture of first-century Galilee, including herds of peasants who toil ceaselessly, slipping into peonage and beggary as they lose their tiny plots to taxes and debt while Zapata-like bandits raise armies of the dispossessed. Far up the social ziggurat, bosses feast and count their gold, pan-Mediterranean "patrons" dispense favors, and Romans crack the whip. Into this grim agrarian vista—which Crossan may have derived from his observations of life on the untenured lower rungs of a university faculty ladder—walks Jesus, a dirt-poor, illiterate social reformer who might have borrowed his clothing style and mode of existence from the Cynics. Trailing in his wake is a band of equally disreputable disciples, whom Crossan calls "the hippies" of the first century, contrasting them with the nouveau "yuppies" of the exploiting classes. In Crossan's books, Jesus' healings are a kind of peasant magic wherein exorcising demons is a symbolic way of destroying the Romans. Crossan's Jesus is essentially an advocate of "the brokerless kingdom," an egalitarian, anti-patriarchal society in which there are no hierarchies, political or religious (which was why Jesus ignored Jewish dietary laws).[58] The heart of Jesus' praxis is in fact "open commensality," or breaking bread with social outcasts:

> Commensality was . . . a strategy for rebuilding peasant community on radically different principles from those of honor and shame, patronage and client. It was based on an egalitarian sharing of spiritual and material power at the grass-roots level.[59]

Jesus' death, in Crossan's view, was a ghastly accident: He had ventured into Judea for Passover, where his unusual style alarmed the Romans, and they dispatched him as they did other public nuisances.

The only Seminar activist to take the sage-Jesus seriously as a *religious* figure is Marcus Borg. Although his scholarly work abounds with peasants, patriarchy, honor, shame, and other American New Quest jargon, he does describe Jesus as "a spirit-filled person in the charismatic stream of Judaism"[60] who actually prayed, meditated, had visions, made pilgrimages, and functioned like a prophet. Nearly alone among the Seminar partisans, Borg believes that the historical Jesus did something besides spout aphorisms and make Galilean outcasts feel socially acceptable, including genuine acts of healing. In the end, however, Borg's Jesus is yet another counterculturalist whose aims are as much political as spiritual: "He saw conventional wisdom, with its focus on the securities offered by culture, even though sanctioned by Scripture and hallowed by practice, as the chief rival to centering in God."[61] One of the loci of "conventional wisdom" that Jesus opposes—and seeks to reform—is the traditional Judaism to which he belongs, which in Borg's view stresses "holiness" instead of "compassion." As for Jesus' "kingdom," Borg wrote in 1994, "it was a symbol."[62] Somehow the first-century "spirit-filled person" had become a 20th-century symbolist poet.

Even amateur biblical scholars have joined the American New Quest and reconstructed versions of the minimalist, highly secularized sage-Jesus. In 1986, Thomas Sheehan, a philosophy professor at the University of Illinois, published *The First Coming,* in which he theorized that Jesus' main objective was to rid the world of religion. In 1991, the poet and translator Stephen Mitchell issued his *Gospel of Jesus,* a conscious imitation of Thomas Jefferson's razored-down canonicals, declaring that he was omitting all "sectarian passages" in the Gospels so that "we can recognize that Jesus speaks in harmony with the supreme teachings of all the great religions: the Uphanishads, the Tao TeChing, the Buddhist Sutras, the Zen and Sufi and Ḥasidic Masters."[63] Mitchell also candidly admitted that he had followed his own literary and spiritual instincts in deciding what Gospel material was authentic. In 1996, I interviewed (for *Lingua Franca* magazine) James Carse, a retired New York University religion professor who was in the process of writing his own gospel. Carse's Jesus is so out of communication with God that he never even prays. "There's a danger in people thinking of themselves as being directly addressed by God," Carse told me. "It gives them this absolutist attitude on political issues."[64]

As I stated above, the New Quest Jesus of history was also a Christ of faith—and the faith turned out to be liberation theology. In 1967, while the Vietnam War was raging and Western Europe was about to explode in student rebellions, Ernst Käsemann, the father of the German New Quest, delivered a startling lecture in Hanover titled "The Presence of the Crucified One," in which he vividly portrayed the historical Jesus as a model for revolutionary political action in the here and now. Käsemann's lecture, which was subsequently published under the title *Der Ruf der Freiheit,* was translated into English in 1968 as *Jesus Means Freedom.* (The literal translation, "the cry of freedom," was unable to convey the subtle pun attached to the word *"Ruf,"* an allusion to John the Baptist's description of himself in canonical Gospels as "one crying out in the wilderness," which is a direct quotation from the prophet Isaiah.)[65]

In Käsemann's view, authentic religion—the religion of Jesus—was also prophetic, in the sense of speaking out against the power that be. In defining Jesus as a "liberal . . . by the standards of his religious environment,"[66] he made it clear that he was not talking about the "liberal" of the bourgeois 19th century. Instead, he was describing a figure whose opposition to authority gave him a distinct 1960s cast. While at first glance Käsemann might well be accused of the crude anti-Judaism that characterized the 19th century, he was actually consolidating the religious and political leadership of Jesus' time, along with its social restrictions, into a single structure of oppression:

> The guiding ideal here was the priestly nation, which, through its holiness, would stand continuously before God. Thus Jesus, through his associations, infringed not only a social and political taboo, nor even simply the presiding moral order. He repeatedly attacked what was regarded as God's will, and in so doing seemed to attack God the Father himself.[67]

Among Jesus and his first followers, Käsemann maintained, "exuberant vitality breaks through every dike and stops for no bourgeois taboo. Thus, at any rate, the problem of the emancipation of slaves and women appears on the horizon, although not in its modern version."[68] Jesus was a liberator. Anticipating Theissen's sociological model of Christianity, Käsemann contended that the church had calcified after Jesus' death into exactly the sort of oppressive, establishment-supporting institution that he had fought against while on earth. "[W]e can no longer make a clean break between the gospel and politics," Käsemann declared.[69] (His outspoken theology of liberation had a tragic personal aftermath when his daughter Elisabeth was killed in 1977, at age 30, in the Argentinean military junta's "Dirty War.")

Although liberation theology is widely believed to be an indigenous "Latin American" Christian variant, it was actually of German provenance, as witnessed by Käsemann's speech. During the 1960s, two Catholic theologians at the University of Münster, Johann Baptist Metz and Karl Rahner, the latter of whom had masterminded some of the ecclesial changes of the Second Vatican Council, worked out what they called a "political theology," or religious *Ostpolitik,* directed at Communist-controlled East Germany. In attempting a dialogue with Marxism that would merge notions of revolutionary class struggle with the traditional Gospel mandate of ministering to the poor, Metz developed a theological concept known as "orthopraxis," which was based on the Marxist principle of direct action. The model of orthopraxis was to be the historical Jesus, colored by New Quest minimalism and interpreted along Käsemann-like lines as a social outcast and rebel. Not surprisingly, one of the leading liberation theologians of Latin America was a European with a German education, the Spanish-born Jesuit priest Jon Sobrino, who had obtained his doctorate at the Hochschule Sankt Georgen in Frankfurt in 1975.

The 1960s and 1970s could also be described as the time when Catholics discovered the historical Jesus. There had already been some movement in this direction among Catholic Modernists of the early 20th century, as exemplified by Alfred Loisy, the priest whose immersion in liberal theory had led to his repudiation of the creeds and also the eucharist, although he continued to enjoy the pomp of the liturgy. George Tyrrell, an English Jesuit, adopted Johannes Weiss's view of Jesus as an eschatology-obsessed fanatic. Both clerics became apostles of German scholarship in the face of what they viewed as antediluvian Catholic supernaturalism, alarming Pope Pius X, who issued a 1907 encyclical condemning Modernism in sweeping language, and barring Catholics from all biblical scholarship that was not rigidly monitored by a Vatican commission. Both Loisy and Tyrrell were excommunicated. Pius XII, who was fascinated by science and archaeology, relaxed the interdict somewhat in 1943, but until the Second Vatican Council, Catholic biblical scholars by and large confined their work to archival and textual studies, such as piecing together and translating the Dead Sea Scrolls.

The climate changed drastically when the Second Vatican Council wound up its proceedings in 1965 with a *Dogmatic Constitution on Divine Revelation,* that explicitly allowed Catholic exegetes to consider all existing sources, traditions, and literary forms in analyzing the Gospels. As a consequence, a number of scholars who had spent their entire professional lives toiling in obscure pontifical libraries soon embraced the most extreme speculations of the Protestant post-Bultmannians. At age 43, Raymond E. Brown, an American Catholic priest and New Testament expert who had spent most of his teaching career at a Catholic seminary in Baltimore, suddenly found himself on the faculty of Union Theological Seminary, the bastion of liberal Christianity, where he submerged himself in trajectory theory. In 1979, he published *The Community of the Beloved Disciple,* in which he used John's Gospel and three New Testament letters attributed to him to sketch out a 100-year history and a separatist theology for the evangelist's church, an endeavor that would have been unheard of 15 years earlier.

The most enthusiastic Catholic Johnny-come-lately was Hans Küng, a priest and theologian at the University of Tübingen. Born in 1928, Küng had spent much of his life on the cutting edge of Catholicism, pioneering the custom among priestly scholars of wearing suits and ties instead of Roman collars. A gifted analyst of Protestant theology, in 1957 he wrote his doctoral dissertation on Karl Barth at the Sorbonne at a time when few Catholics had ever heard of Barth. In 1974, when he was 48, Küng published a 600-page book, *On Being a Christian,* whose ramblings bore all the earmarks of a middle-aged man's sudden (and slightly behind-the-curve) discovery of sixties youth culture: quotations from *Hair,* allusions to *Jesus Christ Superstar* and the Beatles, and fawning adulation of everyone under the age of 30. While Küng's academic specialty was systematic theology and not biblical studies, he devoted half his book to "the earthly Jesus," retailing everything he had learned, or thought he had learned, from New Quest literature, including the theory of Jesus' anti-authoritarianism, which he thought was more relevant to the young than church teachings. "Jesus did not belong to the ecclesiastical and social establishment," Küng declared.[70]

Another Catholic systematic theologian, Belgian-born Edward Schillebeeckx, discovered the historical Jesus similarly late in life. In his 1974 *Jesus,* which was even longer than *On Being a Christian,* he explored the historical Jesus' subjective relationship with God the father, which he called his "*abba*-experience." Filled with 1970s buzz words such as "praxis" and "liberated," *Jesus* became required reading among liberal Catholics, and his "*abba*-experience" the subject of many a sermon. Although Schillebeeckx was investigated by the Vatican on charges that his use of experiential language meant that he did not really believe that Jesus was divine, he was eventually cleared. Küng, however, was censured by Pope John Paul II in 1979, not for his biblical theories but for denying the doctrine of papal infallibility.

As the writings of Küng and Schillebeeckx indicate, the phrase "historical Jesus" quickly lost its original connection to New Testament research and became a touchstone for whatever anti-establishment theology could be associated with "liberation," "oppression," or "exploitation." In Jon Sobrino's words, "The Christ who cannot be co-opted by accommodationists and opportunists is the historical Jesus."[71] In a jacket blurb for one of Sobrino's books, Robert McAfee Brown, a professor of ecumenics at Union, praised the Jesuit for "showing the basic connection between the radical historicity of Jesus and the suffering pain of oppressed people."[72] Neither Sobrino nor Brown was talking about Jesus as a historical figure, even in New Quest terms, but rather as a mental construct or symbol of group suffering, or perhaps revolution.

While liberation theology suffered a mortal blow in the 1990 elections in Nicaragua when the people decided they did not want to be ruled by high-minded Marxists, it had long before become customary for anyone claiming a grievance to invoke the historical Jesus. In 1969, James H. Cone, a professor of systematic theology at Union, published a book in which he asserted that Jesus was black. "Christ is black because he is oppressed, and oppressed because he is black," concluded Cone.[73] Another African-American, Joseph Johnson, wrote of the "quest for the black Jesus."[74]

New Testament scholar Elisabeth Schüssler Fiorenza of the Harvard Divinity School began recasting Jesus as an androgynous personage of feminist leanings who conceived of himself as an emissary of Sophia, the female personification of divine wisdom from the Book of Proverbs. As Schüssler Fiorenza could not quite bring herself to say that Jesus had assumed an active feminist stance at a time when the notion of women's equality was virtually unknown, she declared instead that "the historical Jesus, *as remembered by his female followers,* was a feminist." [Italics mine][75] She called her efforts a new "imagining" of Christian origins. Two other feminist scholars, Joanne Carlson Brown of St. Andrew's College in Saskatchewan, and Rebecca Parker of the Starr King School for the Ministry in Berkeley, have similarly re-imagined out of existence the historicity of Jesus' crucifixion on the anti-patriarchal grounds that the doctrine of atonement amounts to "divine child abuse."[76] Still other feminist theologians have reconstructed a re-imagined historical Jesus on the cross as a woman suffering from menstrual cramps.

Process theology, one of the latest fashions to influence biblical scholarship, maintains that God evolves along with mankind in a fluid and reciprocal process, recalling Feuerbach's old dictum, appropriated by Marx, that God is nothing more than our own projections. Both theories may well have been the basis for the seventies liberationist trend—which has continued unabated through the nineties—of relating the historical Jesus to the causes of identity politics. In any case, the Jesus who lived in history was not black, nor did he identify himself with women, except in metaphorical terms that are comprehensible through Christian spirituality, not historical methodology. Ironically, the search for the "historical" Jesus in the end has yielded a figure who is not historical at all, and to whom historical reality is quite irrelevant.

11

THE RETURN

Over the past 40-odd years, the New Quest has produced a number of different—and possibly inconsistent—portraits of Jesus, including those of a Cynic-like sage, a peasant revolutionary, a gay magician, a teacher of subversive wisdom, a class-warrior, and a "woman-identified" prophet of Sophia. All of the variations have one thing in common: They are not particularly Jewish. In fact, among the most prominent new-questers, only Marcus Borg and Elisabeth Schüssler Fiorenza have taken Jesus' Jewishness seriously. Norman Perrin and his "criterion of dissimilarity," which barred all Jewish-sounding sayings of Jesus from qualifying for authenticity, may have been the culprits.

Nevertheless, the New Quest certainly does not represent the only recent scholarship on Jesus. Throughout the 20th century, a varied array of researchers who never bought into Bultmannian and post-Bultmannian theory have worked on the sidelines to explore the role that Jesus played in the world of Second Temple Judaism where he actually conducted his ministry. Jewish scholars in particular have become fascinated by the figure whom Jews once regarded as an apostate, and are seeking to "reclaim" him for Judaism.

Furthermore, the discovery of the Dead Sea Scrolls in the Judean desert during the late 1940s and early 1950s has provided solid evidence that the religious imagery of the New Testament—angels and demons, heavenly ascents, eschatological dramas, divine emanations, light-and-darkness metaphors, and even the title "son of God"—was not a Christian innovation, or a Hellenistic accretion, but instead an important component of Jewish spirituality during the Second Temple period. Archaeological excavations in the Holy Land, including the unearthing of the Scrolls, have also tended to support the historical value of the Gospels, at least as sources of information about the conditions of their times. The Gospel of John, for example, which was long dismissed as a historically worthless and highly "Hellenistic" theological tract, has undergone radical reappraisal. A number of researchers nowadays view John as a document of solidly Jewish origin that demonstrates an uncannily accurate knowledge of first-century Palestinian geography and customs. Indeed, some experts consider John a more reliable source for the chronology of Jesus' ministry and passion than the Synoptic Gospels. Finally, a group of scholars in Germany, Britain, the United States, and elsewhere have arrived at a loose consensus on the historical Jesus that differs markedly from that of the politicized New Quest, regarding him as a primarily religious figure who was drenched in the Judaism of his time, but who was so startlingly original that he may well have inspired his followers—who were almost all Jews themselves—to call him "Lord" and "Messiah" and "Son of Man" after his death or even during his lifetime. This new accord entails a far more nuanced understanding of the interplay between Judaism and Hellenism in Second-Temple Palestine. Moreover, there has been a revival of the theory that Jesus' preaching of his "kingdom" and of coming judgment did in fact have an eschatological dimension. This new "third quest" (as it has been called in some quarters) views the Gospels not only as distillations of their authors' own theologies but as genuine efforts to write narrative accounts of Jesus' life, on the theory that the earliest Christians were interested in the story of Jesus as well as his teachings and his role as a salvation figure.

After the Roman conquest of Jerusalem in 70 C.E., the variegated Judaism of the Second Temple period reconstituted itself as the rabbinic Judaism that is nearly universally practiced by today's Jews. The rabbis traced their spiritual lineage to a single branch of the Pharisees who followed the teachings of Hillel, a famous Pharisaic scholar of Jerusalem who died in 10 C.E. The founder of rabbinic Judaism, the long-lived Pharisee Yoḥanan ben Zakkai, was said to have studied with Hillel.

Like Pharisaism, rabbinic Judaism is centered on devotion to Torah, holding in equal value the Pentateuch, or "written Torah," said to have been given by God to Moses in the first five books of the Hebrew Bible, and the "oral Torah," the body of rabbinic traditions and scriptural interpretation, part of which is said to date back to Moses. The traditions were eventually codified around the year 200 C.E. in the legal code known as the Mishnah, as well as in the Tosefta, a collection of Tannaitic (early oral) material similar in scope to that of the Mishnah. Later on came the Jerusalem Talmud (ca. 400 C.E.) and the Babylonian Talmud (ca. 500 C.E.), each of which contains the Mishnah, along with a massive stratum of later rabbinic commentary called the Gemara. (While the Mishnah is the same for both Talmuds, the Gemara is markedly different.) For rabbinic Jews, Torah *is* Judaism, and the study of Torah in both its written and oral manifestations is the reason that God created the human race.

Christianity, by contrast, centers itself on Jesus, who may be said to represent for Christians what Torah does for Jews. According to the rabbis of the first centuries after Jesus' birth, the first Christian converts had known the Torah as Jews but had deliberately apostatized from it at the urging of Jesus. On their part, Christians held the theological contempt for Judaism that has prevailed to this very day. The anti-Jewish polemic that flowed from pulpit and scriptorium was grounded in the belief that the Jews had known Jesus, but had deliberately rejected him. The Christian community, which was already extensive, gained considerable political power after the emperor Constantine's ascendancy. The Jews, on the other hand, were relatively few in number and extremely vulnerable. Their legal rights were increasingly circumscribed, and even their places of residence were dependent on the whims of Christian rulers.

On the intellectual front, however, the rabbis were a match for the best of the Christian theologians. The Judaism they crafted in the shadow of Jerusalem's rubble and the triumph of the cross was designed to withstand any political setback: Its center of observance would become the home, not the temple, and every Jew would be a priest, in contrast to a corruptible Temple caste. As for Christianity, the rabbis in their writings tended to ignore it entirely.

After the fall of Jerusalem, much of the Jewish apocalyptic and mystical literature that had been part of the intellectual backdrop of Jesus' ministry fell into disuse, surviving as Jewish mysticism and rabbinic poetry (the Messiah is an eschatological figure in rabbinic Scriptures). While Jews continued to relish the visionary and eschatological material in the books of the Hebrew prophets that had inspired the apocalyptic texts, the rabbinic exaltation of Torah reflected a suspicion of miracles and claims to prophetic powers.

As the Hebrew Bible gradually coalesced into the standard "canon" of Pentateuch, prophets, and writings, the texts that we know today as Apocrypha and Pseudepigrapha were omitted, and the concept of the Messiah was subtly altered. In Jesus' day, most Jews envisioned the Messiah as a militaristic savior king who would raise an army and rescue Israel from her Roman oppressors. In the rabbinic texts, which postdated the fiasco of the Bar Kokhba rebellion and the failure of other Jewish messianic leaders, the Messiah evolved into a strictly teleological personage whose coming ultimately depended on strict observance of Torah.

By and large, the few oblique references to Jesus in rabbinic writings tended to be quite hostile. Perhaps in reaction to Christian persecution and anti-Judaism, Talmudic stories often painted him as a bastard, a sorcerer, and a false prophet. A passage from the Babylonian Talmud declared: "And a Master has said, 'Jesus the Nazarene practiced magic and led Israel astray.' "[1]

The most detailed Talmudic reference to Jesus is a Tannaitic *baraita* from the Babylonian Talmud (a *baraita* is a written redaction of an oral tradition that may date to the earliest sessions of the Yavneh academy despite its exclusion from the Mishnah):

> It was taught: On the eve of the Passover Yeshu . . . was hanged. For forty days before the execution took place, a herald went forth and cried, 'He is going forth to be stoned because he has practiced sorcery and enticed Israel to apostasy. Anyone who can say anything in his favour, let him come forward and plead on his behalf.' But since nothing was brought forward in his favour he was hanged on the eve of Passover . . . !—Ulla retorted: Do you suppose that he was one for whom a defence could be made? Was he not a *mesit,* concerning whom Scripture says, 'Neither shalt thou spare, neither shalt thou conceal him?' With Yeshu however it was different, for he was connected with the government.[2]

The *baraita,* which emphasizes the fairness of the legal proceedings against Jesus, was most likely a response to the anti-Jewish rhetoric of the Gospel passion stories, and as such has little or no historical value. However, Rabbi Ulla's retort does accord with the rabbinic tradition of viewing Jesus as a *mesit,* or prophet of a false religion, who justly deserved his execution. Other parts of the Babylonian Talmud refer to Jesus in veiled terms as the deceiver Balaam, and to his mother as a hairdresser named Miriam who traduces her husband. Nonetheless, one of the cryptic Talmudic tales seems to place Jesus in a sympathetic light, telling the story of a sage who visited one of the

Nazarene's followers in order to be healed. There may well have been more of those stories, but the rabbis of Christian Europe censored most allusions to Jesus in the Talmud out of fear of reprisal from Christian authorities.

In Jewish folklore, Jesus was the *taluy,* or the "hanged one." The *Toledot Yeshu,* a medieval parody of the Gospels, details the seduction of the married Miriam during her menstrual period (a time of ritual uncleanliness) by Joseph Pandera, (a variant spelling of "Pantera") as well as the career of their illicitly conceived son, Yehoshua, or Yeshu. As a boy, Yeshu sasses the rabbis; when he reaches adulthood, he steals the Name of God from the Jerusalem Temple, which he writes on a scrap of leather and sews into his thigh so that he can work miracles, including raising the dead. He also proclaims himself the virgin-born son of God and Messiah. After the spy Yeḥuda Iskariotes betrays him, he is arrested by the Sages of Israel, and then stoned and hanged on a cabbage stalk because no tree will consent to bear him. A gardener steals his body from the tomb, inspiring his disciples to proclaim him risen from the dead. After his corpse is eventually discovered in a ditch, it is tied to the tail of a horse and dragged in front of Queen Helena (perhaps the mother of Constantine), who has become one of Yeshu's believers. The disciple Shimeon Kepha, who learns the Name of God himself, founds a new, non-Jewish religion, supposedly in Yeshu's name. The *Toledot Yeshu,* with its bitter tone and sly humor, is an indictment of the contemptuous Christian treatment of Jews during the Middle Ages, and an expression of the very real Jewish fear of forced conversion. As such, it is a clear indication of the mutual demonization that marked the tenor of Jewish-Christian relations during the Middle Ages.

Interestingly, rather than denying the veracity of the Gospel stories about Jesus, the rabbinic tales and Jewish folklore offered their own interpretations, including the hypothesis that Jesus was born not of the Holy Spirit but of the seed of a Palestinian Romeo. Moreover, his miracles were real but were performed by means of sorcery or blasphemy. Although the Jews did not deny their own involvement in Jesus' death, they maintained that he had deserved it. Certain of the stories in the *Toledot,* as well as references to Jesus in rabbinic texts, corroborate the accusations of illegitimate birth (via the Roman soldier Pantera) and practice of sorcery that the pagan Celsus leveled at Jesus during the second century, suggesting that the Jewish traditions about Jesus were indeed very old.

Despite mutual theological and cultural hostility, there were always Jews who found themselves drawn to Jesus as a human being. The Karaites, who flourished in Persia from the eighth to the 12th century, were a schismatic Jewish sect that not only rejected the Talmud, but also viewed Jesus as an important Jewish martyr. While Moses Maimonides (Moses Ben Maimon; 1135–1204), the renowned physician and philosopher from Cordoba, condemned Jesus (without mentioning his name) for altering the Torah, he nonetheless believed that Christianity had a providential mission in acquainting others with Jewish religious principles. Isaac of Troki, a 16th-century Polish Jew, attempted to accord Jesus a positive place in Jewish history, maintaining that in calling God his "father," Jesus was not claiming divine status for himself, but simply expressing conventional Jewish piety.

The real sea-change in Jewish scholarly attitudes toward Jesus did not come about until the dawn of modernity. The Enlightenment in Christian Europe had a rationalistic Jewish analogue, the Haskalah, which sought to relax the authority of rabbinic tradition, which governed every aspect of daily existence, as well as to secularize Jewish learning and bring Jews into the cultural and political mainstream, particularly in light of the intense pressure on emancipated Jews (as in France after the Revolution) to conform to the mores of secularized society.

The leading exponent of "Liberal" or "Reform" Judaism was Abraham Geiger (1810–1874), a Semitics scholar who became the chief rabbi of Berlin. In addition to advocating the simplification of Jewish observances, he downplayed the theology of the Jews' election as God's chosen people, emphasizing instead a more universalistic Jewish mission of promulgating monotheism and morality to the world at large. Geiger even went so far as to allow instrumental music at Jewish services, a novelty for rabbinic Judaism, although he did draw the line at Sunday worship, which some of the most assimilationist Reform rabbis of the time were urging.

In Reform Judaism, the written and oral Torahs have no absolute authority and are binding only insofar as they reflect the essence of Judaism, which is usually defined as its ethical content. It was therefore natural that Reform Jews, like liberal Protestants, would want to shape a Jesus who primarily taught an ethical gospel. The first to do so was Moses Mendelssohn (1729–1786), a philosopher, Haskalah leader, and promoter of Jewish cultural assimilation who was also a close friend of Gotthold Lessing. Mendelssohn believed that Christians and Jews could make common cause by focusing on the ethic of Jesus. In a series of letters to friends and patrons, Mendelssohn proposed a Jesus who would be acceptable to both Jews and Christians as a faithful observer of Jewish law who was in no way superhuman. As for the *Toledot Yeshu,* which was an embarrassment to liberal Jews, Mendelssohn condemned it as *eine Missgeburt,* or a "literary freak."[3]

The Jewish Enlightenment was still in its infancy, and most Orthodox rabbis were not receptive to Mendelssohn's attempted rehabilitation of Jesus. It did not help when Mendelssohn's son Abraham converted to Christianity, or when his grandson, the composer Felix Mendelssohn (1809–1847), spearheaded a revival of interest in the music of that quintessentially Christian composer, Johann Sebastian Bach.

However, other Jewish intellectuals soon followed Moses Mendelssohn's lead. During the 1820s, the historian Isaac Markus Jost published a nine-volume history of the Jewish people in which he reiterated Mendelssohn's observation that Jesus had faithfully observed the Jewish law. He even referred to Jesus as a rabbi, although he noted that Jesus' teachings about mankind's relationship with God were novel, and that the Pharisees' opposition to them was justified. In 1838, Joseph Salvador, whose father was descended from Spanish Jews but whose mother was Catholic, published the first Jewish book devoted solely to Jesus and his teachings, as part of his efforts to promote the emergence of a universal religion that would amalgamate Judaism and Christianity. Whereas his treatise reiterated the Talmudic tradition that Jesus had been born out of wedlock, had learned magic in Egypt, where his mother had fled to escape the shame of his birth, and later used sorcery to work miracles while allowing people to worship him as a god, Salvador insisted that Jesus' ethical teaching was wholly Jewish. Like himself, Salvador's Jesus stood somewhere between Judaism and Christianity.

Abraham Geiger also emphasized Jesus' Jewishness, following Jost's lead in referring to him as "a Pharisaic Jew with Galilean coloring."[4] In a series of lectures on Jewish history published in 1864, Geiger took an extremely ambivalent stand toward Jesus. Asserting that while Jesus had taught nothing that was not consistent with Judaism, Geiger maintained that he had allowed his disciples, who were the actual founders of Christianity, to disregard the law. The German-Jewish historian Heinrich Grätz (1817–1891) developed the theme of Jesus' Galilean provenance by arguing that the inferior brand of Judaism in Galilee, a region far from Jerusalem and close to pagan Syria, had contaminated Jesus' teachings. Although he contended that Jesus was a second-rate Hillel who worked spells and came to believe wrongly that he was the Messiah, Grätz also spoke of Jesus in positive terms as someone who sought to impart greater meaning to the precepts of Judaism.

Both Grätz and Geiger were influenced by Hegelian theories of history, particularly by Ferdinand Christian Baur's rewriting of Christian history in Hegelian terms. In their view, Jesus was a sincere, if somewhat unorthodox rabbi (Grätz considered Jesus an Essene), while Christianity represented a "Hellenized" distortion of his message. Grätz and Geiger received reinforcement from their liberal Protestant colleagues, who believed as well that dogmatic Christianity had festooned Jesus with supernaturalism and obscured his central ethical message.

By the early 20th century, most liberal Jewish scholars had succeeded in transforming Jesus into a Reform rabbi. Israel Abrahams (1858–1925), a Talmudist at Cambridge University in England, wrote a two-volume treatise titled *Studies in Pharisaism and the Gospels* (1889–1907), whose intent was not only to vindicate the Pharisees, but also to rehabilitate Jesus as a Pharisee in good standing. One of Abrahams's close friends, Claude Joseph Goldsmid Montefiore (1858–1938), went even further in recasting Jesus as a liberal rabbi. Educated at Oxford, where his mentor had been the famous classicist Benjamin Jowett (1817–1893), Montefiore had a benign disposition toward all things English, including Christianity. Whereas Geiger and Grätz in Germany had demonstrated ambivalence about Jesus, Montefiore harbored no such feelings. As a liberal Jew (he became president of the World Union for Progressive Judaism in 1926), he regarded Christianity as a daughter religion of Judaism. "The daughter learnt from the Mother; why should not the Mother learn also from the Daughter?" he asked in a 1920 essay titled "Has Judaism a Future?"[5]

Montefiore believed that Jesus' mission had been the "universalisation of some fundamental tenets of Judaism" among the Gentiles, in particular its code of morality.[6] In fact, Jesus' message was so much in line with rabbinic teaching that he was not even original. At a time when many scholars were contending that Jesus had never existed, and when influential liberal Christian theologians such as Adolf von Harnack were trying to distance Jesus from Judaism, Montefiore attempted to counter both theories in a commentary on the Synoptic Gospels based on the parallels between Jesus' sayings and those of the early rabbis. For example, Jesus' Golden Rule—"Do to others as you would have them do to you"[7]—is an analogue of Hillel's directive as recorded in the Babylonian Talmud: "What is hateful to yourself, do not do to your enemies; that is the entirety of the Torah."[8]

In 1935, Montefiore reiterated his admiration for Jesus in a book titled *What a Jew Thinks about Jesus.* If there was fault to be found with Christianity, he theorized, it should be laid at the feet of Paul of Tarsus, whose theology of sin, death, and atonement was morbid and rigid, in contrast to the tolerant and forgiving message of Jesus. Although Paul had called himself a "Pharisee" in his letter to the Christians of Philippi,[9] Montefiore believed that he could never have been such because he was simply not liberal enough. Instead of merely bringing Judaism to the Gentiles as Jesus had done, Paul had founded the new faith of Christianity, "a religion poorer than, and even inferior to, the typical and average rabbinic Judaism," Montefiore noted.[10]

In 1922, Joseph Klausner (1874–1960), a Lithuanian-born Jewish scholar who had received his doctoral degree at the University of Heidelberg, published what might be called the first Jewish "liberal life" of Jesus. As an Orthodox Jew, Klausner was critical of Montefiore's genial assimilationism. However, his years at Heidelberg, where he specialized in philosophy and Semitic languages, had implanted in him a passion for modernity. Early in life, he had come under the influence of Ahad Ha-am (1856–1927), a Ukrainian-born Zionist philosopher (and another critic of Montefiore, because like most Reform Jews of that period, Montefiore was not a Zionist). Ahad's Zionism was more cultural than political, and he did not emigrate to Palestine until a few years before his death. His primary concern was not so much the creation of a Jewish state as the building of a new Jewish culture grounded in the Hebrew language that would replace the Yiddish mentality of the Eastern European ghetto. Accordingly, he helped promote modern Hebrew as a living language (his own name had been Asher Ginzberg until he changed it in 1889 to Ahad Ha-Am, which means "one of the people"). Like his mentor Ahad, Klausner embraced Zionism and cultural revival, moving to Palestine in 1920 to teach at the newly founded Hebrew University in Jerusalem, where he became another important force in the creation of modern Hebrew. He wrote his *Jesus of Nazareth* in Hebrew.

Klausner's avowed purpose in writing his life of Jesus was to take a fresh look at the Nazarene from the perspective of someone living in the Jewish homeland, far away from Christian anti-Jewish polemic and countervailing Jewish polemic against Jesus. For the first time in the history of Jewish literature, Klausner gave Jesus a legal (if nonsupernatural) birth, noting that "[his] father was Joseph and his mother Mary."[11] He went on to describe the family's ethic of hard work and piety, and the rudimentary education in Torah and the prophets that Jesus most likely received from the local synagogue. In the spirit of the 19th-century Jesus-biographers (whose work Klausner had undoubtedly encountered at Heidelberg), he reveled in painting the Galilean setting of Jesus' ministry. Once again in the liberal German tradition, he used the Gospel of Mark as his narrative outline and main source, although he drew on additional material from the Gospels of Matthew—especially the Sermon on the Mount—and Luke. He also rationalized Jesus' miracles, variously attributing them to psychosomatic cures, mercurial Galilean weather conditions, and a simple-minded populace who expected Jesus to act like a prophet.

Drawing on his own extensive knowledge of rabbinic learning, Klausner demonstrated how thoroughly concordant with Judaism Jesus' ethic really was. Indeed, at the beginning of his ministry, Jesus was "a 'Rab' and preacher, a 'Galilean itinerant', differing from others of that type only in certain peculiarities," Klausner wrote in an assessment much like Montefiore's.[12] Later on, however, Jesus came to believe that he was in fact the Messiah, following a latent and unfortunate tendency to transform his Judaism into absolutism. "The main strength of Jesus lay in his ethical teaching," Klausner concluded. "If we omitted the miracles and a few mystical sayings which tend to deify the Son of man, and preserved only the moral precepts and parables, the Gospels would count as one of the most wonderful collections of ethical teachings in the world."[13] In *From Jesus to Paul,* which he published in 1939, Klausner echoed certain of Montefiore's themes in *What a Jew Thinks about Jesus,* particularly with regard to Jesus' stance as a Jewish reformer, in contrast to that of Paul, who had founded a completely new religion.

While Klausner and Montefiore disagreed on the question of Zionism, their views about Jesus were strikingly similar, including their belief in dissonance between Jesus and Paul, and their exclusion of the Gospel of John as a source of historical information. They both portrayed Jesus as a liberal rabbi whose main mission was that of a teacher of ethics, and rejected as inauthentic all Gospel material that depicted him as an opponent of the Pharisees. An earlier scholar such as Isaac Jost would have argued that the Pharisees had good reason to oppose Jesus' somewhat unorthodox interpretations of Jewish law, but Klausner and Montefiore had made liberals of the Pharisees as well. Their views have prevailed in much 20-century Jewish scholarship on Jesus. The Jewish scholar Paul Winter (1904–1969) went so far as to declare: "Yet in historical reality Jesus was a Pharisee. . . . In the whole of the New Testament we are unable to find a single historically reliable instance of religious differences between Jesus and members of the Pharisaic guilds, let alone evidence of a mortal conflict."[14]

Klausner's view of Jesus was influential in another way: He had made him so completely Jewish a figure that he had no interest whatsoever in Gentiles (it was Paul who had preached to non-Jews). Among later scholars who elaborated the theory that Jesus had conceived of himself as having a message only for Jews was David Flusser, a professor of comparative religion at Hebrew University, who wrote in 1968: "The picture preserved for us by the first three gospels is clear: Jesus the Jew worked among Jews and wanted to work only among them."[15]

The Dead Sea Scrolls expert Geza Vermes took Flusser one step further. In *Jesus the Jew,* published in 1973 Vermes, who had built a towering reputation as a scrolls scholar, turned his attention to the historical Jesus. He maintained that Jesus actively disliked Gentiles, refusing to visit Galilean urban centers such as Sepphoris and Tiberias, where large numbers of Gentiles resided. Vermes's Jesus was a *Ḥasid,* a type of charismatic, miracle-working rabbi whose flouting of certain rabbinic customs and informal familiarity with God scandalized some of the Pharisees. Vermes pointed to two *Ḥasidim* mentioned in the Mishnah who conformed to his typology: Ḥoni the Circle Drawer (also mentioned in Josephus), born sometime before 63 B.C.E., who ended a drought by drawing a ring around himself into which God poured rain; and Ḥanina ben Dosa, born around 20 C.E., who lived just 10 miles south of Nazareth, practiced total poverty (to the discomfiture of his wife), had power over demons, could stop a rainstorm, and effected a long-distance cure of one of the sons of the Pharisee Gamaliel I in Jerusalem.

Vermes also maintained that when Jesus died and his body disappeared from his tomb, his followers construed the happenstance as yet another of the supernatural events connected with his mission. He also tied Jesus' lifelong celibacy to his prophetic function, pointing to a Talmudic passage declaring that Moses had ceased sexual relations with his wife after receiving his call from God. As for Jesus' references to himself as "son of man," he noted that in Aramaic the phrase was simply a synonym for human being, and as such had no eschatological connotation. Vermes concluded that Jesus, "so distorted by Christian and Jewish myth alike, was in fact neither the Christ of the Church, nor the apostate and bogey-man of Jewish popular tradition."[16]

In the course of rescuing Jesus from his bogey-man status in Jewish folklore, nearly all the Jewish reclamations had made a bogey-man out of Paul. Just as Jesus the opponent of the Pharisees in the Gospels had become a Pharisee, Paul the self-described Pharisee had become a non-Pharisee. Samuel Sandmel (1911–1979), a Reform rabbi and Judaic scholar who taught for many years at the Hebrew Union College–Jewish Institute of Religion in Cincinnati, saw the humor in this paradox (which was also prevalent in Gentile scholarship) and summed it up in a little rhyme:

A Jew Named Saul
Later Called Paul
Came and spoiled it all.[17]

However, Sandmel's shrewd and very readable *We Jews and Jesus* (1965), in which that rhyme appeared, offered virtually the same assessment of Jesus as had Vermes, Flusser, Winter, Klausner, and Montefiore: While Jesus was a good Jewish teacher, in no sense could he be considered an innovator:

> I own to seeing no originality in the teachings of Jesus, for I hold that those passages which deal with his supernatural role reflect not his authentic words but the piety of the developing Church. As to those teachings which are conceivably his, they seem to me to be of a piece with Jewish teaching, and that they range from the commonplaces of Jewish teaching through a sporadic flash of insight that other Jewish teachers also achieved. Yet I feel that all too often the question of originality is a misguided one, for it can often resolve itself into the unimportant question of mere priority. To my mind the crux of the issue about the Golden Rule is not the question of whether Hillel said it before Jesus, or Jesus before Hillel (Hillel chances to be a little earlier than Jesus), nor whether Hillel's formula in the negative is superior or inferior to Jesus' formula in the affirmative . . . nor whether both are, or are not derived from Leviticus 19. To my mind the issue is that of value, not priority; I find that there is more in the teachings of Jesus that I admire than that I do not.[18]

Indeed, there was so little difference between Jesus and Hillel in Sandmel's mind that the only discrepancies he discerned between Judaism and Christianity were cultural. Judaism was for Jews, and Christianity was for Christians, and it was a tragedy that the two faiths had been enemies for so many centuries. "I do not regard Judaism as objectively superior to Christianity nor Christianity to Judaism," Sandmel wrote. "Rather, Judaism is mine, and I consider it good, and I am at home in it, and I love it, and want it. That is how I want Christians to feel about their Christianity."[19]

The Jewish reclamation of Jesus has contributed much of value to 20th-century New Testament scholarship, and to Christians' understanding of Judaism. Today's Gentile-dominated New Quest tends to disregard or denigrate Jesus' Jewish backdrop, treating Temple worship and Pharisaic preoccupations with holiness as "legalistic," "hypocritical," "oppressive," or just plain irrelevant. Taking Jesus' Jewishness seriously—for the first time since the earliest days of Christianity—is in itself an important achievement. Furthermore, the Jewish texts on Jesus, particularly Klausner's, can serve for non-Jews as cogent introductions to Judaism, about which many are vastly ignorant. Even the most philo-Semitic Christians tend to regard Jews as religious coelecanths, or living Old Testament fossils. Jewish Jesus-research has introduced Christians to the wholeness of Judaism, its completeness as a system of salvation, the loving and merciful nature of its God, the central function of rabbinic teaching in Jewish spiritual life, and the positive, nourishing role of Jewish law as a reflection of the covenant between God and Israel.

Before the Jewish reclamation, far fewer Christians were aware of the thoroughly Jewish nature of many of Jesus' ethical preachments, or of rabbinic parallels and overlaps to his parables. The 19th-century "liberal lives" had always presumed that Jesus' ethic was superior to that of Judaism (the only German scholar of the time who gave Jesus' teachings a sympathetic Jewish context was Alfred Edersheim, a Jew who had converted to Lutheranism). Moreover, there is something touching about the Jewish insistence on Jesus' legitimate birth, particularly when the most au courant Gentile scholars these days have decided that he was conceived out of wedlock! Finally, it makes more historical sense to think of Jesus as a pious first-century Jew than as an impudent Cynic philosopher. In one of the most recent Jewish Jesus-reconstructions, Irving M. Zeitlin paints an appealing picture of a "charismatic religious virtuoso"[20] who was intensely prayerful, knew the Jewish Scriptures backwards and forwards, and felt an especially close relationship with the divine.

The Jewish reclamation of Jesus has also come under criticism, however, not the least of which has come from Jewish scholars themselves. Samuel Sandmel, who kept up with trends in New Testament scholarship among Christians, complained that Jewish reclaimers of Jesus were inclined to accept the face-value historicity of the Gospels far more than their liberal Gentile counterparts, ignoring the Synoptic Problem and other questions of literary dependency, not to mention form criticism. Sandmel also noted that Jewish scholars' criteria for deciding which parts of the Gospels were true to Jesus and which were Christian inventions have tended to be idiosyncratic. In point of fact, most of the Jewish reclaimers (including Sandmel) have adopted Perrin's "criterion of dissimilarity," but in only one direction: While they have rejected all sayings of Jesus that sound Christian, they have retained in toto his Jewish-sounding sayings.

The most glaring error of Jewish reclaimers, as noted by Montefiore and Sandmel, and more recently by Jacob Neusner, has been their tendency to use Talmudic materials anachronistically, retrojecting into the early first century Jewish teachings and customs recorded as late as the fifth century. Geza Vermes has been one of the leading offenders in this respect. The Talmudic references to the miracles of Ḥoni and Ḥanina date from more than 250 years after Ḥoni's lifetime and a century and a half after Ḥanina's. Paul Winter's assertion that "Jesus was a Pharisee" was also pure speculation: As Neusner has demonstrated, very little is known about the Pharisees of the early first century beyond the fact that there is a generational link between Hillel's Pharisaic Judaism and rabbinic Judaism. Furthermore, the historical Hillel is even more elusive than the historical Jesus. Hillel's sayings, and those of his contemporary Shammai, survive only in anecdotes embedded in the Talmud hundreds of years later. Whereas scholars of a generation or so ago freely delved into the Mishnah to discern supposed Jewish customs and religious practices of Jesus' time, most are now extremely cautious about Talmudic statements purporting to describe first-century Jewish life in Palestine.

Neusner has characterized the reclaimers' inclination to recast Jesus as "Rabbi Jesus the Reformer"[21] as not only anachronistic, but also condescending to all but the most liberal Christians who do not believe in Jesus' divinity:

> Facing a wider world professedly interested in Judaic views, the Judaic theologians found impolitic the retelling of the malicious gossip about the bastard wanton, the bad disciple. Not only so but, for some at least, a reading of the Gospel record yielded more than a few passages worthy of genuine respect: the power of the tale itself, the moral message—these have always won assent from outsiders to Christian faith. So, quite naturally, in place of the disreputable philanderer, son of a philanderer, Judaic theologians produced the figure they could admire most at the least cost: a rabbi. Since . . . at this very same time Christian theologians pointed to the Jewishness of Jesus—discovering, after so long a spell of inadvertence, that Jesus and his mother, as well as Joseph, John the Baptist, and all the disciples, were Jews—the Judaic Christology (if that is what it can be called) found a sympathetic hearing.
>
> What made at all possible a Judaic reading of Jesus was, of course, the separation of "the historical Jesus" from "the Christ of faith." Judaism then could

> pay its respects but still concede nothing when it praised his teachings. Obviously, the Gospels' allegations that Jesus Christ was crucified on the cross (by the Romans), died, was buried, and in three days rose from the dead to be enthroned on high—these have no bearing on the historical Jesus and may therefore be set aside in the "Christ-of-faith" file, which we . . . do not consult. And the "son-of-Man" sayings could be read to mean merely "man," however Christians understood the phrase. It would go without saying that we can distinguish, moreover, between what Jesus really said and "words attributed to Jesus by the developing Church."[22]

Neusner viewed the Jewish concession that Jesus was a good man as a vacuous equivalent to the now-common Christian concession that Jesus was a Jew and Jews are good people, both of which concessions are true, but neither of which contributes much to genuine Jewish-Christian dialogue about Jesus.

The extent of Jewish involvement in Jesus' death has been the most troubling aspect of the Jewish reclamation of Jesus. During the many centuries in which Jews adopted the Talmudic view of Jesus as a false prophet and sorcerer, to some degree they acquiesced to the Gospel accounts of Jesus' trial and passion, which variously portrayed the chief priests, the scribes, the Sanhedrin (the court of Jerusalem religious officials), and the Pharisees as having had a hand in Jesus' execution, even though the order for his death came from the Roman official Pontius Pilate. The Gospels portray Pilate as willing to have Jesus flogged, but reluctant to crucify him until a Jerusalem mob, egged on by the priests, howls for his death.

When recent Jewish scholarship recast Jesus as a rabbi, or uncontroversial teacher, there was no longer any rationale for Jewish participation in his crucifixion, an accusation that had been tragically exploited in the Christian persecution of Jews. No other rabbi (or Pharisee) of the early first century is known to have been so religiously offensive as to warrant capital punishment. It is difficult indeed to plot a trajectory for a Pharisaic Jesus that would end with his being nailed to a cross.

The Jewish reclaimers who have dealt with the problem of Jesus' death have uniformly recast him as a *political* revolutionary, or at the very least as someone who gave the appearance of such. As Joseph Klausner declared: "It is certain that the priests did not see in Jesus anything more than an ordinary rebel: they did not recognize his special spiritual nature; what they did they did, in all simplicity, in order to save the people from the cruel vengeance of

Pilate, who was on the watch for some possible excuse to demonstrate the power of Rome and the nugatory nature of Jewish autonomy in any matter of political importance."[23] He also emphasized that crucifixion was a Roman punishment that was repugnant to all Jews (he was writing before the discovery of the Dead Sea Scrolls, which contain references to crucifixion as a form of Jewish punishment). He thus adopted the Talmudic (and the Gospels') position that Jewish authorities played a role in Jesus' crucifixion—probably a brief hearing before the Sanhedrin—without actually blaming them for what they did.

In 1914, however, a Jewish scholar named Jean Juster had published *Les Juifs dans l'Empire Romain* (*The Jews in the Roman Empire*), which took the position that no Sanhedrin proceeding had ever occurred. In so doing, he had addressed a major polemical issue: It was one thing for the high priest Caiaphas, a Roman puppet who owed his appointment to Pilate's predecessor, Valerius Gratus, or even for the entire class of priests and Temple sectaries to oppose Jesus. However, the involvement of the Sanhedrin (as recounted in the three Synoptics) or the Pharisees (as related in John) seemed to imply the involvement, at least symbolically, of the entire Jewish people. In fact, throughout the 19th century, there had been a running debate over whether the Sanhedrin had afforded Jesus a fair trial. The Gospel of Mark reported nighttime proceedings and a double hearing, which would have violated the Mishnah's rules of legal procedure. Jewish scholars such as Jost and Salvador argued that the Sanhedrin had acted legally, while Christians insisted that the trial had violated Jewish conceptions of due process.

Juster had taken a completely different tack. He contended that the Sanhedrin possessed the right to mete out the death penalty in Second Temple times, which meant that had the Sanhedrin been involved in Jesus' trial, there would have been no need to go to Pilate to execute Jesus. Moreover, because Jesus had died on a Roman cross, it could not have been the Sanhedrin that condemned him. To support his position, Juster cited the Mishnah, which declared that the Sanhedrin possessed the requisite capital powers, as well as several instances of Jewish religious executions recorded in Josephus and the New Testament, including the stoning of the deacon Stephen in the Acts of the Apostles. Juster's theories were adopted by the German Gentile scholar Hans Lietzmann in *Der Prozess Jesu* (*The Trial of Jesus*), published in 1931. In Lietzmann's view, the passion story in Mark's Gospel was simply a collection of anti-Jewish traditions that had served as a model for the narratives in the other three Gospels.

In *We Jews and Jesus,* Samuel Sandmel reaffirmed Juster and Lietzmann's contention that the Gospel reports of a Sanhedrin proceeding were an anti-Jewish fiction, and that Pontius Pilate was solely responsible for Jesus' death: "Cannot one discern the palpable shift of responsibility [in the Gospels] from Pilate through the patent devices by which Pilate is portrayed as reluctantly giving in to Jewish malevolence?"[24] However, Sandmel conceded that his own motive for denying Jewish involvement in Jesus' crucifixion had more to do with combating anti-Semitism than with strict regard for historical truth:

> Perhaps we might be willing to say to ourselves that it is not at all impossible that some Jews, even leading Jews, recommended the death of Jesus to Pilate. We are adverse to saying this, for so total has the charge been against us that we have been constrained to make a total denial. Yet if we admit—admit, not confess!—that some Jews were involved, then why blame us all, both then and now? And since Jesus was a Jew, is it not more reasonable to say that people killed Jesus, than to put the statement as though Jesus were not a Jew, but his opponents were? Is it not equally unfair to say the Americans killed Lincoln and Kennedy?[25]

While David Flusser did not go so far as Sandmel in his 1968 study of Jesus (he believed that the high priest Caiaphas and the Temple police had played a role in turning Jesus over to Pilate), he did argue that there had never been a trial under either Jewish or Roman auspices. He noted that Jesus' Jewish contemporary Philo of Alexandria had complained to the emperor Gaius that Pilate had a history of "constant executions" of suspected troublemakers "without passing judgment."[26] In Flusser's words, "It would seem, therefore, that Jesus' tragic end was preceded by no verdict of any earthly judiciary. It was the outcome of the grisly interplay of naked spheres of interest, in the shadow of brutal antagonisms, and to outward appearance, it had no real connection with the man Jesus and his cause."[27] In *Jesus the Jew,* Geza Vermes also bypassed the question of Jesus' trial, concluding that he was probably summarily crucified as a Zealot because he was from Galilee, home to Judas the Galilean and other bandit chiefs.

Others who wrote on the subject contended that the Romans must have had good reason to think that Jesus was a political revolutionary. In his best-selling *Passover Plot* (1965), the British writer Hugh J. Schonfield theorized that Jesus had decided early on that he wanted to be the political liberator of his people, and deliberately arranged to provoke the priests, fulfill the messianic prophecies in the Scriptures, be crucified at Passover, and be taken down from the cross alive so that he could "rise" from the tomb and preside over his new kingdom. All went well until shortly after his interment, when he accidentally died from loss of blood. His followers then secretly disposed of his body, displayed his empty tomb to the faithful, and persuaded others to simulate his post-resurrection appearances.

In a more serious work of scholarship, titled *Jesus and the Zealots* (1967), S. G. F. Brandon, a professor of comparative religion at the University of Manchester, asserted that although Jesus himself was not a Zealot, he was very close in spirit to the nationalist Jewish guerrilla group (one of his disciples was in fact called "Zelotes"). In Brandon's view, Jesus was not a pacifist as is commonly thought, but rather a religious militant, a Robin Hood who hated the rich, loved the poor, and was executed by Pilate after he drove the money-changers from the Temple in defiance of the priestly upper class who collaborated with Rome: "The attack upon the Temple trading system constituted, therefore, a most radical challenge to the authority of the sacerdotal aristocracy, and it was also a truly revolutionary act, for the high priest held his office and authority from the Romans, and was thus an essential factor of the Roman government in Judaea. . . . To challenge the role of the high priest was thus, in effect, to challenge the Roman rule."[28]

In *Revolution in Judaea* (1973), the most elaborate reconstruction of Jesus as a Jewish resistance leader, British Talmudist Hyam Maccoby portrayed him as both a Pharisee and a political rebel, arguing that Pilate executed him for his efforts to restore a theocracy in the Holy Land. Maccoby also speculated that Jesus of Nazareth and Jesus Barabbas, the condemned insurrectionist whom the Gospels report Pilate as freeing in Jesus' stead, were in reality one and the same person.

The most widely read and influential of all the Jewish evaluations of Jesus' death was Paul Winter's *On the Trial of Jesus* (1961). Winter's mother, sister, and other close relatives were killed in the Holocaust and he dedicated his book in searing language "to the dead in Auschwitz, Izbica, Majdanek, Treblinka, among whom are those who are dearest to me."[29] Born in 1904, he had studied philosophy and ancient languages at the University of Vienna and law at the University of Prague. After graduation, he was a successful international lawyer in Prague until 1939, when Hitler annexed Czechoslovakia. Winter managed to escape through Hungary and the Balkans to Palestine, where he joined the Free Czech Army and served under the British and American command until the end of the Second World War. His last tour of duty was at the German headquarters of the United States First Army, where his task was the care and repatriation of some 80,000 survivors of Nazi concentration and forced-labor camps. After the war, he became legal advisor to the United Nations Displaced Persons Operations, participating in the drafting of legislation under which the German government would indemnify victims of political or racial persecution by the Third Reich.

In 1947, Winter moved to London, became a British citizen, and worked for a time for the British Broadcasting Corporation's overseas service. Then he dropped out of public life completely, spending the next two decades in solitary penury, eking out a living with low-paying jobs as a railroad porter, mail sorter, and night watchman while he haunted the public libraries of London researching the Gospels. He admired Jesus greatly, and his trial had fascinated him since boyhood. *On the Trial of Jesus* brought Winter worldworld acclaim and numerous lecture invitations. Cardinal Augustin Bea, author of the Second Vatican Council's pathbreaking declaration that the Jews were not guilty of deicide with respect to Jesus' death, was said to have studied his book. Nonetheless, Winter continued to live in isolation and near-destitution, plagued by poor health until he died of a heart attack in 1969.

On the Trial of Jesus essentially adopted Juster's argument that the Sanhedrin had the power to order capital punishment for a religious offense, and would therefore not have involved itself in a Roman crucifixion. However, as Winter had taught himself form criticism while pursuing his New Testament studies in the libraries of London, he was able to present his case in more sophisticated fashion than Juster. Winter contended that the very irregularities reported by the Gospels—deviations from the Mishnah's rules—proved that the accounts of Jesus' Sanhedrin trial were fictional.

Winter surmised that the evangelist Mark had invented almost the entire passion story, drawing partly on strands of tradition already in circulation and partly on his own editorial and theological resources. As evidence for his supposition, Winter pointed to the many Old Testament parallels to the events of Jesus' passion, which seemed to fulfill Old Testament prophecies. For example, Mark's account of the chief priests and scribes passing by the cross where Jesus is hanging and taunting him by saying, "He saved others; he cannot save himself,"[30] echoes the following lines of Psalm 22: "All who see me mock at me; they make mouths at me, they shake their heads; / 'Commit your cause to the Lord; let him deliver—let him rescue the one in whom he delights!'"[31] Along the lines of David Friedrich Strauss, Winter concluded that Mark had searched the Jewish Scriptures for prophetic material to work into his rendition of Jesus' death. Consequently, neither the mockery of Jesus nor any of the other events in Mark's passion narrative had ever taken place.

Because Winter believed that Jesus' teachings resembled those of other Pharisees, he argued that the Gospel accounts of disputes between Jesus and other Jews merely represented the antagonisms faced by the early Christian communities at various stages in their development. "All the Marcan 'controversy stories,' without exception, reflect disputes between the 'Apostolic Church' and its social environment, and are devoid of roots in the circumstances of the life of Jesus," he wrote emphatically, adding, "Some of the controversy stories have simply been constructed by the Second Evangelist himself, who presented certain traditional items by framing them as a disputation."[32]

Winter also maintained that since the hostility between the early Christians and their Jewish neighbors only increased over time, each of the Gospels that followed Mark—Matthew, Luke, and John—became more anti-Jewish in its reworking of the passion-story materials, gradually placing the entire blame on the Jews for Jesus' death and portraying Pilate as a sympathetic character. In Winter's view, Jesus' trial and death had essentially been a Roman affair, and in all likelihood Pilate himself issued Jesus' arrest warrant. However, the high priests and Jerusalem aristocracy, who were constantly worried about insurrections that might result in restraints on local autonomy, probably played some role in the proceedings, such as a preliminary hearing on the part of the Sanhedrin (as in Luke's version of the story). Moreover, although Jesus did not consider himself to be the Messiah and had almost no Jewish enemies, in Winter's view, he had inadvertently given the *impression* of political insurgency, provoking Roman and priestly authorities to take swift action against him in order to avoid unrest in a city swollen with high-spirited Passover pilgrims celebrating Israel's liberation from Egypt.

Winter's book provoked a great deal of criticism from other scholars who were sympathetic toward his efforts to combat anti-Semitism but dubious about his historical conclusions. The most trenchant of his detractors was David R. Catchpole of the University of Lancaster, who pointed out that Winter had used the Mishnah anachronistically in presuming that a Jewish legal code finalized in 200 C.E. reflected procedures of Jesus' time. In fact, the Sanhedrin of the Mishnah, a rabbinic court that issued strictly religious rulings, bore little resemblance to the pre–70 C.E. council of the local elite that adjudicated a variety of civil and religious matters, Catchpole pointed out. Catchpole also questioned Winter's assumption that the incorporation of Old Testament material into New Testament passages necessarily meant that the New Testament passages were unhistorical. With regard to Jesus' crucifixion, he contended that Winter had failed to explain why anyone would mete out a felon's death to an innocuous and unprovocative rabbi. Finally, Catchpole, who was no mean form critic himself, criticized Winter's supposition that the four Gospels were progressively less historical and more tendentious. Catchpole himself believed that Luke's Gospel preserved certain traditions that were older, more authentic, and less anti-Jewish than those in Mark, such as the likelihood that the Sanhedrin proceedings against Jesus were a mere preliminary examination rather than a full trial.

John A. T. Robinson (1919–1983), the Anglican bishop of Woolwich and a former Oxford University dean, took issue specifically with Winter's assumption that the Gospel passion stories displayed an increasing tendency to "canonize" Pilate at the expense of the Jews. Robinson noted that in John's Gospel, which is in some ways the least anti-Jewish of the four, there were no Sanhedrin proceedings against Jesus, but merely a brief inquisition at the house of the high priest Caiaphas. Nor was John's Pilate any saint, but a complex character whose personality was consistent with that of Philo's portrait: a hardhead who liked to annoy his Jewish subjects, until someone reminded him what the emperor Tiberius might think. Pilate was, after all, a protégé of the ruthless Praetorian Guard commander Aelius Sejanus, who eventually made so many political enemies that he was executed for conspiracy in 31 C.E. "'Perhaps the tremors that presaged the fall of Sejanus were already felt by sensitive political observers, and Pilate feared that soon he would have no protection at court,'" Robinson wrote, quoting from a commentary on John's Gospel written by Raymond E. Brown.[33] "'A shrewd ecclesiastical politician like Caiaphas would have been quite aware of the prefect's vulnerability and prompt to probe it.'"[34]

In the wake of the Holocaust, it has been painful for many scholars to offer alternatives to Winter's analysis of Jesus' crucifixion. Nonetheless, in 1994, Brown published a detailed two-volume commentary on the passion stories titled *The Death of the Messiah,* whose more than 1,500 pages were the result of 20 years of research. Despite his adventurous forays into trajectory theory, Brown is in good standing with the Vatican. However, his moderately liberal views—deeming certain parts of the Gospels legendary and expressing sympathy with the cause of women's ordination to the priesthood—have made him the target of conservative Catholics, and he could hardly be called a biblical reactionary. While he found a good deal of legendary and strictly theological material in the passion stories, he rejected Winter's theory that the stories were entirely fictional. On the contrary, he viewed a good number of the reported events as historically plausible, such as the mocking of Jesus on the cross (although perhaps not by priests or the Sanhedrin), despite the interpretive overlay of Old Testament allusions that accompanied each of them.

Brown concluded that a broad spectrum of Jewish authorities had probably played a role in assuring Jesus' death, arguing that even if the Sanhedrin possessed the death penalty, it was highly unlikely that it would have carried out an execution with incendiary political overtones during the Passover season without first obtaining Pilate's approval. To corroborate the Gospel accounts, Brown alluded to a passing reference to Jesus' death in one of Josephus's histories: "Pilate, upon hearing him accused by men of the highest standing amongst us, had condemned him to be crucified,"[35] as well as to Talmudic tradition and Celsus and other pagan authors. He also contended that many religious Jews would have considered Jesus a genuinely blasphemous figure and voted in perfectly good faith to condemn him:

> On the one hand, Jesus is portrayed as consorting frequently and pleasantly with public sinners who take no offense at him. On the other hand, he criticizes scathingly a religious outlook that many would judge laudable, e.g., condemning as unjustified before God a Pharisee who has taken care not to break the commandments, who observes pious practices and prays, and who is generous to religious causes (Luke 18:11–14). To the accumulated teaching of his era Jesus at times offers a sovereign challenge, the sole authority for which seems to be his claim that he can speak for God. If one takes the Gospels at face value (and even if one examines them through the microscope of historical criticism), there emerges a Jesus capable of generating intense dislike.[36]

Despite Brown's restrained tone and his candid concession that there is indeed an anti-Jewish polemic strain in the Gospels, other scholars jumped all over *The Death of the Messiah.* John Dominic Crossan promptly published a riposte, a 1995 text titled *Who Killed Jesus? Exposing the Roots of Anti-Semitism in the Gospel Story of the Death of Jesus.* Crossan theorized that the apocryphal Gospel of Peter, which is far more anti-Jewish than the canonicals, was the real source of all four canonical passion stories. Like David Flusser, he maintained that Jesus' crucifixion was not preceded by any sort of legal action, much less one involving the Jews:

> Imagine, for example, that Caiaphas and Pilate had standing agreements and orders concerning Passover whereby any subversive action involving the Temple and its crowds would beget instant punishment with no need to go very high up the chain of command for a peasant nuisance nobody like Jesus, no need for even a formal interrogation before Caiaphas, let alone a detailed trial before Pilate. In the case of Jesus, there may well have been Arrest and Execution, but no Trial whatsoever in between.[37]

Shortly after Crossan's book appeared, Elaine Pagels published *The Origin of Satan* (1995), using Winter's schema (each Gospel is more anti-Jewish than the last, and all are mostly fictional) to link Christian anti-Semitism to a growing conviction that the Jews were the devil's people. Efforts like Pagels's or Crossan's may be laudable insofar as they heighten Christians' awareness of their treatment of Jews, but one wonders whether condemning out of hand Brown's sensitive effort to view the passion stories from another perspective serves the historian's goal of trying to shed genuine light on the past.

It is now virtually impossible, for example, to discuss Judas Iscariot, the renegade disciple whom the Gospels identify as having betrayed Jesus to the authorities, without raising issues of anti-Semitism. In his *Judas Iscariot and the Myth of Jewish Evil,* published in 1992, Hyam Maccoby insisted that Judas, whose Hebrew name *Yeḥudah* is the root-word of both "Judea" and "Judaism," was yet another hate-filled Christian fiction. (With his penchant for finding doubles, Maccoby concluded that the historical Iscariot and another of Jesus' disciples who was also named Judas—known to English-speaking Christians as St. Jude—were one and the same person, and probably Jesus' younger brother.) Apparently with the aim of softening the New Testament's anti-Jewish implications, the Jesus Seminar's *Five Gospels* translates the Greek *ioudaioi* as "Judaeans" instead of "Jews," thereby confusing the reader whenever "Judaeans" appear as residents of Galilee. Again, the goal may be laudable, but the translation is not true to the text.

The effort to combat anti-Semitism has at times approached the absurd. In a review of Norman Mailer's fictional "autobiography" of Jesus titled *The Gospel According to the Son* (1997), the self-proclaimed former Christian A. N. Wilson chided the Jewish Mailer for not pinning sufficient blame for Jesus' death on Pontius Pilate. "Here . . . we read of the Pharisees improbably collaborating with the Romans and urging them to kill Jesus," Wilson lectured.[38] "It remains the Jews, in the accounts of Jesus/Mailer, who are guilty of crucifying the innocent Galilean prophet—a fiction that has had an incomparably damaging historical effect, and which is both the origin and supposed justification of European anti-Semitism."[39] Following the lead of Winter, Maccoby, and others, Wilson declared that "the historical Jesus was likely to have been [the] ally [of the Pharisees], if not a Pharisee himself," adding that the "real Pilate crucified 2,000 Pharisees in a single day."[40] (Pilate actually did nothing of the kind; Wilson evidently confused him with the Hasmonean king Alexander Jannaeus.)

Certain scholars have gone so far as to denounce all Christology, or theological claims about Jesus, as *ipso facto* anti-Semitic. "Is it possible to say 'Jesus is Messiah' without, implicitly or explicitly, saying at the same time 'and the Jews be damned'?" asked the Catholic theologian Rosemary Radford Ruether rhetorically in 1974.[41] As a solution, Ruether proposed that Christians forsake their "absolutist" claims about Jesus, and view him simply as one among many Jewish men of faith. The Ebionites have made yet another appearance in this connection, as model early Christians who regarded Jesus as just another good Jew and preserved his teachings more faithfully then did the orthodox. Robert Graves's *Nazarene Gospel Restored,* published in 1946 as a reconstruction of a supposed first-century Ebionite life of Jesus, is now enjoying a resurgence of popularity in many avant-garde circles. Wilson, Crossan, Maccoby, and Gerd Lüdemann have all recently promoted Ebionitism, or "Jewish Christianity," as the true religion of Jesus. As I have said several times before, there is no evidence that such a community existed in the first century.

According to Maccoby, Paul of Tarsus was the "originator of Christian anti-Semitism"[42] because in inventing Christianity he had also invented Christology. Maccoby essentially depicts Paul as a tormented megalomaniac who had briefly converted to Judaism and who lied about having been a Pharisee. Poorly educated and lacking a capacity for logical argument, he was rejected by Gamaliel I's school in Jerusalem and became a lowly Temple policeman instead, whereupon he suffered a nervous breakdown. After turning against Judaism, he stitched together his own faith out of a melange of themes from the Hellenistic mystery religions of his native Asia Minor, which he then attached to Jesus, who had appeared to him in "visions" during his psychological crisis:

> Paul was the greatest fantasist of all. He created the Christian myth by deifying Jesus, a Jewish Messiah figure whose real aims were on the plane of Jewish political Utopianism. Paul transformed Jesus' death into a cosmic sacrifice in

> which the powers of evil sought to overwhelm the power of good, but, against their will, only succeeded in bringing about a salvific event. This also transforms the Jews, as Paul's writings indicate, into the unwitting agents of salvation, whose malice in bringing about the death of Jesus is turned to good because this death is the very thing needed for the salvation of sinful mankind. The combination of malice and blindness described here is the exact analogue of the myth of Balder, in Norse mythology, in which malice is personified by the wicked god Loki and blindness by the blind god Hother, and both together bring about the salvific death which alone guarantees a good crop and salvation from death by famine.
>
> Paul took the cosmic drama of good and evil from Gnosticism, and so took over the dramatization of the Jews as the representatives of cosmic evil. . . . The Jews became not just the opponents of the figure descended from the world of light, but the performers of the cosmic sacrifice by which the heavenly visitant brings salvation. The Jews thus became identified as the dark figure which in myths of the deaths of gods bring about the saving death—Set, Mot, Loki; and the stage is prepared for the long career of the Jews in the Christian imagination as the people of the Devil. The elements which Paul took over from Judaism to embellish his myth—the religio-historical elements which set the death of Jesus in a panorama of world history—only intensified the resultant anti-Semitism, because there was now an aspect of usurpation in the Pauline myth, an incentive to blacken the Jewish record in order to justify the Christian take-over of the Abrahamic 'promises.' The career of the Jews in history began to be seen as a prefiguring of their central role, the murder of the divine sacrifice; they were separated from their prophets, now regarded as proto-Christs, hounded, like Jesus, by the Jews.[43]

As this bizarre Hellenistic/Gnostic/Nordic syncretism did not sit well with the Judaic church of James in Jerusalem, Paul peddled his myths to the Gentiles. The Hellenistic churches he founded turned the myths into narratives, which in turn became Gospels. For Maccoby, the Jewish reclamation of Jesus has evolved into a scathing polemic against Christianity.

Maccoby's ideas have gained wide circulation mainly because A. N. Wilson has used them for ammunition in his own continuing diatribe against Christianity. A writer of fiction and literary critic by trade, Wilson has borrowed nearly all his historical theories about Jesus and Paul from Maccoby and Vermes, as evidenced by his much-publicized *Jesus: A Life* (1992) and more recent *Paul: The Mind of the Apostle* (1997). From Vermes, he adopted the theory that Jesus was a wonder-working rabbi like Ḥoni and Ḥanina, and from Maccoby the notion that Paul was a lowly Temple thug with an outsize neurotic ego. Wilson's own contribution to the enterprise has been by way of novelistic (and sometimes zany) detail, averring for instance that Paul was the "Malchus" whose ear Peter cut off in Gethsemane, and that the disciples on the road to Emmaus thought they had encountered the risen Jesus but had really run into his lookalike brother James.

Several scholars have already condemned Wilson for carelessness with facts and an imagination run amok (in purported nonfiction). Although Wilson's Jesus is supposed to be a first-century Jewish holy man, he is actually a nondenominational 20th-century therapy-group facilitator whose specialty is "enabling [people] to become themselves,"[44] and whose message is: "Suppress if you can the yang and exalt the yin! Keep down the urge the dominate, to score, to triumph, to fight, and exalt the urge to conciliate, to understand, to value."[45] Wilson's "Jewish" Jesus seems more attracted to the Far East and the New Age than to Judasim.

The discovery in 1947 of a cache of Jewish religious documents near the Wadi Qumran in Judea has similarly led certain researchers to believe they have at last found the historical Jesus in the Holy Land, even though it is most unlikely that any of the hundreds of manuscripts refers to Jesus or was written by Christians.

The Wadi Qumran (a *wadi* is a dried-up stream bed) lies in a moonscape of rocky cliffs near the northwest shore of the Dead Sea, a forbidding, uninhabitable, below-sea-level terrain some seven and a half miles south of Jericho and 15 miles east of Jerusalem. In early 1947, three Bedouin goatherds discovered a cave in one of the cliff-faces just south of an ancient ruin whose identity was then unknown. Inside were a number of tall pottery jars, one of which contained three bundles wrapped in cloth and leather. Once opened, the seven parcels that were eventually recovered revealed brittle, tightly coiled old manuscripts. Months later, working through a cobbler they knew in Bethlehem who had an antiquities business on the side, the Bedouin sold four of the scrolls for only a few pounds to Mar Athanasius Yeshua Samuel, the Syrian Orthodox archbishop associated with St. Mark's monastery in Jerusalem.

The sale of these documents coincided with the last months of the British Mandate in Palestine, during which there was bitter three-way fighting among the British, the Jewish underground army called the Haganah, and Palestinian Arabs who were determined that there should never be a Jewish state. Samuel recognized the language of the scrolls as Hebrew; he also knew that no one had lived in the vicinity of Qumran since the early Christian era. However, when he sought help at Hebrew University and the École Biblique, a Catholic archaeological institute in East Jerusalem, he found that experts at both places either had abandoned the city or refused to risk their lives by visiting St. Mark's. Others who examined the scrolls viewed them merely as disused Torahs that had probably been stolen from synagogue storerooms during the Arab-Jewish conflict.

Unlike Egypt, whose year-round dry climate facilitates the preservation of ancient documents, the deserts of the Holy Land have an annual rainy season that is corrosive to parchment and paper. Until the Dead Sea discoveries, the oldest Hebrew text of the Bible dated only to the ninth century. When a librarian from Hebrew University finally went to the monastery to look at the scrolls, he decided they were relatively recent Samaritan manuscripts.

As Samuel fretted over how to dispose of his four scrolls, E. L. Sukenik, an archaeologist at Hebrew University (and father of the famous Israeli archaeologist Yigael Yadin, who was then commander of the Jewish armed forces), learned that the other three were for sale in Bethlehem. Despite the fact that the city lay in Arab territory, he managed to locate the documents and acquire them for the university. The date of the sale, according to Sukenik, was November 29, 1947, the very day on which the United Nations voted to partition Palestine and create the state of Israel.

After the departure of the British, East Jerusalem became a virtual battle zone. By that time, however, Samuel had arranged for three of the four scrolls at St. Mark's to be photographed by John Trever, a young scholar attached to the American School of Oriental Research in Jerusalem, who identified one of the manuscripts as a copy of the Book of Isaiah. In superb condition, it was written in a script that predated the oldest known sample of biblical Hebrew, which dated from the second century C.E. Trever mailed one of his photographs to W. F. Albright of Johns Hopkins University, a leading expert on ancient writing, who confirmed that he had stumbled upon the greatest manuscript discovery of the 20th century.

While Sukenik was negotiating with Samuel to buy the four scrolls in his possession for Hebrew University, the archbishop sold the American School the publication rights to the photographs of the documents, whereupon he left for the United States with the originals in mid-1948, eventually taking up residence in Hackensack, New Jersey. As Jordan (in whose domain Qumran and Jerusalem lay) and Israel bickered over which country had a proper claim to Jewish antiquities, the scrolls toured America, including the Library of Congress. Samuel, who could not return to Jerusalem because he was persona non grata with the Jordanian government, tried without success to sell the scrolls to Harvard and Duke universities. In mid-1954, he placed an advertisement in *The Wall Street Journal* that described the documents as "an ideal gift to an educational or religious institution." Working through an American intermediary, Sukenik's son, Yigael Yadin, bought the scrolls on behalf of the Israeli government, persuading the archbishop to drop his asking price from $1,000,000 to $250,000. Although the money was designated for the "Archbishop Samuel Trust" to aid Syrian Orthodox churches, the legal papers were not properly drawn. The U.S. Internal Revenue Service took the position that the amount was Samuel's personal income and ended up with most of it.

The seven documents from the original Bedouin discovery, together with a copper-foil scroll listing the treasures of the Jerusalem Temple that had been found in another Qumran cave in 1952, and a ninth manuscript, the *Temple Scroll,* which was spirited into private hands and confiscated in Bethlehem by Yadin after the Six Day War of 1967, are the only intact texts to have emerged from Wadi Qumran. The rest of the material, from a total of 11 different caves in the area, consists of fragments of more than 800 different documents in Hebrew, Aramaic, and Greek (in one, Cave 7). Approximately one-fourth are complete or partial versions of every book of the Hebrew Bible except Esther, together with Hebrew and Aramaic transcriptions of several works of Old Testament Apocrypha and Pseudepigrapha. The rest of the manuscripts were most likely composed by the Qumran sect itself. Archaeologists also excavated the ruin, Khirbet Qumran, which proved to be the remains of a large communal settlement that may well have been an Essene monastery. (Certain scholars maintain, however, that the Qumran residents were not Essene, but rather Sadducees or Zealots; Norman Golb of the University of Chicago believes that the Qumran library actually came from Jerusalem, and thus represented mainstream Judaism.) During the 1960s, architectural teams lead by Yadin also unearthed troves of documents (including Qumran sectarian texts) at Masada, the rebel fortress that fell to the Romans in 73 C.E., and caches of religious and secular writings connected to the Bar Kokhba rebellion in a series of caves south of Qumran.

From the very beginning, researchers hoped that the Dead Sea Scrolls would reveal the key to the historical Jesus and Christian origins. Among the first experts to examine the manuscripts was André Dupont-Sommers, who announced in 1950 that he had found a template for Jesus at Qumran. One of the scrolls that had been photographed by Trever was an interpretation, or *pesher,* of the Book of Ḥabakkuk, one of the prophets of the Hebrew Bible. The *Ḥabakkuk Commentary,* as it came to be known, referred to a "Teacher of Righteousness" who preached penitence and love of one's neighbor but was persecuted and killed by a "Wicked Priest." The author of the commentary believed that these events had fulfilled certain of Ḥabakkuk's prophecies.

The "Teacher of Righteousness," and his enemy, the "Man of Scoffing," had also figured in a tattered medieval codex called the *Damascus Document,* which had been discovered in 1897 by Cambridge University Talmudic scholar Solomon Schechter (a good friend of Claude Montefiore) inside the *genizah,* or repository for disused holy writings, of a centuries-old synagogue in Cairo. Coincidentally, several of the Qumran caves excavated in 1952 also contained fragments of the *Damascus Document,* which described a communal Jewish brotherhood of the Second Temple era and its flight to Damascus after persecution by Jewish leaders in Jerusalem. The *Damascus Document* and the *Ḥabakkuk Commentary* seemed to refer to the same group, as did another of Samuel's scrolls, dubbed by scholars the *Manual of Discipline,* which was a series of moral teachings and rules for monastic living. Finally, one of the scrolls that Sukenik had purchased from the Bedouins in 1947 (later known as the *War Scroll*) described an eschatological war between the "Sons of Light," who appeared to be the Qumran community, and the "Sons of Darkness," an alliance of Jerusalem enemies that possibly included the Romans.

The pottery and coins discovered at Khirbet Qumran indicate that in all probability its earliest settlement occurred between 140 and 100 B.C.E. (Its last period of occupation was most likely around 70 C.E., the year in which the Romans destroyed the Jerusalem Temple, and the Qumran residents hid their scrolls before abandoning their settlement or being forcibly dispersed.) The allusions to an intra-Jewish conflict contained in the *Ḥabakkuk Commentary,* the *Damascus Document,* and the *War Scroll* could possibly have stemmed from the claim of Hasmonean kings of Judea during the late second century B.C.E. that they were high priests as well as secular rulers, which contravened the First Temple tradition in which all high priests were descendants of Zadok, the high priest of King David. The *Damascus Document* refers to the "sons of Zadok," and the *Manual of Discipline* speaks of the coming of a priest-Messiah as well as a royal Messiah. For these reasons, most scholars have assumed that the "Wicked Priest" was one of the Hasmonean kings, probably the ruthless Alexander Jannaeus, and the "Teacher of Righteousness" was the priest-founder of the Qumran community, evidently of the Zadokite line.

Several of the scrolls and scroll fragments reflect tantalizing parallels to Christian beliefs and practices. The *Manual of Discipline* in particular refers to "living water," to a "new covenant," to communally held possessions, to a sacred meal of bread and wine, and to the return of the "Teacher of Righteousness" as Messiah. One of the most extraordinary of the fragments, nine double-columned lines of Aramaic discovered in Cave 4 in 1952, links together the prophet Daniel, the "Spirit," an eschatological battle in which God will prevail, and amazingly, a figure identified with the Messiah who "will be called the son of God; they will call him the son of the Most High."[46] As early as 1910, shortly after Schechter had published the Cairo text of the *Damascus Document,* certain experts were speculating that the first Christians had modeled Jesus after the "Teacher of Righteousness," while others maintained that John the Baptist was the "Teacher," and that the "Man of Scoffing" was Paul, the villain who had Hellenized Christianity.

Dupont-Sommers was merely propagating a more sophisticated version of these turn-of-the-century speculations when he claimed to have found intimations of Jesus' crucifixion in the *Ḥabakkuk Commentary*. "The Galilean Master, as he is presented to us in the writings of the New Testament, appears in many respects as an astonishing reincarnation of [the Teacher of Righteousness]," he wrote in a 1950 essay.[47] "Like him He was the object of the hostility of the priests, the party of the Sadducees. Like him He was condemned and put to death. Like him He pronounced judgement on Jerusalem, which was taken and destroyed by the Romans for having put Him to death. Like him, at the end of time, He will be the supreme judge."[48]

While most of Dupont-Sommers's colleagues disputed his interpretation of the *Ḥabakkuk Commentary*, the literary critic Edmund Wilson's widely read *New Yorker* article and best-selling book titled *The Scrolls from the Dead Sea* (1955) hinted—misleadingly—that certain other scholars were coming around to the Dupont-Sommers version of the origins of Christianity. In portentous language Wilson adopted Dupont-Sommers's theories about Qumran: "The monastery, this structure of stone that endures, between the bitter waters and the precipitous cliffs, with its oven and its inkwells, its mill and its cesspool, its constellation of sacred fonts and the unadorned graves of its dead, is perhaps, more than Bethlehem or Nazareth, the cradle of Christianity."[49] Wilson regarded the Dead Sea texts as a grave threat to the uniqueness of Jesus and hoped that increasing numbers of experts would join Dupont-Sommers in viewing Christianity as merely a rogue offshoot of the Essenes, who were themselves a rogue branch of Judaism.

To this day, the majority of researchers have declined to walk down Dupont-Sommers and Wilson's road, arguing that although there are startling similarities between Christian and Qumran theological vocabularies and eschatological outlooks (along with some probable direct borrowing by Christians of Qumran's ecclesial organization), their teachings show significant divergences as well. The Christian doctrine of atonement, for example, is completely missing from Qumran, as is Jesus' concern for the plight of sinners. There is, however, general agreement that Christianity and the Qumran sect drew on some of the same Second Temple Jewish religious imagery.

Thus far, the caves have produced no undisputedly Christian texts. The only possible texts of Christian provenance are a few scraps of Greek-language papyrus from Cave 7. In 1972, José O'Callaghan, a Spanish priest and papyrologist, identified fragment 7Q5 as part of two lines from the Gospel of Mark, written in a Greek script that dated no later than 50 C.E. If correct, O'Callaghan's conclusions about 7Q5 would be revolutionary. Indeed, if Mark actually wrote his Gospel less than 20 years after Jesus' death, many of the "layering" theories of form and redaction criticism would be totally invalidated. It should be noted, however, that O'Callaghan's entire hypothesis is based on no more than a few nearly illegible letters in a minuscule fragment. Moreover, only a handful of scholars agree with his readings. Others of his New Testament identifications among Cave 7 fragments have engendered even less enthusiasm.

Despite the consensus among Christian and Jewish scholars that the Dead Sea Scrolls are far more informative about first-century Judaism than about Jesus, several experts have continued to insist that they contain certain materials pertaining to the Nazarene that avowedly Christian researchers have conspired to suppress, citing in particular a scandalous delay in printing some of the scroll contents, which they view as a Vatican cover-up. The scandal is real enough: It has taken some 50 years for the entire manuscript contents of the Qumran caves to be published. Until the late 1980s, only half of the texts had appeared in print.

The reasons for this state of affairs are somewhat complex. Of the more than 500 texts recovered from Cave 4, not a single one was intact. Instead, they lay in a jumble of about 15,000 fragments, some of which were as small as computer chips. As the Jordanian government refused to allow Jewish scholars to work on manuscripts located in its jurisdiction, in 1956 a consortium of foreign archaeological schools located in East Jerusalem bought the Cave 4 cache from the Bedouin with funds provided by the Vatican (which has ties to the École Biblique) and other sources. Under the supervision of Jordan's Department of Antiquities, the documents were moved to what is now the Rockefeller Museum in East Jerusalem, where Roland de Vaux, a priest-scholar from the École Biblique, assembled a team of experts, most of whom were Catholic priests, to piece them together for eventual publication. Even after the Israelis seized the Old City during the Six Day War, they chose not to alter the all-Gentile composition of the Cave 4 team.

As the decades passed, very few of the Cave 4 manuscripts saw publication, which meant that they were inaccessible to other scholars. Upon his death in 1971, de Vaux himself left behind a mass of unpublished data. Others in the group developed drinking and other problems that impaired their ability to work. The most dilatory editor of all was a Polish cleric named Jozef T. Milik, who was a genius at correlating the tiniest of scroll particles. When he abandoned the priesthood for marriage and life in Paris after the Second Vatican Council, he also neglected to finish his assignment. In contrast to the Nag Hammadi situation, where the United Nations had been able to break the scholarly embargo during which manuscripts had gone unpublished for more than three decades, the complexities of Arab-Israeli geopolitics made it impossible for the organization to intervene in Jerusalem.

In 1987, John Strugnell of the Harvard Divinity School, the new chief editor of the Cave 4 project, invited more than half a dozen prominent Israeli and American Jewish scholars to work along with him. He also managed to persuade Milik to part with about a third of his unpublished hoard so that other experts could take over, and accelerated the editing timetable. Most significant, he released for limited publication a concordance to the scrolls that allowed other researchers to explore what the still unpublished manuscripts contained. In the end, however, Strugnell was beset by some of the same problems that had plagued his predecessors, as well as a few of his own, including alcohol, separation from his wife, and episodes of extreme depression.

In 1990, Israel's Antiquities Authority appointed Hebrew University professor Emmanuel Tov as co-editor-in-chief of the project. At about the same time, Strugnell, who was a Catholic convert, gave a highly publicized interview to a Tel Aviv newspaper in which he described Judaism as "a horrible religion" because it had not accepted Christ, adding that he was "against the state of Israel as a political question."[50] At the request of Strugnell's colleagues, the Authority removed him from the top position, although not from the team itself. It was later revealed that despite his professional openness toward Jews, Strugnell had a reputation at the Museum for anti-Semitic ragging. He and certain other Catholics on the Cave 4 team, who had maintained a running rivalry with Yadin and other Israeli scroll experts, had refused to enter Jewish West Jerusalem or otherwise recognize post-1967 Israeli jurisdiction over the city.

In the meantime, outside experts had begun running the concordance through their computers in order to reconstruct the unpublished Cave 4 manuscripts and break the Jerusalem monopoly. Photographs of other Cave 4 documents mysteriously appeared, a number of which were published by the Biblical Archaeology Society in Washington, D.C. The new Cave 4 team wrested even more texts from Milik, and the entire contents of Cave 4 were finally released to the public.

The tale of Cave 4, with its mix of scholarly malfeasance, political squabbling, and religious bigotry, was a motherlode of source-material for those who were convinced that the Catholic Church was working covertly to hinder publication of Dead Sea Scrolls data that undermined Christian beliefs. In 1991, two British journalists, Michael Baigent and Richard Leigh, published *The Dead Sea Scrolls Deception,* which took sinister note of the large number of Catholics on the original team and pointed out that the École Biblique was closely affiliated with the Pontifical Biblical Commission. The commission's head was Cardinal Joseph Ratzinger, a staunch theological conservative who was close to the equally conservative Pope John Paul II. Ratzinger's other role as head of the Congregation for the Doctrine of the Faith, the modern successor to the Inquisition, only fed fuel to the fire. Leigh insisted that de Vaux and his colleagues had done away with incriminating Qumran documents, and that the unpublished Cave 4 material contained disturbing information about Jesus that Catholic authorities were determined to squelch.

Along with a third writer named Harry Lincoln, Baigent and Leigh had already published their own ideas about the historical Jesus in two books, *Holy Blood, Holy Grail* (1982) and *The Messianic Legacy* (1986). Like Karl Friedrich Bahrdt, Karl Venturini, Friedrich Schleiermacher, and Hugh Schonfeld—as well as Robert Graves in his *Nazarene Gospel Restored* and D. H. Lawrence in his novel *The Man Who Died*—the three authors believed that Jesus had survived his crucifixion. Their particular theory was that Jesus had married Mary Magdalene and fled with her to the south of France, where he had founded the Merovingian dynasty, which ruled France until the rise of Charlemagne. They further contended that a shadowy French organization called the "Prieuré de Sion," whose goal was to restore the Merovingian monarchy (its last active king, Dagobert I, had died in 639), was the actual lineal successor to Jesus and his band of disciples. Although it was a secret society, over the centuries the Prieuré's membership had possibly included such notable artistic and political names as Leonardo da Vinci, Victor Hugo, André Malraux, Charles de Gaulle, and Jean Cocteau, according to the three authors.

Perhaps the weakest point in the Baigent-Leigh-Lincoln argument involved a Provençal count named Pierre Plantard de Saint-Clair, whom they had identified as one of the last living descendants of Jesus. However, the so-called Saint-Clair may well have been a commoner named Pierre Plantard, who had concocted the Prieuré himself during the 1950s. In any case, the trio of journalists concluded that there had to be a French connection: As Jesus had originally been a member of the Qumran community, his teachings lived on, not only among the Ebionites (who the successors of Qumran)and at the Prieuré, but also in Celtic Christianity. Baigent and Leigh worked their theory that Jesus had lived at Qumran into *The Dead Sea Scrolls Deception*.

Another dissident scholar, Robert Eisenman, a professor of Middle Eastern religions at California State University–Long Beach, also became convinced that the Catholic papyrologists at the École Biblique were concealing information about the Qumran sect and its relationship to Jesus. Eisenman was certain, for example, that the then-unpublished fragments of the *Damascus Document* found in Cave 4 contained explicit references to New Testament figures and Pauline theology. At one time a leading figure in the breaking of the Jerusalem embargo on the Cave 4 fragments, including the forwarding of photographs of unpublished texts (whose provenance he has never revealed) to the Biblical Archaeology Society, in 1990 Eisenman took a group of his students to Qumran to search for their own scroll fragments (the group apparently came home empty-handed).

Eisenman's theories wove Jesus and the Ebionites into the struggle between the "Teacher of Righteousness" and the enemies alluded to in the *Damascus Document,* the *Ḥabakkuk Commentary*, and other Qumran writings. In his view (which was also adopted by Baigent and Leigh in *The Dead Sea Scrolls Deception*), these documents referred not to events during the reign of the Hasmonean kings, but rather to early Christian disputes centered on James, described as the "brother of the Lord" in the New Testament, whom many

Ebionite promoters had identified as the Qumran sect's founder. The "Wicked Priest" was Ananus, the high priest of Jerusalem whom Josephus reported as having ordered James's execution.

Paul of Tarsus was also to be found at Qumran, according to Eisenman, as the figure that the *Ḥabakkuk Commentary* identifies as "the Liar," because he had attempted to turn Jesus into a god. Moreover, James, his brother Jesus, John the Baptist, and even Judas Maccabeus and the prophet Ezra had all belonged to a "Zadokite" sect that became the Jesus movement during the first century under James's leadership. (The Zadokites, according to Eisenman, were militant anti-Roman nationalists like the rebels of Masada, devoted to the Torah and haunted by messianic apocalypticism, in contrast to the pacifist and cosmopolitan Gentile churches that Paul had founded.) In light of the above, Eisenman theorized that the Catholic-dominated first generation of Qumran scholars had "safely" dated the *Damascus Document* and the *Ḥabakkuk Commentary* more than two centuries before Jesus' time—dates that were blatantly fraudulent.

So confident was Eisenman of his theory about the deliberate misdating of the Dead Sea documents that he petitioned the Israeli Department of Antiquities in 1989 to perform state-of-the-art carbon-14 testing. The test results, which were made public in 1991, showed instead that most of the documents in question dated to the second and first centuries B.C.E. (just as the earlier scholars had contended) with only one text dating to the period after Jesus' birth. These negative findings did not faze Eisenman in the least. "[The testing] process is still in its infancy, subject to multiple variables, and too uncertain to be applied with precision to the kind of materials we have before us," he wrote in a 1992 book titled *The Dead Sea Scrolls Uncovered.*[51] "As always in this field, one is finally thrown back on the areas of literary criticism, textual analysis, and a sure historical grasp—debatable enough quantities in any field—to make determinations of this kind," he added.[52] Such statements prompted Geza Vermes, who did not sign onto Eisenman's theories, to remark dryly: "No further comment is required."[53] One of the unpublished Qumran texts that Eisenman had hoped would name New Testament figures turned out only to list Hasmonean monarchs.

Eisenman is not the only Dead Sea dissident to have interpreted the Scrolls as cryptograms about Jesus. In 1992, Barbara Thiering, an academic attached to the University of Sydney in Australia, published *Jesus and the Riddle of the Dead Sea Scrolls,* in which she also assigned later dates to the *Ḥabakkuk Commentary,* certain of the other biblical commentaries, and the *Temple Scroll* in particular, in order to make them products of the Herodian/Roman period of Jesus' birth and death. Thiering concluded that the "Teacher of Righteousness" was John the Baptist, and that Jesus was the "Wicked Priest." According to her reading, Jesus married Mary Magadalene, with whom he had three children; after surviving his crucifixion (not in Jerusalem but at Qumran), he divorced her to marry another woman, named Lydia. He then traveled around the Mediterranean in the company of Peter and Paul until he arrived in Rome, where he died of natural causes at age 70.

The most outrageous Dead Sea readings of all have come from John M. Allegro, an Englishman who was the only agnostic on the 1950s Cave 4 team (there was also a single Protestant, Frank Moore Cross of McCormick Theological Seminary and later Harvard University). Allegro managed to alienate his Jerusalem colleagues in an incident involving the *Copper Scroll,* which had been sent to the Manchester College of Technology in 1955 for opening and photographing. Milik, who held the formal publication rights to the scroll, was scheduled to bring out an edition during the early 1960s. Allegro took it upon himself to rush off to Manchester, where he observed the sawing open of the scroll in 1955 and 1956. After publishing his own unauthorized edition of the *Copper Scroll* in 1960, two years before Milik's official version emerged, he went back to Jerusalem to hunt for the treasure listed in it, which further irritated his colleagues.

Although Allegro was the only member of the Jerusalem team to publish his entire assignment on time (in 1968), Strugnell considered his scholarship so poor that he issued a set of corrections that was more than 100 pages long. While nearly all scrolls scholars both on and off the team have agreed that Strugnell's criticisms were justified, certain of them, including Eisenman, insist that Strugnell had a personal vendetta against Allegro, who constantly twitted him about the scrolls' potential to demolish his Catholic faith.

In 1970, Allegro published *The Sacred Mushroom and the Cross,* a true collector's item for aficionados of the search for the historical Jesus. Allegro contended that Jesus was not a human being, but rather a mushroom. More specifically, he was a psilocybin-like species known as *Amanita muscaria,* which produces hallucinations when ingested. As this rodlike fungus with a brilliant red cap flecked with white specks is an obvious phallic symbol, Allegro decided that it had been the center of a Near Eastern congeries of drug and fertility cults, including Judaism and Christianity, which involved ritualistic copulation and the shedding of menstrual blood in the fields to ensure an abundant harvest.

Along the same line, Allegro surmised that the Jewish revolt against Rome in 66 C.E. was probably drug-induced. He also associated the Sumerian phoneme "U" with fertility rites, maintaining that *Yehoshua,* the ancient Hebrew form of Jesus' name, was derived from the Sumerian *"IA-U=shU-A"* (which contained two U-phonemes). Jesus and the Israelite hero Joshua, as well as the Greek god Dionysius (whose name also contained two U-phonemes), were therefore cultic divinities associated with tumescence. Accordingly, the blood-stained lintels of the first Jewish Passover celebrated menstruation, Easter was an erection festival, the Lord's Prayer was an orgasmic wail, and the Messiah, or "Anointed One," was actually smeared with either real or simulated semen.

Allegro viewed both the Jewish sacrificial rites on the Day of Atonement (prescribed in the Book of Leviticus) and the Catholic Mass as recapitulations of primeval Canaanite sacred fornication. In the words of his X-rated exegesis: "The priest, dressed as a penis, anointed with the various saps and resins as representing the divine semen, enters through the doors of the Porch, the 'labia' of the womb, past the veil or 'hymen' and so into the Hall."[54] The early Christians, who had invented the human being Jesus and his death on the cross as a hoax in order to hide their mushroom-worship from the Romans, over time had come to believe the stories they had concocted. In his 1979 book *The Dead Sea Scrolls and the Christian Myth,* Allegro further elaborated the relationship between Christianity and cultic sex, finding connections between the Essenes of Qumran and the more libertine branches of the Gnostics, and hypothesizing à la Morton Smith that the baptismal rituals of both Essenes and Gnostics involved ejaculatory fluid rather than water.

In any case, one need not agree with Allegro that early Christianity consisted of ceremonial orgies, or with Thiering that the Dead Sea Scrolls reveal that Jesus was divorced, or with Eisenman that the Dead Sea community represented early Christianity, in order to glean from the scrolls how deeply rooted the first Christians' theological language and cultic life were in the Judaism of their time. The angel Gabriel's prophecy to Mary in Luke's Gospel, "The Holy Spirit will come upon you, and the power of the Most High will overshadow you; therefore the child to be born will be holy; he will be called Son of God,"[55] does not derive from a Greek myth. The evangelist John did not draw on Gnostic dualism when he wrote of the cosmic contrast between light and darkness: "The light shines in the darkness, and the darkness did not overcome it."[56] The imagery of both these Gospel texts is similar enough to that of the scrolls to have sprung from the same font of Jewish religiosity.

The Christian sacraments of eucharist and baptism also have parallels at Qumran. Moreover, Otto Betz of the University of Tübingen believes that John the Baptist lived at Qumran for a while. A passage from the *Temple Scroll* may be able to shed light on the charges of blasphemy that prompted Jesus' crucifixion: "If a man slanders his people and delivers his people to a foreign nation and does evil to his people, you shall hang him on a tree and he shall die."[57] If Norman Golb is correct in assuming that the Dead Sea Scrolls represent a mainstream pre-70 Jewish library, it is easy to imagine how Qumran's religious typology might have been part of the spiritual background of many Jews of Jesus' time. Both Josephus and Philo testify that there were Essenes throughout Palestine, and the existence of an "Essene Gate" in one of Second Temple Jerusalem's walls might indicate that substantial numbers of Essenes lived there as well. The Qumran community might not have been a paranoid sect but instead an eccentric yet widely respected religious institution analogous to clusters of distinctively garbed monks or holy men in other religious traditions. The Qumranites' soaring apocalyptic imagery and their hope for immediate deliverance by God might have been on the minds of more than a few Jews in Roman-occupied Palestine. Finally, the large and variegated library of spiritual documents at Qumran makes one wonder whether the physically and spiritually isolated early Christian communities envisioned by the form and redaction critics—each devoted to a single religious text—had any basis in first-century Palestinian reality.

The discovery of the Dead Sea Scrolls forces one to contemplate Jesus' relationship to Judaism in a far more sophisticated way than either the new-questers or most of the Jewish reclaimers have done. In his critique of Paul Winter's book, David Catchpole pointed out that the reclaimers who had transformed Jesus into a modern-sounding liberal rabbi had failed to take into account "one basic fact: Jesus stood in tension with Judaism."[58] He chided Gentile scholars for failing to illuminate this tension without making a caricature out of Judaism.

However, there has existed a tradition of against-the-grain Jesus-research since the early part of this century whose objective is precisely to shed light on Jesus' complex relationship with Judaism. In 1922, the German scholars Hermann L. Strack and Paul Billerbeck published a massive commentary on the New Testament that used rabbinic writings to elucidate certain customs and religious practices referred to in the Gospels. Although their approach was wrongheaded (today's scholars take the opposite tack in employing the New Testament to illuminate first-century events referred to in rabbinic documents), they were pioneers in the examination of Jesus' Jewish world. Ernst Lohmeyer, another early-20th-century German scholar, adopted a moderate version of form criticism that tried to place the original "forms" of the Gospel stories in a specifically Aramaic-speaking context rather than resorting to theoretical presumptions about how early Christian communities might have developed. While Norman Perrin's mentor at Göttingen, Joachim Jeremias, participated in the New Quest, in essence he was looking for sayings of Jesus that also reflected Aramaic speech-patterns.

There has also been a recent effort to acknowledge the Jewishness—and historicity—of John's Gospel. Since the 19th century, it has been commonplace to regard the Fourth Gospel as a theological essay rather than a work of history. For Rudolf Bultmann, John's Gospel was pure *kerygma,* the point at which the pre-Christian Gnostic redeemer myth finally settled into Christianity, while for the new-quester Ernst Käsemann, John's Gospel presented a thoroughly bloodless and unhuman Jesus.

For many of the Jewish reclaimers of Jesus, John's Gospel is merely Pauline theology in narrative form. For the Jesus Seminar, John's Gospel is the stuff of consistently negative votes. In his *Community of the Beloved Disciple* (1979), Raymond Brown assumed that John's Gospel was no more than a history of the evangelist's church, and that the various disciples John had named stood for Christian communities with differing theologies from his own. Acting on the assumption that John's Gospel was a "layered" production similar to that of Q, another scholar, Robert Tompson Fortna, reconstructed one of its hypothetical sources of John in 1970 in a work titled "The Gospel of Signs."

Certain facts concerning John's Gospel have now become embarrassingly evident. For one thing, it was written in the late first century rather than the late second century, far earlier than most scholars had assumed. Second, John's knowledge of first-century Palestinian geography is detailed and complete. Whereas it was once more or less universally assumed that the "five porticos"[59] described by John as surrounding the pool of Beth-zatha (or Bethesda) in Jerusalem were strictly symbolic, excavations carried out during the 1950s unearthed not only the first-century pool but also the remains of the five porticos themselves. In other instances as well, John revealed himself as being highly familiar with the layout of Jerusalem and its environs. For a supposed Gentile Gnostic, he also proved to be extremely knowledgeable about Jewish religious practices and feast days. In 1963, the British scholar C. F. Dodd's *Historical Tradition in the Fourth Gospel* took detailed note of the Gospel of John's surprising historical meticulousness.

Then along came John A. T. Robinson. He had had a reputation as a religious skeptic in an Anglican mitre, and during the height of the "Death of God" movement in the 1960s, he had written a shocking book titled *Honest to God,* in which he claimed to prefer atheists to Christians who held superficial views about the deity. In 1985, however, he reversed his course with *The Priority of John,* which tore apart every fashionable assumption about Gospel composition that had ever prevailed (and still prevails) in New Testament circles. He characterized as ridiculous the form-critical dictum that "communities" had corporately composed the Gospels out of whole cloth. "The early Christian congregations are nowhere described in our sources as grey masses of unnamed equals," Robinson wrote. "Everywhere we see that certain persons have greater authority than others. And clearly one of the factors that gave a man authority in the early church was what he knew about Jesus."[60]

Robinson also concluded that John of Zebedee, the Galilean fisherman, had actually written the Gospel bearing his name. Everything seemed to fit: the grammatically correct but syntactically simplified schoolboy Greek the son of a successful tradesman would have learned in order to do business in a bilingual society; the vivid personalities and scenes of Palestinian life; the lingo of fish-wholesaling (John uses the word *ōpsaria* for cooked fish, in contrast to *ichthyes* for those that are still swimming, a distinction that modern Greek still preserves in the word *psaria*); and most of all, the genuine "feel" of some of the Fourth Gospel's scenes.

In the Gospel's epilogue (John 21), seven disciples go night-fishing in the Sea of Galilee after Jesus' resurrection and see their master standing on the beach just after daybreak. The apostle Peter gets so excited when he recognizes Jesus that he throws on some clothes (he is fishing naked), jumps off the boat, and wades ashore. While many scholars view the epilogue as an allegory about the early church, for Robinson it was "as vivid in its details of name and place and number as anything in this or any other Gospel." Moreover, he believed that John's chronology of Jesus' ministry was so precise that it was possible to figure out the year, the month, and sometimes even the day of the week in which many events had occurred, as evidenced by the wedding at Cana (where Jesus turned water into wine), which occurred "on the third day, without divulging the event that the three days were supposed to have followed."[61] Robinson surmised that "the third day" *(tēi hēmerai tēi tritēi)* actually meant Tuesday, a lucky day for weddings in the ancient world.

Robinson considered John's Gospel such a seamless, stylistically consistent narrative that it clearly had no written sources, and was probably a major source for the three Synoptics. While his adventurous redating of John has not found many scholarly takers, his fresh look at it as literature has persuaded many a lay reader that even if John's Gospel is fiction, it is realistic fiction of the highest order.

During the late 1960s, Martin Hengel, a colleague of Ernst Käsemann at Tübingen, launched a series of studies that dismissed the rigid distinctions between early Jewish and Hellenistic culture that had fueled so many of the "conflict models" of Christian origins, as the artificial constructs of certain scholars. Convinced that Hellenistic modes of thinking had penetrated every corner of Palestine, including Qumran, Hengel wrote:

> Since after a more than three-hundred-year history under the influence of Greek culture Palestinian Judaism can also be described as "Hellenistic Judaism," the term "Hellenistic" as currently used no longer serves to make any meaningful differentiation in terms of the history of religions within the history of earliest Christianity. . . . We must stop attaching either negative or positive connotations to the question of "Hellenistic" influence. It may again become popular to play off the (Old Testament) Jewish spirit against the Greek (and vice versa) but such evaluations do not get us any further. . . . We should therefore be more cautious in using the adjective "Hellenistic" in descriptions of earliest Christianity. It says too much, precisely because it says too little.[62]

Not only did Jews and Greeks live side by side in Palestine, especially in Galilee, but the predominance of Greek inscriptions in Jewish cemeteries, as well as Greek letters and documents found among the possessions of the Jews in the Bar Kokhba caves (including documents from the nationalist hero's own hand), indicates a high level of bilingualism during Jesus' time.

Hengel's studies paved the way for a new understanding of Paul of Tarsus that has come to regard his theology—and that of early Christianity itself—as specifically Jewish, rather than Gentile and "Hellenistic." In a 1990 treatise on Paul's conversion to Christianity, Alan Segal, a Judaic scholar at Barnard College, examined the sociological and psychological factors that might have prompted his joining the Christians. Segal concluded that Paul was essentially a mystic whose religious visions, including an ascension into heaven, paralleled the Merkavah mysticism of the early rabbis that the famous authority Gershom Sholem had explored. In worshipping Jesus as divine, Paul was simply drawing on the rich Jewish scriptural tradition of imagining God in human form or postulating an intermediary—an angel or an exemplary human being—as sitting on God's throne. "A human figure on the divine throne is described in Ezekiel 1, Daniel 7, and Exodus 24, among other places, and was blended into a consistent picture of a principal mediator figure who, like the angels of the Lord in Exodus 23, embodied, personified, or carried the name of God, YHWH, the tetragrammaton," Segal wrote, adding that "this figure, elaborated on by Jewish tradition, would become a central metaphor for Christ in Christianity."[63]

The religious themes that engrossed both Paul and the Merkavah mystics, including the figure who mediates between God and the human race and who is elevated to the divine throne and the sacred Tetragrammaton, all figure in that earliest extant Christian hymn that I cited in my introduction to this book. As N. T. Wright, an Oxford University scholar and dean of Lichfield Cathedral in England, has noted: "All early Christianity was Jewish Christianity. All early missionary work among Gentiles was undertaken by Jewish Christians. The decision not to require circumcision of Gentile converts has as much right to be labeled 'Jewish Christian' as does the position of those who bitterly opposed it."[64] Wright was arguing, *contra* the Ebionite revivalists, that there was no distinction between "Jewish Christians" and other kinds of early Christians.

Obviously, it was impossible for many first-century Jews to embrace the radical permutation of Judaism that early Christianity ultimately represented. The adoration of Jesus would have scandalized many Jews who viewed obedience to Torah as the heart of their religion. While early Christianity was as thoroughly Jewish as Merkavah mysticism, it also represented a radical break from Judaism by placing Jesus as Christ above Torah.

Jesus himself as presented in the Gospels embodied this paradox: He kept the Jewish law, and yet he was a radical figure within Judaism. As a teacher, he transmitted as many beautiful ethical insights as the rabbis (even speaking in parables, as they did, if the Gospels are correct), but he also abrogated to himself a frightening divine authority that placed him above—and in tension with—family, secular laws, and even Torah itself. As such, Jesus was not without parallels in Jewish religiosity. In the Hebrew Bible, figures like him are known as prophets. They were aware of being divinely inspired, they had reputations as miracle-workers (including raisings from the dead), they experienced visions filled with eschatological content (but were not deluded, as Albert Schweitzer had thought), they could be outcasts among their own people, even killed, and they could ascend directly to the kingdom of God, as Elijah had done. Jesus, of course, claimed to be more than a prophet, to play a sacrificial role as "ransom for many," but this, too, has extraordinary Jewish parallels in the Yom Kippur liturgy outlined in Leviticus.[65]

The "third quest" is essentially an effort to delineate a Jesus who worked in this mode, which seems truer to the context of his time and his place than the portrayal of the pallid, secularized figures who have so regularly emerged from the New Quest and the original German quest. The "third-questers" are a group of scholars of varying ideologies and religious affiliations, including Wright, Hengel, James H. Charlesworth of Princeton, E. P. Sanders of Duke, John P. Meier of the Catholic University of America, and Richard A. Horsley of the University of Massachusetts, all of whose depictions of Jesus are radically different from one another. Horsley's prophetic Jesus has a liberation-theology edge, while Sanders's is more Pharisaic: a Jesus who is killed because he took a public stand against Temple sacrifice. (Horsley and Sanders are also famous for their scholarly wrangles over social conditions in first-century Palestine.) Meier, a Catholic priest who "prescinds" from his faith when researching Jesus and tries to limn a consensus Jesus in his *A Marginal Jew* (1991 and 1994), has been criticized for trying to be too many things to too many people: Catholics, Protestants, Jews, agnostics, and atheists. Hengel's Jesus has a distinct—and very traditionalist—messianic consciousness. Nonetheless, the third-questers do agree on the historicity of much of the canonical Gospels as the creations of individuals who took an active interest in the narrative shape of Jesus' ministry and death, and who might have had access to eyewitnesses to his deeds.

In 1960, Alfred B. Lord, a professor of comparative literature at Harvard University, published a monograph titled *The Singer of Tales,* which was the product of years of research in the Balkans on the way in which long and complicated stories were transmitted intact, via formulaic passages, by the oral cultures of the 20th century. He concluded that the narrative methodology he had investigated yielded the clue to the composition of the *Iliad* and the *Odyssey.* Certain of the third-questers, in particular Wright and Horsley, have been exploring the possibility of applying Lord's theories of oral transmission to the Gospels to determine to what extent they preserve authentic memories—or very early legends—concerning a very tangible Jesus.

With its emphasis on the continuity between the Jewish worlds of Jesus and Paul and the Judaism-infused Christian theology of the crucified Messiah, the third quest seems to promise some results of lasting value—perhaps because it represents the full-circle return to which I alluded in my introduction. Jews and Christians will probably never reach a religious consensus on who Jesus *was,* but the importance placed by the third-questers on the ancient Jewish prophetic tradition offers a way in which Jews and Christians might reach a historical consensus on what Jesus *was like.* In the Gospels (specifically in Q), Jesus laments, "Jerusalem, Jerusalem, the city that kills the prophets and stones those who are sent to it!"[66] With this cry of prescient sorrow, Jews and Christians might reach some genuine reconciliation.

NOTES

INTRODUCTION

1. Deut. 21:23.
2. Phil. 1:2–6.
3. Isa. 53:5, 12.
4. Isa. 53:12, 45:23.
5. Gen. 1:2.
6. Dan. 7:13.
7. James H. Charlesworth, *Jesus within Judaism: New Light from Exciting Archaeological Discoveries* (Garden City, N.Y.: Doubleday, 1988), p. 31.
8. George Tyrrell, *Christianity at the Cross-Roads* (London: Longmans, Green, 1909), p. 44.

CHAPTER 1: JESUS' JEWISH WORLD

1. Tacitus, *Histories,* bk. 5, chap. 9, trans. Clifford H. Moore (Cambridge, Mass.: Harvard University Press and London: William Heinemann Ltd., 1931), 2:190–191.
2. Ibid., chap. 10, p. 193.
3. E. Mary Smallwood, *The Jews under Roman Rule: From Pompey to Diocletian* (Leiden: E. J. Brill, 1981), p. 16.
4. Meeks, Wayne A., *The First Urban Christians: The Social World of the Apostle Paul* (New Haven: Yale University Press, 1983), p. 17.
5. Luke 13:32.
6. See, for example, Burton L. Mack, *The Lost Gospel: The Book of Q and Christian Origins* (San Francisco: HarperCollins, 1993), pp. 58–59.
7. J. N. Sevenster, *Do You Know Greek? How Much Greek Could the First Jewish Christians Have Known?,* trans. J. de Bruin (Leiden: E. J. Brill, 1968), pp. 96–175.
8. E. P. Sanders, *Judaism: Practices and Beliefs, 63 BCE–66 CE* (London: SCM Press Ltd.; Valley Forge, Pa.: Trinity Press International, 1992), pp. 123–124.
9. Fernand Braudel, *The Mediterranean and the Mediterranean World in the Age of Philip II,* trans. Siân Reynolds (Berkeley: University of California Press, 1995), p. 234.
10. Seán Freyne, *Galilee from Alexander the Great to Hadrian, 235 B.C.E.. to 135 C.E.: A Study of Second Temple Judaism* (Wilmington, Del.: Michael Glazier; Notre Dame, Ind.: Notre Dame University Press, 1980), p. 174.
11. Joachim Jeremias, *Jerusalem in the Time of Jesus: An Investigation into Economic and Social Conditions during the New Testament Period,* trans. M. E. Dahl (Philadelphia: Fortress Press, 1969), p. 9.
12. E. P. Sanders, *Judaism: Practice and Belief, 63 BCE–66 CE* (London: SCM Press and Valley Forge, Pa.: Trinity Press International, 1994), p. 128.

13. Jacob Neusner, preface to *Judaisms and Their Messiahs,* ed. Jacob Neusner, William Scott Green, and Ernest S. Frerichs (Cambridge: Cambridge University Press, 1987), pp. xi–xii.
14. Josephus, *Jewish Antiquities,* vol. 17, trans. Ralph Marcus (Cambridge, Mass.: Harvard University Press and London: William Heinemann Ltd., 1965), 8:9.
15. Charlesworth, *Jesus within Judaism,* pp. 31–32.
16. Lester L. Grabbe, *Judaism from Cyrus to Hadrian* (Minneapolis: Fortress Press, 1992), 2:539.
17. Jacob Neusner, *From Politics to Piety: The Emergence of Pharisaic Judaism* (Englewood Cliffs, N.J.: Prentice-Hall, 1973), p. 152.
18. Ibid., p. 154.

CHAPTER 2: THE QUARRELS OF THE ANCIENTS

1. Minucius Felix, *The Octavius of Minucius Felix,* (9:5–6, trans. G. W. Clarke, in *Ancient Christian Writers: The Works of the Fathers in Translation,* no. 39 (New York and Paramus, N.J.: Newman Press, 1974), p. 65.
2. Ibid., 9:3, p. 65.
3. Suetonius, *Nero,* bk. 16, chap. 1, trans. J. C. Rolfe (Cambridge, Mass.: Harvard University Press and London: William Heinemann Ltd., 1979), 2:110–111.
4. *Annales,* bk. 15, chap. 44, in *Tacitus,* trans. John Jackson (Cambridge, Mass.: Harvard University Press and London: William Heinemann Ltd., 1981), 5:282–283.
5. *The Passing of Peregrinus,* 2:51, in *Lucian,* vol. 5, trans. A. M. Harmon (Cambridge, Mass.: Harvard University Press and London: William Heinemann Ltd., 1962), 14–15.
6. Origen, *Dialogue with Heraclides and His Fellow Bishops on the Father, the Son, and the Soul,* trans. Robert J. Daly, in *Ancient Christian Writers: The Works of the Fathers in Translation,* no. 54 (New York and Mahwah, N.J.: Paulist Press, 1992), p. 75.
7. *The First Apology,* chap. 22, in *The Writings of Saint Justin Martyr,* trans. Thomas B. Falls (New York: Christian Heritage, 1948), p. 58.
8. Matt. 1:23.
9. *Dialogue with Trypho,* chap. 67, in *The Writings of Saint Justin Martyr,* p. 254.
10. *Alexander, the False Prophet,* pp. 38–39, in *Lucian,* vol. 4, trans. A. M. Harmon (Cambridge, Mass.: Harvard University Press and London: William Heinemann Ltd., 1962), pp. 175–252.
11. Celsus, *On the True Doctrine,* trans. R. Joseph Hoffman (New York and Oxford: Oxford University Press, 1987), p. 37.
12. Ibid., p. 53.
13. Ibid., p. 57.
14. Ibid., p. 119.
15. Ibid., pp. 67–68.
16. Ibid., p. 64.
17. John 1:1, 14.
18. H. W. C. Frend, *The Rise of Christianity* (Philadelphia: Fortress Press, 1984), pp. 237–238.
19. Gal. 1:7.
20. 2 Cor. 11:13.
21. 2 John :7.
22. 1 John 1:7.
23. Tertullian, *Adversus Marcionem,* bk. 3, sec. 10, 11, ed. and trans. Ernest Evans (London and New York: Oxford University Press, 1972), p. 201.
24. "Apocalypse of Peter," trans. James Brashler, in *The Nag Hammadi Library in English,* ed. James M. Robinson (San Francisco: HarperCollins, 1990), p. 377.
25. Luke 2:52.
26. E. M. Forster, *Alexandria: A History and a Guide* (London: Michael Haag, 1982), pp. 80–81.
27. J. Stevenson, ed., *Creeds, Councils, and Controversies: Documents Illustrative of the History of the Church A.D. 337–461* (London: S.P.C.K., 1966), p. 337.

28. Edward Gibbon, *The History of the Decline and Fall of the Roman Empire,* ed. J. B. Bury (London: Methuen and New York: Doran, 1938), 2:352.
29. Adolf von Harnack, *History of Dogma,* trans. Neil Buchanan (New York: Dover, 1961), 1:330.
30. A. N. Wilson, *Jesus: A Life* (New York: Norton, 1992), p. 253.
31. Gregory of Nyssa, *On the Deity of the Son* (*Patrologia Gracea.,* xivi, 557B), quoted in Timothy Ware, *The Orthodox Church* (Harmondsworth: Penguin, 1982), p. 44.
32. Rowan A. Greer, "The Leaven and the Lamb: Christ and Gregory of Nyssa's Vision of Human Destiny," in *Jesus in History and Myth,* ed. R. Joseph Hoffmann and Gerhard A. Lance (Buffalo, N.Y.: Prometheus Press, 1986), pp. 170–171.
33. John of Damascus, "First Apology against Those Who Attack the Divine Images," in *On the Divine Image: Three Apologies against Those Who Attack the Divine Images,* trans. David Anderson (Crestwood, N.Y.: St. Vladimir's Seminary Press, 1980), p. 23.
34. Ware, *The Orthodox Church,* p. 41.
35. Stevenson, *Creeds, Councils,* p. 317.
36. V. A. Kolve, *The Play Called Corpus Christi* (Stanford: Stanford University Press, 1966), p. 174.
37. Thomas Aquinas, *Treatise on the Passion of Christ, Summa Theologica,* pt. III. Q. 46, art. 12, trans. Fathers of the English Dominican Provinces (Westminster, Md.: Christian Classics, 1981), p. 2271.
38. "The Dream of the Rood," in *Bright's Anglo-Saxon Reader,* rev. and enl. James R. Hulbert (New York: Holt, Rhinehart & Winston, 1964), p. 185.
39. Rosemary Woolf, "Doctrinal Influences in the Dream of the Rood," in *Art and Doctrine: Essays on Medieval Literature,* ed. Heather O'Donoghue (London and Ronceverte: Hambledon Press, 1986), p. 46.
40. Ignatius of Antioch, Letter to the Ephesians, chap. 19, in *Early Christian Writings: The Apostolic Fathers,* trans. Maxwell Staniforth (Harmondsworth: Penguin, 1968), p. 81.
41. Mircea Eliade, *Myth and Reality,* trans. Willard R. Trask (New York: Harper & Row, 1963), pp. 172–173.

CHAPTER 3: THE PARADIGM SHIFT

1. Albert Schweitzer, *The Quest of the Historical Jesus: A Critical Study of Its Progress from Reimarus through Wrede,* trans. W. Montgomery (London: A & C Black, Ltd. and New York: Macmillan, 1910), p. 1.
2. Ibid., p. 13.
3. *Reimarus: Fragments,* trans. Ralph S. Fraser and ed. Charles H. Talbert (Philadelphia: Fortress Press, 1970), p. 245.
4. Schweitzer, *Quest,* p. 15.
5. Robert W. Funk, Roy W. Hoover, and the Members of the Jesus Seminar, *The Five Gospels: The Search for the Authentic Words of Jesus* (New York: Macmillan, 1993), p. 2.
6. Ibid., pp. 6–7.
7. Peter Gay, ed., *The Enlightenment: A Comprehensive Anthology* (New York: Simon & Schuster, 1973), p. 145.
8. Peter Gay, ed., *Deism: An Anthology* (Princeton, N.J.: D. Van Nostrand, 1968), p. 10.
9. Thomas Chubb, *The True Gospel of Jesus Christ, Asserted* (London: Thomas Cox, 1735), p. 105.
10. William Baird, *History of New Testament Research,* vol. 1: *From Deism to Tübingen* (Minneapolis: Fortress Press, 1992), p. 55.
11. Rudolf Bultmann, *New Testament and Mythology and Other Basic Writings,* ed. and trans. Schubert M. Ogden (Philadelphia: Fortress Press, 1984), p. 4.
12. Jacques Ellul, *The New Demons,* trans. C. Edward Hopkin (New York: Seabury Press, 1975), p. 102.
13. Gotthold Lessing, "On the Proof of the Spirit and the Power," in *Lessing's Theological Writings,* trans. Henry Chadwick (Stanford: Stanford University Press, 1956), p. 52.
14. Charlotte Allen, "Away with the Manger," *Lingua Franca* 5, no. 2 (1995): 25.
15. Irenaeus, *Adversus Haereses* III.xi.8, quoted in Bruce Metzger, *The Canon of the New Testament: Its*

Origin, Development, and Significance (Oxford and New York: Oxford University Press, 1987), pp. 154–155.

16. Ibid., p. 313.
17. James L. Kugel and Rowan A. Greer, *Early Biblical Interpretation* (Philadelphia: Westminster Press, 1986), p. 200.
18. Hans Frei, *The Eclipse of Biblical Narrative: A Study in Eighteenth and Nineteenth Century Hermeneutics* (New Haven: Yale University Press, 1974), pp. 1–3.
19. Matt. 16:16.
20. Ibid., 17.
21. Augustine, *On the Harmony of the Gospels,* bk. 3, chap. 13, par. 43, trans. S. D. F. Salmond, ed. M. B. Biddle, in *A Select Library of the Nicene and Post-Nicene Fathers,* ed. Philip Schaff, vol. 6 (Grand Rapids, Mich.: William B. Eerdmans Publishing Company, 1980), p. 199.
22. Marshall McLuhan, *The Gutenberg Galaxy: The Making of Typographic Man* (Toronto: University of Toronto Press, 1962), pp. 105–107.

CHAPTER 4: THE TALK OF THE COFFEE HOUSES

1. Isaac Newton to Richard Bentley, 17 January 1793, in *The Correspondence of Isaac Newton,* ed. H. W. Turnbull (Cambridge: Cambridge University Press, 1961), 3:238.
2. Francis Bacon, *"Proem," The Great Instauration,* in *The New Organon and Related Writings,* ed. Fulton H. Anderson (Indianapolis: Bobbs-Merrill, 1960), p. 4.
3. Isaac Newton, *Opticks,* bk. 3, pt. 1 (New York: Dover, reprint ed., 1952), p. 405.
4. "Letter to Caroline, Princess of Wales, November 1715," in *The Leibniz-Clarke Correspondence,* ed. H. G. Alexander, quoted in Peter Gay, *The Enlightenment: An Interpretation,* vol. 2: *The Science of Freedom* (New York: Knopf, 1969), p. 143.
5. Psalm 139:13.
6. G. Lessing, *Lessing's Theological Writings,* trans. Henry Chadwick (Stanford: Stanford University Press, 1956), pp. 53, 55.
7. Voltaire, *Correspondence,* 5:281, quoted in Gay, *The Enlightenment,* 2:129.
8. Ibid., pp. 128–133.
9. Ibid., p. 128.
10. Ibid., p. 126.
11. Thomas Hobbes, *Leviathan,* pt. 1, chap. 13, ed. Robert Tuck (Cambridge and New York: Cambridge University Press, 1991), p. 89.
12. Ibid., pt. 2, chap. 19, p. 130.
13. Ibid., chap. 12, p. 79.
14. John Locke, *Two Treatises of Government,* bk. 1, chap. 6, sec. 58, ed. Peter Laslett (Cambridge: Cambridge University Press, 1967), p. 200.
15. Ibid., bk. 2, chap. 8, sec. 124, p. 348.
16. Ibid., chap. 5, sec. 36, p. 311.
17. Leo Strauss, *Natural Right and History* (Chicago: University of Chicago Press, 1971), p. 242.
18. Locke, *Two Treatises,* bk. 1, chap. 9, sec. 92, p. 227.
19. L. Strauss, *Natural Right and History* (Chicago: University of Chicago Press, 1953), pp. 242–243.
20. John Locke, *The Reasonableness of Christianity,* par. 178, ed. and abr. I. T. Ramsey (Stanford: Stanford University Press, 1958), p. 45.
21. Ibid., par. 245, p. 70.
22. Peter Gay, ed., *Deism: An Anthology* (Princeton, N.J.: D. Van Nostrand, 1968), p. 26.
23. John Toland, "Christianity Not Mysterious," in ibid., p. 61.
24. Ibid., pp. 63–64.
25. John Toland, *Nazarenus: Or Jewish, Gentile, and Mahometan Christianity* (London: J. Brotherton, J. Roberts, A. Dodd, 1720), p. vii.

26. Ibid., p. iii.
27. Anthony Collins, "A Discourse of Free-Thinking," in Gay, *Deism,* pp. 80–81.
28. Ibid., p. 80.
29. "Christianity As Old As the Creation," in ibid., p. 119.
30. Gay, ed., *Deism,* p. 24.
31. Thomas Woolston, *A Discourse on the Miracles of Our Saviour,* 6th ed. (London, 1728), p. iv.
32. Thomas Woolston, *Sixth Discourse on the Miracles of Our Saviour* (London, 1729), p. 33.
33. Thomas Chubb, "Of the Personal Character of Jesus Christ," in *The Posthumous Works of Thomas Chubb,* vol. 2, sec. 9 (London: R. Baldwin and Salisbury: E. Easton, 1748), p. 267.
34. Thomas Chubb, *The True Gospel of Jesus Christ Asserted* (London: Thomas Cox, 1737), p. 81.
35. Baron Paul Henri Thiry d'Holbach, *Systèmes de la nature,* in *The Enlightenment: A Comprehensive Anthology,* ed. Peter Gay (New York: Simon & Schuster, 1973), p. 108.
36. "What Is Enlightenment?" trans. Peter Gay, in Gay, *The Enlightenment: A Comprehensive Anthology,* p. 384.
37. Ibid., p. 389.
38. Charles H. Talbert, introduction to *Reimarus: Fragments,* trans. Ralph S. Fraser (Philadelphia: Fortress Press, 1970), p. 25.
39. Ibid., p. 69.
40. Ibid., p. 72.
41. Ibid., p. 141.
42. Ibid., p. 243.
43. Ibid., p. 62.
44. Ibid., p. 63.
45. Ibid., p. 232.
46. Julien Weill, "Un texte de Montesquieu sur le Judaïsme," quoted in Arthur Hertzberg, *The French Enlightenment and the Jews* (New York: Columbia University Press and Philadelphia: Jewish Publication Society of America, 1968), p. 275.
47. Voltaire, *Oeuvres complètes,* pp. 159–163, in ibid., pp. 302–303.
48. Marquis Jean Baptiste d'Argens, *Lettres juives,* in ibid., p. 279.
49. Rudolph Reuss, "L'antisémitisme dans le Bas-Rhin pendant la révolution," in ibid., p. 367.
50. Thomas Paine, "The Age of Reason," in Gay, *Deism,* p. 169.
51. Charles T. Cullen, ed., *Jefferson's Extracts from the Gospels: The Papers of Thomas Jefferson,* 2d series (Princeton: Princeton University Press, 1983), p. 409.
52. Ibid., p. 352.

CHAPTER 5: A GERMAN PHILOSOPHICAL HERO

1. Jean-Jacques Rousseau, *Emile* (New York: Dutton, 1974), p. 229.
2. Ibid., pp. 272–273.
3. Vincent A. McCarthy, *Quest for a Philosophical Jesus: Christianity and Philosophy in Rousseau, Kant, Hegel, and Schelling* (Mercer, Ga.: Mercer University Press, 1986), p. 31.
4. Ibid., p. 53.
5. Immanuel Kant, *Religion within the Limits of Reason Alone,* trans. Theodore M. Green and Hoyt H. Hudson (New York: Harper Torchbooks, 1960), p. 77.
6. Matt. 7:12; see also Luke 6:31.
7. Kant, *Religion.*
8. J. C. O'Neill, "The Study of the New Testament," in *Nineteenth-Century Religious Thought in the West,* eds. Ninian Smart, John Clayton, Steven Katz, and Patrick Sherry (Cambridge: Cambridge University Press, 1985), 2:143.
9. Ibid.
10. Daniel L. Pals, *The Victorian "Lives" of Jesus* (San Antonio: Trinity University Press, 1982), p. 140.
11. Johann Salomo Semler, *Treatise on the Free Investigation of the Canon,* quoted in Werner Georg Küm-

mel, *The New Testament: The History of the Investigation of Its Problems,* trans. S. McLean Gilmour and Howard C. Kee (Nashville: Abingdon Press, 1972), p. 63.

12. Johann Gottfried Eichhorn, *Introduction to the New Testament,* quoted in Kümmel, *New Testament,* p. 79.
13. Ibid., p. 101.
14. Johann Philipp Gabler, "On the Distinction between Exposition and Explanation, Illustrated by the Various Modes of Treatment of the Narrative of the Temptation of Jesus," quoted in Kümmel, *New Testament,* p. 103.
15. A. Schweitzer, *The Quest of the Historical Jesus,* trans. W. Montgomery (New York: Macmillan, 1910), p. 29.
16. Matt 5:4.
17. *History of the Last Three Years of the Life of Jesus,* quoted in Schweitzer, *Quest,* p. 30.
18. Johann Gottfried Herder, *Collected Works,* ed. B. Suphan, quoted in Kümmel, *New Testament,* p. 83.
19. Karl Hase, *Life of Jesus: A Manual for Academic Study,* trans. James Freeman Clarke (Boston: Walker, Wise, and Company, 1860), p. 201.
20. Ibid., p. 119.
21. Ibid., p. 160.
22. John 14:6.
23. Friedrich Schleiermacher, *The Life of Jesus,* trans. S. McLean Gilmour and ed. Jack C. Verheyden (Philadelphia: Fortress Press, 1971), p. 102.
24. Ibid., p. 205.
25. Ibid., p. 471.
26. Ibid., p. 428.
27. Ibid., p. 469.

CHAPTER 6: THE TRIUMPH OF MATERIALISM

1. Georg Wilhelm Friedrich Hegel, *Lectures on the Philosophy of Religion,* trans. R. F. Brown, Peter Hodgson, and J. M. Stewart, ed. Peter Hodgson (Berkeley: University of California Press, 1984), p. 122.
2. V. A. McCarthy, *Quest for a Philosophical Jesus* (Mercer, Ga.: Mercer University Press, 1986), p. 145.
3. Ferdinand Christian Baur, "Die Christuspartei in der korinthischen Germeinde, der Gegensatz des petrinischen und paulinischen Christenthums in der ältesten Kirche, der Apostel Petrus in Rom," in *Tübinger Zeitschift für Theologie,* vol. 4 in G. Kümmel, *The New Testament: The History of the Investigation of Its Problems,* trans. S. McLean Gilmour and Howard C. Kee (Nashville: Abingdon Press, 1972), pp. 129–130.
4. Ferdinand Christian Baur, *The Church History of the First Three Centuries,* trans. Allan Menzies (London: Williams and Norgate, 1878), 1:1.
5. Matt. 5:3.
6. Baur, *Church History,* 1:28–29.
7. Ibid., pp. 38, 41.
8. David Friedrich Strauss, *In Defense of My Life of Jesus against the Hegelians,* trans. and ed. Marilyn Chapin Massey (Hamden, Conn.: Archon Books, 1983), p. 6.
9. David Friedrich Strauss, *The Life of Jesus Critically Examined,* trans. George Eliot and ed. Peter C. Hodgson (Philadelphia: Fortress Press, 1972), p. 296.
10. A. Schweitzer, *Quest of the Historical Jesus,* trans. W. Montgomery (New York: Macmillan, 1910), p. 68.
11. Strauss, *Life of Jesus,* p. 445.
12. Ibid., p. 518.
13. Schweitzer, *Quest,* p. 89.
14. Strauss, *Life of Jesus,* p. 742.

15. Richard S. Cromwell, *David Friedrich Strauss and His Place in Modern Thought* (Fair Lawn, N.J.: Burdick, 1974), p. 218.
16. Johann August Neander, *The Life of Jesus Christ in Its Historical Connection and Historical Development,* trans. John McClintock and Charles E. Blumenthal (London: George Bell and Sons, 1892), p. 35.
17. Ibid., p. 81.
18. Gordon S. Haight, *George Eliot: A Biography* (New York: Oxford University Press, 1968), p. 42.
19. Ibid., p. 54.
20. Herbert Spencer, *Social Statics* (New York: Roger Schalkenbach Foundation, 1995), p. 60.

CHAPTER 7: A GOOD LIBERAL

1. Christian Hermann Weisse, *The Present Position of the Problem of the Gospels,* quoted in A. Schweitzer, *The Quest of the Historical Jesus,* trans. W. Montgomery (New York: Macmillan, 1910), p. 13.
2. Heinrich Julius Holtzmann, quoted in W. G. Kümmel, *The New Testament,* trans. S. McLean Gilmour and Howard C. McKee (Nashville: Abingdon Press, 1972), p. 152.
3. Ibid., p. 153.
4. Schweitzer, *Quest,* p. 206.
5. Theodor Keim, *The History of Jesus of Nazara: Considered in Its Connection with the National Life of Israel, and Related in Detail,* trans. Arthur Ransom and Edward Martin Geldart (London: Williams and Norgate, 1873–1881), 1:22.
6. Ibid., 3:x.
7. Julius Wellhausen, *Prologomena to the History of Israel* (Atlanta: Scholars Press, 1994), pp. 509, 510.
8. David Friedrich Strauss, *A New Life of Jesus* (London: Williams and Norgate, 1865), p. v.
9. Ibid.
10. Ibid., pp. 282–283.
11. Ibid., p. 282.
12. David Friedrich Strauss, *The Christ of Faith and the Jesus of History: A Critique of Schleiermacher's Life of Jesus,* trans. Leander E. Keck (Philadelphia: Fortress Press, 1971), pp. 167, 169.
13. David Friedrich Strauss, *The Old Faith and the New,* quoted in Horton Harris, *David Friedrich Strauss and his Theology* (Cambridge: Cambridge University Press, 1973), p. 241.
14. Karl Barth, *From Rousseau to Ritschl* (Philadelphia: Fortress Press, 1959), pp. 370–371.
15. Wilhelm Hermann, *The Communion of the Christian with God,* trans. J. Sandys Stanton (Philadelphia: Fortress Press, 1971), p. 79.
16. Adolf von Harnack, *What Is Christianity?* trans. Thomas Bailey Saunders (Philadelphia: Fortress Press, 1987), p. 38.
17. Ibid.
18. Gustav Frenssen, *Holyland,* trans. Mary Alice Hamilton (Boston: Dana Estes & Company and London: Archibald Constable & Company, 1906), pp. 287, 300.
19. Ibid., pp. 288, 300.
20. Alfred Loisy, *The Birth of the Christian Religion and the Origins of Christianity,* trans. L. P. Jacks (London: George Allen & Unwin Ltd., 1948), pp. 97–98.
21. Matthew Arnold, *Essays in Criticism,* quoted in Stephen Neill, *The Interpretation of the New Testament, 1861–1961* (London: Oxford University Press, 1964), p. 25.
22. Richard Davies Hanson, *The Jesus of History* (London: Williams and Norgate, 1869), p. xviii.
23. Shailer Mathews, *The Gospel and the Modern Man* (New York: Macmillan, 1910), p. 6.
24. Ibid.
25. S. Mathews, *The Social Teaching of Jesus: An Essay in Christian Sociology* (New York: Macmillan, 1897), p. 54.
26. Mathews, *The Gospel and the Modern Man,* pp. 104–105.
27. Walter Rauschenbusch, *The Social Principles of Jesus* (New York and London: Association Press, 1916), p. 91.

28. James E. Freeman, *The Man and the Master* (New York: Thomas Whittaker, 1906), p. 59.
29. Shirley Jackson Case, *Jesus: A New Biography* (1927; reprint ed., New York: Greenwood Press, 1968), p. 371.
30. Ibid., pp. 387, 429.
31. Lloyd C. Douglas, *The Robe* (Boston: Houghton Mifflin, 1944), p. 555.

CHAPTER 8: SEX AND DEATH FOR THE CINEMA

1. Ernest Renan, *The History of the Origins of Christianity, Book I: Life of Jesus,* trans. from the 13th edition (London: Mathieson & Company), p. 223.
2. Ibid., pp. 13–14.
3. H. W. Wardman, *Ernest Renan: A Critical Biography* (London: University of London Press, 1964), p. 77.
4. Charles Higham, *Cecil B. DeMille* (New York: Charles Scribner's Sons, 1973), p. 167.
5. Renan, *History,* p. 249.
6. Ibid.
7. Ibid., pp. 158–159.
8. E. Renan, *Letters from the Holy Land: The Correspondence of Ernest Renan with M. Berthelot While Gathering Material in Italy and the Orient for the "Life of Jesus,"* trans. Lorenzo O'Rourke (New York: Doubleday, Page, 1904), p. 176.
9. Renan, *Life of Jesus,* p. 23.
10. Ibid., pp. 129, 137.
11. Ibid., p. 96.
12. Ibid., p. 97.
13. Ibid., p. 111.
14. Daniel L. Pals, *The Victorian Lives of Jesus* (San Antonio: Trinity University Press, 1982), p. 38.
15. Renan, *Letters from the Holy Land,* p. 160.
16. Ibid.
17. Renan, *Life of Jesus,* pp. 321–322.
18. H. W. Wardman, *Ernest Renan,* pp. 54–55.
19. Ibid., p. 54.
20. Renan, *Life of Jesus,* p. 30.
21. Ibid.
22. Timothée Colani, "Examen de la vie de Jésus de M. Renan," quoted in A. Schweitzer, *Quest of the Historical Jesus,* trans. W. Montgomery (New York: Macmillan, 1910), p. 189.
23. Ibid., p. 182.
24. Camille Paglia, *Sexual Personae: Art and Decadence from Nefertiti to Emily Dickinson* (New Haven, Conn.: Yale University Press, 1990), p. 33.
25. Gustave Flaubert, *Madame Bovary,* trans. Francis Steegmuller (New York: Random House, 1957), p. 40.
26. "The First Epistle of Clement to the Corinthians," in *Early Christian Writings: The Apostolic Fathers,* trans. Maxwell Staniforth (Harmondsworth: Penguin, 1982), p. 26.
27. Eusebius, *The History of the Church,* trans. G. A. Williamson (Harmondsworth: Penguin, 1983), p. 200.
28. François-René de Chateaubriand, *The Genius of Christianity,* trans. Charles L. White (Baltimore: John Murphy & Co., 1875), p. xxx.
29. François-René de Chateaubriand, *The Martyrs,* trans. and ed. O. M. Wright (New York: Howard Fertig, 1976), p. vii.
30. Ibid., p. 390.
31. Ibid., p. 438.
32. Carl E. Schmöger, ed., *The Life of Our Lord and Saviour Jesus Christ, Combined with the Bitter Passion and*

the Life of Mary, from the Revelations of the Venerable Anna Catharina Emmerick as Recorded in the Journals of Clemens Brentano, translation (Fresno, Calif.: Academy Library Guild, 1954), 4:245–246.

33. Ibid., p. 273.
34. Edward Said, *Orientalism* (New York: Vintage Books, 1994), p. 98.
35. Ibid., p. 177.
36. Gustave Flaubert, "Notes de voyages," quoted in Benjamin Bart, *Flaubert* (Syracuse, N.Y.: Syracuse University Press, 1967), p. 220.
37. James Jacques Joseph Tissot, *Biblical Paintings* (New York: Jewish Museum, 1982), p. 25.
38. Ibid.
39. Ernest Renan, *The History of the Origins of Christianity, Book II: The Apostles,* translation (New York: Carleton, 1875), p. 119.
40. Ibid., *Book IV: Antichrist,* trans. and ed. Joseph Henry Allen (Boston: Roberts Brothers, 1897), pp. 151, 156, 157–158.
41. Gustave Flaubert, "Hérodias," in *Three Tales,* trans. A. J. Krailsheimer (New York: Oxford University Press, 1991), pp. 94–95.
42. Oscar Wilde, *De Profundis,* ed. Jacques Barzun (New York: Vintage Books, 1964), p. 117.
43. Ibid., pp. 113–114.
44. Helen Kazantzakis, ed., *Nikos Kazantzakis: A Biography Based on His Letters* (New York: Simon & Schuster, 1970), p. 136.
45. Ibid., p. 515.

CHAPTER 9: THE LIBERAL CHURCH CRUMBLES

1. Albert Kalthoff, *The Rise of Christianity,* trans. Joseph McCabe (London: Watts & Co., 1907), p. 187.
2. Ibid.
3. Ibid., p. 13.
4. Martin Kähler, *The So-Called Historical Jesus and the Historic Biblical Christ,* trans. Carl E. Braaten (Philadelphia: Fortress Press, 1964), p. 56.
5. Ibid., p. 57.
6. Ibid., p. 88.
7. Ibid., p. 51.
8. Ibid., p. 80.
9. Ibid., p. 26.
10. Johannes Weiss, *Jesus' Proclamation of the Kingdom of God,* trans. and ed. Richard Hyde Hiers and David Larrimore Holland (Philadelphia: Fortress Press, 1971), p. 132.
11. Ibid., p. 135.
12. Richard Reitzenstein, *The Hellenistic Mystery-Religions: Their Basic Ideas and Significance,* trans. John E. Steely (Pittsburgh: Pickwick Press, 1978), p. 496.
13. Wilhelm Bousset, *Kyrios Christos: A History of the Belief in Christ from the Beginnings of Christianity to Irenaeus,* trans. John E. Steely (Nashville: Abingdon Press, 1970), p. 155.
14. Wilhelm Wrede, *The Messianic Secret,* trans. J. C. G. Greig (London: James Clarke & Co., 1971), p. 236.
15. A. Schweitzer, *The Quest for the Historical Jesus,* trans. W. Montgomery (New York: Macmillan, 1910), p. 401.
16. Mark 10:45.
17. Schweitzer, *Quest,* pp. 368–369.
18. Hermann Gunkel, *The Psalms: A Form-Critical Introduction,* trans. Thomas M. Horner (Philadelphia: Fortress Press, 1967), passim.
19. Rudolf Bultmann, "The Significance of the Historical Jesus," *Faith and Understanding,* quoted in Alister E. McGrath, *The Making of Modern German Christology: From the Enlightenment to Pannenberg* (Oxford, New York: Basil Blackwell, 1986), p. 140.

20. Rudolf Bultmann, "On the Problem of Demythologizing," quoted in David Fergusson, *Bultmann* (Collegeville, Minn.: Liturgical Press, 1992).
21. 2 Cor. 5:17.
22. Rudolf Bultmann, *Jesus and the Word,* trans. Louise Pettibone Smith and Erminie Huntress Lantero (New York: Charles Scribner's Sons, 1958), p. 14.
23. Ibid., p. 14.

CHAPTER 10: AVANT-GARDE FASHIONS

1. Mark 7:15.
2. Günther Bornkamm, *Jesus of Nazareth,* trans. Irene and Fraser McLuskey with James M. Robinson (New York: Harper & Row, 1960), p. 26.
3. Ibid., p. 105.
4. Ibid., p. 24.
5. Ernst Fuchs, *Studies of the Historical Jesus,* trans. Andrew Scobie (Naperville, Ill.: Alec R. Allenson, 1964), p. 29.
6. Ibid., p. 31.
7. Gerhard Ebeling, *Word and Faith,* trans. James M. Leitch (London: SCM Press Ltd., 1963), p. 290.
8. Ibid., p. 303.
9. Rudolf Bultmann, *The History of the Synoptic Tradition,* in Heikki Raisanen, *The "Messianic Secret in Mark,"* trans. Christopher Tuckett (Edinburgh: T&T Clark Ltd., 1990), p. 3.
10. 2 Cor. 11:13.
11. Walter Bauer, *Orthodoxy and Heresy in Earliest Christianity,* trans. Philadelphia Seminar on Christian Origins (Philadelphia: Fortress Press, 1971), p. 77.
12. Ibid., p. 292.
13. "Gospel of Thomas," trans. Thomas O. Lambdin, in *The Nag Hammadi Library in English,* ed. James M. Robinson (San Francisco: HarperCollins, 1990), p. 126.
14. Ibid., p. 138.
15. James M. Robinson, *A New Quest of the Historical Jesus* (London: SCM Press, Ltd., 1971), p. 86.
16. Ibid., p. 93.
17. Norman Perrin, *Rediscovering the Teachings of Jesus* (New York: Harper & Row, 1967), p. 220.
18. Ibid., p. 246.
19. Ibid., p. 247.
20. Ibid., p. 248.
21. Norman Perrin, *What Is Redaction Criticism?* (Philadelphia: Fortress Press, 1969), p. 71.
22. Ibid.
23. Ibid.
24. Ibid.
25. J. A. Baker, *The Foolishness of God,* in John Hick, ed., *The Myth of God Incarnate* (Philadelphia: Westminster Press, 1977), p. 6.
26. Frances Young, "A Cloud of Witnesses," in Hick, *Myth,* p. 47.
27. Dennis Nineham, epilogue, in Hick, *Myth,* p. 202.
28. Mark 14:51.
29. Mark 14:13.
30. Morton Smith, *The Secret Gospel: The Discovery and Interpretation of the Secret Gospel According to Mark* (London: Victor Gollancz, 1974), pp. 112–113.
31. M. Smith, *Jesus the Magician* (San Francisco: Harper & Row, 1978), p. 146.
32. Matt. 6:24; Luke 16:13.
33. Matt. 11:5; Luke 7:22.
34. John S. Kloppenborg, *The Formation of Q: Trajectories in Ancient Wisdom Collections* (Philadelphia: Fortress Press, 1989), p. 27.
35. Luke 14:26; see also Matt. 10:37.

36. Luke 10:4; see also Matt. 10:9 and Mark 6:8.
37. David D. Gilmore, "Anthropology of the Mediterranean Area," quoted in John Dominic Crossan, *The Historical Jesus: The Life of a Mediterranean Jewish Peasant* (San Francisco: HarperCollins, 1992), p. 7.
38. Bruce J. Malina, *The New Testament World: Insights from Cultural Anthropology* (Louisville, Ky.: Westminster/John Knox Press, 1993), p. xii.
39. Max Weber, *The Sociology of Religion,* trans. Ephraim Fischoff (Boston: Beacon Press, 1964), p. 46.
40. Gerd Theissen, *Sociology of Early Palestinian Christianity,* trans. John Bowder (Philadelphia: Fortress Press, 1978), p. 8.
41. Matt. 5:44; Luke 6:27.
42. Luke 6:29; see also Matt. 5:39.
43. Robert W. Funk, Roy W. Hoover, and the Jesus Seminar, *The Five Gospels: The Search for the Authentic Words of Jesus* (New York: Macmillan, 1993), p. 32.
44. Ibid., p. 33.
45. Ibid.
46. Charlotte Allen, "Away with the Manger," *Lingua Franca* 5, no. 2 (1995): 25.
47. C. Allen, "Rising Son," *Lingua Franca* 5, no. 4 (1995): 5.
48. Robert Funk, *Honest to Jesus: Jesus for a New Millennium* (San Francisco: HarperCollins, 1996), p. 302.
49. Ibid., p. 314.
50. Burton L. Mack, *A Myth of Innocence: Mark and Christian Origins* (Philadelphia: Fortress Press, 1988), p. 62.
51. Ibid., p. 64.
52. Ibid., p. 73.
53. Ibid., p. 63.
54. B. Mack, *The Lost Gospel: The Book of Q and Christian Origins* (San Francisco: HarperCollins, 1993), p. 57.
55. Ibid., p. 9.
56. B. Mack, *Who Wrote the New Testament? The Making of Christian Origins* (San Francisco: HarperCollins, 1995), pp. 39–40.
57. C. Allen, "The Search for a No Frills Jesus," *Atlantic Monthly* 278, no. 6 (1996). 67.
58. Crossan, *Historical Jesus,* p. 304.
59. Ibid., p. 344.
60. Marcus J. Borg, *Jesus, A New Vision: Spirit, Culture, and the Life of Discipleship* (San Francisco: HarperCollins, 1987), p. 25.
61. Ibid., p. 104.
62. M. Borg, *Jesus in Contemporary Scholarship* (Valley Forge, Pa.: Trinity Press International, 1994), p. 55.
63. Stephen Mitchell, *The Gospel According to Jesus: A New Translation and Guide to His Essential Teachings for Believers and Unbelievers* (New York: Harper Perennial, 1993), p. 9.
64. C. Allen, "The Gospel According to Carse," *Lingua Franca* 7, no. 2 (1997):13.
65. Matt. 3:3, Mark 1:3, Luke 3:4, John 1:23; see also Isaiah 40:3.
66. Ernst Käsemann, *Jesus Means Freedom,* trans. Frank Clarke (Philadelphia: Fortress Press, 1968), p. 17.
67. Ibid., p. 28.
68. Ibid.
69. Ibid., p. 64.
70. Hans Küng, *On Being a Christian,* trans. Edward Quinn (Garden City, N.Y.: Doubleday & Company, 1976), p. 197.
71. Jon Sobrino, *Christology at the Crossroads: A Latin American Approach,* trans. John Drury (Maryknoll, N.Y.: Orbis Books, 1980), p. 274.
72. Ibid., jacket.
73. James H. Cone and Graynaud S. Wilmore, *Black Theology: A Documentary History* (Maryknoll, N.Y.: Orbis Books, 1993), 1:71.
74. Ibid., 1:207.

75. Elisabeth Schüssler Fiorenza, *In Memory of Her: A Feminist Reconstruction of Christian Origins* (New York: The Crossroad Publishing Company, 1994), p. xxviii.
76. Joanne Carlson Brown and Rebecca Parker, "For God So Loved the World?" *Christianity, Patriarchy, and Abuse: A Feminist Critique,* ed. J. C. Brown and Carole R. Bohn (Cleveland: Pilgrim Press, 1989), p. 26.

CHAPTER 11: THE RETURN

1. Babylonian Talmud Sanhedrin 107b, in Jacob Neusner, *Telling Tales: Making Sense of Christian and Jewish Nonsense* (Louisville, Ky.: Westminster/John Knox Press, 1993), p. 66.
2. Sanhedrin 43a, in David R. Catchpole, *The Trial of Jesus: A Study in the Gospels and Jewish Historiography from 1770 to the Present Day* (Leiden: E.J. Brill, 1971), p. 4.
3. Letter, in Catchpole, *Trial of Jesus,* pp. 13–14.
4. Abraham Geiger, "Das Judenthum und seine Geschichte," in Catchpole, *Trial of Jesus,* p. 36.
5. Claude Joseph Goldsmid Montefiore, "Has Judaism a Future?" in Donald A. Hagner, *The Jewish Reclamation of Jesus: An Analysis and Critique of Modern Jewish Study of Jesus* (Grand Rapids, Mich.: Zondervan Publishing House, 1984), p. 29.
6. C. Montefiore, "The Significance of Jesus for His Own Age," in Hagner, *Jewish Reclamation,* p. 295.
7. Luke 6:31; see also Matt. 7:31.
8. Babylonian Talmud Shabbat 31a, in J. Neusner, *Telling Tales,* p. 48.
9. Phil. 3:5.
10. Claude Joseph Goldsmid Montefiore, *Judaism and St. Paul: Two Essays* (New York: Arno Press, 1973), p. 81.
11. Joseph Klausner, *Jesus of Nazareth,* trans. Herbert Danby (New York: Macmillan, 1956), p. 232.
12. Ibid., p. 381.
13. Ibid.
14. Paul Winter, *On the Trial of Jesus* (Berlin and New York: Walter de Gruyter, 1974), p. 186.
15. David Flusser, *Jesus,* trans. Ronald Walls (New York: Herder and Herder, 1969), p. 64.
16. Geza Vermes, *Jesus the Jew: A Historian's Reading of the Gospels* (New York: Macmillan, 1974), p. 17.
17. Samuel Sandmel, *We Jews and Jesus* (New York: Oxford University Press, 1965), p. 79.
18. Ibid., p. 109.
19. Ibid., p. 151.
20. Irving M. Zeitlin, *Jesus and the Judaism of His Time* (Cambridge: Polity Press, 1988), p. 61.
21. J. Neusner, *Telling Tales,* p. 81.
22. Ibid., pp. 86–88, quoting S. Sandmel, *We Jews,* p. 34.
23. J. Klausner, *Jesus of Nazareth,* p. 345.
24. S. Sandmel, *We Jews,* p. 139.
25. Ibid., p. 141.
26. Philo of Alexandria, *Legatio ad Gaium,* 299–305, in D. Flusser, *Jesus,* p. 129.
27. Ibid.
28. S. G. F. Brandon, *Jesus and the Zealots: A Study of the Political Factor in Primitive Christianity* (New York: Charles Scribner's Sons, 1967), p. 232.
29. P. Winter, *Trial of Jesus,* dedication page.
30. Mark 15:31.
31. Psalm 22:7–8.
32. P. Winter, *Trial of Jesus,* p. 175.
33. Raymond E. Brown, *The Gospel According to John,* quoted by John A. T. Robinson, *The Priority of John,* ed. J. F. Coakley (London: SCM Press Ltd., 1985), p. 260.
34. Ibid.
35. Flavius Josephus, *Jewish Antiquities,* 18:64, trans. Louis H. Feldman (Cambridge: Harvard University Press, 1965), pp. 50–51.
36. Raymond E. Brown, *The Death of the Messiah* (New York: Doubleday, 1994), vol. 1, p. 392.

37. John Dominic Crossan, *Who Killed Jesus? Exposing the Roots of Anti-Semitism in the Gospels* (San Francisco: HarperCollins, 1995), p. 117.
38. A. N. Wilson, "Jesus Wept," *Slate,* April 29, 1997, p. 3.
39. Ibid.
40. Ibid.
41. Rosemary Radford Ruether, *Faith and Fratricide* (New York: Seabury Press, 1974), p. 247.
42. Hyam Maccoby, *The Myth-Maker: Paul and the Invention of Christianity* (San Francisco: Harper & Row, 1986), pp. 203–204.
43. Ibid., pp. 204–205.
44. A. N. Wilson, *Jesus: A Life* (New York and London: W. W. Norton & Company, 1992), p. 149.
45. Ibid., p. 161.
46. 4Q246, col. 2, line 1, in *The Dead Sea Scrolls Uncovered,* ed. and trans. R. Eisenman and M. Wise (New York and London: Penguin Books, 1993), p. 70.
47. André Dupont-Sommers, *The Dead Sea Scrolls: A Preliminary Survey,* quoted by James C. VanderKam, in *Understanding the Dead Sea Scrolls,* ed. Hershel Shanks (New York: Random House, 1992), p. 182.
48. Ibid.
49. Edmund Wilson, *The Scrolls from the Dead Sea* (New York: Oxford University Press, 1955), pp. 97–98.
50. Avi Katzman, "Interview with Chief Scroll Editor John Strugnell," in *Understanding the Dead Sea Scrolls,* p. 261.
51. R. Eisenman and M. Wise, *The Dead Sea Scrolls Uncovered,* p. 13.
52. Ibid.
53. Geza Vermes, "Brother James's Heirs?" quoted by Otto Betz and Rainer Riesner, *Jesus, Qumran and the Vatican: Clarifications,* trans. John Bowden (New York: Crossroad, 1994), p. 75.
54. John M. Allegro, *The Sacred Mushroom and the Cross: A Study of the Nature and Origins of Christianity Within the Fertility Cults of the Near East* (London: Hodder and Stoughton, 1970), p. 25.
55. Luke 1:35.
56. John 1:5.
57. II QT 64, in Geza Vermes, ed., *The Dead Sea Scrolls in English* (Sheffield: ISOT Press, 1987), p. 156.
58. D. Catchpole, *Trial of Jesus,* p. 267.
59. John 5:2.
60. J. A. T. Robinson, *Priority of John,* p. 97.
61. John 2:1.
62. Martin Hengel [in collaboration with Christoph Markschies], *The "Hellenization" of Judaea in the First Century after Christ,* trans. John Bowden (London: SCM Press; Philadelphia: Trinity Press International, 1989), p. 53.
63. Alan F. Segal, *Paul the Convert: The Apostolate and Apostasy of Saul the Pharisee* (New Haven and London: Yale University Press, 1990), p. 41.
64. N. T. Wright, *The New Testament and the People of God* (Minneapolis: Fortress Press, 1992), p. 453.
65. The author thanks Mark J. Mirsky for his contribution to this insight during the course of an e-mail exchange in October 1997.
66. Matt. 23:37; Luke 13:34.

BIBLIOGRAPHY

Abbott, Edwin Abbott. *Philochristus: Memories of a Disciple of the Lord.* 2d ed. (Boston: Roberts Brothers, 1878).

Adams, Dickinson W., ed. *Jefferson's Extracts from the Gospels.* Papers of Thomas Jefferson, Second Series (Princeton: Princeton University Press, 1983).

Albright, William Foxwell. *The Archaeology of Palestine.* Rev. ed. (Harmondsworth: Penguin, 1954).

———. *From the Stone Age to Christianity: Monotheism and the Historical Process* (Baltimore: Johns Hopkins Press, 1940).

Allegro, John M. *The Dead Sea Scrolls and the Christian Myth* (Buffalo: Prometheus Books, 1984).

———. *The Sacred Mushroom and the Cross: A Study of the Nature and Origins of Christianity within the Fertility Cults of the Near East* (London: Hodder and Stoughton, 1970).

Allen, Charlotte. "Away with the Manger." *Lingua Franca* 5, no. 2 (1995): 25.

———. "The Gospel According to Carse." *Lingua Franca* 7, no. 2 (1997): 13.

———. "Rising Son." *Lingua Franca* 5, no. 1 (1995): 5.

Allison, Henry E. *Benedict de Spinoza: An Introduction.* Rev. ed. (New Haven, Conn.: Yale University Press, 1987).

———. *Lessing and the Enlightenment: His Philosophy of Religion and Its Relation to Eighteenth-Century Thought* (Ann Arbor: University of Michigan Press, 1966).

Altizer, Thomas J. *The Gospel of Christian Atheism* (London: Collins, 1967).

Altizer, Thomas J., and Hamilton, William. *Radical Theology and the Death of God.* (Indianapolis: Bobbs-Merrill, 1966).

Anderson, Hugh, ed. *Jesus: Great Lives Observed* (Englewood Cliffs, N.J.: Prentice-Hall, 1967).

Anderson, Janice Capel, and Moore, Stephen D., eds. *Mark and Method: New Approaches in Biblical Studies* (Minneapolis: Fortress Press, 1992).

Aquinas, Thomas. "Treatise on the Passion of Christ." In *Summa Theologica.* Translated by the Fathers of the English Dominican Province in 1911. Rev. ed., 1920 (reprint ed., Westminster, Md.: Christian Classics, 1981).

Asch Sholem. *The Nazarene.* 1939. Translated by Maurice Samuel (reprint ed., New York: Caroll & Graf, 1996).

Atkins, Dorothy. *George Eliot and Spinoza.* Salzburg Studies in English Literature. Romantic Reassessment no. 78 (Salzburg: Institut für englische Sprache und Literatur, Universität Salzburg, 1978).

Aubrey, Edwin E., et al. *Through Jesus to God* (Chicago: American Institute of Social Literature, 1931).

Augustine of Hippo. *The Harmony of the Gospels.* Translated by S. D. F. Salmond. Edited by M. B. Biddle. 1887 (reprint ed., Grand Rapids, Mich.: William B. Eerdmans Publishing Co., 1980).

Bacon, Francis. *The New Organon and Related Writings.* Edited by Fulton H. Anderson (Indianapolis: Bobbs-Merrill, 1960).

Baigent, Michael; Leigh, Richard; and Lincoln, Henry. *Holy Blood, Holy Grail* (New York: Delacorte Press, 1982).

———. *The Messianic Legacy* (New York: Holt, 1987).

Baird, William. *History of New Testament Research,* vol. 1: *From Deism to Tübingen* (Minneapolis: Fortress Press, 1992).

Ballo, Tino, ed. *The American Film Industry* (Madison: University of Wisconsin Press, 1976).

Bammel, Ernst, and Moule, C. F. D., eds. *Jesus and the Politics of His Day* (Cambridge: Cambridge University Press, 1984).

Barclay, William. *Jesus As They Saw Him: New Testament Interpretations of Jesus* (Grand Rapids, Mich.: William B. Eerdmans Publishing Company, 1978).

Barnard, L. W. *Justin Martyr: His Life and Thought* (Cambridge: Cambridge University Press, 1967).

Barrett, Wilson. *The Sign of the Cross* (Philadelphia: Lippincott, 1904).

Bart, Benjamin F. *Flaubert* (Syracuse: Syracuse University Press, 1967).

Barth, Karl. *Protestant Theology in the Nineteenth Century: Its Background and History.* English translation (Valley Forge, Pa.: Judson Press, 1973).

———. *The Word of God and the Word of Man.* Translated by Douglas Horton (New York: Harper, 1957).

Barth, Karl, and Bultmann, Rudolf. *Letters, 1922–1966.* Edited by Bernd Jaspert. Translated and edited by Geoffrey W. Bromley (Grand Rapids, Mich.: William E. Eerdmans Publishing Company, 1981).

Barton, Bruce. *The Man Nobody Knows: A Discovery of the Real Jesus* (New York: Triangle Books, 1940).

Bauer, Bruno. *Christus und die Caesaren: Der Ursprung des Christenthums aus den römischen Griechenthum* (Berlin, 1877).

———. *Kritik des evangelischen Geschichte der Synoptiker.* 1841 (reprint ed., Hildesheim: Georg Olms, 1974).

———. *Philo, Strauss und Renan: und das Urchristentum.* 1874 (reprint ed., Darmstadt: Scientia Verlag Aalen, 1972).

Bauer, Walter. *Orthodoxy and Heresy in Earliest Christianity.* Translated by a team from the Philadelphia Seminar on Christian Origins. Edited by Robert A. Kraft and Gerhard Krodel (Philadelphia: Fortress Press, 1971).

Baur, Ferdinand Christian. *The Church History of the First Three Centuries.* Translated by Allan Menzies (London: Williams and Norgate, 1878).

———. *On the Writing of Church History.* Edited and translated by Peter C. Hodgson (New York: Oxford University Press, 1968).

Beecher, Henry Ward. *The Life of Jesus the Christ.* 2 vols. (New York: J. B. Ford; Edinburgh: Thomas Nelson & Sons, 1871).

Bellinzoni, Arthur, L. ed. *The Two-Source Hypothesis: A Critical Appraisal* (Atlanta, Ga.: Mercer University Press, 1985).

Bennett, J. A. W. *The Poetry of the Passion: Studies of Twelve Centuries of English Verse* (Oxford: Clarendon Press, 1982).

Bentley, Jerry H. *Humanists and Holy Writ: New Testament Scholarship in the Renaissance* (Princeton: Princeton University Press, 1983).

Berger, Peter L. *The Heretical Imperative: Contemporary Possibilities of Religious Affiliation* (Garden City, N.Y.: Anchor Press/Doubleday, 1979).

Betz, Otto. *What Do We Know about Jesus?* Translated by Margaret Kohl (Philadelphia: Westminster Press, 1968).

Betz, Otto, and Riesner, Rainer. *Jesus, Qumran and the Vatican.* Translated by John Bowden (New York: Crossroad Publishing Company, 1994).

Beyschlag, Willibald. *New Testament Theology or Historical Account of the Teachings of Jesus and of Primitive Christianity According to the New Testament Sources.* Translated by Neil Buchanan. 2 vols. (Edinburgh: T&T Clark, 1895).

Bigler, Robert M. *The Politics of German Protestantism: The Rise of the Protestant Church Elite in Prussia, 1815–1848* (Berkeley and Los Angeles: University of California Press, 1972).

Boers, Hendrikus. *What Is New Testament Theology? The Rise of Criticism and the Problem of a Theology of the New Testament* (Philadelphia: Fortress Press, 1979).

———. *Who Was Jesus? The Historical Jesus and the Synoptic Gospels* (San Francisco: Harper & Row, 1989).

Boethius. *The Theological Tractates* (Cambridge: Harvard University Press; London: W. Heinemann, Ltd., 1973).

Borg, Marcus J. *Jesus: A New Vision* (San Francisco: HarperCollins, 1987).

———. *Jesus in Contemporary Scholarship* (Valley Forge, Pa.: Trinity Press International, 1994).

———. *Meeting Jesus Again for the First Time: The Historical Jesus and the Heart of Contemporary Faith* (San Francisco: HarperCollins, 1994).

Bornkamm, Günther. *Jesus of Nazareth.* Translated by Irene and Fraser McLuskey with James M. Robinson (New York: Harper & Row, 1960).

Bosc, Ernest. *Vie esoterique de Jesus de Nazareth: et origines orientales du christianisme* (Paris: Libraire Dorbon Aine, 1902).

Bousset, Wilhelm. *Jesus.* Translated by W. D. Morrison (New York: G. Putnam's Sons; London: Williams & Norgate, 1906).

———. *Kyrios Christos: A History of the Belief in Christ from the Beginnings of Christianity to Irenaeus.* 1913. Translated by John E. Steely (Nashville: Abingdon Press, 1970).

Bowman, John Wick. *Which Jesus?* (Philadelphia: Westminster Press, 1970).

Boyd, Gregory A. *Cynic Sage or Son of God? Recovering the Real Jesus in an Age of Revisionist Replies* (Wheaton, Ill.: Victor Books/SP Publications, 1995).

Braaten, Carl, ed. *The Historical Jesus and the Kerygmatic Christ: Essays on the New Quest* (New York: Abingdon Press, 1964).

Brandon, S. G. F. *Jesus and the Zealots: A Study of the Political Factor in Primitive Christianity* (New York: Charles Scribner's Sons, 1967).

Braudel, Fernand. *The Mediterranean and the Mediterranean World in the Age of Philip II.* Translated by Siân Reynolds (Berkeley: University of California Press, 1995).

Braun, Herbert. *Jesus of Nazareth: The Man and His Time.* Translated by Everett R. Kalin (Philadelphia: Fortress Press, 1979).

Bright's Anglo-Saxon Reader. 1891. Rev. and enl. by James R. Hulbert (New York: Holt, Rinehart & Winston, 1964).

Brown, David. *Walter Scott and the Historical Imagination* (London: Routledge & Kegan Paul, 1979).

Brown, Joanne Carlson, and Bohn, Carole R., eds. *Christianity, Patriarchy, and Abuse: A Feminist Critique* (Cleveland: Pilgrim Press, 1989).

Brown, Raymond E. *The Birth of the Messiah: A Commentary on the Infancy Narratives in the Gospels of Matthew and Luke.* Updated ed. (Garden City, N.Y.: Doubleday, 1993).

———. *The Death of the Messiah: A Commentary on the Passion Narratives in the Four Gospels.* 2 vols. (Garden City, N.Y.: Doubleday, 1994).

———. *An Introduction to the New Testament* (Garden City, N.Y.: Doubleday, 1997).

Brown, Raymond E.; Donfried, Karl P.; Fitzmyer, Joseph A.; and Reumann, John, eds. *Mary in the New Testament* (Philadelphia: Fortress Press; New York: Paulist Press; Toronto: Ramsey, 1978).

Bultmann, Rudolf. *The History of the Synoptic Tradition.* Translated by John Marsh (Oxford: Basil Blackwell, 1963).

———. *Jesus and the Word.* 1926. Translated by Louise Pettibone Smith and Erminie Huntress Lantero (New York: Scribner and Sons, 1958).

———. *Kerygma and Myth: A Theological Debate.* Edited by Hans Werner Bartsch and Herbert Reich. Translated by Reginald H. Fuller. Rev. ed. (New York: Harper Torchbooks, 1961).

———. *New Testament and Mythology and Other Writings.* Edited and translated by Schubert M. Ogden (Philadelphia: Fortress Press, 1984).

Bultmann, Rudolf, and Kundsin, Karl. *Form Criticism: Two Essays on New Testament Research.* 1934. Translated by Frederick C. Grant (republished, New York: Harper & Row, 1962).

Burridge, Richard A. *Four Gospels, One Jesus?* (Grand Rapids, Mich.: William B. Eerdmans Publishing Company, 1994).

Burrow, J. W. *Gibbon* (Oxford: Oxford University Press, 1985).

Bushnell, T. L. *The Sage of Salisbury: Thomas Chubb, 1697–1747* (New York: Philosophical Library, 1967).

Cadbury, Henry J. *The Peril of Modernizing Jesus.* 1937 (London: SPCK, 1962).

Case, Shirley Jackson. *Jesus: A New Biography.* 1927 (reprint ed., New York: Greenwood Press, 1968).

Catchpole, David R. *The Quest for Q* (Edinburgh: T&T Clark, 1993).

———. *The Trial of Jesus: A Study in the Gospels and Jewish Historiography from 1770 to the Present Day* (Leiden: E. J. Brill, 1971).

Celsus. *On the True Doctrine: A Discourse against the Christians.* Translated by R. Joseph Hoffmann (New York: Oxford University Press, 1987).

Cerfaux, Lucien. *Christ in the Theology of St. Paul.* Translated by Geoffrey Webb and Adrian Walker (New York: Herder and Herder, 1959).

Chadbourne, Richard M. *Ernest Renan* (New York: Twyane, 1968).

Chadwick, Henry. *Early Christian Thought and the Classical Tradition: Studies in Justin, Clement, and Origen* (Oxford: Oxford University Press, 1996).

———. *The Early Church* (Harmondsworth: Penguin, 1967).

———. *Heresy and Orthodoxy in the Early Church* (Aldershot: Variorum Reprints, 1991).

———. *History and Thought of the Early Church* (London: Variorum Reprints, 1982).

Chadwick, Owen. *From Bossuet to Newman.* 2d ed. (Cambridge: Cambridge University Press, 1987).

———. *The Secularization of the European Mind in the Nineteenth Century* (Cambridge: Cambridge University Press, 1975).

Charlesworth, James H. *Jesus within Judaism: New Light from Exciting Archaeological Discoveries* (Garden City, N.Y.: Doubleday, 1988).

Charlesworth, James H., ed., with Blisard, Frank X., and Siker, Jeffrey S., asst. eds. *Jews and Christians: Exploring the Past, Present, and Future* (New York: Crossroad, 1990).

Charlesworth, James H., ed., with Brownson, J.; Davis, M. T.; Kraftchick, S. J.; and Segal, A. F. *The Messiah: Developments in Earliest Judaism and Christianity.* First Princeton Symposium on Judaism and Christian Origins, 1987, Princeton Theological Seminary (Minneapolis: Fortress Press, 1992).

Charlesworth, James H., and Weaver, Walter P., eds. *Images of Jesus Today.* Faith and Scholarship Colloquies 3, Florida Southern College (Valley Forge, Pa.: Trinity Press International, 1994).

Chateaubriand, François René. *The Genius of Christianity: Or the Spirit and Beauty of the Christian Religion.* 1802. Translated by Charles L. White (Baltimore: John Murphy & Co.; Philadelphia: J. B. Lippincott & Co., 1875).

———. *The Martyrs.* 1809. English translation edited by O. M. Wright (1859) (reprint ed., New York: Howard Fertig, 1976).

Chilton, Bruce, and Evans, Craig A., eds. *Studying the Historical Jesus: Evaluations of the State of Current Research* (Leiden: E. J. Brill, 1994).

Chubb, Thomas. *The Posthumous Works of Thomas Chubb* (London: R. Baldwin; Salisbury: E. Easton, 1748).

———. *The True Gospel of Jesus Christ Asserted* (London: Thomas Cox, 1735).

Clark, Robert T., Jr. *Herder: His Life and Thought* (Berkeley and Los Angeles: University of California Press, 1955).

Cobb, John B., Jr. *God and the World* (Philadelphia: Westminster Press, 1969).

Cochem, Martin von. *Life of Christ* (*Life and Sufferings of Our Lord Jesus Christ and his Mother Mary*). Abridged and adapted by Bonaventure Hamner (New York: Benziger Brothers, 1897).

Cohn, Haim. *The Trial and Death of Jesus* (New York: Harper & Row, 1971).

Collins, Raymond F. *Introduction to the New Testament* (Garden City, N.Y.: Doubleday, 1983).

Cone, James, and Wilmore, Graynaud S. *Black Theology: A Documentary History.* Vol. 1: *1966–1979.* 2d. ed. rev. (Maryknoll, N.Y.: Orbis Books, 1993).

Conzelmann, Hans. *History of Primitive Christianity.* Translated by John E. Steely (Nashville: Abingdon Press, 1973).

———. *Jesus.* Translated by John Reumann (Philadelphia: Fortress Press, 1973).

———. *The Theology of St. Luke.* Translated by Geoffrey Buswell (1961) (reprint ed., Philadelphia: Fortress Press, 1982).

Costain, Thomas. *The Silver Chalice* (Garden City, N.Y.: Doubleday, 1952).

Court, John, and Court, Kathleen. *The New Testament World* (Englewood Cliffs, N.J.: Prentice-Hall, 1990).

Cromwell, Richard S. *David Friedrich Strauss and His Place in Modern Thought* (Fair Lawn, N.J.: R. E. Burdick, 1974).

Crossan, John Dominic. *The Essential Jesus: Original Sayings and Earliest Images* (San Francisco: HarperCollins, 1994).

———. *The Historical Jesus: The Life of a Mediterranean Jewish Peasant* (San Francisco: HarperCollins, 1991).

———. *In Fragments: The Aphorisms of Jesus* (San Francisco: Harper & Row, 1983).

———. *Jesus: A Revolutionary Biography* (San Francisco: HarperCollins, 1994).

Cullen, Charles T., ed. *Jefferson's Extracts from the Gospels.* Papers of Thomas Jefferson, Second Series (Princeton: Princeton University Press, 1983).

Cumont, Franz. *The Mysteries of Mithra.* 1900. Translated from the 2d rev. French ed. of 1902 by Thomas J. McCormack (New York: Dover, 1956).

———. *The Oriental Religions in Roman Paganism.* Authorized English translation, with an introduction by Grant Showerman (Chicago: Open Court Publishing Company; London: Kegan, Paul, Trench, Trubner & Co., 1911).

Davies, W. D. *Invitation to the New Testament: A Guide to Its Main Witnesses* (Garden City, N.Y.: Doubleday, 1966).

———. *Paul and Rabbinic Judaism: Some Rabbinic Elements in Pauline Theology.* 3d ed. (London: SPCK, 1970).

———. *The Territorial Dimension of Judaism* (Berkeley and Los Angeles: University of California Press, 1982).

Dibelius, Martin. *A Fresh Approach to the New Testament and Early Christian Literature.* English translation (London: Ivor Nicholson and Watson, 1936).

———. *From Tradition to Gospel.* Translated from the 2d ed. of 1919 by Bertram Lee Woolf (Cambridge: James Clarke & Co., 1971).

———. *Jesus.* Translated by Charles B. Hedrick and Frederick C. Grant (Philadelphia: Westminster Press, 1949).

———. *The Message of Jesus Christ: The Tradition of the Early Christian Communities.* Translated by Frederick C. Grant (New York: Charles Scribner's Sons, 1939).

Didon, Henri. *Jesus Christ: Our Saviour's Person, Mission, and Spirit.* English translation edited by Bernard O'Reilly (New York: D. Appleton and Company, 1891).

———. *The Life of Christ.* 6th ed. in 1 vol. (London: Kegan, Paul, Trench, Trubner & Co.; St. Louis: B. Herder Book Co., 1928).

Dillistone, F. W. *C. H. Dodd, Interpreter of the New Testament* (Grand Rapids, Mich.: William B. Eerdmans Publishing Company, 1977).

Dodd, C. H. *Historical Tradition in the Fourth Gospel* (Cambridge: Cambridge University Press, 1963).

———. *History and the Gospel.* 1938 (reprint ed., London: Nisbet & Co. 1952).

Dodd, Valerie A. *George Eliot: An Intellectual Life* (New York: St. Martin's Press, 1990).

Doty, William C. *Contemporary New Testament Interpretation* (Englewood Cliffs, N.J.: Prentice-Hall, 1972).

Douglas, Lloyd C. *The Robe* (Boston: Houghton Mifflin, 1942).

Durkheim, Emile. *The Elementary Forms of the Religious Life.* Translated by Joseph Ward Swan (New York: Free Press, 1915).

Ebeling, Gerhard. *Word and Faith.* Translated by James W. Leitch (London: SCM Press Ltd., 1963).

Edersheim, Alfred. *The Life and Times of Jesus the Messiah.* 2 vols. (New York: Longmans, Green, and Co., 1896).

Edwards, David L., ed. *The Honest to God Debate* (Philadelphia: Westminster Press, 1963).

Ehrman, Bart D. *The Orthodox Corruption of Scripture: The Effect of Early Christological Controversies on the Text of the New Testament* (New York: Oxford University Press, 1993).

Ehrman, Bart D., and Holmes, Michael W. *The Text of the New Testament in Contemporary Research: Essays on the Status Quaestionis* (Grand Rapids, Mich.: William B. Eerdmans Publishing Company, 1995).

Eisenman, Robert, and Wise, Michael. *The Dead Sea Scrolls Uncovered* (London: Penguin Books, 1993).

Eliade, Mircea. *Myth and Reality.* Translated by Willard R. Trask (New York: Harper & Row, 1963).

Ellman, Richard. *Oscar Wilde* (New York: Alfred A. Knopf, 1988).

Ellul, Jacques. *The New Demons.* Translated by C. Edward Hopkin (New York: Seabury Press, 1975).

Emmerich, Anna Katharina. *The Life of Our Lord and Savior Jesus Christ, Combined with The Bitter Passion and The Life of Mary, as Recorded in the Journals of Clemens Brentano.* Arranged and edited by Carl E. Schmoeger. 4 vols. (Fresno: Academy Library Guild, 1954).

Eusebius. *The History of the Church from Christ to Constantine.* Translated by G. A. Williamson (Harmondsworth: Penguin, 1965).

Evans, C. Stephen. *The Historical Christ and the Jesus of Faith: The Incarnational Narrative as History* (Oxford: Oxford University Press, 1996).

Farmer, William R. *The Gospel of Jesus: The Pastoral Relevance of the Synoptic Problem* (Louisville: Westminster/ John Knox Press, 1994).

———. *The Synoptic Problem: A Critical Analysis* (New York: Macmillan, 1964).

Feine, Paul, and Behm, Johannes. *Introduction to the New Testament.* Reedited by Werner Georg Kümmel. 14th rev. ed. Translated by A. J. Mattill, Jr. (Nashville: Abingdon Press, 1967).

Ferguson, Everett, ed. *Doctrines of God and Christ in the Early Church.* Studies in Early Christianity, vol. 9 (New York: Garland, 1993).

———, ed. *Orthodoxy, Heresy, and Schism in Early Christianity.* Studies in Early Christianity, vol. 4 (New York: Garland, 1993).

Fergusson, David. *Bultmann* (Collegeville, Minn.: Liturgical Press, 1992).

Finegan, Jack. *The Archaeology of the New Testament: The Life of Jesus and the Beginning of the Early Church* (Princeton, N.J.: Princeton University Press, 1969).

Fiorenza, Elisabeth Schüssler. *But She Said: Feminist Practices of Biblical Interpretation* (Boston: Beacon Press, 1992).

———. *In Memory of Her: A Feminist Theological Perspective of Christian Origins.* 1983. Tenth anniversary ed. (New York: Crossroad Publishing Company, 1994).

———. *Jesus: Miriam's Child, Sophia's Prophet: Critical Issues in Feminist Christology* (New York: Continuum Publishing Company, 1995).

Flaubert, Gustave. *Madame Bovary.* 1856. Translated by Francis Steegmuller (New York: Random House, 1957).

———. *Salammbô.* 1862. English translation (New York: Modern Library, 1929).

———. *The Temptation of Saint Antony.* Translated by Kitty Mrosovsky (Ithaca, N.Y.: Cornell University Press, 1981).

———. *Three Tales.* 1877. Translated by A. J. Krailsheimer (Oxford: Oxford University Press, 1991).

Flusser, David. *Jesus.* Translated by Ronald Walls (New York: Herder and Herder, 1969).

Forster, E. M. *Alexandria: A History and a Guide.* 1922 (republished, London: Michael Haag, 1982).

Fortna, Robert Tomson. *The Fourth Gospel and Its Predecessor* (Philadelphia: Fortress Press, 1989).

———. *The Gospel of Signs: A Reconstruction of the Narrative Source Underlying the Fourth Gospel* (Cambridge: Cambridge University Press, 1970).

Fouard, Constant. *The Christ the Son of God: A Life of Our Lord and Saviour Jesus Christ.* Translated from the 5th ed. by George F. X. Griffith. 2 vols. (New York: London: Longmans, Green, 1891).

Fox, Robin Lane. *Pagans and Christians* (New York: Knopf, 1987).

———. *The Unauthorized Version: Truth and Fiction in the Bible* (New York: Knopf, 1992).

Frazer, James George. *The Golden Bough: A Study in Magic and Religion.* 1-vol. abridged ed. (New York: Macmillan, 1992).

Freeman, James E. *The Man and the Master* (New York: Thomas Whittaker, 1906).

Frei, Hans W. *The Eclipse of Biblical Narrative: A Study in Eighteenth and Nineteenth Century Hermeneutics* (New Haven: Yale University Press, 1974).

Frend, W. H. C. *Archaeology and History in the Study of Early Christianity* (London: Variorum Reprints, 1988).

———. *Martyrdom and Persecution in the Early Church: A Study of a Conflict from the Maccabees to Donatus* (Oxford: Basil Blackwell, 1965).

———. *The Rise of Christianity* (Philadelphia: Fortress Press, 1984).

———. *The Rise of the Monophysite Movement* (Cambridge: Cambridge University Press, 1972).

Frenssen, Gustav. *Holyland.* Translated by Mary Agnes Hamilton (Boston: Dana Estes & Company; London: Archibald Constable & Company, Ltd., 1906).

Freyne, Seán. *Galilee from Alexander the Great to Hadrian, 235 B.C.E. to 135 C.E: A Study of Second Temple Judaism* (Wilmington, Del.: Michael Glazier; Notre Dame, Ind.: Notre Dame University Press, 1980).

Froelich, Karlfried, trans. and ed. *Biblical Interpretation in the Early Church* (Philadelphia: Fortress Press, 1984).

Frye, Northrop. *The Great Code: The Bible and Literature.* 1981 (London: Ark Paperbacks, 1983).

Fuchs, Ernst. *Studies of the Historical Jesus.* Translated by Andrew Scobie (Naperville, Ill.: Alec R. Allenson, 1964).

Fuller, Reginald. *The New Testament in Current Study: Some Trends in the Years 1941–1962* (London: SCM Press Ltd., 1963).

Fuller, Reginald, and Perkins, Pheme. *Who Is This Christ? Gospel Christology and Contemporary Faith* (Philadelphia: Fortress Press, 1983).

Funk, Robert W. *Honest to Jesus: Jesus for a New Millennium* (San Francisco: HarperCollins, 1996).

Funk, Robert W.; Hoover, Roy; and the Members of the Jesus Seminar. *The Five Gospels: The Search for the Authentic Words of Jesus* (New York: Macmillan, 1993).

Gager, John G. *The Origins of Anti-Semitism: Attitudes toward Judaism in Pagan and Christian Antiquity* (New York: Oxford University Press, 1983).

Gallup, George, and Castelli, Jim. *The People's Religion: American Faith in the 90s* (New York: Macmillan, 1989).

Gay, Peter, ed. *Deism: An Anthology* (Princeton: D. Van Nostrand Company, 1968).

———, ed. *The Enlightenment: A Comprehensive Anthology* (New York: Simon & Schuster, 1973).

———. *The Enlightenment: An Interpretation,* vol. 1: *The Rise of Modern Paganism* (New York: Knopf, 1967).

———. *The Enlightenment: An Interpretation,* vol. 2: *The Science of Freedom* (New York: Knopf, 1969).

Georgi, Dieter. *The Opponents of Paul in Second Corinthians.* Translated under the author's supervision (Philadelphia: Fortress Press, 1986).

Gibbon, Edward. *The Decline and Fall of the Roman Empire and Other Selected Writings.* Edited and abridged and with an introduction by Hugh R. Trevor-Roper (New York: Twayne, 1963).

———. *The History of the Decline and Fall of the Roman Empire.* Edited by J. B. Bury (London: Methuen; New York: Doran, 1938).

Giergielewicz, Miecyslaw. *Henryk Sienkiewicz* (New York: Twayne, 1968).

Gilmore, David D., ed. *Honor and Shame and the Unity of the Mediterranean* (Washington, D.C.: American Anthropological Association, 1987).

Goguel, Maurice. *Jesus the Nazarene: Myth of History?* Translated by Frederich Stephens (New York: Appleton and Company, 1927).

———. *The Life of Jesus.* Translated by Olive Wyon (New York: Macmillan, 1933).

Goodman, Martin. *State and Society in Roman Galilee, A.D. 132–212* (Totowa, N.J.: Rowman & Allanheld, 1983).

Goulder, Michael. *Midrash and Lection in Matthew* (London: SPCK, 1974).

———. *St. Paul versus St. Peter: A Tale of Two Missions* (Louisville, Ky.: Westminster John Knox Press, 1995).

Grabbe, Lester L. *Judaism from Cyrus to Hadrian* (Minneapolis: Fortress, 1992).

Grabowski, John S. "Newton, Hume and the Ethics of the Closed System." *Irish Theological Quarterly* 2 (1995): 138–158.

Grant, Michael. *Jesus: An Historian's View of the Gospels* (New York: Charles Scribner's Sons, 1977).

———. *The Jews in the Roman World* (New York: Charles Scribner's Sons, 1973).

Grant, Robert M. *Augustus to Constantine: The Thrust of the Christian Movement into the Roman World* (New York: Harper & Row, 1970).

———. *Early Christianity and Society* (San Francisco: Harper & Row, 1976).

———. *Jesus after the Gospels* (Louisville, Ky.: Westminster/John Knox Press, 1989).

Graves, Robert. *King Jesus* (New York: Minerva Press, 1946).

Graves, Robert, and Podro, Joshua. *The Nazarene Gospel Restored* (Garden City, N.Y.: Doubleday, 1954).

Gray, Douglas. *Themes and Images in the Medieval Religious Lyric* (London: Routledge & Kegan Paul, 1972).

Gray, James R. *Modern Process Thought: A Brief Ideological History* (Lanham, Md.: University Press of America, 1982).

Green, Joel B., and Turner, Max, eds. *Jesus of Nazareth, Lord and Christ: Essays on the Historical Jesus and New Testament Christology* (Grand Rapids, Mich.: William B. Eerdmans Publishing Company, 1984; Carlisle: Paternoster Press, 1994).

Griffin, David R. *A Process Christology* (Philadelphia: Westminster Press, 1973).

Gunkel, Hermann. *The Influence of the Holy Spirit: The Popular View of the Apostolic Age and the Teaching of Paul the Apostle.* 1888. Translated by Roy A. Harrisville and Philip A. Quanbeck II (Philadelphia: Fortress Press, 1979).

———. *Israel and Babylon: The Influence of Babylon on the Religion of Israel.* English translation (Philadelphia: John Jos. McVey, 1904).

———. *The Legends of Genesis: The Biblical Saga and History.* 1901. Translated by W. H. Carruth (reprint ed., New York: Schocken Books, 1964).

———. *The Psalms: A Form-Critical Introduction.* Translated by Thomas H. Horner (Philadelphia: Fortress Press, 1967).

Hagner, Donald A. *The Jewish Reclamation of Jesus: An Analysis and Critique of Modern Jewish Study of Jesus* (Grand Rapids, Mich.: Zondervan Publishing House, 1984).

Hahn, Paul; Lohff, Wenzel; and Bornkamm, Günther. *What Can We Know about Jesus?* 1962. Translated by Gover Foley (Philadelphia: Fortress Press, 1969).

Haight, Gordon S. *George Eliot: A Biography* (New York: Oxford University Press, 1968).

Hanna, William. *The Last Day of Our Lord's Passion* (New York: Robert Coute & Brothers, 1864).

———. *The Life of Christ.* New and enl. ed. arranged by Charles H. Morgan (New York: American Tract Society, 1913).

Hanson, Paul D. *The Dawn of Apocalyptic: The Historical and Sociological Roots of Jewish Apocalyptic Imagery.* Rev. ed. (Philadelphia: Fortress Press, 1979).

Hanson, Richard Davies. *The Jesus of History* (London: Williams and Norgate, 1869).

Harnack, Adolf von. *History of Dogma.* Translated from the 3d German ed. by Neil Buchanan (1897; republished, New York: Dover, 1961).

———. *What is Christianity?* 1900. Translated by Thomas Bailey Saunders (New York: Harper & Brothers, 1957; republished, Philadelphia: Fortress Press, 1987).

Harris, Holton. *David Friedrich Strauss and His Theology* (Cambridge: Cambridge University Press, 1973).

Hart-Davis, Rupert. *The Letters of Oscar Wilde* (New York: Harcourt, Brace & World, 1962).

Hartin, P. J., and Prizer, J. H. *Text and Interpretation: New Approaches in the Criticism of the New Testament* (Leiden: E. J. Brill, 1991).

Hase, Karl. *Life of Jesus: A Manual for Academic Study.* Translated from the 3d and 4th eds. by James Freeman Clarke (Boston: Walker, Wise, and Company, 1860).

Hayne, Donald, ed. *The Autobiography of Cecil B. DeMille* (Englewood Cliffs, N.J.: Prentice-Hall, 1959).

Hefelbower, S. G. *The Relation of John Locke to English Deism* (Chicago: University of Chicago Press, 1918).

Hegel, Georg Wilhelm Friedrich. *Lectures on the Philosophy of Religion.* Translated by R. F. Brown, Peter Hodgson, and J. M. Stewart; edited by Peter Hodgson (Berkeley: University of California Press, 1984).

Heitmüller, Wilhelm. *In Namen Jesu.* (Göttingen: Vandenhoeck & Ruprecht, 1903).

Hengel, Martin. *Acts and the History of Earliest Christianity.* Translated by John Bowden. (Philadelphia: Fortress Press, 1980).

———. *Between Jesus and Paul: Studies in the Earliest History of Christianity.* Translated by John Bowden (Philadelphia: Fortress Press, 1983).

———. *The Charismatic Leader and His Followers.* Translated by James Grieg (New York: Crossroad, 1981).

———. *The Cross of the Son of God.* Translated by John Bowden (London: SCM Press Ltd., 1986).

———. *Crucifixion: In the Ancient World and the Folly of the Message of the Cross.* Translated by John Bowden (London: SCM Press, Ltd.; Philadelphia: Fortress Press, 1977).

———. *Jews, Greeks and Barbarians: Aspects of the Hellenization of Judaism in the Pre-Christian Period.* Translated by John Bowden (Philadelphia: Fortress Press, 1980).

———. *Studies in the Gospel of Mark.* Translated by John Bowden (Philadelphia: Fortress Press, 1985).

———. *Victory over Violence: Jesus and the Revolutionists.* Translated by David E. Green (Philadelphia: Fortress Press, 1973).

Hengel, Martin, in collaboration with Christoph Markschies. *The "Hellenization" of Judaea in the First Century after Christ.* Translated by John Bowden (London: SCM Press Ltd.; Philadelphia: Trinity Press, 1989).

Hennecke, Edgar. *Gospels and Related Writings.* English translation edited by R. McL. Wilson (Philadelphia: Fortress Press, 1963–1966).

Hennell, Charles C. *An Inquiry Concerning the Origins of Christianity and Christian Theism* (London: Trubner and Co., 1852).

Hermann, Wilhelm. *The Communion of the Christian with God: Described on the Basis of Luther's Statements.* 1892. Translated by J. Sandys Stanyon, rev. in 1906 by R. W. Stewart in accordance with the 4th German ed. of 1903 (New York: G. P. Putnam's Sons; London: Williams & Norgate, reprint ed., edited by Robert T. Voelkel, Philadelphia: Fortress Press, 1971).

Hertzberg, Arthur. *The French Enlightenment and the Jews* (New York: Columbia University Press, 1968).

Hick, John, ed. *The Myth of God Incarnate* (Philadelphia: Westminster Press, 1977).

Higham, Charles. *Cecil B. DeMille* (New York: Charles Scribner's Sons, 1973).

Hilprecht, H. V. *Explorations in Bible Lands during the Nineteenth Century* (Philadelphia: A. J. Holman and Company, 1903).

Hobbes, Thomas. *Leviathan* (Cambridge: Cambridge University Press, 1991).

Hoehner, Harold W. *Herod Antipas* (Cambridge: Cambridge University Press, 1972).

Hoffmann, Manfred, ed. *Martin Luther and the Modern Mind: Freedom, Conscience, Toleration, Rights.* Toronto Studies in Theology, vol. 22 (New York: Edwin Mellen Press, 1985).

Hoffmann, R. Joseph, and Lance, Gerald A., eds. *Jesus in History and Myth* (Buffalo: Prometheus Press, 1986).

Holbach, Paul Henri Thiery, baron d'. *Ecce Homo! An Eighteenth Century Life of Jesus.* Translated by George Houston. Revised and edited by Andrew Hunwick (Berlin: Mouton de Gruyter, 1995).

Horsley, Richard A. *Galilee: History, Politics, People* (Valley Forge, Pa.: Trinity Press International, 1995).

———. *Jesus and the Spiral of Violence: Popular Jewish Resistance in Roman Palestine* (San Francisco: Harper & Row, 1987).

Horsley, Richard A., and Hanson, John S. *Bandits, Prophets, and Messiahs: Popular Movements in the Time of Jesus* (Minneapolis: Winston, 1985).

Hughes, Thomas. *The Manliness of Christ* (Boston: Houghton Mifflin, n.d.).

Hultgren, Arland. *The Rise of Normative Christianity* (Minneapolis: Fortress Press, 1994).

Ingraham, Joseph H. *The Prince of the House of David, or Three Years in the Holy City.* 1897. Rev. ed. (Reprint ed., Folcroft: Folcroft Library Editions, 1978).

Jacobson, Arland D. *The First Gospel: An Introduction to Q.* (Sonoma, Calif.: Polebridge Press, 1992).

James, M. R. ed. *The Apocryphal New Testament: A Collection of Apocryphal Christian Literature in English Translation* (Oxford: Oxford University Press, 1993).

Jaubert, Annie. *The Date of the Last Supper.* Translated by Isaac Rafferty (Staten Island, N.Y.: Alba House, 1965).

Jeremias, Joachim. *The Eucharistic Words of Jesus.* Translated by Norman Perrin (New York: Scribner Brothers, 1966).

———. *Jerusalem in the Time of Jesus: An Investigation into Economic and Social Conditions during the New Testament Period.* Translated from the 3d ed. by M. E. Dahl (Philadelphia: Fortress Press, 1969).

———. *The Parables of Jesus.* Translated from the 6th ed. by S. H. Hooke (New York: Charles Scribner's Sons, 1963).

———. *The Rediscovery of Bethesda: John 5:2.* New Testament Archaeology Monograph no. 1. Edited by Jerry Vardaman (Louisville, Ky.: Southern Baptist Theological Seminary, 1966).

Jervell, Jacob. *The Continuing Search for the Historical Jesus.* 1962. Translated by Harris E. Kaasa (Minneapolis: Augsburg Publishing House, 1965).

John of Damascus. *The Divine Images: Three Apologies against Those Who Attack the Divine Images.* Translated by David Anderson (Crestwood, N.Y.: St. Vladimir's Seminary Press, 1980).

Johnson, Luke Timothy. *The Real Jesus: The Misguided Quest for the Historical Jesus and the Truth of the Traditional Gospels* (San Francisco: HarperCollins, 1996).

———. *The Writings of the New Testament: An Interpretation* (Philadelphia: Fortress Press, 1986).

Jones, Alan. *Independence and Exegesis: The Study of Early Christianity in the Work of Alfred Loisy (1857–1940), Charles Guignebert (1857–1939) and Maurice Goguel (1880–1955).* Beiträge zur Geschichte der Biblischen Exegese, no. 26. (Tübingen: J. C. B. Mohr, 1983).

Josephus, Flavius. *Jewish Antiquities.* Vols. 15–17. Translated by Ralph Marcus (Cambridge: Harvard University Press, 1963).

———. *Jewish Antiquities.* Vols. 18–20. Translated by Louis H. Feldman (Cambridge: Harvard University Press, 1965).

———. *The Jewish War.* Translated by G. A. Williamson (1959). Revised and with a new introduction, notes, and appendix by E. Mary Smallwood (London: Penguin, 1981).

Joy, Charles, ed. *Albert Schweitzer: An Anthology* (New York: Harper Brothers; Boston: Beacon Press, 1947).

Jülicher, Adolf. *Einleitung in das Neue Testament* (Freiburg: Akademische Verlagbuchhandlung von. J. C. B. Mohr, 1894).

———. *Die Gleichnisreden Jesu.* 3 vols. (Tübingen: J. C. B. Mohr, 1910). Reprinted in 1 vol. (Darmstadt: Wissenchaftliche Buchgesellschaft, 1976).

Jussim, Estelle. *Slave to Beauty: The Eccentric Life and Controversial Career of F. Holland Day, Photographer, Publisher, Aesthete* (Boston: David R. Godine, 1981).

Justin. *The Writings of Saint Justin Martyr.* Translated by Thomas B. Falk (New York: Christian Heritage, 1948).

Kähler, Martin. *The So-Called Historical Jesus and the Historic, Biblical Christ.* Translated by Carl E. Braaten, with a forward by Paul J. Tillich (Philadelphia: Fortress Press, 1964).

Kalthoff, Albert. *The Rise of Christianity.* 1902. Translated by Joseph McCabe (London: Watts & Co., 1907).

Kamesar, Adam. *Jerome, Greek Scholarship, and the Hebrew Bible* (Oxford: Clarendon Press, 1993).

Kant, Immanuel. *Religion within the Limits of Reason Alone.* Translated by Theodore M. Greene and Hoyt H. Hudson (New York: Harper Torchbooks, 1960).

Käsemann, Ernst. *Essays on New Testament Themes.* Translated by J. M. Montague (London: SCM Press Ltd.; Naperville, Ill.: Alec R. Allenson, 1964).

———. *Jesus Means Freedom.* Translated by Frank Clarke (Philadelphia: Fortress Press, 1968).

———. *New Testament Questions of Today.* Translated by W. J. Montague and Wilfred F. Bunge (Philadelphia: Fortress Press, 1969).

Kazantzakis, Helen. *Nikos Kazantzakis: A Biography Based on His Letters* (New York: Simon & Schuster, 1970).

Kazantzakis, Nikos. *The Last Temptation.* Translated by P. A. Bien (Oxford: Bruno Cassirer, 1961).

Keck, Leander E. *A Future for the Historical Jesus: The Place of Jesus in Preaching and Theology* (Nashville: Abingdon Press, 1971).

Keck, Leander E., and Martyn, J. Louis, eds. *Studies in Luke-Acts* (Nashville, Tenn.: Abingdon Press, 1966).

Kee, Howard Clark. *Jesus in History: An Approach to the Study of the Gospels.* 2d ed. (New York: Harcourt Brace Jovanovich, 1977).

———. *What Can We Know About Jesus?* (Cambridge: Cambridge University Press, 1990).

Keim, Theodor. *The History of Jesus of Nazara.* Translated by Arthur Ransom (London: William and Norgate, 1883).

Kelly, George A. *The New Biblical Theorists: Raymond E. Brown and Beyond* (Ann Arbor; Mich.: Servant Books, 1983).

Kesich, Vladimir. *The First Day of the New Creation: The Resurrection and the Christian Faith* (Crestwood: St. Vladimir's Seminary Press, 1982).

Kissinger, Warren S. *The Lives of Jesus: A History and Bibliography* (New York: Garland, 1985).

Klassen, William. *Judas: Betrayer or Friend of Jesus?* (Minneapolis: Fortress Press, 1996).

Klausner, Joseph. *Jesus of Nazareth: His Life, Times, and Teaching.* 1925. (New York: Macmillan, 1959).

Klijn, A. F. J., trans. and ed. *The Acts of Thomas* (Leiden: E. J. Brill, 1962).

———. *An Introduction to the New Testament.* Translated by M. Van der Vathorst-Smit (Leiden: E. J. Brill, 1967).

Kloppenborg, John S. *The Formation of Q: Trajectories in Ancient Wisdom Collections* (Philadelphia: Fortress Press, 1987).

———. *Q Parallels: Synopsis, Critical Notes and Concordance* (Sonoma, Calif.: Polebridge Press, 1988).

———, ed. *Conflict and Invention: Literary, Rhetorical, and Social Studies on the Sayings Gospel Q* (Valley Forge, Pa.: Trinity Press International, 1995).

Kloppenborg, John S.; Meyer, Marvin W.; Patterson, Stephen J.; and Steinhauser, Michael G. *Q Thomas Reader* (Sonoma, Calif.: Polebridge Press, 1990).

Knight, W. S. M. *The Life and Works of Hugo Grotius* (London: Sweet & Maxwell, 1925).

Knoepflmacher, *Religious Humanism and the Victorian Novel: George Eliot, Walter Pater, and Samuel Butler* (Princeton: Princeton University Press, 1965).

Kodell, Jerome. *The Eucharist in the New Testament* (Wilmington, Del.: Michael Glazier, 1988).

Koester, Helmut. *Ancient Christian Gospels: Their History and Development* (Philadelphia: Trinity Press International; London: SCM Press Ltd., 1990).

Kolve, V. A. *The Play Called Corpus Christi* (Stanford: Stanford University Press, 1966).

Kors, Alan Charles, and Korshin, Paul J. *Anticipations of the Enlightenment in England, France, and Germany* (Philadelphia: University of Pennsylvania Press, 1987).

Kugel, James L., and Greer, Rowan. *Early Biblical Interpretation.* Library of Early Christianity, vol. 3 (Philadelphia: Westminster Press, 1986).

Kümmel, Werner Georg. *The New Testament: The History of the Investigation of Its Problems.* Translated by S. McLean Gilmour and Howard C. Kee (Nashville: Abingdon Press, 1972).

Küng, Hans. *On Being a Christian.* Translated by Edward Quinn (Garden City, N.Y.: Doubleday, 1976).

Lagerqvist, Pär. *Barabbas.* 1950. Translated by Alain Blair (New York: Vintage Books, 1989).

Lambe, Patrick J. "Biblical Criticism and Censorship in Ancien Régime France: The Case of Richard Simon." *Harvard Theological Review* 78 (1985): 149–177.

Lapide, Pinchas. *The Resurrection of Jesus: A Jewish Perspective.* English translation (Minneapolis: Augsburg Publishing House, 1983).

Lawler, Edwina G. *David Friedrich Strauss and His Critics: The Life of Jesus Debate* in *Early Nineteenth-Century German Journals.* American University Studies, series 7, Theology and Religion, vol. 16 (New York: Peter Lang Publishing, 1986).

Lawrence, D. H. *The Man Who Died.* (Hopewell, N.J.: Ecco Press, 1994).

Leaney, A. R. C. *The Jewish and Christian World, 200 B.C. to A.D. 200* (Cambridge: Cambridge University Press, 1984).

Lednicki, Waclaw. *Henryk Sienkiewicz: A Retrospective Synthesis* (Gravenhage: Mouton & Co., 1960).

Lenski, Gerhard E. *Power and Privilege: A Theory of Social Stratification* (New York: McGraw-Hill, 1966).

Lerou, Emilie ("Pierre Nahor"). *Jesus.* Translated by S. L. Lee (New York: Abbey Press, 1903).

Lessing, Gotthold. *Lessing's Theological Writings.* Selected and translated by Henry Chadwick (Stanford: Stanford University Press, 1956).

Lietzmann, Hans. *Der Prozess Jesu* (Berlin: Walter de Gruyter, 1931).

Lightfoot, R. H. *The Gospel Message of St. Mark* (London: Oxford University Press, 1950).

Linnemann, Eta. *Is There a Synoptic Problem? Rethinking the Literary Dependence of the First Three Gospels.* Translated by Robert W. Yarbrough (Grand Rapids, Mich.: Baker Book House, 1992).

———. *Parables of Jesus: Introduction and Exposition.* English translation (London: SPCK, 1966).

Locke, John. *The Reasonableness of Christianity,* with *A Discourse on Miracles* and part of *A Third Letter Concern-*

ing Toleration. Edited, abridged, and introduced by J. T. Ramsey (Stanford: Stanford University Press, 1958).

———. *Two Treatises of Government.* Edited by Peter Laslett (Cambridge: Cambridge University Press, 1960).

Lohmeyer, Ernst. *The Lord's Prayer.* Translated by John Bowden (London: Collins; New York: Harper, 1965).

Loisy, Alfred. *The Birth of the Christian Religion.* Translated by L. P. Jacks (London: George Allen & Unwin Ltd., 1948).

———. *The Origins of the New Testament.* Translated by L. P. Jacks (London: George Allen and Unwin Ltd., 1950).

Lord, Albert B. *The Singer of Tales* (New York: Atheneum, 1960).

Love, Nicholas. *Mirror of the Blessed Life of Jesus Christ.* Edited by Michael G. Sargent (New York: Garland, 1992).

Lowe, Margaret. *Towards the Real Flaubert: A Study of Madame Bovary* (Oxford: Clarendon Press, 1984).

Lucian of Samosata. *Alexander, the False Prophet.* In *Lucian,* vol. 4. Translated by A. M. Harmon (Cambridge: Harvard University Press; London: William Heinemann, Ltd., 1925).

———. *The Passing of Peregrinus.* In *Lucian,* vol. 5. Translated by A. M. Harmon (Cambridge: Harvard University Press; London: William Heinemann, Ltd., 1936).

Lüdemann, Gerd. *Heretics: The Other Side of Early Christianity.* Translated by John Bowden (Louisville, Ky.: Westminster/John Knox Press, 1996).

———. *The Resurrection of Jesus: History, Experience, Theology.* Translated by John Bowden (Minneapolis: Fortress Press, 1994).

Lüdemann, Gerd, in collaboration with Alf Özen. *What Really Happened to Jesus? A Historical Approach to the Resurrection.* Translated by John Bowden (Louisville, Ky.: Westminster/John Knox Press, 1995).

Lührmann, Dieter. *An Itinerary of New Testament Study.* Translated by John Bowden (London: SCM Press Ltd.; Philadelphia: Trinity Press International, 1989).

Lukacs, Georg. *The Historical Novel.* Translated by Hannah and Stanley Mitchell (London: Merlin Press, 1962).

McCarthy, Vincent A. *Quest for a Philosophical Jesus: Christianity and Philosophy in Rousseau, Kant, Hegel, and Schelling* (Macon, Ga.: Mercer University Press, 1986).

McClelland, Charles E. *State, Society, and University in Germany, 1700–1914* (Cambridge: Cambridge University Press, 1980).

Maccoby, Hyam. *Judas Iscariot and the Myth of Jewish Evil* (New York: Free Press, 1992).

———. *The Mythmaker: Paul and the Invention of Christianity* (New York: Harper & Row, 1987).

———. *Paul and Hellenism* (London: SCM Press Ltd.; Philadelphia: Trinity Press International, 1991).

———. *Revolution in Judaea: Jesus and the Jewish Resistance.* (New York: Taplinger Publishing Co., 1980).

———. *The Sacred Executioner: Human Sacrifice and the Legacy of Guilt* (London: Thames and Hudson, 1982).

McGrath, Alister. *The Making of Modern German Christology: From the Enlightenment to Pannenberg* (London: Basil Blackwell, 1986).

McKnight, Gerald. *Verdict on Schweitzer: The Man behind the Legend of Lambaréné* (London: Frederick Muller Limited, 1964).

McLuhan, Marshall. *The Gutenberg Galaxy: The Making of Typographic Man* (Toronto: University of Toronto Press, 1962).

Mack, Burton L. *The Lost Gospel: The Book of Q and Christian Origins* (San Francisco: HarperCollins, 1993).

———. *A Myth of Innocence: Mark and Christian Origins* (Philadelphia: Fortress Press, 1988).

———. *Who Wrote the New Testament? The Making of the Christian Myth* (San Francisco: HarperCollins, 1995).

Mailer, Norman. *The Gospel According to the Son* (New York: Random House, 1997).

Maisels, Charles Keith. *The Near East: Archaeology in the "Cradle of Civilization"* (London: Routledge, 1993).

Malherbe, Abraham. *Social Aspects of Early Christianity* (Philadelphia: Fortress Press, 1983).

Malina, Bruce J. *The New Testament World: Insights from Cultural Anthropology.* Rev. ed. (Louisville, Ky.: Westminster/John Knox Press, 1993).

———. *Windows on the World of Jesus: Time Travel to Ancient Judea* (Louisville: Westminster/John Knox Press, 1993).

Marshall, Bruce. *Christology in Conflict: The Identity of a Saviour in Rahner and Barth* (London: Blackwell, 1987).

Martin, Luther H. *Hellenistic Religions: An Introduction* (London: Oxford University Press, 1987).

Marty, Martin E. *A Short History of Christianity* (Philadelphia: Fortress Press, 1959).

Marxsen, Willi. *Jesus and the Church: The Beginnings of Christianity.* Selected, translated, and introduced by Philip E. Devenish (Philadelphia: Trinity Press International, 1992).

———. *Jesus the Messiah: The Synoptic Tradition of the Revelation of God in Christ.* English translation (London: Hodder and Stoughton, 1943).

———. *Mark The Evangelist: Studies on the Redaction History of the Gospel.* 1956. Translated by James Boyce, Donald Juel, and William Poehlmann, with Roy A. Harrisville (Nashville: Abingdon Press, 1969).

———. *The New Testament as the Church's Book?* 1966. Translated by James E. Mignard (Philadelphia: Fortress Press, 1972).

———. *The Resurrection of Jesus of Nazareth.* Translated by Margaret Kohl (Philadelphia: Fortress Press, 1970).

Massey, Marilyn Chapin. *Christ Unmasked: The Meaning of Life of Jesus in German Politics* (Chapel Hill: University of North Carolina Press, 1983).

Mathews, Shailer. *The Gospel and the Modern Man* (New York: Macmillan, 1910).

———. *Jesus on Social Institutions.* 1928. Edited and with an introduction by Kenneth Cauthen (Philadelphia: Fortress Press, 1971).

———. *The Social Teaching of Jesus: An Essay in Christian Sociology* (New York: Macmillan, 1897).

Matyjasckiewicz, Krystyna, ed. *James Tissot* (New York: Abbeville Press, 1985).

Mead, George Robert Stow. *Did Jesus Live 100 B.C.? An Inquiry into the Talmudic Jesus Stories, the Toldoth Jeschu, and Some Curious Statements of Epiphanius—Being a Contribution to the Study of Christian Origins.* 1903. (Reprint ed., Hyde Park: University Books, 1968).

Meeks, Wayne A. *The First Urban Christians: The Social World of the Apostle Paul* (New Haven: Yale University Press, 1983).

Meeks, Wayne, and Wilken, Robert L. *Jews and Christians in Antioch in the First Four Centuries of the Common Era* (Missoula: Scholars Press, 1978).

Meier, John P. *A Marginal Jew: Rethinking the Historical Jesus.* 2 vols. (Garden City, N.Y.: Doubleday, 1991, 1994).

Meinardus, Otto F. A. *St. Paul in Greece.* 6th ed. (Athens: Lycabettus Press, 1992).

Mercer, Calvin R. *Norman Perrin's Interpretation of the New Testament* (Macon, Ga.: Mercer University Press, 1986).

Metz, Johann Baptist. *Faith in History and Society: Toward a Fundamental Practical Theology.* Translated by David South (New York: Seabury Press, 1980).

Metzger, Bruce. *The Canon of the New Testament: Its Origin, Development, and Significance* (Oxford: Clarendon Press, 1987).

———. *Manuscripts of the Greek Bible: An Introduction to Greek Paleography* (New York: Oxford University Press, 1981).

———. *The Text of the New Testament: Its Transmission, Corruption, and Restoration* (New York: Oxford University Press, 1992).

Metzger, Bruce, and Coogan, Michael D., eds. *The Oxford Companion to the Bible* (New York: Oxford University Press, 1993).

Meyer, Marvin, trans. *The Gospel of Thomas: The Hidden Sayings of Jesus* (San Francisco: HarperCollins, 1992).

Miller, Robert J., ed. *The Complete Gospels: Annotated Scholars Version* (San Francisco: HarperCollins, 1994).

Mills, C. Wright. *The Power Elite* (New York: Oxford University Press, 1956).

Minucius Felix. *The Octavius of Minucius Felix.* Translated by G. W. Clarke. Ancient Christian Writers: The Works of the Fathers in Translation, no. 39 (New York: Newman Press, 1974).

Mitchell, Stephen. *The Gospel According to Jesus: A New Translation and Guide to His Essential Teachings for Believers and Unbelievers* (New York: HarperCollins, 1991).

Mollenauer, Robert, ed. *Introduction to Modernity: A Symposium on Eighteenth-Century Thought* (Austin: University of Texas Press, 1965).

Montefiore, Claude Joseph Goldsmid. *Judaism and St. Paul: Two Essays* (New York: Arno Press, 1973).

Moore, Stephen D. *Mark and Luke in Poststructuralist Perspectives: Jesus Begins to Write* (New Haven: Yale University Press, 1992).

———. *Post-Structuralism and the New Testament: Derrida and Foucault at the Foot of the Cross* (Minneapolis: Fortress Press, 1994).

Morgan, Robert, ed. and trans. *The Nature of New Testament Theology: The Contribution of William Wrede and Adolf Schlatter* (Naperville, Ill.: Alec R. Allenson; London: SCM Press, Ltd., 1973).

Morley, Charles, ed. and trans. *Portrait of America: Letters of Henryk Sienkiewicz* (New York: Columbia University Press, 1959).

Morsberger, Robert E., and Morsberger, Katharine M. *Lew Wallace: Militant Romantic* (New York: McGraw-Hill, 1980).

Neander, August. *The Life of Jesus Christ: In its Historical Connexion and Historical Development.* 1837. Translated by John McClintock and Charles E. Blumenthal from the 4th ed. of 1845 (London: George Ballard and Sons, 1892).

Neill, Stephen. *The Interpretation of the New Testament, 1861–1961* (London: Oxford University Press, 1964).

Neill, Stephen, and Wright, Tom. *The Interpretation of the New Testament, 1861–1986* (Oxford: Oxford University Press, 1988).

Neusner, Jacob. *From Politics to Piety: The Emergence of Pharasaic Judaism* (Englewood Cliffs, N.J.: Prentice-Hall, 1973).

———. *Jews and Christians: The Myth of a Common Tradition* (London: SCM Press Ltd.; Philadelphia: Trinity Press International, 1991).

———. *Judaism in the Beginning of Christianity* (Philadelphia: Fortress Press, 1984).

———. *Telling Tales: Making Sense of Christian and Judaic Nonsense* (Louisville: John Knox Press, 1993).

Neusner, Jacob; Green, William Scott; and Frerichs, Ernest S., eds. *Judaisms and Their Messiahs* (Cambridge: Cambridge University Press, 1987).

———. *The Social World of Formative Judaism* (Philadelphia: Fortress Press, 1988).

Newton, Isaac. *Opticks.* (Reprint ed., New York: Dover, 1952).

Nietzsche, Friedrich. *Untimely Meditations.* Translated by R. J. Hollingdale (Cambridge: Cambridge University Press, 1983).

Notovitch, Nicolas. *The Unknown Life of Jesus.* English translation. (reprint ed., Joshua Tree, Calif.: Tree of Life Publications, 1996).

O'Neill, J. C. *The Bible's Authority: A Portrait Gallery of Thinkers from Lessing to Bultmann* (Edinburgh: T&T Clark, 1991).

Origen. *Treatise on the Passover and Dialogue with Heracleides.* Translated by Robert J. Daly. Ancient Christian Writers: The Works of the Fathers in Translation, no. 54 (New York: Paulist Press, 1992).

Oursler, Fulton. *The Greatest Story Ever Told: A Tale of the Greatest Life Ever Lived* (Garden City, N.Y.: Doubleday, 1950).

Pagels, Elaine. *The Gnostic Gospels* (New York: Random House, 1979).

———. *The Origin of Satan* (New York: Random House, 1995).

Paglia, Camille. *Sexual Personae: Art and Decadence from Nefertiti to Emily Dickinson* (Yale University Press, 1990).

Painter, George D. *Chateaubriand: A Biography.* 2 vols. (New York: Alfred A. Knopf, 1978).

Pals, Daniel L. *Seven Theories of Religion* (New York: Oxford University Press, 1996).

———. *The Victorian "Lives" of Jesus.* (San Antonio, Texas: Trinity University Press, 1982).

Pannenberg, Wolfhart. *Jesus—God and Man.* Translated by Lewis L. Wilkens and Duane A. Priebe (Philadelphia: Westminster Press, 1968).

Park, Paul. *The Gospel of Corax* (New York: Soho Press, 1996).

Pater, Walter. *Marius the Epicurean: His Sensations and Ideas.* 2 vols. (London: Macmillan, 1885).

Pelikan, Jaroslav. *Jesus Through the Centuries* (New Haven: Yale University Press, 1985).

Penzel, Klaus, ed. *Philip Schaff: Historian and Ambassador of the Universal Church: Selected Writings* (Macon, Ga.: Mercer University Press, 1991).

Perrin, Norman. *Jesus and the Language of the Kingdom: Symbol and Metaphor in New Testament Interpretation* (Philadelphia: Fortress Press, 1976).

———. *The Kingdom of God in the Teaching of Jesus* (Philadelphia: Westminster Press, 1963).

———. *Rediscovering the Teachings of Jesus* (New York: Harper & Row, 1967).

———. *The Resurrection According to Matthew, Mark, and Luke* (Philadelphia: Fortress Press, 1977).

———. *What Is Redaction Criticism?* (Philadelphia: Fortress Press, 1969).

Pfleiderer, Otto. *Primitive Christianity: Its Origins and Teachings in Their Historical Connections.* Translated by W. Montgomery from the 2 ed. of 1902. 2 vols. (Republished, Clifton, N.J.: Reference Book Publishers, 1965).

Philo Judaeus. *The Essential Philo.* Edited by Nahum N. Glatzer (New York: Schocken, 1971).

Pliny the Younger. *Letters and Panegyricus,* vol. 2. Translated by Betty Radice (Cambridge: Harvard University Press; London: William Heinemann, Ltd., 1969).

Powelson, Mark, and Riegert, Ray, eds. *The Lost Gospel Q: The Original Sayings of Jesus* (Berkeley, Calif.: Ulysses Press, 1996).

Price, Reynolds. *Three Gospels. The Good News According to Mark, The Good News According to John, An Honest Account of a Memorable Life* (New York: Scribner, 1996).

Raisanen, Heikki. *The "Messianic Secret" in Mark.* 1976. Translated by Christopher Tuckett (Edinburgh: T&T Clark Ltd., 1990).

Rauschenbusch, Walter. *Selected Writings.* Edited by Winthrop S. Hudson (New York: Paulist Press, 1984).

———. *The Social Principles of Jesus* (New York: Association Press, 1916).

Redeker, Martin. *Schleiermacher: Life and Thought.* Translated by John Wallhausser (Philadelphia: Fortress Press, 1973).

Redwood, John. *Reason, Ridicule and Religion: The Age of Enlightenment in England, 1660–1750* (Cambridge: Harvard University Press, 1976).

Reimarus, Hermann Samuel. *Reimarus: Fragments.* Translated by Ralph S. Fraser. Edited by Charles H. Talbert (Philadelphia: Fortress Press, 1970).

Reitzenstein, Richard. *The Hellenistic Mystery-Religions: Their Basic Ideas and Significance.* Translated by John E. Steely (Pittsburgh: Pickwick Press, 1978).

Renan, Ernest. *The History of the Origins of Christianity.* Book 1: *The Life of Jesus.* 1864. Translated from the 13th ed. with modifications by the author (London: Mathieson & Company, n.d.).

———. *The History of the Origins of Christianity.* Book 2: *The Apostles.* English translation (New York: Carleton, 1875).

———. *The History of the Origins of Christianity.* Book 4: *Antichrist.* Translated and edited by Joseph Henry Allen (Boston: Roberts Brothers, 1897).

———. *The History of the Origins of Christianity.* Book 5: *The Gospels.* English translation (London: Mathieson & Company, n.d.).

———. *The History of the Origins of Christianity.* Book 6: *The Christian Church, Comprising the Reigns of Hadrian and Antoninus Pius (A.D. 117–161).* English translation (London: Mathieson & Company, n.d.).

———. *The History of the Origins of Christianity.* Book 7: *Marcus-Aurelius.* Translated into English (London: Mathieson & Company, n.d.).

———. *Letters from the Holy Land.* Translated by Lorenzo O'Rourke (Garden City, N.Y.: Doubleday, Page & Company, 1904).

Reventlow, Henning Graf. *The Authority of the Bible and the Rise of the Modern World.* Translated by John Bowden (Philadelphia: Fortress Press, 1984).

———. *Problems of Biblical Theology in the Twentieth Century.* Translated by John Bowden (Philadelphia: Fortress Press, 1986).

Reventlow, Henning Graf, and Farmer, William, eds. *Biblical Studies and the Shifting of Paradigms, 1850–1914.* Journal for the Study of the Old Testament, Supplement Series 192 (Sheffield: Sheffield Academic Press, 1995).

Rhodes, Royal W. *The Lion and the Cross: Early Christianity in Victorian Novels* (Columbus: Ohio State University Press, 1995).

Riches, John. *A Century of New Testament Study* (Valley Forge, Pa.: Trinity Press International, 1993).

———. *The World of Jesus: First-Century Judaism in Crisis* (Cambridge: Cambridge University Press, 1990).

Rist, John M. *On the Independence of Matthew and Mark.* Society for New Testament Studies Monograph Series, no. 32 (Cambridge: Cambridge University Press, 1978).

Robinson, James M. *A New Quest of the Historical Jesus.* Studies in Biblical Theology, no. 25 (London: SCM Press Ltd., 1959).

———, gen. ed. *The Nag Hammadi Library in English.* 3d ed. (San Francisco: HarperCollins, 1990).

Robinson, James, M., and Koester, Helmut. *Trajectories Through Early Christianity* (Philadelphia: Fortress Press, 1971).

Robinson, John A. T. *Honest to God* (Philadelphia: Westminster Press, 1963).

———. *The Priority of John.* Edited by J. F. Coakley (London: SCM Press Ltd., 1985).

Rosenzweig, Franz. *The Star of Redemption.* Translated from the 2d ed. 1930 by William W. Mallo (New York: Holt, Rinehart and Winston, 1970, 1971).

Rousseau, Jean-Jacques. *Émile.* 1762. English translation (New York: Dutton, 1974).

Rousseau, John J., and Arav, Rami. *Jesus and His World: An Archaeological and Cultural Dictionary* (Minneapolis: Fortress Press, 1995).

Ruether, Rosemary Radford. *Faith and Fratricide: The Theological Roots of Anti-Semitism* (New York: Seabury Press, 1974).

Said, Edward. *Orientalism.* 1978 (Republished with a new afterword, New York: Vintage Books, 1994).

Sanders, E. P. *The Historical Figure of Jesus* (London: Allen Lane, Penguin Press, 1993).

———. *Jesus and Judaism.* (Philadelphia: Fortress Press, 1985).

———. *Judaism: Practices and Beliefs, 63 BCE–66 CE* (London: SCM Press Ltd.; Valley Forge, Pa.: Trinity Press International, 1992).

———. *Paul and Palestinian Judaism: A Comparison of Patterns of Religion* (London: SCM Press Ltd.; Philadelphia: Fortress Press, 1977).

———. *Paul, the Law, and the Jewish People* (Philadelphia: Fortress Press, 1983).

Sanders, E. P., and Davies, Margaret. *Studying the Synoptic Gospels* (London: SCM Press Ltd.; Philadelphia: Trinity Press International, 1989).

Sandmel, Samuel. *Judaism and Christian Beginnings* (New York: Oxford University Press, 1978).

———. *Philo of Alexandria: An Introduction* (New York: Oxford University Press, 1979).

———. *We Jews and Jesus* (New York: Oxford University Press, 1965).

Saramago, José. *The Gospel According to Jesus Christ.* Translated by Giovanni Pontiero (San Diego: Harcourt Brace & Company, 1994).

Schaberg, Jane. *The Illegitimacy of Jesus: A Feminist Theological Interpretation of the Infancy Narratives* (New York: Crossroad, 1990).

Schillebeeckx, Edward. *Jesus: An Experiment in Christology.* Translated by Herbert Hoskins (New York: Seabury Press, 1979).

Schleiermacher, Friedrich. *The Life of Jesus.* 1864. Translated by S. Gilmour. Edited by Jack C. Verheyden (Philadelphia: Fortress Press, 1975).

Schonfield, Hugh J. *The Passover Plot: New Light on the History of Jesus* (New York: Bernard Geis Associates, 1965).

Schubert, Kurt. *The Dead Sea Community.* Translated by John W. Doberstein (New York: Harper & Brothers, 1959).

Schürer, Emil. *Das messianische Selbstbewusstein Jesu Christi* (Göttingen: Vandenhöck & Ruprecht, 1903).

Schweitzer, Albert. *The Kingdom of God and Primitive Christianity.* Translated by L. A. Garrard (New York: Seabury Press, 1968).

———. *The Mystery of the Kingdom of God: The Secret of Jesus' Messiahship and Passion.* Translated by William Lowrie. 1914 (reprint ed., Buffalo: Prometheus Books, 1985).

———. *The Mysticism of Paul the Apostle.* Translated by William Montgomery, 1931 (Reprint ed., New York: Seabury Press, 1968).

———. *Paul and His Interpreters: A Critical History.* Translated by W. Montgomery (London: Adam and Charles Black, 1912).

———. *The Psychiatric Study of Jesus: Exposition and Criticism* (Boston: Beacon Press, 1948).

———. *The Quest of the Historical Jesus: A Critical Study of Its Progress from Reimarus to Wrede.* Translated by W. Montgomery (London: A&C Black, Ltd.; New York: Macmillan, 1910).

Scott, Burton Easton. *The Gospel before the Gospels* (New York: Charles Scribner's Sons, 1928).

Seeley, John R. *Ecce Homo: A Survey of the Life and Work of Jesus Christ* (London: J. M. Dent & Sons Ltd.; New York: E. P. Dutton & Co., 1908).

Segal, Alan F. *The Other Judaisms of Late Antiquity.* Brown Judaic Studies, no. 127 (Atlanta: Scholars Press, 1987).

———. *Paul the Convert: The Apostolate and Apostasy of Saul the Pharisee* (New Haven: Yale University Press, 1990).

Sevenster, J. N. *Do You Know Greek? How Much Greek Could the First Jewish Christians Have Known?* Translated by J. de Bruin (Leiden: E. J. Brill, 1968).

Seydel, Rudolf. *Bhudda und Christus* (Breslau: Schhottlaender, 1884).

———. *Das Evangelium von Jesu: in seinem Verhältnissen zu Buddha-Sage und Buddha-Hehre mit fortlaufender Rücksicht auf andere Religionskreise* (Leipzig: Breitkopf & Hartel, 1882).

Shanks, Hershel. *Understanding the Dead Sea Scrolls: A Reader from the Biblical Archaeology Review* (New York: Random House, 1992).

Sheehan, Thomas. *The First Coming: How the Kingdom of God Became Christianity* (New York: Random House, 1986).

Sherrard, Philip. *The Greek East and the Latin West: A Study in the Christian Tradition.* 1959. Reprinted with amendments and additions (Limni, Evia, Greece: Denise Harvey & Company, 1992).

Sienkiewicz, Henryk. *Quo Vadis.* 1896. Translated by W. S. Kuniczak (New York: Macmillan, 1993).

Smalley, Beryl. *The Study of the Bible in the Middle Ages* (Oxford: Basil Blackwell, 1952).

Smallwood, E. Mary. *The Jews under Roman Rule: From Pompey to Diocletian* (Leiden: E. J. Brill, 1981).

Smart, L. Ninian; Clayton, John; Katz, Steven; and Sherry, Patrick, eds. *Ninteenth Century Religious Thought in the West* (Cambridge: Cambridge University Press, 1985).

Smith, Christian. *The Emergency of Liberation Theology: Radical Religion and Social Movement Theory* (Chicago: University of Chicago Press, 1991).

Smith, Morton. *Jesus the Magician* (San Francisco: Harper & Row, 1978).

———. *The Secret Gospel: The Discovery and Interpretation of the Secret Gospel According to Mark* (London: Victor Gollancz Ltd., 1974).

Sobrino, Jon. *Christology at the Crossroads: A Latin American Approach.* Translated by John Drury (Maryknoll, N.Y.: Orbis Books, 1978).

———. *Jesus the Liberator: A Historical-Theological Reading of Jesus of Nazareth.* Translated by Paul Burns and Francis McDonagh (Maryknoll, N.Y.: Orbis Books, 1994).

Speirs, John. *Medieval English Poetry: The Non-Chaucerian Tradition* (London: Faber & Faber, 1957).

Spencer, Herbert. *Social Statics.* 1850 (reprint ed., New York: Roger Schalkenbach Foundation, 1995).

Spong, John Shelby. *Born of a Woman: A Bishop Rethinks the Birth of Jesus* (San Francisco: HarperCollins, 1992).

———. *Resurrection: Myth or Reality? A Bishop's Search for the Origins of Christianity* (San Francisco: HarperCollins, 1994).

———. *This Hebrew Lord* (New York: Seabury Press, 1974).

Staley, Jeffrey L. *Reading with a Passion: Rhetoric, Autobiography and the American West in the Gospel of John* (New York: Continuum Publishing Company, 1995).

Staniforth, Maxwell, ed. *Early Christian Writings* (Harmondsworth: Penguin, 1968).

Stark, Rodney. *The Rise of Christianity: A Sociologist Reconsiders History* (Princeton: Princeton University Press, 1996).

Stark, Rodney, and Bainbridge, William Sims. *A Theory of Religion.* Toronto Studies in Religion, vol. 2 (New York: Peter Lang Publishing, 1987).

Stauffer, Ethelbert. *Jesus and His Story.* Translated by Richard and Clara Winston (New York: Knopf, 1960).

Stevenson, J., ed. *Creeds, Councils and Controversies: Documents Illustrative of the History of the Church A.D. 337–461* (London: SPCK, 1966).

Strachey, Lytton. *Eminent Victorians* (Garden City, N.Y.: Garden City Publishing Co., 1918).

Strauss, David Friedrich. *The Christ of Faith and the Jesus of History: A Critique of Schleiermacher's Life of Jesus.* Translated by Leander E. Keck (Philadelphia: Fortress Press, 1971).

———. *In Defense of My Life of Jesus against the Hegelians.* Translated and edited by Marilyn Chapin Massey (Hamden, Conn.: Shoe String Press, 1983).

———. *The Life of Jesus Critically Examined.* 1835. Translated from the 4th German ed. by George Eliot. Edited by Peter G. Hodgson (Philadelphia: Fortress Press, 1971).

———. *A New Life of Jesus.* English translation in 2 vols. (London: Williams and Norgate, 1865).

———. *The Old Faith and the New.* Translated by Mathilde Blind (Amherst, N.Y.: Prometheus Books, 1997).

Strauss, Leo. *Natural Right and History* (Chicago: University of Chicago Press, 1953).

Streeter, Bernard Hillman. *The Four Gospels: A Study of Origins* (New York: Macmillan, 1925).

Stuhlmacher, Peter, ed. *The Gospel and the Gospels.* (Grand Rapids, Mich.: William B. Eerdmans Publishing Company, 1991).

Suetonius. *Nero.* Vol. 2. Translated by J. C. Rolfe (Cambridge: Harvard University Press; London: William Heinemann, Ltd., 1914).

Sykes, Stephen. *Friedrich Schleiermacher* (Richmond, Va.: John Knox Press, 1971).

Tacitus. *The Annals.* Book 15. Translated by John Jackson (Cambridge: Harvard University Press; London: William Heinemann, Ltd., 1937).

———. *The Histories.* Books 5 and 9. Translated by Clifford H. Moore (Cambridge: Harvard University Press; London: William Heinemann, Ltd., 1931).

Talbert, Charles H. *What Is a Gospel? The Genre of the Canonical Gospels* (Philadelphia: Fortress Press, 1977).

Tertullian. *Against Marcion.* Edited and translated by Ernest Evans (New York: Oxford University Press, 1972).

Theissen, Gerd. *The Shadow of the Galilean: The Quest of the Historical Jesus in Narrative Form.* Translated by John Bowden (Philadelphia: Fortress Press, 1987).

———. *Social Reality and the Early Christians: Theology, Ethics, and the World of the New Testament.* Translated by Margaret Kohl (Minneapolis: Fortress Press, 1992).

———. *The Social Setting of Pauline Christianity: Essays on Corinth.* Translated by John H. Schuetz (Philadelphia: Fortress Press, 1989).

———. *Sociology of Early Palestinian Christianity.* Translated by John Bowden (Philadelphia: Fortress Press, 1978).

Thiede, Carsten Peter. *The Earliest Gospel Manuscript? The Qumran Fragment 7Q5 and Its Significance for New Testament Studies* (London: Paternoster Press, 1992).

Thiering, Barbara. *Jesus and the Riddle of the Dead Sea Scrolls: Unlocking the Secrets of His Life Story* (San Francisco: HarperCollins, 1992).

Thompson, J. A. *The Bible and Archaeology.* 3d ed. (Grand Rapids, Mich.: William B. Eerdmans Publishing Co., 1982).

Tissot, James Joseph Jacques. *Biblical Paintings* (New York: Jewish Museum, 1982).

Tödt, H. E. *The Son of Man in the Synoptic Tradition.* Translated by Dorothea M. Barton (Philadelphia: Westminster Press, 1965).

Toland, John. *Nazarenus: or Jewish, Gentile, and Mahometan Christianity* (London: J. Brotherton, J. Roberts, A. Dodd, 1720).

Torrance, Thomas F. *Karl Barth, Biblical and Evangelical Theologian* (Edinburgh: T&T Clarke, 1990).

Troeltsch, Ernst. *The Absoluteness of Christianity and the History of Religions.* 1929. Translated by David Reid with an introduction by James Luther Adams (Richmond, Va.: John Knox Press, 1971).

———. *Religion in History.* Translated by James Luther Adams and Walter F. Bense (Minneapolis: Fortress Press, 1991).

———. *The Social Teaching of the Christian Churches.* Vol. 1. Translated by Olive Wyon (New York: Macmillan, 1931).

———. *Writings on Theology and Religion.* Translated and edited by Robert Morgan and Michael Pye (Atlanta: John Knox Press, 1977).

Trollope, Anthony. *The Bertrams.* 1859. Edited by Geoffrey Harvey (Oxford: Oxford University Press, 1991).

Tuckett, Christopher M. *Q and the History of Early Christianity: Studies on Q* (Edinburgh: T&T Clarke Ltd., 1996).

———. *Reading the New Testament: Methods of Interpretation* (Philadelphia: Fortress Press, 1987).

Turnbull, H. W. *The Correspondence of Isaac Newton* (Cambridge: Cambridge University Press, 1961).

Tyrrell, George. *Christianity at the Cross-Roads* (London: Longmans, Green and Co., 1909).

———. *Tradition and the Critical Spirit: Catholic Modernist Writings.* Selected and introduced by James C. Livingston (Minneapolis: Fortress Press, 1991).

Vaage, Leif E. *Galilean Upstarts: Jesus' First Followers According to Q* (Valley Forge, Pa.: Trinity Press International, 1994).

Vermes, Geza. *The Dead Sea Scrolls: Qumran in Perspective.* 2d ed. (Philadelphia: Fortress Press, 1981).

———. *The Dead Sea Scrolls in English.* 3d ed. (Sheffield: JSOT, 1987).

———. *Discovery in the Judean Desert* (New York: Desclee Company, 1956).

———. *Jesus and the World of Judaism* (London: SCM Press Ltd., 1983).

———. *Jesus the Jew: A Historian's Reading of the Gospels* (New York: Macmillan, 1974).

Volkmar, Gustav. *Die Religion Jesu und ihre erste Entwickelung* (Leipzig: F. A. Brodhaus, 1857).

Voragine, Jacobus de. *The Golden Legend: Readings on the Saints.* Translated by William Granger Ryan. 2 vols. (Princeton: Princeton University Press, 1993).

Wallace, Lew. *An Autobiography.* 2 vols. (New York: Harper & Brothers, 1906).

———. *Ben-Hur: A Tale of the Christ.* 1880 (republished, Pleasantville: Reader's Digest Association, 1992).

Waller, John H. *Gordon of Khartoum: The Saga of a Victorian Hero* (New York: Atheneum, 1988).

Walsh, Michael. *The Triumph of the Meek: Why Early Christianity Succeeded* (San Francisco: Harper & Row, 1986).

Wardman, H. W. *Ernest Renan: A Critical Biography* (London: University of London, 1964).

Ware, Timothy. *The Orthodox Church.* Rev. ed. (Harmondsworth: Penguin, 1982).

Weathersby, Robert W., II. *J. H. Ingraham* (Boston: Twayne, 1980).

Weaver, Richard M. *Ideas Have Consequences* (Chicago: University of Chicago Press, 1948).

Weber, Max. *The Protestant Ethic and the Spirit of Capitalism.* Translated by Talcott Parsons (New York: Charles Scribner's Sons, 1958).

Wedderburn, A. J. M., ed. *Paul and Jesus: Selected Essays.* Journal for the Study of the New Testament, Supplement Series no. 37 (Sheffield: JSOT Press, 1989).

Wegener, Thomas. *Sister Anne Katherine Emmerich of the Order of St. Augustine: The Marvelous Interior and Exterior Life of this Servant of God.* Translated by Francis X. McGowan (New York: Benziger Brothers, 1898).

Weiffenbach, Wilhelm. *Die Frage der Wiederkunft Jesu* (Friedberg: Carl Bindernagel, 1901).

Weiss, Bernhard. *The Life of Christ.* Translated by John Walter Hope. 3 vols. (Edinburgh: T&T Clark, 1888–1892).

Weiss, Johannes. *Earliest Christianity: A History of the Period A.D. 30–150.* 1937. Translated by Frederick C. Grant. 2 vols. (New York: Harper & Row, 1959).

———. *Jesus' Proclamation of the Kingdom of God.* Translated and edited by Richard Hyde Hiers and David Larrimore Holland (Philadelphia: Fortress Press, 1971).

Weiss-Rosmarin, Trude. *Judaism and Christianity: The Difference.* 1943. (Middle Village, N.Y.: Jonathan David Publishers, 1981).

Wellhausen, Julius. *Prolegomena to the History of Israel.* 1895 (reprint ed., Atlanta: Scholars Press, 1994).

Wilde, Oscar. *De Profundis.* 1897. Edited by Jacques Barzun (New York: Vintage Books, 1964).

Wilken, Robert L. *The Christians As the Romans Saw Them* (New Haven: Yale University Press, 1984).

Williams, Walter G. *Archaeology in Biblical Research* (New York: Abingdon Press, 1965).

Wilson, A. N. *Jesus: A Life* (New York: Norton, 1992).

———. *Paul: The Mind of the Apostle* (New York: Norton, 1997).

Wilson, Edmund. *The Scrolls from the Dead Sea* (New York: Oxford University Press, 1955).

Winter, Paul. *On the Trial of Jesus.* 2d. ed. Revised and edited by T. A. Burkill and Geza Vermes (Berlin and New York: Walter de Gruyter, 1974).

Witherington, Ben, III. *The Jesus Quest: The Third Search for the Jew of Nazareth* (Downers Grove, Ill.: Inter-Varsity Press, 1995).

Wood, Christopher. *Tissot: The Life and Works of Jacques Joseph Tissot, 1836–1920* (London: Weidenfeld and Nicholson, 1986).

Wood, Diana, ed. *Martyrs and Martyrologies* (London: Blackwell Publishers, 1993).

Woolf, Rosemary. *Art and Doctrine: Essays on Medieval Literature.* Edited by Heather O'Donoghue (London: Hambledon Press, 1986).

Woolston, Thomas. *A Defence of the Discourses on Miracles*. 2d ed. (London: 1729).

———. *A Discourse on the Miracles of Our Saviour.* 6th ed. (London: 1728).

———. *Sixth Discourse on the Miracles of Our Saviour* (London: 1729).

Worrall, Peter. "St. Thomas and Arianism" (Dissertation, Pontifical Institute "Angelicum," 1957).

Wrede, Wilhelm. *The Messianic Secret.* Translated by J. C. G. Greig (London: James Clarke & Co., 1971).

Wright, N. T. *The New Testament and the People of God* (Minneapolis: Fortress Press, 1992).

———. *Who Was Jesus?* (Grand Rapids, Mich.: William B. Eerdmans Publishing Company, 1993).

Yadin, Yigael. *Bar Kokhba: The Rediscovery of the Legendary Hero of the Second Jewish Revolt against Rome* (New York: Random House, 1971).

Zeitlin, Irving M. *Jesus and the Judaism of His Time* (Cambridge: Polity Press, 1988).

Zeitlin, Solomon. *Who Crucified Jesus?* 1947 (facsimile of 2d ed., Ann Arbor: Xerox University Microfilm, 1975).

INDEX

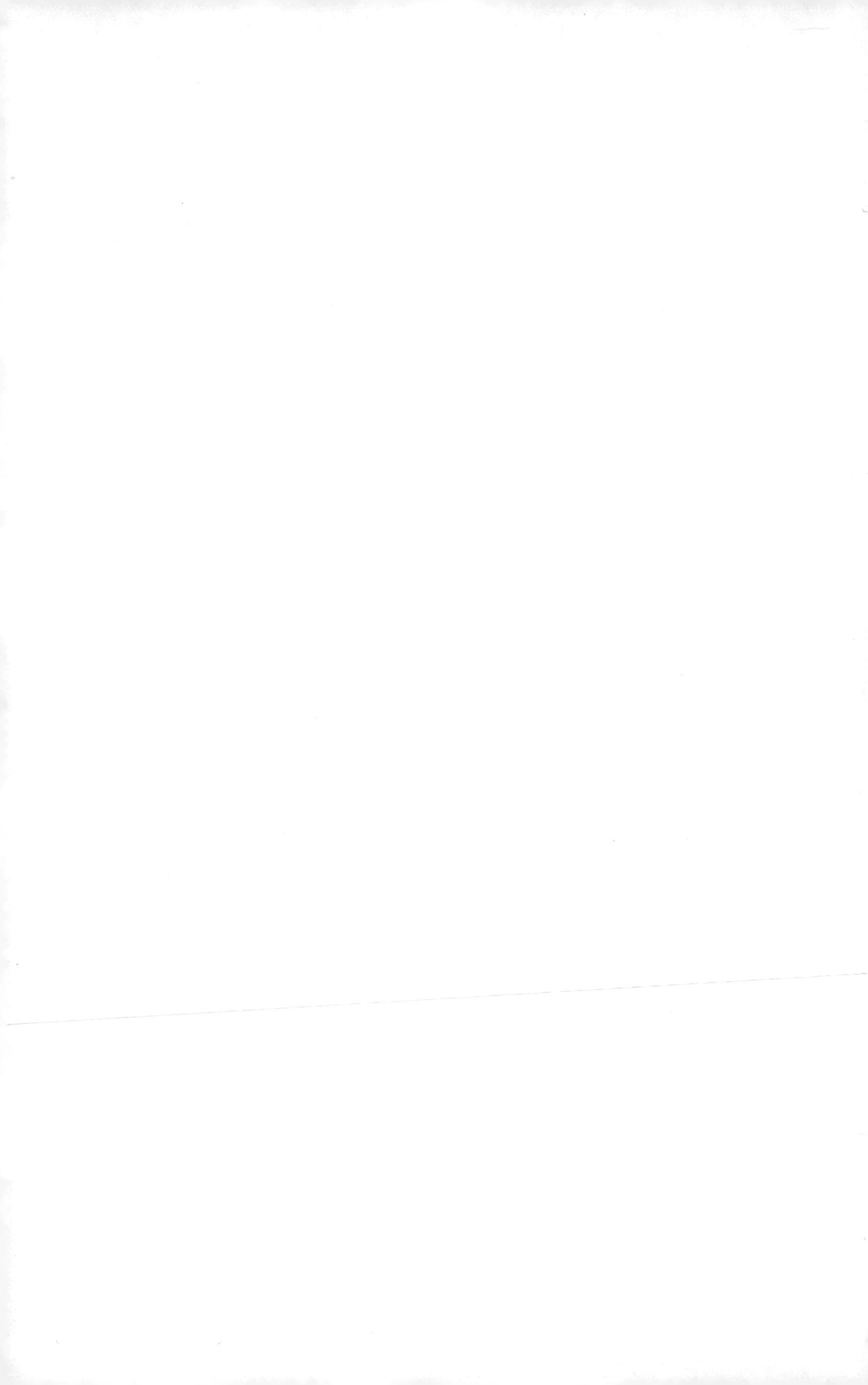